Jam Baldwin Review

Volume Seven

Contents

⌐JamesBaldwinReview

James Baldwin Review (*JBR*) is an annual journal that brings together a wide array of peer-reviewed critical and creative non-fiction on the life, writings, and legacy of James Baldwin. In addition to these cutting-edge contributions, each issue contains a review of recent Baldwin scholarship and an award-winning graduate student essay. *James Baldwin Review* publishes essays that invigorate scholarship on James Baldwin; catalyze explorations of the literary, political, and cultural influence of Baldwin's writing and political activism; and deepen our understanding and appreciation of this complex and luminary figure.

It is the aim of *James Baldwin Review* to provide a vibrant and multidisciplinary forum for the international community of Baldwin scholars, students, and enthusiasts.

Copyright © 2021, James Baldwin Review
ISSN 2056-9203 (Print) ISSN 2056-9211 (Online)
ISBN 978 1 5261 6277 9

Published by Manchester University Press and the University of Manchester Library

Manchester University Press, Oxford Road, Manchester, M13 9PL, UK
Tel: +44 (0)161 275 2310
Email: mup@manchester.ac.uk
Web address: www.manchesteruniversitypress.co.uk

University of Manchester Library, Oxford Road, Manchester, M13 9PP, UK
Tel: +44 (0)161 275 3751
Web address: www.library.manchester.ac.uk

James Baldwin Review is a collaborative venture made possible by support from
The New School and The University of Manchester.

Subscriptions

JBR is an Open Access journal, freely available at: www.manchesteropenhive.com/jbr

Articles

The editors encourage the submission of cross disciplinary articles on the life, writings, and legacy of James Baldwin. Possible contributors are welcome to discuss an article proposal or outline with the Managing Editor (joyceja@newschool.edu) before committing to a full submission.

Articles should be a minimum of 5,000 words and not exceed 10,000 words, including notes. Submissions should be made via email to the Managing Editor, Justin A. Joyce (joyceja@ newschool.edu).

Typeset by Sunrise Setting Ltd, Brixham
Printed in Great Britain by Bell & Bain Ltd, Glasgow

Manchester University Press

The University of Manchester

INTRODUCTION

Walk with the Wind

Justin A. Joyce   The New School

Abstract

Recalling the insurrectionary violence that descended upon the US Capitol on 6 January 2021, reflecting on the baser instincts left unchecked in America by an absence of common communication and a paradigmatic shift in our media apparatuses, Justin A. Joyce introduces the seventh volume of *James Baldwin Review*.

Keywords: James Baldwin, 2020 election, DC insurrection, Donald Trump, Abraham Lincoln, Joe Biden, *No Name in the Street*, social media

James Baldwin Review, Volume 7, 2021, © The Authors. Published by Manchester University Press and The University of Manchester Library
http://dx.doi.org/10.7227/JBR.7.1

The weight of this sad time we must obey,
Speak what we feel, not what we ought to say.
The oldest hath borne most; we that are young
Shall never see so much, nor live so long.

William Shakespeare, King Lear[1]

People who treat other people as less than human must not be surprised when the bread they have cast on the waters comes floating back to them, poisoned.

James Baldwin, No Name in the Street[2]

In the prologue to his 1998 memoir *Walking with the Wind*, Congressman and civil rights icon John Lewis tells a remarkable story from his childhood about persistence and the power of a group working together. The story concerns a windstorm that rose up on a four-year-old Lewis and some fourteen playmates on a Saturday afternoon in Alabama, quickly gathering strength and forcing them to shelter in his Aunt Sevena's rather modest house. Terribly frightened, the previously boisterous children huddled together, suddenly very quiet as the winds howled. Sevena, the only adult present, was frightened too, Lewis recalls, as the storm grew louder still, shook and swayed the house, and began to lift it from its foundation. At Sevena's prudent instruction, the children gathered hands and marched toward that lifting corner, weighing down the house, bolstering it against the power of the wind that threatened its integrity. When the wind shifted, their collective presence was required to hold down a different section of the trembling house. This continued, Lewis reports, "back and forth, fifteen children walking with the wind, holding that trembling house down with the weight of our small bodies."[3]

Recalling the story more than fifty years later, Lewis employs it as an analogy for the American struggle:

> It has struck me more than once over those many years that our society is not unlike the children in that house, rocked again and again by the winds of one storm or another, the walls around us seeming at times as if they might fly apart ... But the people of conscience never left the house. They never ran away. They stayed, they came together and they did the best they could, clasping hands and moving toward the corner of the house that was the weakest.
>
> And then another corner would lift, and we would go there ... Children holding hands, walking with the wind. That is America to me.[4]

It's an inspiring story and a powerful metaphor, no doubt. But I'm worried this tale may no longer cohere with the America we have seen of late. For what happens when the winds that threaten to tear the house apart come not from without, but from the bellicose bullies among these proverbial playmates? How do we walk with them? If the people of conscience let go their hold upon other hands, leave the house and run away, will there be enough walkers left to withstand the winds?

If we can't stay together and we don't do the best we can, will our walking adrift to separate corners still hold the house together? If our responses to the inevitable winds evince an absence of decency, are devoid of any dignity, utterly bereft of any sense of brotherhood, which way do we walk then?

Despite these misgivings, I've chosen to open with Lewis's tale because I'm a fan of unifying metaphors. Not just within an ideal public sphere wherein we all work toward a common goal, but also within a single piece of writing. A written journey, if you will, whereby we together—the writer and the reader—travel along a path bestrewn with consistent rhetorical reminders of the theme that ties us together on our journey. Ever the traveler, Baldwin knew about such journeys. Writing to his agent, Jay Acton, in 1979, he reveals that journeys are often themselves revelatory: "I am saying that a journey is called that because you cannot know what you will discover on the journey, what you will do with what you find, or what you find will do to you."[5]

I'd like to take us on such a journey, to traverse together the written page, but I'll admit this desire is somewhat self-centered because I am also searching for something on this journey. As Toni Morrison has noted, beyond the deadlines or the obligations, writing is occasionally the best way to find an answer:

> Sometimes you're nudged; and sometimes you're just searching. To make the writing interesting to me. It's not *just* writing. It's, "I don't know what this means." But I have to find out. And I have to explore all the characters' attitudes and so on. I got to know. And the only way I can know, and *own* what I know, is to write it. And then let you read it. So we both know.[6]

I'm hoping we find not only a metaphor, but also that together we find hope. Along the way I'm trusting as well that I can find my own "better angels," such as those Lincoln implored when he closed his first inaugural on the eve of civil war with an oft-quoted call for unity:

> We are not enemies, but friends. We must not be enemies. Though passion may have strained, it must not break our bonds of affection … when again touched, as surely they will be, by the better angels of our nature.[7]

Lincoln, though, was hardly the last to call for unity in a bitterly divided nation. The sentiments appear with predictable regularity seemingly every time a group of entitled white men are enabled to run roughshod over the pillars of decency, decorum, and dignity that underlie our democracy—though these high-minded calls are notably absent when people of color in this nation call for something as basic as the respect of their fundamental rights. A mere fourteen days after the US Capitol was attacked, the "better angels" of Lincoln were explicitly invoked in President Biden's call for forgiveness and unity during his own inauguration. Something about unity, "hope," and the "better angels" of our nature, then, is what I am *supposed* to be saying. But that's not, in truth, what I'm feeling.

Figure 1   Selma to Montgomery March, 1965: James Baldwin third from left in front row; John Lewis (then President of SNCC) sixth from left in front (Photograph by Stephen F. Somerstein/Getty Images)

I'm not ready to count those denying truth and sowing division for partisanship or profit as my "enemies," per se, but my feelings are far from friendly. Writing after numerous assassinations of prominent figures in the civil rights struggle in the 1960s, a struggle that united Baldwin and John Lewis as they appeared together on several high-profile marches, Baldwin commented upon his own faltering faith in the future of the United States, lamenting that "something has altered in me, something has gone away."[8]

Baldwin pointed out that "incontestably, alas, most people are not, in action worth very much; and yet every human being is an unprecedented miracle. One tries to treat them as the miracles they are, while trying to protect oneself against the disasters they've become."[9] Something has altered in me as well after witnessing the 6 January insurrection in Washington DC. Something has gone far away after watching the marauders peacefully escorted out once their vulgar debauch had subsided; going further away still upon seeing congressional representatives whose very lives were threatened failing to hold accountable their colleagues who whipped up such misguided fury. As I write this, Republican obstinacy festers still. It was bad enough that hours after the attack more than one hundred members of the House voted against certifying the election results; that many are now actively working to dismiss the attack on Congress and whitewash over it as merely an act of protest is a shameless dereliction of duty, conscience, and history. In his first inaugural address in 2009, Barack Obama pledged that we should extend our hands to those on the wrong side of history, if they were willing to unclench their fists.[10] Amid talk of bridge building and high rhetoric about coming together in some putative middle, I feel we'd do just as well to remember that a divide can also be bypassed via a tunnel. If the intractable among us won't meet us halfway, then it's high time we went around them.

Alas, I fear my provincial Americanness must be showing. I'm feeling more than a bit tribal and polarized myself as of late and I'm feeling most American in the moments when I have the least interest in compromise and the most invest-ment in "justice." Terry K. Aladjem has written that when Americans talk about justice, "they want something angry and punitive."[11] In his essay "Stranger in the Village" from 1953, Baldwin wrote that "people are trapped in history and history is trapped in them."[12] I'd like to tell you that they are wrong, but I've watched too many Westerns and lived too long in this democracy to deny their truths. I'm no stranger in this village; I, too, am a product of the culture in which I was raised. I'd be lying to you, and myself, were I to deny that each time charges are announced for another participant in the January insurrection I scoff at the absence of charges for sedition, treason, and terrorism against the mob of mutineers. Focusing unduly on the American scene presents its own conundrum too in a journal devoted to a man as cosmopolitan as Baldwin, for *James Baldwin Review* seeks to expand our international readership. As of this volume, we've had visitors to our open access website from 80 different countries around the world, a readership we hope to expand further, not alienate with additional focus on the "exceptionalism" of America. The fragility of American democracy, though, bodes ill for the whole world if we let it falter still.

Forgive me, dear reader, as I'm having some troubles tying this all together. For one, to even make a tentative list of all that has transpired since last I penned the introduction to *James Baldwin Review* is bound to be exhausting for us both, and yet not nearly exhaustive enough. Rarely does Shakespeare get accused of under-stating things, but I've selected our first epigraph from *King Lear* as a nod to all that we've been through this past year. Old or young, I'd say, will never see as much nor have a year lived so long as 2020. There are too many threads upon which to comment. When you have this many threads, your garment is just as likely to be a Gordian snarl of knots as it is to be a beautifully, luxuriously dense weave of 500 strands of the finest Egyptian cotton. Finally, I'll acknowledge that as I write this I'm having trouble focusing on the task at hand chiefly because I'm also simulta-neously switching between five different browser windows, constantly refreshing the same webpage in a hexagonal dance of resubmitting the same medical info and the same zip codes, desperately trying to secure my spot in line for a vaccine.

Let's focus, then, on a notion Baldwin seems to have misjudged, the strength of our social bond. Not to say that he "got it wrong," exactly, but to note that the times and circumstances have fundamentally, paradigmatically changed since he wrote. I'm not suggesting that he should somehow have seen the future with which we grapple, nor be faulted for not anticipating the fourth industrial revolution. Rather, I submit that when we bring the power of his words to bear on our own moments, unpacking the contextual, historical distances between us can be especially illuminating. Baldwin's long essay *No Name in the Street* (1972) concludes with a gambit about one's desire to live in harmony among one's fellow citizenry:

> A person does not lightly elect to oppose his society. One would much rather be at home among one's compatriots than be mocked and detested by them. And there is a level on which the mockery of the people, even their hatred, is moving because it is so blind; it is terrible to watch people cling to their captivity and insist on their own destruction.[13]

This is both profoundly true, in the elemental human sense of our fear of alienation and desire to be connected, and also unhelpfully bound to the time in which Baldwin first penned it. Simply put, the technological revolution since he wrote this in 1972 means that today, in a mash of posts, one can quite easily oppose one's society; what's more, one can do so without much consequence.

For the opposition Baldwin speaks of occurred in a sphere far more public, far more accountable, than our own online forums where anonymity and isolation reign. In 1972, to be oppositional might mean that you would be shunned, isolated and apart from your peers. Taken further, you might be branded a "radical" and lose privacy due to surveillance. Kept at a distance by leaders during the civil rights movement, spurned by Black Power—in both cases because of his sexuality—and harassed by the FBI, Baldwin would surely have known this. But when you're already isolated and anonymous, when your privacy has already been freely traded for access to platforms, what's one got to lose by being oppositional in 2021? A few social media followers, perhaps? The sad fact is you may well stand to gain quite a bit. Opposition, after all, courts offense, offense begets attention, and attention generates advertising revenue. Certainly you needn't worry about any legal consequences, for you can always resort to claiming your opposition, no matter how outlandish, is merely "opinion." You're not denying reality, you're "simply asking questions." Commit yourself to being oppositional enough, and you might be asked to co-host a show with Tucker Carlson or fill Rush Limbaugh's now vacant talk radio space, to say nothing of the conspiratorial corners of the internet.

It's a sad irony that this same long essay by Baldwin, his most sobering look at the failure of the country to heed the warnings of the civil rights era, begins with an epigraph from an African American spiritual, what he terms in the book a "slave song," with the refrain, "If I had-a-my way I'd tear this building down."[14] Though the January 2021 coup attempt failed, the dystopian desires so brazenly displayed have been too easily dismissed. Considering America's ills, we are sadly still stuck, as Baldwin noted in 1969, "believing that the empty and criminal among our children are the result of some miscalculation in the formula (which can be corrected); that the bottomless and aimless hostility which makes our cities among the most dangerous in the world is created, and felt, by a handful of aberrants."[15] Some take solace in the idea that the looters were led astray, writing and pontificating about "the big lie," but the harsh truth is that Donald Trump received more than seventy million votes in November. Four years of a monstrously misleading administration and half a million deaths from a mismanaged pandemic, and yet close to half of the voters voted for more of the same. That so many refused to accept the results, boorishly breaking into the Capitol in bizarre costumes in pursuit of an absurd premise, a pursuit that left more than 100 injured and five dead, should give us every reason to calculate with a different formula.

At the time of this writing, deaths due to COVID-19 are nearing 600,000 in the US, over 3 million worldwide.[16] Hunkered down at home, we've learned a lot of medical terminology this year. The term "comorbidity" refers primarily to the existence of two simultaneous ailments. This coexistence is not an issue of causality; it is an issue of consequences. Whether we term them conditions, disorders, or diseases is less important than the notion that more than one of these, in combination, is more likely to lead to serious illness or death. I'd like to propose that we examine the political impact of Trump and his hold on not just the public but especially the Republican party with the same terminology. Not an issue of cause or symptom, but as a comorbidity. Was it Trump's racism and disdain for authority that called out to his voters and the politicians and pundits that did his bidding, or was he simply a witless but all too willing accomplice to America's persistent white supremacy and willed ignorance? That, to me, is less important than the fact, which I perceive to be as plain as day, that this combination, these comorbidities in the American political and governmental system, are making our democracy measurably ill. One can only hope that should the morbidity turn mortal it will mean the death of so-called "Republican" politics in America, and not of the American republic.

Comorbidity also may be a useful lens through which to understand the January insurrection, as we're forced now more than ever before to ponder the impact of social media on public discourse and democracy. Are the antisocial impetuses revealed in the meteoric rise of social media platforms amplifying or merely revealing our tendencies to separate into cordoned-off, warring camps? Surely the scions of social media would prefer to lay the blame at our feet and claim that they are merely providing "what the users want." Messrs Zuckerberg, Pichia, and Dorsey have all repeatedly proclaimed so, whenever Facebook, Google, or Twitter are brought before Congress concerning the impact of their platforms. Resisting regulation at every turn, they either push responsibility onto users or claim they're unable to do anything about the beasts they've unleashed. Say what you will about the desire to play God and cheat death, but at least Dr. Frankenstein had the decency to chase his monster to the ends of the earth when it got free and started killing people.

Baldwin, speaking of the television Western *Gunsmoke*, rightly points to the inseparability between culture and society, undermining the notion that art or society "reflects" one or the other, and insisting that they are, instead, intertwined:

> I am less appalled by the fact that *Gunsmoke* is produced than I am by the fact that so many people want to see it ... The people who run the mass media and those who consume it are really in the same boat. They must continue to produce things they do

not really admire, still less love, in order to continue buying things they do not really
want, still less need ... The trouble is that serious things are handled (and received)
with the same essential lack of seriousness.[17]

Our current media culture is far more diverse and diversified—two different
things, after all—than the broadcast media apparatus that reigned when Baldwin
wrote this essay in 1959, a time when there were only a handful of channels, and
Westerns like *Gunsmoke* accounted for an inordinate amount of programming. In
our narrowcasting realm of streaming services and niche selections, though, the
paradigm is eerily similar. One can be forgiven for looking at Mr. Andy Cohen's
television oeuvre with the same appalled apprehension at the state of our "culture"
industry, to say nothing of the absurdities paraded about as "news." All this before
we even begin to see the effects of what Baldwin aptly diagnosed as an "essential
lack of seriousness" be played out as the rejection of mask-wearing mandates, hes-
itancy over a vaccination that will save not only lives but entire economic orders,
or the outright denial of contagion itself during a pandemic.

Though he could not have envisioned the paradigmatic shifts in our media
environments since 1972, Baldwin seems eerily prescient about the calamities to
befall us when we deny the fulness of our complex humanity. In his first major
essay, "Everyone's Protest Novel," an attack on Richard Wright that launched his
career even before his first novel was published, Baldwin worried about a zeal for
categorization leading to confusion that is worth an extended quote:

> Our passion for categorization, life neatly fitted into pegs, has led to an unforeseen,
> paradoxical distress; confusion, a breakdown of meaning. Those categories which
> were meant to define and control the world for us have boomeranged us into chaos;
> in which limbo we whirl, clutching the straws of our definitions. The "protest" novel,
> so far from being disturbing, is an accepted and comforting aspect of the American
> scene, ramifying that framework we believe to be so necessary. Whatever unsettling
> questions are raised are evanescent, titillating; remote, for this has nothing to do with
> us, it is safely ensconced in the social arena, where, indeed it has nothing to do with
> anyone, so that finally we receive a very definite thrill of virtue from the fact that we
> are reading such a book at all. This report from the pit reassures us of its reality and
> its darkness and our own salvation ... But unless one's ideal of society is a race of
> neatly analyzed hard-working ciphers, one can hardly claim for the protest novels the
> lofty purpose they claim for themselves or share the present optimism concerning
> them. They emerge for what they are; a mirror of our confusion, dishonesty, panic,
> trapped and immobilized in the sunlight prison of the American dream.[18]

Writing from Paris in the late 1940s, Baldwin here aptly captures the encapsulated
existences of our cordoned-off, online lives. The unparalleled connectivity we
experience in an utterly mediated reality has paradoxically led us to be less connected than ever before. For most of our connections are meted out by a set of
algorithmic designs that few of us explicitly consented to and even fewer of us
understand. The "ideal" society Baldwin warns of here is precisely the ideal of a

well-functioning algorithm: neatly broken down into discrete units with predictable outputs. What's more, the algorithms that populate our media spheres were designed to capture most of all our attention. And, to put it mildly, we are hooked. As communication theorist and Obama campaign strategist Michael Slaby notes in his manifesto for changing the trajectory of these platforms, *For All the People*, this addiction is by design:

> These systems are intended to be habit forming … They are designed with feedback loops meant to prey on our brain chemistry for rewards and with outrage to keep our attention. They are configured to keep us clicking on more and more content, regardless of whether we are informed or satisfied. Being informed or satisfied is not the goal of these systems—it's not how they are optimized.[19]

To put it simply, as long as we stay logged on the ad revenue piles up. None of this, mind you, is an accident; it has been designed this way. On purpose. For profit. This cannot be overstated. The predictability of the unit and the output feed back upon each other in a loop or echo that is no less predictable, and therefore all the more profitable.

Were it only profits being extracted, the need for modification might not be so dire. When the loop closes in upon itself, authority and expertise are not simply no longer needed, they are, more worrisome still, a burden to the smooth flow of algorithmic sorting. What once was knowledge or wisdom is now noise, friction, a hindrance. The distinction between information and disinformation falls apart when the only marker of impact is popularity. As Baldwin put it, the unforeseen result is "confusion, a breakdown of meaning" as we are "boomeranged into chaos." The chaos is not merely metaphorical, for Slaby usefully points out that the consequences of such indistinguishability are not just dire, they are downright deadly:

> As more and more of our content consumption moves toward online streams and feeds, the platforms benefit more—in terms of maximized attention and continuous engagement—from the indistinguishability of credible versus incredible content than from accuracy … In addition to crumbling trust, the failure of our systems to help us understand and distinguish credible information also results in a decrease in the value of expertise that society needs to function.[20]

Whether it is the promulgation of misinformation about public health, further polarization and division, the lack of a common story to unify, or a shared aim for which to strive, the "price of the ticket" we've paid for all this putatively "free" content is proving, alas, to be rather expensive. Poisoned bread, indeed.

*****

The seventh volume of *James Baldwin Review* contains a mixture of tone, approach, and topic as we continue to strive to deliver material to stimulate appreciation and debate about the writing and impact of our chief subject. Our volume begins with a "Feature Essay" by the esteemed and inimitable Ed Pavlić entitled "'Indisputably Available': The Texture—Gendered, Sexual, Violent—of James Baldwin's Southern Silences." Prompted by his reading of Colson Whitehead's Pulitzer Prize-winning novel *The Nickel Boys* (2019), which is set in Tallahassee, FL, during the 1950s and 1960s, Pavlić presents here an in-depth look at Baldwin's own visit to Tallahassee in May 1960. Considering Baldwin's writings about the South, especially the 1960 essay "They Can't Turn Back," Pavlić puts forth the missing names of Black women in the places marked and unmarked by Baldwin—notably but not limited to Girvaud Roberts, Dorothy Tookes, and Patricia Stevens Due—and puts the May 1959 sexual assault of Betty Jean Owens on the historical map. Pavlić's exploration of issues of race, gender, sex, and violence for their intertwined impacts on historical, and some contemporary, writing offers a deeper consideration of Baldwin's work and the history which he drew upon and to which he contributed so profoundly.

Volume 7 of *James Baldwin Review* presents our first group of guest-edited essays, concentrating our attention on Baldwin and film, considered broadly, in a special section edited by Robert Jackson entitled "Finding Work for the Devil." The essays in this section, from Robert Jackson, Karen Thorsen, D. Quentin Miller, Hayley O'Malley, and Peter Lurie, grew out of a panel hosted by *JBR* at the Modern Language Association's meeting in Seattle in January of 2020. As Jackson notes in his introduction to the section, Baldwin's relationship with film throughout his life was complicated:

> Film is such a big topic in Baldwin's life and career that it can almost be invisible at times, like geological time or climate change or some other pattern whose scale renders it invisible … Baldwin's relationship with film, meanwhile, is not just one thing; it takes many forms, and it changes a great deal over the course of his life.

From Thorsen's remembrance of her lunch with Baldwin in 1986 to O'Malley's deep dig through archival riches, from Miller's innovative reading of *The Devil Finds Work* as a love story to Lurie's examination of the impacts Baldwin's cinematic visions continue to make in current film, this special, guest-edited section of *James Baldwin Review* presents a close focus on a specific topic in Baldwin's life, work, and legacy.

Our Graduate Student Award-winning essay, "'In the Name of Love': Black Queer Feminism and the Sexual Politics of *Another Country*," comes to us from Matty Hemming of the University of Pennsylvania. Hemming explores the sexual politics of Baldwin's 1962 novel from a Black queer feminist perspective, arguing that this critical lens allows us to de-prioritize white gay male eroticism and pursue analyses of a broader range of erotic scenes, thereby reframing *Another Country* as less an idealization of gay male intimacy, reading it, instead, as a troubling, unsettling vision of sex within, as Hemming puts it, a "messy terrain of pleasure, pain, and political urgency."

The "Dispatches" section includes two interviews and a review. William J. Maxwell interviewed Bill Mullen about Mullen's latest book, *James Baldwin: Living in Fire* (2019), and their discussion naturally includes a consideration of Baldwin's internationalism and his relevance to the current pitfalls—and possibilities—within our contemporary racial moment. The second interview was conducted over email by *JBR* editors Douglas Field and Justin A. Joyce with James Campbell. Campbell, whose biography of Baldwin, *Talking at the Gates*, will be reissued in an expanded edition later this year, provides readers with an expansive consideration of a number of topics and time periods. The resulting interview is, perhaps, the record of a man of letters, whose career of reading and writing, I hazard, we all might wish to emulate. Our "Dispatches" closes with a review essay by Herb Boyd, "White Lies Matter," wherein Boyd evaluates Eddie S. Glaude, Jr.'s best-selling *Begin Again: James Baldwin's America and Its Urgent Lessons for our Own* (2020) against several other recent works such as Bill Mullen's *James Baldwin: Living in Fire* and Nicholas Buccola's *The Fire Is Upon Us* (2019).

James Baldwin Review is very excited to premiere in this volume our first set of creative works. Swedish writer Aleksander Motturi presents us with "The Fire Inside," translated for *JBR* by award-winning translator Kira Josefsson, a creative spin on the infamous meeting between Baldwin and then US Attorney General Robert Kennedy in 1963. Motturi's piece is followed by a contribution from Maureen Kelleher, private detective and advocate for prisoners wrongly sentenced to death. "Baldwin's Perfect Storm" is a creative reimagining of Baldwin's suicidal depression upon his release from a brief stint in a Parisian jail in 1949. We hope these first creative pieces in *JBR* will not only provoke our readers' imaginations but also generate interest and further submission of creative works for future volumes.

As many of you may have heard, we lost an esteemed colleague in 2020 with the passing of Cheryl Wall. *James Baldwin Review*, with the generous coordination of Cora Kaplan, has collected here numerous tributes to Cheryl's memory, her impact, and her friendship in an *In Memoriam* tribute. Professor Wall didn't simply change the course of African American literary studies with her pioneering work on Black women's fiction—especially that of Zora Neale Hurston—she also touched countless lives through her generous mentorship and inspired teaching. We hope to honor her legacy here.

Our seventh volume finishes with our bibliographic essay, which comes to us from Terrance Dean. Reading works on Baldwin from 2017 to 2019, Dean tracks the significance of Baldwin for the Black Lives Matter movement and our growing need for police reform in conjunction with a revaluation of the lives of racial and ethnic minorities within the oppressive systemic biases of American social and political life.

This year's cover comes to us from Brooklyn-based artist Rico Gatson, whose stunning mural installations adorn the recently remodeled 167th St. subway station in New York City. The Baldwin mural, based off of a photograph by Steve Shapiro, is one of eight murals drawn from Gatson's earlier museum installation, "Icons." The other murals at the Bronx station by Gatson celebrate Gil Scott Heron, Audre Lorde, Celia Cruz, Justice Sonya Sotomayor, Reggie Jackson, Tito Puente, and Maya Angelou. Aptly entitled "Beacons," these murals stand as prominent testaments to the power of cultural and artistic icons to lead and catalyze change and action through their exemplary lives and works. *James Baldwin Review* is grateful to Mr. Gatson and Mr. Shapiro for their generous permission to feature this inspiring public art. Like a lighthouse showing the way safely to shore, or a signal fire lighting the darkness, beacons of hope like James Baldwin can help ensure we are walking in the right direction on whatever paths our journeys create.

Pondering the disarray and discordance wrought by the paradigm shift in our communications and connections, looking to Baldwin's searing witnessing as a beacon in our present darkness, I take solace in Baldwin's notion of being "boomeranged." As I understand it, a boomerang comes back to the thrower at the end of its arc. It's a weapon, after all, a tool intended to wound or kill, but what makes it unique and storied is that after riding the wind on its deadly path, it returns to the point of origin. Unlike other projectiles, the boomerang, that is, comes back. The elliptical path is somewhat predetermined but we have the chance to catch it at a different point. Though we may have been thrown into chaos, perhaps by walking a step toward the arc of the tools and weapons we've deployed, to meet them in a different place from whence we began, we might have the chance to come back. To what, though, depends upon us.

Each of us, then, has much work to do to ensure that the arc of the weapon bends toward not more death or destruction, not more disinformation and division, but instead toward a different use for the tools of our time, in line with the oft-quoted line from Martin Luther King about the arc of the moral universe bending toward justice. Speaking on the occasion of John Lewis's sixty-fifth birthday, Barack Obama noted that this arc needs our work:

> It doesn't bend on its own. It bends because we help it bend that way ... [because] thousands of ordinary Americans with extraordinary courage have helped it bend that way ... we continue to progress as a people because they inspire us to take our own two hands and bend that arc.[21]

As my colleague Julian Hater has put it, "things done on purpose must be undone purposefully."[22]

The purposes before us are many—police reform, expansion of voting rights and access, healthcare reform, climate change and energy reform, gun control, renewing our commitments to not just scientific expertise but higher education as well—but in closing I'd like to bring us back to where we began our journey. One of the striking parts about John Lewis's story is the presence of the lone figure of authority, Aunt Sevena. She's the "adult in the room," you see, and we've been hearing a lot about these adults as of late. How the adults in the room would prevail over irresponsible notions and instill order and calm amid the chaos. Over and again we were assured that the "adults in the room" would temper Trump's tantrums. Instead, they were simply replaced. Whenever one of the "adults" ran counter to impish impulses, a more malleable minion was ushered in to take their place.

As Baldwin pointed out in *The Fire Next Time* (1963), "a civilization is not destroyed by wicked people; it is not necessary that people be wicked but only that they be spineless."[23] The cumulative effect of such a revolving door in so esteemed an office as the White House was that at any one time which adult in the room was supposed to be the voice of reason was unclear, to both the greater public and the other grown-ups in the West Wing. Categorically unchecked, is it any wonder the "child" grew unrulier still? He tried to cheat the election by pressuring numerous officials to overturn results, cried "foul" when he didn't win, and spread false information nearly as fast as specious lawsuits. When all these attempts to rig the game in his favor came up short, are we really surprised that he ultimately resorted to inciting a riot and a revolt, like a brat smashing his toys?

I find solace and, it must be admitted, a bit of hope near the end of our journey, in the image of conscience and courage presented by Aunt Sevena as she guided the children in her care during the windstorm. Certainly, there are children about still who need such courage from us, for the winds have not yet ceased to blow. Baldwin wrote many times about innocence and children—not at all the same thing—often with variations on a central thesis, that "a child cannot afford to be fooled."[24] Writing for *Esquire* in 1980, he elaborates:

> Children, I submit, cannot be fooled. They can only be betrayed by adults, not fooled—for adults, unlike children, are fooled very easily, and only because they wish to be … no child can fool another child the way one adult can fool another.[25]

After the year we've come through, I'd venture that America, young *and* old, can no longer afford to fool ourselves and each other. For whenever this present storm may pass, another will surely rise, threatening to lift again the corners of our house. In these moments, we will need to heed Aunt Sevena's instruction. Each of us, whether we dwell in the American house or no, whether or not we are the designated "adult" in the room, will need to move at least close enough to grasp one another's hand and walk together. Whichever path you walk to secure a healthier, more unified, and more just future, walk well, friends, and walk with the wind.

Grosse Pointe Park, MI, 1 May 2021

Notes

1 William Shakespeare, *King Lear*, Act 5, scene 3, final lines spoken by Edgar.

2 James Baldwin, *No Name in the Street* (1972) (New York, Vintage, 2000), p. 192.

3 John Lewis, *Walking with the Wind: A Memoir of the Movement* (New York, Simon and Schuster, 1998), p. xvi.

4 *Ibid.*, pp. xvi–xvii.

5 James Baldwin, "Letter to Jay Acton," qtd. in *I Am Not Your Negro (Compiled and Edited by Raoul Peck)* (New York, Vintage, 2017), p. 5.

6 Toni Morrison, qtd. in Timothy Greenfield-Sanders (dir.), *Toni Morrison: The Pieces I Am* (USA, Perfect Day Films, 2019).

7 Abraham Lincoln, "Inaugural Address, March 4, 1861," https://millercenter.org/the-presidency/presidential-speeches/march-4-1861-first-inaugural-address (accessed 23 April 2021).

8 Baldwin, *No Name*, p. 9.

9 *Ibid.*, p. 10.

10 Barack Obama, "A New Era of Responsibility," First Inaugural Address, Washington DC, 20 January 2009, in *We Are the Change We Seek: The Speeches of Barack Obama*, ed. E. J. Dionne, Jr., and Joy-Ann Reid (New York, Bloomsbury, 2017), p. 102.

11 Terry K. Aladjem, *The Culture of Vengeance and the Fate of American Justice* (New York, Cambridge University Press, 2008), p. 3.

12 James Baldwin, "Stranger in the Village" (1953), in *Collected Essays*, ed. Toni Morrison (New York, Library of America, 1998), p. 119.

13 Baldwin, *No Name*, pp. 194–5.

14 *Ibid.*, n.p.

15 James Baldwin, "Mass Culture and the Creative Artist: Some Personal Notes" (1969), in *The Cross of Redemption: Uncollected Writings*, ed. Randall Kenan (New York, Pantheon, 2010), p. 5.

16 Statistics from the Johns Hopkins Coronavirus Resource Center, https://coronavirus.jhu.edu/map.html (accessed 23 April 2021).

17 Baldwin, "Mass Culture and the Creative Artist," pp. 4–5.

18 James Baldwin, "Everybody's Protest Novel" (1949), in *Notes of a Native Son* (New York, Beacon Press, 1992), p. 19. I'm indebted to the Quilting Points reading group, led by Joseph Genchi, Izzy Jenkinson, and Craig McDonald at the University of Leeds, for inviting me to participate in their discussions during 2021. Izzy Jenkinson, in particular, deserves credit here for first bringing the contemporary pertinence of this part of Baldwin's essay to my attention.

19 Michael Slaby, *For All the People: Redeeming the Broken Promises of Modern Media and Reclaiming our Civic Life* (New York, Disruption Books, 2021), pp. 168–9.

20 *Ibid.*, pp. 88–9.

21 Barack Obama, "'How Far We've Come,' Remarks at John Lewis's Sixty-fifth Birthday Gala, Atlanta, GA, Feb 21, 2005," in Dionne, Jr., and Reid (eds.), *We Are the Change We Seek*, p. 20.

22 I first heard this from Hater as part of a community discussion sponsored by the Oklahoma Center for the Humanities on Carol Anderson's book *White Rage* on 4 February, 2021. I'm using this quote here with Dr. Hater's permission.

23 James Baldwin, *The Fire Next Time* (1963), in Morrison (ed.), *Collected Essays*, p. 318.

24 James Baldwin, "If Black English Isn't a Language, Then Tell Me What Is" (1979), in Morrison (ed.), *Collected Essays*, p. 783.

25 James Baldwin, "Dark Days" (1980), in Morrison (ed.), *Collected Essays*, p. 794.

Works Cited

Aladjem, Terry K., *The Culture of Vengeance and the Fate of American Justice* (New York, Cambridge University Press, 2008).

Baldwin, James, "Dark Days" (1980), in *Collected Essays*, ed. Toni Morrison (New York, Library of America, 1998), pp. 788–98.

_____ "Everybody's Protest Novel" (1949), in *Notes of a Native Son* (New York, Beacon Press, 1992), pp. 11–18.

_____ *The Fire Next Time* (1963), in *Collected Essays*, ed. Toni Morrison (New York, Library of America, 1998), pp. 286–347.

_____ *I Am Not Your Negro (Compiled and Edited by Raoul Peck)* (New York, Vintage, 2017).

_____ "If Black English Isn't a Language, Then Tell Me What Is" (1979), in *Collected Essays*, ed. Toni Morrison (New York, Library of America, 1998), pp. 780–3.

_____ "Mass Culture and the Creative Artist: Some Personal Notes" (1969), in *The Cross of Redemption: Uncollected Writings*, ed. Randall Kenan (New York, Pantheon, 2010), pp. 3–6.

_____ *No Name in the Street* (1972) (New York, Vintage, 2000).

_____ "Stranger in the Village" (1953), in *Collected Essays*, ed. Toni Morrison (New York, Library of America, 1998), pp. 117–29.

Greenfield-Sanders, Timothy (dir.), *Toni Morrison: The Pieces I Am* (USA, Perfect Day Films, 2019).

Johns Hopkins Coronavirus Resource Center, https://coronavirus.jhu.edu/map.html (accessed 23 April 2021).

Lewis, John, *Walking with the Wind: A Memoir of the Movement* (New York, Simon and Schuster, 1998).

Lincoln, Abraham, "Inaugural Address, March 4, 1861," https://millercenter.org/the-presidency/presidential-speeches/march-4-1861-first-inaugural-address (accessed 23 April 2021).

Obama, Barack, "A New Era of Responsibility," First Inaugural Address, Washington DC, 20 January 2009, in *We Are the Change We Seek: The Speeches of Barack Obama*, ed. E. J. Dionne, Jr., and Joy-Ann Reid (New York, Bloomsbury, 2017), pp. 96–105.

_____ "'How Far We've Come,' Remarks at John Lewis's Sixty-fifth Birthday Gala, Atlanta, GA, Feb 21, 2005," in *We Are the Change We Seek: The Speeches of Barack Obama*, ed. E. J. Dionne, Jr., and Joy-Ann Reid (New York, Bloomsbury, 2017), pp. 14–20.

Slaby, Michael, *For All the People: Redeeming the Broken Promises of Modern Media and Reclaiming our Civic Life* (New York, Disruption Books, 2021).

Contributor's Biography

Justin A. Joyce is one of the founding editors of *James Baldwin Review* and the journal's current managing editor, and he is Research Director at The New School. An interdisciplinary scholar of literature and film, his first monograph was *Gunslinging Justice: The American Culture of Gun Violence in Westerns and the Law* (Manchester University Press, 2018). With Dwight A. McBride, he is the editor of *A Melvin Dixon Critical Reader* (University Press of Mississippi, 2006), Vincent Woodard's Lambda Literary Award-winning book *The Delectable Negro: Human Consumption and Homoeroticism in U.S. Slave Narratives* (NYU Press, 2014), and Lindon Barrett's *Racial Blackness and the Discontinuity of Western Modernity* (University of Illinois Press, 2014). Featured in interviews and discussions on *The Humanities on the High Plains* podcast, the Maryland Lynching Memorial Project, and on *RadioWest*, Joyce's writings on Baldwin have also appeared in *A Historical Guide to James Baldwin* (Oxford University Press, 2009) and *James Baldwin in Context* (Cambridge University Press, 2019).

Manchester University Press

FEATURE ESSAY

"Indisputably Available": The Texture—Gendered, Sexual, Violent—of James Baldwin's Southern Silences

Ed Pavlić   University of Georgia

Abstract

Spurred on by Colson Whitehead's Pulitzer Prize-winning novel *The Nickel Boys* (2019), which is set in Tallahassee, FL, during the 1950s and 1960s, this essay presents a close-up look at James Baldwin's visit to Tallahassee in May 1960. Moving between Baldwin's writings about the South, especially "They Can't Turn Back," published by *Mademoiselle* magazine in August 1960, and subsequent writing about the movement in Tallahassee, and checking off against Whitehead's fictional treatment, we find a lattice of silences obscuring the names and contributions of Black women. Most importantly, we find that the historic case of the rape of Betty Jean Owens in May 1959, and the subsequent trial that summer, appears neither in Baldwin's nor Whitehead's writing about Tallahassee at the time. This essay establishes the missing names of Black women in the places marked and unmarked by Baldwin in his work at the time, and puts the case of Betty Jean Owens on the historical map where it belongs. In so doing, we figure issues of race, gender, sex, and violence for the ways they twist together, ways suppressed in historical (and even some contemporary) writing, ways crucial to our deepening consideration of Baldwin's work and the history which he drew upon and to which he contributed so profoundly.

Keywords: Colson Whitehead, civil rights, Tallahassee, Deep South, rape, Betty Jean Owens, Patricia Stevens Due, Daisy Young, Dorothy Nash Tookes, Girvaud Roberts, Danielle L. McGuire

James Baldwin Review, Volume 7, 2021, © The Authors. Published by Manchester University Press and The University of Manchester Library
http://dx.doi.org/10.7227/JBR.7.2

Colson Whitehead's Pulitzer Prize-winning novel *The Nickel Boys* (2019) had been sitting on my ever-growing stack of books to read for months. Because final grades went in and the Pulitzers were announced on the same morning, early in May 2020, I decided to read it, which I did, in one day. It's a very good novel that tells much in a short space. Whitehead's language is a chiseled economy, a web of phrases honed to purpose and precision. And answering the—silent?—call of certain literary fiction that aspires to popular contemporary success, *The Nickel Boys* succeeds in presenting a tale of trouble and moral—in this case racial—atrocity while tonally and obliquely reassuring otherwise comfortable American readers that they are, indeed, otherwise comfortable American readers. They may look away whenever they like. Stable ground exists outside the frame, for someone. Whitehead's story centers on a fictional correctional facility for boys, the Nickel School, which is loosely based on a historical one, the Arthur G. Dozier School for Boys, both in Florida.

Purpose and precision: pinning down a racial and political point, the hall of torture where physical abuse is doled out to boys who break rules at the Nickel School is called the "White House." After being severely beaten at the White House, the main character, Elwood Curtis, a known nonviolent idealist, is left out of a plan to poison a particularly hated abuser at the school:

> The prank was against his moral conscience. Hard to picture the Reverend Martin Luther King Jr. dousing Governor Orval Faubus with a couple ounces of lye. And Elwood's beating at the White House had him scarred all over, not just his legs. It had weeviled deep into his personality.[1]

That thing about Whitehead's chiseled economy: I hadn't seen "weeviled" as a verb. Even so, it's a little strange that the narration fixes our attention on the Governor of Arkansas. During the narrative present, the early 1960s, Florida Governor Cecil Farris Bryant, a staunch segregationist who had replaced the comparatively liberal Thomas Collins in 1961, would have done just as well for anyone who had lived in Florida at the time.

In a popular novel like *The Nickel Boys*, however, the audience isn't really people who had ever lived in Florida or those with a nuanced historical knowledge. It's written for active reading members of what James Baldwin once called "the great, vast blank generality" in America: "descendants of a barbarous Europe who arbitrarily and arrogantly reserve the right to call themselves Americans."[2] Baldwin would remark upon such American blankness, which, as in *The Fire Next Time* (1963), more than a strictly racial feature of our personalities, or lack of same, he thought signaled "the little connection" many people's "attitudes have with their perceptions or their lives."[3] Concentrated among white people in those decades, and especially, at least in Baldwin's experience at the time, among liberals, I think we could say the twenty-first century has democratized access to "blank generality" as an option among those who aspire to the way its detached numbness feels like safety. We might call that progress, if we're crazy.

Whitehead's novel expertly tickles and trifles with, and here and there lashes out at, the free-floating moral sense—aka the innocence—of this blankly generalized readership. It's the job of popular fiction to tickle and trifle and, at times, to lash out in these ways because it's only in those moments when that moral sense can be felt to exist at all. Late in the novel, one of the novel's key characters, long out of detention, still finds himself trying to pass for one of the blank Americans:

> All these years out of that school and he still spent a segment of his days trying to decipher the customs of normal people. The ones who had been raised happily, three meals a day and a kiss goodnight, the ones who had no notion of White Houses … and white county judges who sentenced you to hell.[4]

This is part of the science of contemporary, popular, literary fiction: a story meant to tickle and lash out at "normal people" who "had been raised happily" so that they can be made sure—by the tickling and lashing—that they themselves exist. In this task, stories of people demonstrably *other* to that blank normal play an important role. *The Nickel Boys* is astonishingly good at doing this.

For me, however, the most interesting things about *The Nickel Boys* are the choices Whitehead makes in setting up the world his main character comes from. Elwood Curtis comes from a very particular time in a very particular place: Tallahassee during the 1950s and early 1960s. I read the first chapters of the book fascinated to see how Whitehead would situate a general—not to say blank—reader in and among particulars that most people know very little about. Tallahassee during those years wasn't Faubus's Little Rock or Bull Connor's Birmingham. In decades since, Tallahassee hasn't accrued the mythology of those battlegrounds. But it was indeed crucial in ways that, at the time, weren't exactly featured even by people very close to the civil rights movement. I wondered if Whitehead would break those silences, a lattice of gendered and sexualized silences. When he didn't I felt compelled to go back and look closely at them myself, silences left in the creases between the histories in fiction and the fictions in history.

In *The Nickel Boys*, Elwood lives with Harriet Johnson, his maternal grandmother. Elwood is a quiet, keenly observant, and studious young Black man. As a child, his attention latches on to a recording of speeches by Martin Luther King, Jr., and the local bus boycott, which started when "he was ten years old."[5] In history the Tallahassee bus boycott began on 26 May 1956 and ended in a truce of sorts that pleased no one on 22 December of that same year. This was two days after a more resolute victory came, about 200 miles to the Northwest, in the more widely known Montgomery bus boycott. In *The Nickel Boys*, refusing to become "the only woman in Frenchtown to take public transportation," Elwood's grandmother reluctantly and fearfully supports the boycott: "she trembled each time Slim Harrison pulled up in his '57 Cadillac and she squeezed into the back with the other downtown-bound ladies."[6]

Six years later, while in high school, age 16, Elwood joins a protest in May 1963 meant to desegregate two movie houses in downtown Tallahassee, the State and Florida Theaters. Also in May of that year, a SNCC-affiliated history teacher even gives Elwood a copy of James Baldwin's 1955 book, *Notes of a Native Son*, which Whitehead quotes. As he reads Baldwin's 1951 essay, "Many Thousands Gone"—"*Negroes are Americans and their destiny is the country's destiny*"—we're told that Elwood's "mind churned."[7] An opportunity to enroll in a nearby college leads Elwood to hitch a ride in what turns out to be a stolen car. This lands him at the Nickel School, and propels the story into what it becomes. All that is set up in about forty pages.

The glance at Tallahassee and its (at the time, nationally visible) local "Freedom Movement" in the first chapters of *The Nickel Boys*, the brief reference to and quote from James Baldwin, and the longer passages from Martin Luther King's speeches that ring in Elwood's mind throughout the book got me thinking. You could say it made *my* mind churn. I knew Baldwin had toured the South a few times during the years of Elwood's fictional adolescence. I also knew Baldwin had visited Tallahassee. Splicing history into fiction, as Whitehead does deftly, if somewhat blankly, in *The Nickel Boys*, I wondered how close Baldwin had come to "Elwood" during his time in Tallahassee, late in the month of May in 1960, exactly sixty years before *The Nickel Boys* would win the Pulitzer Prize—Whitehead's second—for fiction. I also wondered about things that Whitehead and Baldwin both left out of their descriptions of the Tallahassee movement, things Elwood and, especially, Elwood's grandmother and "the other downtown-bound ladies" in the back seat of Slim Harrison's brand-new Caddy must have had in—or perhaps placed carefully just outside—their minds at the time.

I also thought about how it was a little unfortunate that, in *The Nickel Boys*, Elwood's teacher, Mr. Hill, gave Elwood the book he did. While obviously resonant, *Notes of a Native Son* was published before Baldwin had thought seriously about a civil rights movement, and before he'd ever been to the Deep South. What if Mr. Hill had given Elwood *Nobody Knows My Name* (1961), Baldwin's most recent book of essays at that point in Whitehead's novel? Elwood's mind might have churned upon sentences aimed closer to his home and his experience than those in *Notes of a Native Son*. In essays like "A Fly in Buttermilk" and "A Letter From the South," Elwood would have read about students somewhat like himself, students like Gus Roberts in Charlotte, NC, and about the curious tensions in Black families and communities between those who supported the movement, those who joined, and others who refused. In fact, in a letter from the day after he met Gus Roberts, in October 1957, Baldwin asked his friend Mary Painter in Washington DC if she'd buy a paperback copy of *Notes of a Native Son* and send it to the embattled young man. He provided Gus Roberts's address, 512 N. McDowell St., in Charlotte, and told Mary he would have asked his agent or the press to send it "but they ain't reliable."[8]

Strangely, however, in *Nobody Knows My Name*, Elwood wouldn't have learned about Gus Roberts's sister, Girvaud, who, by herself, integrated her middle school the same fall her older brother, by himself, integrated his high school class in September 1957 in Charlotte. Baldwin notes that Gus's "younger brother and sister" were there when he visited the Roberts home, staying till midnight.[9] But he never mentions her by name, nor that she was one of the four students integrating the schools in Charlotte, not a word about it. Did he never think to have Mary Painter send two copies of *Notes of a Native Son*? Now, whenever I re-read "A Fly in Buttermilk"—first published in *Harper's*, in October 1958, titled "The Hard Kind of Courage"—I think about Girvaud Roberts's missing name and I wonder about that silence, as we'll see, one of many.

Some literary silences are harder to break than others. Even had he read all of *Nobody Knows My Name*, Elwood still wouldn't have read Baldwin's account of his time in Tallahassee. "They Can't Turn Back: A Firsthand Report on the Negro Student in the South" was published in the "Back to School" issue of *Mademoiselle* magazine in August 1960. But, strangely, "They Can't Turn Back" wasn't included in *Nobody Knows My Name*. The essay—plus a few typos—would first appear in book form in 1985, in *The Price of the Ticket*, the first edition of Baldwin's collected

Figure 1   Gus and Girvaud Roberts leaving for school on 4 September 1957 (Photograph courtesy of Robinson-Spangler Carolina Room, Public Library of Charlotte and Mecklenburg County)

nonfiction writings, and again—less the typos—in 1998 in the Library of America volume of Baldwin's *Collected Essays*.

Unless Elwood read *Mademoiselle* magazine, he might not have known that Baldwin had ever been to Tallahassee, though he might well have heard about it. He might even have brushed shoulders with Baldwin in Frenchtown, at the corner of fiction and history, and never knew it. Or maybe—however, unlikely—he and his grandmother, in fiction, were there that night in late May, in history, when Baldwin nervously made his return to the pulpit.

During the last week of May in 1960, James Baldwin did visit Tallahassee; he intended to go from there to Atlanta and spend time shadowing Martin Luther King, Jr.—who he had missed in Tallahassee by about ten days—in preparation for a profile of King for *Harper's* magazine. Following his first visit to the region in the fall of 1957, this was Baldwin's second trip to the Deep South. It was in Tallahassee on this trip that Baldwin made his first address from the pulpit of a Black church since he had left his ministry as a teenager in Harlem. In a letter dated 26 May, four years to the day after the beginning of the Tallahassee bus boycott, Baldwin told his friend Mary Painter that he was surprised to find himself standing before "the early Christians here."[10] He told Painter that he recognized the congregants, "the same patient women, the same weary men," from his time in the churches of Harlem.[11] He told the activist church in Tallahassee that those who had been servants in "the great, strange house, called America ... might be able to save the house."[12] Apparently, he left an impression. After his remarks, he told Painter he overheard one of the sisters say: "He's little, ain't he? But he's dynamite."[13] He said, days later, people were still talking about it.

Baldwin's intensity in the pulpit was partly due to his fear of being back in the church as well as his terror at being back in the Deep South. Opening his letter to Painter, he transcribes a letter sent to him care of *Esquire* magazine from Birmingham Police Chief Jamie Moore. Warning off a visit, Chief Moore assured *Esquire* editors that "no good can come from a discussion between me and Mr. Baldwin."[14] Of his plans to go to Alabama—where Martin Luther King was on trial in Montgomery for tax evasion—following his stay in Tallahassee, Baldwin was clear about one thing: he would get in and out of Birmingham without having to stay overnight. His night at the Gaston Motel in Birmingham on 18 October 1957 had been quite enough. The accumulating pressure from his first tour of the South had broken over him that night; he had barely postponed his breakdown until his return to New York City. From Tallahassee, two and a half years later, he told Painter that "when your time comes to die, that's it, that's all. It can happen anywhere, anytime."[15] Still, staying the night in Birmingham, having been personally disinvited by Chief Moore, was *not* in the plan.

As had been the case during his first time in the South in 1957, Baldwin found the subtleties of Southern life and manners almost as disturbing as the ever-present possibility of violence. Even before he left the Tallahassee airport upon arrival, he was already vexed by intricate patterns of Southern silence, a "system of signs and nuances covers the mined terrain of the unspoken—the forever unspeakable."[16] He was in Tallahassee to cover the sit-in movement, what he called "the battle of Negro students for freedom," a struggle through which "the point of view of the subjugated is finally and inexorably being expressed."[17] Part of an emergent national movement, the Student Nonviolent Coordinating Committee (SNCC) having been newly formed just the previous month, this wing was led by members and affiliates of the Congress for Racial Equality (CORE), and students at Florida A&M University (FAMU) and neighboring Florida State University (FSU).

Reviewing recent history in "They Can't Turn Back," Baldwin notes how the Tallahassee bus boycott "began five months after the boycott in Montgomery" and, sparked by "the arrest of two Negro coeds who refused in a crowded bus to surrender their seats to whites on the motorman's order," followed a similar course:

> from cross-burning, fury, and intransigence on the part of the city and bus officials, along with the almost total and unexpected unanimity among the Negroes, to reprisal, intimidation, and near-bankruptcy of the bus company, which took its buses off the streets for a month.[18]

Baldwin interviews Reverend C. K. Steele and Reverend Daniel Speed, who helped organize the boycott and the carpool system that supported it, "with the result that all the windows were blown out of" Speed's grocery store among many other reprisals.[19] Rather than recount the full list, Steele, who in 1957 had become founding Vice President of the Southern Christian Leadership Conference, "preferred that [Baldwin] remain silent about the details."[20] Baldwin also notes that the student movement in Tallahassee that spring was part of a wave of nonviolent direct action beginning in February, less than two weeks after the first student sit-ins happened in Greensboro, NC. He doesn't note, however, that there were actually active CORE members among FAMU students the previous year, some of whom conducted sit-ins testing bus desegregation in the fall of 1959. Even though he talked with several students who were directly involved, and with others who weren't, Baldwin says nothing about sit-in activity in Tallahassee taking place before that in Greensboro, nor does he mention why those Tallahassee sit-ins occurred. What could have instigated student activism among FAMU students pre-dating the historic beginning of sit-ins in Greensboro? We'll see.

In Tallahassee Baldwin was guided by FAMU music professor Richard Haley, who, soon after Baldwin left town, "was dismissed from his position … because he backed the student protest movement."[21] In her memoir, *Freedom in the Family* (2003), leading FAMU activist Patricia Stevens Due notes that Haley was fired despite having been—or because he had been—voted "FAMU's Teacher of the Year" by the "student congress … only a week before he was let go."[22] As was true in Alabama at the time, and as the case of Reverend Speed's store showed, job security wasn't the most immediate worry for organizers in Tallahassee. C. K. Steele told Baldwin that, during the bus boycott, "Every time I drove my car into the garage, I expected a bullet to come whizzing by my head."[23] Baldwin reports that Steele "was not being fanciful: there are still bullet holes in his living room window."[24] Stevens Due reports that Steele's son Henry, who was also a sit-in activist and jail-in participant when still in high school, recalled "that bullet-riddled venetian blinds hung in their window for years after the boycott, lingering evidence of the price his family had paid."[25] In "They Can't Turn Back," Baldwin presents the structure of intricate tensions within and around HBCUs in the years following *Brown v. Board of Education*, a time when new funding was being made available to schools like FAMU, in return for administrators keeping "order," of course. In other words, many of the tensions within Black communities were collateral damage caused by leaders forced to accommodate with strategies of "massive resistance" to integration among Southern state and local governments.

In his essay, Baldwin finds his way across the mined terrain, at times marking the silences *he* must keep. He notes that Haley arrived too late to pick him up at the airport. Haley had brought with him "another member of the F.A.M.U. staff."[26] A few pages later, listing "the four Negro adults most respected by the students," Baldwin names Steele, Speed, Haley, and "one other person whom I cannot, for the person's sake, name," adding: "it strikes me horrendous that such a consideration should be necessary in this country."[27] Later again, listing adults in attendance at a student planning meeting off campus, he names "Haley, Steele, and the warrior to whom I can give no name."[28] In historical hindsight, it appears that all these references are to the same person, Ms. Daisy Young, assistant director of admissions at FAMU and advisor for the college NAACP chapter. In *Freedom in the Family*, Patricia Stevens Due, who, along with her sister Priscilla, formed the FAMU chapter of CORE in the fall of 1959, notes Young's key importance to the student movement. In her turn, in an 1993 interview with Stevens Due, Daisy Young addresses the silence that obscured the reprisals against Reverend Speed: "'A lot of people don't know how that man suffered' … Rev. Speed was not only targeted by vandals, but his grocery suppliers stopped delivering food to him, trying to put him out of business. The minister had to drive to Jacksonville—nearly 160 miles each way—just to stock his store."[29] In this way, at times like voices in a chorus broken over decades, some silences are finally spoken.

Baldwin's greatest achievement in the essay, however, comes in nuanced portraits of the students themselves as well as glimpses of Elwood's neighborhood where Baldwin stayed. In *The Nickel Boys*, Whitehead informs us that Elwood lives with his grandmother on Brevard St. in Frenchtown. In "They Can't Turn Back," Baldwin talks to students who are appalled that people in one of Tallahassee's Black neighborhoods—one which "is always wide open"—didn't join in the fight on 12 March, the most intense night of student demonstrations and unrest: "nobody was in the streets. It was quiet. It was dark. It was like everybody'd died. I couldn't believe it—*nothing*," says one student.[30] Baldwin explains that this student was talking about Black folks in "Frenchtown, the section of town in which I am staying."[31]

Baldwin doesn't mention the name in the essay, but he said enough for me to figure out that he had stayed at the Tookes Hotel at 412 W. Virginia Street, three blocks south of Brevard in Frenchtown. Googling, I found references to a historic Tallahassee hotel that seemed the likely place. More Googling and I was soon speaking with Ronald McCoy, grandson of the woman who had owned the hotel. He texted me a photo of the page in the hotel register that Baldwin had signed, with his distinctive left-handed script, adding his address: "81 Horatio Street, N.Y. 14." At the top of the page it reads May 1960. I asked if the precise dates of Baldwin's stay might be available? "Hey, man, you know it wasn't the Marriott," McCoy said. We laughed.

So, at the intersection of fiction and history, in May 1960 Baldwin was staying just a few blocks from Harriet Johnson's home on Brevard St. in *The Nickel Boys*,

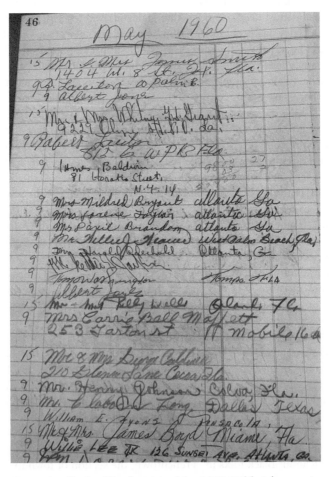

Figure 2   Tookes Hotel register May 1960: Baldwin's name in his distinctive left-hand script and Greenwich Village address clearly visible (Photograph courtesy of Ronald McCoy)

Figure 3 The Tookes Hotel c. 1950 (Photograph courtesy of Florida Memory: State Library and Archives of Florida)

where 14-year-old Elwood lived at the time. In "They Can't Turn Back," Baldwin recounts how Richard Haley drove him to his hotel in Frenchtown. Riding along, Baldwin describes his first glimpses of Elwood's neighborhood:

> One of the two Negro sections of Tallahassee. This section seems to be the more disreputable of the two, judging at least from its long, unpaved streets, the gangs of loud, shabby men and women, boys and girls, in front of the barbershops, the poolrooms, the Coffee House, the El Dorado Café, and the Chicken Shack. It is to this part of town that the F.A.M.U. students come to find whiskey—this is a dry county, which means that whisky is plentiful and drunkards numerous—and women who may or may not be wild but who are indisputably available.[32]

By the end of this essay, Baldwin's line about "women who may or may not be wild but who are indisputably available" will read very differently than it does as the stroke of local color in his portrait that he intended. Baldwin follows the scene in the street with his description of the Tookes Hotel, at once itself and a type, its position in a segregated Southern town, its varied clientele, and its proprietor, Mrs. Dorothy Nash Tookes, whom Baldwin doesn't name:

> My hotel is that hotel found in all small southern towns—all small southern towns, in any case, in which a hotel for Negroes exists. It is really only a rather large frame house run by a widow who also teaches school in Quincy, a town not far away. It is doomed, of course, to be a very curious place, since everyone from NAACP lawyers, visiting

church women, and unfrocked preachers to traveling pimps and the simply, aimlessly, transiently amorous cannot possibly stay anywhere else. The widow knows this, which makes it impossible for her—since she is good-natured and also needs the money—to turn anyone away.[33]

Baldwin's descriptive tone gathers a complex mist of superiority as the New Yorker, the world-traveler, the journalist on assignment for national magazines finds his place on the "more disreputable" Black side of a Southern town. But Baldwin was also a ghetto-born, queer artist and self-described disturber of the peace who, in 1972, would write that he felt "condemned to make [people] uncomfortable."[34] That discomfort, like all viable channels of creative energy, was a two-way street. It had its costs. During his first tours in the South, Baldwin was ill at ease with himself as well as the vexations of middle-class status and responsibility occupied by many of the Black Southerners he met during his early travels. As Baldwin found, and to his confusion, some of these safe-seeming, publicly soft-spoken, maybe middle-class Black Southerners were also disturbers of the peace. The Southern peace—or whatever it might be called—and the complex silences that preserved it also confounded Baldwin. Watching his white cab driver work out payment—in lieu of correct change—with a Black woman upon his arrival in town, Baldwin reported: "They speak together exactly as if they were old friends, yet with this eerie distance between them. It is impossible to guess what they really think of each other."[35]

Part of the brilliance of Baldwin's prose c. 1960 occurs exactly in how it gathers up a volatile tumult of self and other, of self-*as*-other, and at times of other-as-*self* finding its always tenuous order in sentences. Consider the complex mirror he found in the FAMU students he observed while waiting for a taxi to leave campus:

I watch them. Their walk, talk, laughter are as familiar to me as my skin, and yet there is something new about them. They remind me of all the Negro boys and girls I have ever known and they remind me of myself; but, really, I was never like these students. It took many years of vomiting up all the filth I'd been taught about myself, and half-believed, before I was able to walk on earth as though I had a right to be here.[36]

For her part, a home owner who also ran a restaurant called The Hot Spot at 319 N. McComb St., down the block and around the corner from her hotel, Dorothy Nash Tookes was a graduate of FAMU (1928) and was believed to be the first state-registered Black teacher in Florida. She "may have needed the money," sure, but Baldwin doesn't feature how the "widow who also teaches school" was a mainstay in the Black community of Tallahassee, as well as in the neighboring county where she taught, and an important entrepreneur. Dorothy Nash Tookes might have supported the student movement in Tallahassee. There were many in the community who did. And she might well not have. There were many, even in C. K. Steele's church, who didn't. In a way, that's not the point.

No matter her conscious political orientation and her sense of reasonable tactics, Dorothy Nash Tookes knew a lot about her right to be where and who she was that Baldwin sensed but didn't describe. Strictly speaking these weren't legal rights. They were held in place by powers at once more and less stable and dependable than the rights of citizens. Part of what drew Baldwin back to the Deep South, to the Black South, was a kind of power that had no real name in the South and no equivalent in the North. At the close of "Nobody Knows My Name: A Letter From the South," his 1959 essay about his first time in the South, Baldwin came as close as he would come at the time to describing a key—unnamed—factor in that power:

> The really striking thing, for me, in the South was this dreadful paradox, the black men were stronger than the white. I don't know how they did it, but it certainly has something to do with that, as yet, unwritten history of the Negro woman.[37]

As we'll see below, Baldwin himself left most of that history unnamed and unwritten at the time. Girvaud Roberts, Daisy Young, and Dorothy Nash Tookes: Baldwin leaves them unnamed. With the powerful exception of Gus and Girvaud

Figure 4 Dorothy Nash Tookes (at center in white dress, shaking hands with man in suit) greets guests in front of the hotel (Photograph courtesy of Florida Memory: State Library and Archives of Florida)

Figure 5   Dorothy Nash Tookes (Photograph courtesy of Florida Memory:
State Library and Archives of Florida)

Roberts's mother, Elizabeth Gertrude Washington Roberts[38]—who Baldwin left
unnamed and who understood herself to be a descendant of US President George
Washington—all we learn about Black women's particular position from these
essays is that some of them are "indisputably available." Baldwin's later work, especially his final novel *Just Above My Head* (1979), would return to this territory and
at least partially close that yawning gap. Still, in 2020, I was shocked to find key
events in that history still missing even when they're right there between the lines
of a prize-winning novel like *The Nickel Boys*.

Still, with all of the silences, each time I re-read it, Baldwin's account of his brief
time in Tallahassee amazes. One of the most resonant sections of "They Can't Turn
Back" takes place in the Tookes Hotel itself. Of his room, located at the rear of the
house, Baldwin offers that it "was designed for sleeping—possibly—but not for
work."[39] Ever the night owl, Baldwin often worked into the early morning. On this
night, he reports: "I type with my door open, because of the heat."[40] Maybe he was
typing the letter to Mary Painter noted above. Baldwin tells Painter in that letter
that he has to sign off because "the man next door has just come in." In any case,
before long, a young man, identified as "J." in the article, interrupts Baldwin's
work. A "F.A.M.U. student who is visiting a friend and, somewhat improbably,
studying for an exam," J. asks Baldwin if he can borrow a pencil.[41] Baldwin sur-
mises that "he does not really want a pencil, he is merely curious about who would
be sitting at a typewriter so late at night—especially in this hotel."[42] This leads to a

conversation: "I suggest to J. that possibly he and his friend would like a drink and we carry my half-bottle of bourbon down the hall."[43]

In the late 1950s and early 1960s, Baldwin often held that the "private life, his own and that of others, is the writer's subject."[44] His description of his evening with J. and his friend, who "turns out to be really his distant cousin and a gospel singer," carries, "as the bourbon diminishes and the exam begins to be forgotten," a beautiful sense of somewhat vulnerable privacy and half-guarded intimacy.[45] In his version of the conversation with J., Baldwin offers, in fact, a glimpse at almost precisely the young man one imagines Elwood Curtis might have become if fate hadn't jettisoned him from his college-bound path and into the fearful and tragic plot of *The Nickel Boys*.

Talking with J., Baldwin confronts "the really agonizing privacy of the very young."[46] In J., Baldwin sketches a portrait of a young man wrestling, all at once, with his "tormentingly complex" self, apprehensions of a newly "difficult and dangerous" world, for whom "such words as 'honor' and 'truth' conjure up realities more real than the daily bread," and with parents "reading newspapers, listening to the radio, [and] burning up the long-distance wires every time Tallahassee is in the news."[47] J. also deals with a college administration stuck between a segregated rock and a "massive resistance" hard place, who J. is shocked to learn "would like me better if I was more like all the other kids."[48] Indignant, in his gospel singer-cousin's hotel room, J. asks the famous and worldly writer, "Can you imagine that?"[49] And Baldwin, who had never been to college and didn't respect most schools any more than he respected most churches, turns to the reader: "I do not tell him how easily I can imagine that."[50]

On a Monday, Baldwin attends a student-led planning meeting held at a church because "students from Tallahassee's two universities—Florida State, set up for whites, and Florida A. & M. for Negroes—are not allowed to visit each other's campuses."[51] Twenty-five students attend. The plan is to conduct an interracial, "y'all come *prayer* meeting" at the state capitol building. This is the idea of "R., a white student, foreign born, very measured in speech, very direct in manner."[52] In tones sharply contrasting the quiet privacy of J.'s confessions late at night over bourbon at the Tookes Hotel, Baldwin records the public discussion of tactics among student activists who must "summon up the force to face the law and the lawless—who are not, right now in Tallahassee, easily distinguishable": how to "*decide* to have a *spontaneous*" event, how to invite people without tipping off the police, how to involve the police for protection without informing racists in the White Citizens' Council when "'if you tell the police,' said one Negro student, 'it's just as good as telling the White Citizens' Council.'"[53]

As he listens, Baldwin marvels at the difference the fifteen years between his age and the ages of these students makes:

> These students were born at the very moment at which Europe's domination of Africa was ending. I remember, for example, the invasion of Ethiopia and Haile Selassie's vain appeal to the League of Nations, but they remember the Bandung Conference and the establishment of the Republic of Ghana.[54]

He also marvels at the CORE philosophy of nonviolence, in both students and leaders like Richard Haley, who explain again and again, to strangers, to each other, and probably to themselves—allowing Baldwin to explain it to the readership of *Mademoiselle* magazine's "Back to School" issue—how it all was supposed to work:

> "What we're trying to do," [Haley] tells me, "is to sting their consciences a little. They don't want to think about it. Well, we must make them think about it.
>
> "When they come home from work," Haley continues, "and turn on the TV sets and there you are—" he means *you the Negro*— "on your way to jail again, and they know, at the bottom of their hearts, that it's not because you've done anything wrong—something happens in them, something's got to happen in them. They're human beings, too, you know." ... "Most white people in the South don't especially like the idea of integration, but they'll go along with it. By and by they'll get used to it."[55]

Originally from Chicago, Haley knew the professional risks. According to Patricia Stevens Due, he had told Daisy Young: "I'm not concerned about myself, because I can get another job."[56] Haley advised Young to be more careful—and likely advised Baldwin to keep her name out of "They Can't Turn Back"—because she "had family and deeper ties in the [Tallahassee] community."[57] During those years Daisy Young lived at 1314 Pinellas Street, about two blocks from the northeast corner of campus. Clearly, violent reprisals by racists weren't the only dangers Haley and others feared for Young as a consequence of her bravery. In 1993, Daisy Young told Patricia Stevens Due that she was upfront with FAMU colleagues at the time about the coercion she was encountering from upper administration and "her boss in the registrar's office": "Everything I do is after five o'clock. Now, if I'm not free to use my own time, then I know I need to stop fighting crackers and start fighting niggers."[58]

As a visitor in the midst of many levels of turmoil in which Black people were risking their children's education, their jobs, and their lives, Baldwin pauses: "And all this, I think to myself, will only be a page of history."[59] In fact, however, important aspects of that era in Tallahassee would struggle mightily, for decades, to become even that. In *that* struggle, honestly, Baldwin wasn't much help. In "They Can't Turn Back," in addition to withholding the names of powerful women, he stays inexplicably silent about a crucial part of the movement in Tallahassee. As had been the case in Montgomery, the Tallahassee protest movement turned upon the movement against sexual violence. Uncovering the buried foundations of the Montgomery bus boycott in *At the Dark End of the Street* (2010), Danielle McGuire writes:

> the King-centric and male dominated version of events obscures the real history of the Montgomery Bus Boycott as a woman's movement for dignity ... walking hundreds of miles to protest humiliation and testifying publicly about physical and sexual abuse, African Americans—mostly women—reclaimed their bodies and demanded the right to be treated with dignity and respect.[60]

McGuire's research reveals how women like Rosa Parks had been organizing Black women against sexual violence since they instigated a national movement after the rape of Recy Taylor in 1944.

In Tallahassee, and at FAMU, the movement pivoted on the historic case of Betty Jean Owens. In fiction, Elwood's grandmother Harriet might well have been far less ambivalent about *that* movement. Or she might have resisted it even more. In history, the FAMU students and leaders with whom Baldwin spoke while in Tallahassee were exactly those involved in the mass movement in support of Owens and in pursuit of real punishment for her white attackers the previous spring. There's absolutely no question that everyone including Elwood would have known about that; they *all* knew who Owens was. But Elwood, no matter what he read, wouldn't learn about it from Baldwin; and, even more strangely, readers of the 2019 Pulitzer Prize-winning novel *The Nickel Boys* won't hear about Owens from Colson Whitehead. It's also clear that few if any at the time wanted to make the case of Betty Jean Owens part of the national conversation about civil rights. Muted by shame and fear and by patriarchal political imperatives at the time, the story and its importance is still far too little known.

Baldwin's and Whitehead's silences are by no means unique. Even histories of the civil rights movement focused on Tallahassee downplay the importance of Betty Jean Owens's case. The two best books on the Tallahassee movement mention both the rape and the case. But Owens's name doesn't appear in those books either. Glenda Rabby's *The Pain and the Promise* (1999) is the best historical survey of the movement in Tallahassee. Rabby notes that "On 2 May 1959, four armed Tallahassee white men surrounded a parked car near Florida A&M campus and ordered the occupants, all students at the university, out of the car."[61] Rabby explains that one of the women managed to escape and hide but that the "other woman was forced into the car, was taken to the outskirts of town, and was raped by each of the four men."[62] Along with Florida Governor Thomas Collins and Roy Wilkins of the NAACP, Rabby names John Cooke, a "part-time deputy" who aided in the location and recovery of Owens after her assault, "Sheriff Bill Joyce," who filed "formal charges of rape" against all four assailants the next day, and "circuit judge W. May Walker," who presided over the grand jury's indictment.[63]

While none of the other names appear in her account, Rabby notes that FAMU students responded en masse on 4 May, the Monday following the attack. At the rally, students "voted to boycott classes" on Tuesday to "demonstrate their anger over the rape and show solidarity with their classmates."[64] She adds that the "students raised $500 in one day for a fund for the young woman who remained in the hospital."[65] Noting the historical anomaly of charges against white men for rape—in fact these were the first white defendants Judge May had encountered in a dozen or more rape cases during his nineteen years on the bench—Rabby emphasizes the importance of the guilty verdicts and life sentences passed down at the hearing on 22 June. She adds that, on that day also, a Black 16-year-old in a nearby rural county—the county, known for its racism, where Dorothy Nash Tookes taught school—had his death sentence commuted to life imprisonment. Still, improbably, Rabby concludes that the "outcome of the trial had little effect on race relations in the city."[66]

By all accounts, Patricia Stevens Due was one of the most important activists in the Tallahassee movement. In fact, Baldwin arrived in Tallahassee in 1960 just three weeks after Stevens Due and four other FAMU students, including her older sister Priscilla, had been released from jail on 5 May. After being arrested in March during a sit-in, the students had spent 49 days locked up. Refusing to post bail, according to Stevens Due, they'd "pioneered a tactic, becoming the first 'jail-in' of the student protest movement of the 1960s."[67] In *Freedom in the Family*, Stevens Due recounts her coming to racial and political consciousness during the summer of 1959. Following her first year at FAMU, she was home in Miami with Priscilla. She lists major events in her mind leading up to that summer when she and her sister would begin to attend CORE meetings in the city: the 1951 bombing that killed Florida NAACP activist Harry T. Moore and his wife, Harriet; inaction after the *Brown v. Board* decision in 1954; and the national furor surrounding the 1955 murder of Emmett Till. She then mentions: "One incident hit much closer to home." Stevens Due continues:

> In May 1959, shortly before the school term ended for the summer, a nineteen-year-old Negro woman from FAMU had been parked with her date and another couple when four white men forced her from the car with a knife and shotgun, drove away with her into a secluded area in the woods, and raped her seven times.[68]

Despite the convictions and sentences, "a rarity in the South, where usually rapes against Negro women were dismissed," Stevens Due remembers that "the attack had opened up many festering wounds along racial lines in Tallahassee" and that the "shock of the rape had lingered on the FAMU campus of 3,000 students."[69] She adds: "I'd been so enraged about it, in fact, that I'd written a letter to President Eisenhower."[70] She also adds that her Uncle Bertram had had to "sneak out of Kennesaw [Georgia] in the trunk of a car" to escape a false and economically motivated rape charge in the 1920s.[71] But even describing events in following years, noting that her fellow CORE activist Ben Cowins had "first come to campus in the wake of the FAMU student's rape case," Stevens Due never mentions the name Betty Jean Owens.[72]

So it fell to Danielle McGuire, a survivor of sexual violence herself, in *At the Dark End of the Street*, to focus upon Owens's case and its place as the first sentencing of white men to life in prison for the rape of a Black woman in the South. In the wake of the Tallahassee bus boycott from 1956, which—unlike the one in Montgomery—hadn't ever firmly and publicly concluded in victory, McGuire argues that Owens's case represented a crucial early victory in Black political mobilization in the city. McGuire clarifies that "fifteen hundred students filled Lee Auditorium" on campus during the rally on Monday 4 May.[73] That's about half the total enrolled student body. Interviewed by McGuire in 1999, Stevens Due stressed how the attack reinforced the feeling of students as a collective: "We all felt violated, male and female … It was like all of us had been raped."[74] McGuire recounts the 12 June trial. Four hundred people packed the segregated courtroom to listen to Betty Jean Owens detail her terrifying ordeal, concluding: "I was on the ground for two or three hours before the one with the knife pushed me back into the car."[75]

In McGuire's telling, the case for the defense was almost as terrifying and insane as the attack itself. Together with the usual blaming of the victim whose very survival was said to testify to a twisted form of consent, the defense brought in a psychiatrist from Pensacola who argued that one of the defendants, William Ted Collinsworth, should be excused from culpability due to his Native heritage. Dr. W. M. C. Wilhoit testified that "it is a known fact that individuals of the Indian race react violently and primitively when psychotic or intoxicated."[76] Meanwhile, McGuire reports, paranoia and projection spread through white neighborhoods in Tallahassee: "white women around Tallahassee began to speak openly about their 'fear of retaliation,' while young couples avoided parking 'in the country moonlight,' as one said, 'lest some Negroes should be out hunting in a retaliatory mood.'"[77] The conviction of the four men led to widespread reactions among white people in Tallahassee who feared that the verdict signaled turning tides in a racial power struggle. McGuire lists one petition for leniency sent to the judge by a Mrs. Bill Arens, who wrote that "Negro women like to be raped by the white men."[78] Mrs. Arens believed that verdicts "like this will help the Supreme Court force this low bred race ahead, making whites live and eat with him and allow his children to associate with the little apes, grow up and marry them."[79]

At the time the combination of race, sex, and violence in the Betty Jean Owens rape case opened up a window into realms of experience many people refused to look at closely in private and almost no one seriously discussed in public. The comparative victory in the verdict and sentencing seemed not to override the chaos and pain accompanying the convergence of volatile elements of American life: race, sex, and violence. McGuire does slightly overstate the case's immediate impact. She contends that momentum from the victory in the case led directly to an organized student movement, and that, "in the spring of 1960, they successfully desegregated local lunch counters, theaters, and department stores, as did black college students throughout the South."[80] In fact, in May of 1963, FAMU students would still be demonstrating and going to jail by the hundreds in attempts to desegregate, among other things, the Florida and State Theaters in Tallahassee. In *The Nickel Boys*, young Elwood Curtis is right there elbow to elbow with them. The struggle to desegregate buses, lunch counters, theaters, public schools, and pools in Tallahassee would drag on for years into the late 1960s and beyond. But the place of Betty Jean Owens, like that of Mrs. Dorothy Nash Tookes, Patricia Stevens Due, Daisy Young and many others, should have names in history and in fiction. Ronald McCoy agrees. He's leading an effort to restore the Tookes Hotel and make it a museum documenting the history of the Black community in Frenchtown.

Having read and re-read *At the Dark End of the Street* in recent years, the silence covering this central piece of the Tallahassee movement was almost visible to me on the pages of *The Nickel Boys*. It followed me like a shadow as I read the novel while half wondering if some reference to the case might appear before the book ended. Maybe, I thought, *that* was the big reveal, the kind that often awaits readers of popular fiction? Nope. More than once I stopped reading to wonder if Colson Whitehead didn't know about Betty Jean Owens. Had he not encountered her story and that of her attackers when he did the research for the book? Or maybe he thought it too insignificant to weave into the book? How? These questions were so vivid while I read because for years I'd wondered about Baldwin's own silence about Owens in "They Can't Turn Back." As I thought about that, I could see a lattice of gendered silences linking young Girvaud Roberts in Charlotte to Dorothy Nash Tookes to Daisy Young to Patricia Stevens Due to Betty Jean Owens and to "the unwritten history of the Negro woman" generally in writings, including Baldwin's, about the South from those years. And, against those silences, but especially with Owens in mind, Baldwin's sentence about the Black women of Frenchtown, "women who may or may not have been wild but who were indisputably available," rings and burns with particularly disturbing twists.

Clearly the volatility created when the subjects of sex, sexual violence, and race come together and come into speech and action was too much at the time. As a result, a silent web of unsayability, unthinkability, and undoability was lain and fixed and forcibly held over these regions of experience. Maybe the subject of sex and sexual violence was just too volatile? As Darlene Clark Hine in the 1980s wrote about how historically "rape and the threat of rape influenced the development of a culture of dissemblance among Black women," maybe respectability was the best—maybe it was the *only*—option at the time.[81] Maybe part of the movement itself was to protect women from an intrusive and abusive white world, and this vein of silence was part of that protection? Or maybe the silence was to protect Black men who felt shamed and personally violated, too, by what happened to Betty Jean Owens and so many others, and so sought silence as a refuge from that reckoning? Maybe it had to do with all of that. But those causes for silence surely can't obtain in contemporary fiction. Can they?

As the popular slogan goes, it's been time to "Say Her Name." And in saying it, might we realize that it's been time to acknowledge that the history of race is the history of sex, the history of racial violence is the history of sexual violence, and the future of racial liberation depends on the history of sexual liberation. As I wrote this essay, the killings in Tallahassee, in late May and early June 2020, of Tony McDade, Oluwatoyin Salau, and Victoria Sims etched again, in my mind and in our world, the present danger of sexual violence in terrifying and vivid terms. These crimes and others that twist sex, gender, and race violently together into inextricable combinations constitute a direct challenge to our ability to address, to expand, what's thinkable, sayable, and doable. Writers like Colson Whitehead, and of course James Baldwin, give us so much; that's why we need to push against their silences—along with our own and each other's—above all.

Notes

1 Colson Whitehead, *The Nickel Boys* (New York, Doubleday, 2019), p. 121.

2 James Baldwin, *No Name in the Street* (1972), in *Collected Essays*, ed. Toni Morrison (New York, Library of America, 1998), p. 358.

3 James Baldwin, *The Fire Next Time* (1963), in *Collected Essays*, ed. Toni Morrison (New York, Library of America, 1998), p. 320.

4 Whitehead, *The Nickel Boys*, p. 190.

5 *Ibid.*, p. 32.

6 *Ibid.*, p. 33.

7 *Ibid.*, p. 37.

8 James Baldwin, Letter to Mary Garin-Painter, Yale Collection of American Literature, Beinecke Rare Book & Manuscript Library, Yale University, October, 1957.

9 James Baldwin, "A Fly in Buttermilk," in Morrison (ed.), *Collected Essays*, pp. 188–9.

10 Letter to Mary Garin-Painter, Yale Collection of American Literature, Beinecke Rare Book & Manuscript Library, Yale University, 26 May 1960.

11 *Ibid.*

12 *Ibid.*

13 *Ibid.*

14 *Ibid.*

15 *Ibid.*

16 James Baldwin, "They Can't Turn Back," in Morrison (ed.), *Collected Essays*, p. 622.

17 *Ibid.*, pp. 622–3.

18 *Ibid.*, p. 627.

19 *Ibid.*

20 *Ibid.*

21 *Ibid.*, p. 625.

22 Tananarive Due and Patricia Stevens Due, *Freedom in the Family: A Mother–Daughter Memoir of the Fight for Civil Rights* (London, One World, 2003), p. 101.

23 Baldwin, "They Can't Turn Back," p. 627.

24 *Ibid.*

25 Qtd. in Due and Stevens Due, *Freedom in the Family*, p. 144.

26 Baldwin, "They Can't Turn Back," p. 625.

27 *Ibid.*, p. 632.

28 *Ibid.*, p. 633.

29 Daisy Young, qtd. in Due and Stevens Due, *Freedom in the Family*, p. 80.

30 Baldwin, "They Can't Turn Back," p. 631.

31 *Ibid.*, p. 632.

32 *Ibid.*, pp. 627–8.

33 *Ibid.*

34 Baldwin, *No Name in the Street*, p. 365.

35 Baldwin, "They Can't Turn Back," p. 625.

36 *Ibid.*, p. 636.

37 James Baldwin, "Nobody Knows My Name: A Letter From the South," in Morrison (ed.), *Collected Essays*, p. 208.

38 "Girvaud Justice Oral History Interview 1, August 6, 2006," J. Murrey Atkins Library, University of North Carolina-Charlotte.

39 Baldwin, "They Can't Turn Back," p. 628.

40 *Ibid.*

41 *Ibid.*

42 *Ibid.*

43 *Ibid.*, p. 630.

44 James Baldwin, "A Word from Writer Directly to Reader" (1959), in *The Cross of Redemption: Uncollected Writings*, ed. Randall Kenan (New York, Vintage, 2011), p. 8.

45 Baldwin, "They Can't Turn Back," p. 630.

46 *Ibid.*, p. 628.

47 *Ibid.*, pp. 628, 631.

48 *Ibid.*, p. 631.

49 *Ibid.*

50 *Ibid.*

51 *Ibid.*, p. 633.

52 *Ibid.*

53 *Ibid.*, p. 635.

54 *Ibid.*, p. 637.

55 *Ibid.*, p. 635.

56 Due and Stevens Due, *Freedom in the Family*, p. 45.

57 *Ibid.*, p. 45.

58 Young, qtd. in Due and Stevens Due, *Freedom in the Family* [1993 interview], p. 104.

59 Baldwin, "They Can't Turn Back," p. 635.

60 Danielle McGuire, *At the Dark End of the Street: Black Women, Rape, and Resistance—A New History of the Civil Rights Movement from Rosa Parks to the Rise of Black Power* (New York, Vintage, 2010), pp. 132, 134.

61 Glenda Rabby, *The Pain and the Promise: The Struggle for Civil Rights in Tallahassee Florida* (Athens, GA, University of Georgia Press, 1999), p. 77.

62 *Ibid.*

63 *Ibid.*

64 *Ibid.*

65 *Ibid.*

66 *Ibid.*, p. 79.

67 Due and Stevens Due, *Freedom in the Family*, p. 70.

68 *Ibid.*, p. 40.

69 *Ibid.*

70 *Ibid.*

71 *Ibid.*, p. 41.

72 *Ibid.*, p. 132.

73 McGuire, *At the Dark End of the Street*, p. 165.

74 *Ibid.*, p. 166.

75 *Ibid.*, p. 176.

76 *Ibid.*, p. 180.

77 *Ibid.*, p. 170.

78 *Ibid.*, p. 185.

79 *Ibid.*

80 *Ibid.*, p. 188.

81 Darlene Clark Hine, "Rape and the Inner Lives of Black Women in the Middle West: Preliminary Thoughts on the Culture of Dissemblance," *Signs: Journal of Women in Culture and Society*, 14:4 (1989), p. 912.

Works Cited

Baldwin, James, *The Fire Next Time* (1963), in *Collected Essays*, ed. Toni Morrison (New York, Library of America, 1998), pp. 285–347.

_____ "A Fly in Buttermilk" (1958), in *Collected Essays*, ed. Toni Morrison (New York, Library of America, 1998), pp. 187–96.

_____ *No Name in the Street* (1972), in *Collected Essays*, ed. Toni Morrison (New York, Library of America, 1998), pp. 349–475.

_____ "Nobody Knows My Name: A Letter From the South" (1959), in *Collected Essays*, ed. Toni Morrison (New York, Library of America, 1998), pp. 197–208.

_____ "They Can't Turn Back" (1960), in *Collected Essays*, ed. Toni Morrison (New York, Library of America, 1998), pp. 622–37.

_____ "A Word from Writer Directly to Reader" (1959), in *The Cross of Redemption: Uncollected Writings*, ed. Randall Kenan (New York, Vintage, 2011), pp. 7–8.

Due, Tananarive, and Patricia Stevens Due, *Freedom in the Family: A Mother-Daughter Memoir of the Fight for Civil Rights* (New York, One World/Random House, 2003).

Hine, Darlene Clark, "Rape and the Inner Lives of Black Women in the Middle West: Preliminary Thoughts on the Culture of Dissemblance," *Signs: Journal of Women in Culture and Society*, 14:4 (1989), pp. 912–20.

McGuire, Danielle, *At the Dark End of the Street: Black Women, Rape, and Resistance—A New History of the Civil Rights Movement from Rosa Parks to the Rise of Black Power* (New York, Vintage, 2010).

Rabby, Glenda, *The Pain and the Promise: The Struggle for Civil Rights in Tallahassee, Florida* (Athens, GA, University of Georgia Press, 1999).

Whitehead, Colson, *The Nickel Boys* (New York, Doubleday, 2019).

Contributor's Biography

Ed Pavlić is author of thirteen books. His most recent books include *Let It Be Broke* (Four Way Books, 2020), *Another Kind of Madness* (Milkweed Editions, 2019), *Live at the Bitter End* (Saturnalia Books, 2018), and *Who Can Afford to Improvise: James Baldwin and Black Music, the Lyric and the Listener* (Fordham University Press, 2016). His forthcoming books are *Outward: Adrienne Rich's Expanding Solitudes* (University of Minnesota Press, 2021) and *Call It in the Air* (Milkweed Editions, 2023). He is Distinguished Research Professor of English, African American Studies, and Creative Writing at the University of Georgia.

SPECIAL SECTION ON BALDWIN AND FILM

"Finding Work for the Devil"

curated by   Robert Jackson

James Baldwin Review

Previous page: Bette Davis in *20,000 Years in Sing Sing* (1932) (Courtesy Getty Images)

Manchester University Press

INTRODUCTION

James Baldwin and Film Beyond the American Century

Robert Jackson   University of Tulsa

Abstract

This article provides an introduction to this special section of *James Baldwin Review* 7 devoted to Baldwin and film. Jackson considers Baldwin's distinct approach to film criticism by pairing him with James Agee, another writer who wrote fiction as well as nonfiction in several genres, and who produced a large body of film criticism, especially during the 1940s. While Agee, a white southerner born almost a generation before Baldwin, might seem an unlikely figure to place alongside Baldwin, the two shared a great deal in terms of temperament and vision, and their film writings reveal a great deal of consensus in their diagnoses of American pathologies. Another important context for Baldwin's complex relationship to film is television, which became a dominant media form during the 1950s and exerted a great influence upon both the mainstream reception of the civil rights movement and Baldwin's reception as a public intellectual from the early 1960s to the end of his life. Finally, the introduction briefly discusses the articles that constitute this special section.

Keywords: James Baldwin, James Agee, film criticism, television, race, civil rights movement

James Baldwin Review, Volume 7, 2021, © The Authors. Published by Manchester University Press and
The University of Manchester Library
http://dx.doi.org/10.7227/JBR.7.3

I, nevertheless, was the eldest, a responsibility I did not intend to fail, and my first conscious calculation as to how to go about defeating the world's intentions for me and mine began on that Saturday afternoon in what we called *the movies*, but which was actually my first entrance into the cinema of my mind.

James Baldwin, The Devil Finds Work[1]

To see his two loves, movies and books, fused together was, I believe, one of the great ambitions of his life. I'm sure that if pressed Jimmy would have admitted that he craved an Oscar almost as much as he did a Pulitzer. Yet he found a way to participate vicariously in the cinema and he certainly found a way to live in the glamorous lifestyle of its leading actors. But—and this is to his great credit—despite his many frustrations and disappointments, not all of which, by any means, could be attributed to his disdain for legal paperwork, Jimmy never lost his innocent pleasure in the cinema.

Caryl Phillips, A New World Order[2]

Perhaps it's simply that I see the world differently just now, having recently survived 2020, a plague year in several senses of the word. But even the usual line, that *James Baldwin is an essential writer for our time*, feels inadequate, shallow. More than that, though, I find myself musing on our ability to see more deeply into the world when we are living through a crucible of some sort—a pandemic, a reign of terror, a freedom struggle. Not so much a crisis of what Rob Nixon has called slow violence, since that might leave the trauma invisible to the naked eye; but just the reverse, a crisis that clarifies and orders the workings of the world into a spectacle, one whose pattern, whose raw dramatic power, had not always been so plain to witness in ordinary time.[3]

The film writer who most reminds me, just now, of Baldwin is James Agee, and there is a part of me that is surprised that I hadn't made the connection earlier. There are, of course, reasons why the two wouldn't be grouped together. They never met personally; one arrived as a public figure not long before the other departed. Baldwin, fifteen years younger, was a wide-eyed student of the early sound era of the 1930s. Agee's birth year, 1909, made him a child of the silent era, and left him captivated for his too-brief life by such fossils as Charlie Chaplin and Buster Keaton, and by the film he considered the greatest of all time—or, as he put it, "the one great epic, tragic film": D. W. Griffith's *The Birth of a Nation* (1915).[4] Of the same film, an unfortunate but inexorable fact of history which to Baldwin had "the Niagara force of an obsession"—a phrase Agee likely would have appreciated, despite the chasm between the two men in what they took from the film—Baldwin put it bluntly: "*The Birth of a Nation* is really an elaborate justification of mass murder."[5] How could these men be reconciled?

When Agee looked at motion pictures, even during his run as a film critic for *Time* and *The Nation* in the 1940s, he did so in much the way the old silent directors who flourished in the sound era did—King Vidor, John Ford, Alfred

Hitchcock, René Clair, Fritz Lang, Ernst Lubitsch, and Chaplin himself. Which is to say, he continued to see silent films, even when they spoke, sang, or otherwise made noise. But Agee was not—or not simply—an antiquarian, nor a primitivist; he longed for something new, if it could cut through the malaise of the business. "Music can be well used in movies," he wrote in 1945:

> and indeed I think the greatest possibilities have hardly yet been touched. But music is just as damaging to nearly all fiction films as to nearly all fact films, as it is generally used in both today. Its ability to bind together a succession of images, or to make transitions between blocks of them—not to mention "transitional" and "special-effect" and "montage" passages—inevitably makes for laziness or for slackened imagination in making the images and setting them in order, and in watching them. Still worse, it weakens the emotional imagination both of maker and onlooker, and makes it virtually impossible to communicate or receive ideas. It sells too cheaply and far too sensually all the things it is the business of the screen itself to present. The rough equivalent might be a poet who could dare to read aloud from his own work only if the lights were dimmed and some Debussy was on, very low.[6]

This is a passage, not atypical of Agee in his film writing, of diagnosis. His attitude toward the broad run of film he was required to sit through week after week is one of nearly exhausted patience. And while those bygone days are never mentioned, it is clear that the old knowledge, the intricately grained memory of the silents, and Agee's loyalty to that memory, have shaped his identity and vision as few other experiences did or could. This is the task Agee set out for himself: to articulate an ideal of aesthetic dignity and possibility, and in doing so to take the whole industry to task for failing to honor it, or indeed, even to understand its existence. Agee is after honesty, emotional truth, maturity; what he finds instead, all too frequently, is corruption. "Laziness" and "slackened imagination," a weakened "emotional imagination" that is shared by auteur and viewer alike—these are not simply lapses by the purveyors of popular entertainment, but signs of moral failure and dehumanization.

And here, despite their differences in age and race and so much else, is where Agee and Baldwin come together. "Slackened imagination" might well have been one of Baldwin's phrases, pertaining not simply to the movies' impact on the emotional lives of moviegoers but also to the atrophied inner lives of Americans across all their works and days. In this respect, Baldwin's litany of Hollywood's underachievement in *The Devil Finds Work* (1976), a long personal history of moviegoing littered with painful knowledge and thwarted love, is entirely of a piece with his jeremiads against religious hypocrisy and militant ignorance in *The Fire Next Time* (1963). "It is the innocence which constitutes the crime," he wrote in the latter book; and Agee, had he survived to read the words, would have understood and agreed: for he had said much the same thing across the years of his film reviews.[7]

It strikes me as well, in these after times of 2021, that each man had his crucible.[8] Both of these events arrived at nearly the same moment in their lives, around the age of thirty. For Agee, it was World War II; for Baldwin, the civil rights movement. Both men identify a deeply American strain of dishonesty and evasion, of lethal sentimentality, of mass-market conformity that leads to poor habits of mind and heart. These are, in the judgment of both writers, mortal sins. Late in 1943, Agee warned of America's "unique and constantly intensifying schizophrenia which threatens no other nation involved in the war."[9] Its cause: the geographic isolation of Americans from the battlefields, which was making the entire nation, already "a peculiarly neurotic people," even less capable of confronting the realities of the world.[10] "Our predicament is bad enough as it stands," Agee lamented; "the civil and international prospect is unimaginably sinister."[11] Such worries were all in a week's work; Agee's column addressed the squandered opportunities of American motion pictures, from obscure Army Orientation films to Hollywood frauds like *The North Star* (1943)—"something to be seen more in sorrow than in anger and more in the attitude of the diagnostician than in any emotion at all"—to enlist the intelligence and courage of their audience.[12] Of such hokum Agee wrote pessimistically: "I am afraid the general public will swallow it whole. I insist, however, that the public must and can be trusted and reached with a kind of honesty difficult, in so mental-hospital a situation, to contrive; impossible, perhaps, among the complicated pressures and self-defensive virtuosities of the great studios."[13] For Baldwin, similar sentiments more frequently included his analyses of race, a topic that consumed him, but the conclusion was the same: Americans were almost hopelessly addicted to the "corroboration"—a term he used over and over again— of their own fantasies, prejudices, and childish expectations.[14] He himself might have borrowed Agee's lines to describe *The Defiant Ones* (1958), an absurd fantasy of the unconditional Black love that exists for white people, or *The Exorcist* (1973), a horror film most frightening for "the mindless and hysterical banality of the evil" it presents even as it evades the much deeper and more threatening evil that resides as potential within all of us.[15] Unlike most of their fellow citizens—that is, if the evidence of American culture and institutions were to be considered—Agee and Baldwin apprehended a moral urgency in the quotidian matter of lived, and living, history.

As Agee's columns accumulated in the 1940s and Baldwin developed the half-century story of his life at the movies in *The Devil Finds Work* in the 1970s, both struggled to keep their ideals intact in the face of so much terrible product, even as they shared a childlike faith in the possibilities of the form itself. Their continuing to show up for work, armed with the hope of encountering something humane and transformative, is all the more impressive because of their investment in a popular form rather than a "high" one. The sordid origins and heavy-fisted proprietors of the industry, as well as the enormous proletarian audiences of the movies, added, paradoxically, to their import. This was not so much by choice as by inheritance.

They reveled in the lowest of genres, from slapstick to soap opera. Agee, in his truncated childhood in the hills of east Tennessee, and Baldwin, in his own Harlem predicament as a young boy, both discovered almost as early as they could see that they had as much access to this world of light and shadow as anyone else did. Agee grew into himself in his earliest memories sitting in the dark next to his father (whom he would lose in 1915) as they took in Chaplin's sacred pratfalls. With the very space of the theater marking the yawning distance between Baldwin and his holy, disapproving father, the very young Baldwin lived, comparably, in the orbit of Bette Davis's ferocious gaze in *20,000 Years in Sing Sing* (1932), the same gaze featured on this special section's opener. With her "pop-eyes popping," he saw his own face, and incipient ferocity, reflected.[16] "I had discovered that my infirmity might not be my doom," he writes. "My infirmity, or infirmities, might be forged into weapons."[17] Through this disquieting white starlet, who ran the gamut from ingénue to femme fatale—usually all at once—he began to fathom his own multiplicity. A decade later, he writes, Davis's performance as a spoiled southern belle who debases herself before her Black chauffeur in *In This Our Life* (1942) "had the effect, rather, of exposing and shattering the film, so that she played in a kind of vacuum."[18] Davis became "the toast of Harlem," for she graphically exposed the white racial hypocrisy that American culture—not least of all, the Hollywood assembly line—worked tirelessly to hide:

> The blacks have a song which says, *I can't believe what you say, because I see what you do.* No American film, relating to blacks, can possibly incorporate this observation. This observation—set to music, as are so many black observations—denies, simply, the validity of the legend which is responsible for these films: films which exist for the sole purpose of perpetuating the legend.[19]

With "the truth about the woman revealed," Baldwin writes, Davis has pierced through this institutionalized racial mythology from the inside, reminding him of the possibilities of subversion and humanization latent in American film.[20] Baldwin's highest compliment to Davis—a phrase Agee might well have written—was to describe her performance of southern white womanhood as "ruthlessly accurate."[21]

For both writers, and irreversibly, the cinema challenged and supplanted the church; and just as both men lapsed in the formal religious lives they had been assigned as children, and became, somehow, more devout in their apostasy and profanity, their faith in the cinema deepened with each holy horror they encountered on the screen. For both men, the promise of the cinema remained, not unlike the "New Jerusalem" that Baldwin insisted, against all the violent evidence of American history, could still be wrought by people who groped across the abyss that divided them.[22]

They both forged a wicked sense of humor, and it accompanied them like a shield through the lonelier stretches, which were frequent. Agee eventually self-destructed, succumbing to a heart attack in 1955. His fall may have been accelerated by several years of journeyman's work as a screenwriter, when he enjoyed the mainstream success that came far more easily to white writers in Jim Crow Hollywood than to those seen as non-white. Enjoyment, for Agee, was no simple matter, however, and might well consist of compulsive overwork, impossibly high aesthetic expectations, and dangerous sorts of self-medication. Baldwin himself, despite a series of near misses in Hollywood and elsewhere, never abandoned the hope of producing his own films. His sensitivity left him vulnerable, too, especially in a Hollywood setting in which he was hired, in 1968, to imagine Malcolm X not as a friend he had known and mourned but as a generic, and substantially deracinated, action hero. (Charlton Heston, riding high on the success of *Planet of the Apes* (1968), was among the list of names producers suggested for the title role. Baldwin, reading the writing on the studio wall, took his screenplay and left town.) Despite his own occasional self-destructive impulses, Baldwin had other compulsions, too, including his involvement in the civil rights movement, and a wide network of friends, family, and more than a few movie stars, which drew him beyond himself in ways that sustained him. And he understood his fame, in part, as an opportunity not simply to muse on the jagged pattern of history in front of an audience, but to intervene in that history in direct ways that might alter its course for the better. "There is never time in the future in which we will work out our salvation," he wrote in the late 1950s, not about film or celebrity, but about the freedom struggle. "The challenge is in the moment, the time is always now."[23] The show, and the struggle, must go on, with Baldwin as producer as much as star.

Agee had rather less the street activist in him; and his death in 1955 delivered him from the more activist years of the struggle to come. But he, too—and in ways that Baldwin might have appreciated—had a sort of stage presence, and strained to do his part. He chafed under the impositions of Henry Luce, the mogul who employed him as a staff writer at *Fortune* and *Time*. Luce revealed his own priorities in "The American Century" (1941), a *Life* editorial in which he advocated an updated, but not really new, model of American nationalism and imperialism, in which the United States should use the world crisis of the moment to establish itself at the center of the global order. Indeed, Agee's chronic depression might be read as the cost of his ongoing exposure to Luce's all-American brew of military might and earnest shallowness. Working for Luce at *Fortune* in the 1930s, Agee said, left him with feelings ranging from "a hard masochistic liking to direct nausea."[24] A typical reply came in the form of Agee's almost mystically reverent treatment of Alabama tenant farmers in a routine *Fortune* assignment; deemed completely unsuitable for publication in a business magazine, this work became the basis for Agee's classic collaboration with photographer Walker Evans, *Let Us Now Praise Famous Men* (1941). Agee also articulated his support for civil rights legislation, as he wrote to his former teacher and mentor Father James Flye in May 1945: "I dislike the forms of discrimination which this kind of legislation is trying to combat. There are very few ways of combatting it, and on the whole I am afraid they are worse than useless; but such as the ways are, and poor as they are, I am for them."[25] Such a stance as this might have been surprising ten or even twenty years later among most white southerners. In the 1940s it was utterly remarkable; and coming from the same writer who would publish a lengthy tribute to D. W. Griffith in 1948, insisting that the late Griffith, in making *The Birth of a Nation,* had gone "to almost preposterous lengths to be fair to the Negroes as he understood them," and defending Griffith against the calumnies of the "contemporary abolitionists," Agee's antiracism takes on an almost surreal quality.[26] Perhaps, though—and again, in ways Baldwin would recognize—it was more instinctive than intentional, the expression of an uncomplicated humanism in a complicated world.

In the last year of World War II, Agee wrote to Father Flye of his halcyon vision:

> I begin to want to write a weekly column for some newspaper or magazine—very miscellaneous but in general, detailed topical analysis of the very swift and sinister decline and perversion of all that might be meant by individualism, a sense of evil, a sense of tragedy, a sense of moral vigilance or discrimination; the perversion of virtually all nominal rationalism to the most irrational sort of uses and ends; the fear of the so-called irrational, the mock-revival of mock-religion; and well, etc. etc.[27]

To a great extent, this miscellany is what he was already producing in his film criticism, especially in the longer reviews for *The Nation,* but even, with some regularity, in the haiku-like buckshot of his *Time* coverage. Agee's film writing provided persistent autobiographical traces of the sort that left little doubt as to the tenacity of his perception and belief. "Decline and perversion" were mere evidence of the potential for human grandeur; "evil" and "tragedy," reminders of the dignity of man; "moral vigilance," the highest aim of his work. So too with Baldwin, whose ambition and commitment are everywhere in these lines. From backgrounds starkly different—or perhaps not—these men shared a civilization in flight from itself, and as they bore witness to its misdeeds and attempted escapes, they suffered dearly for the insights they carried within themselves.

My own halcyon vision, tailored to my own after times: to discover in the archives some grainy old television footage, the two of them sitting at the table and talking movies, shaking their heads in disbelief and amusement, shoring up their shared humanism, and ours—the New Jerusalem on celluloid.

* * * * *

Film is such a big topic in Baldwin's life and career that it can almost be invisible at times, like geological time or climate change or some other pattern whose scale renders it, most of the time, invisible. He had a lifelong relationship with the movies, a relationship every bit as complicated as his relationships with literature and with many of the people in his family and inner circle. Baldwin's relationship with film, meanwhile, is not just one thing; it takes many forms, and it changes a great deal over the course of his life. What's more, it seems to have changed considerably, or we have changed enough to see it anew, in the decades since his death.

Baldwin's career also coincided with the rise of television, which necessarily transformed his relationship with the movies of his youth. Television was met with utopian fantasies by some Blacks who knew the indignities of the Jim Crow studio system all too well. Perhaps the new medium, which was not subject to the same forces of censorship and self-regulation that had contorted the Black face into a grotesque minstrel rictus, would bring about better portraits of Black lives, and better opportunities for Black performers. This was a widely shared hope at mid-century, just as Baldwin was beginning to publish his writing. Baldwin's celebrity in the following years would owe a great deal to his television appearances, which were numerous and varied, and went well beyond the talk-show circuit: from his 1963 interview with Kenneth Clark on New York's WGBH to *Take This Hammer* (1964), produced for national broadcast by San Francisco's KQED; from his 1965 debate with William F. Buckley at Cambridge to his spirited repartee with Dick Gregory and West Indian students in London in *Baldwin's Nigger* (1968). And even as Baldwin's fiction and drama went unproduced by Hollywood, there were several television adaptations of his work, from a German-language production of his play *Blues für Mister Charlie* (1969), which was filmed in Vienna, to the PBS production of *Go Tell It on the Mountain* (1985) that Baldwin enjoyed not least because it received prominent coverage in that all-important organ of American intellectual life, *TV Guide*.

Television created an identity crisis for Hollywood, and over the course of the 1960s and 1970s the movies struggled to reinvent themselves amid the very forces of American discontent that Baldwin was documenting in his writings and television appearances. While *The Devil Finds Work* did not address television in much detail or explicitness, it was published during a major upheaval in American cinema, and Baldwin experienced the moment as an opportunity—yet another one, as the civil rights movement had been—slipping away. The studios struggled with bankruptcies. Longtime industry leaders no longer trusted themselves to predict what audiences wanted to watch, even as televised images of civil rights protests and the Vietnam War were broadcast, daily, into the living rooms of millions of Americans. An insurgency of film school brats and other outsiders seized the opening and became "canonical" in due time: Francis Ford Coppola, George Lucas, Steven Spielberg, Woody Allen, Martin Scorsese, Hal Ashby, Robert Altman; but also the likes Melvin Van Peebles and Gordon Parks, who proved considerably more bankable than the radical, genre-defying L.A. Rebellion cohort coming out of UCLA. Television exerted its own gravitational force, providing a venue for commentary and critique of Hollywood's mythology even as it shaped Hollywood simply by virtue of its own huge presence in American life. In the context of this blue light, Baldwin's appearances on *The Dick Cavett Show*, in which he continued to disturb the peace amid an early 1970s hangover of benign neglect, suggest that television, more than the big screen, may have been his most apt medium, even as he pined for that elusive Oscar. This was appropriate, too, in the sense that television had served, far better than the cinema, as the medium of the civil rights movement. Baldwin washed his hands of Hollywood's adaptation of, and to, civil rights in such evasive, snail-paced vehicles as *In the Heat of the Night* and *Guess Who's Coming to Dinner* (both 1967). Meanwhile, and despite his occasional reservations about the lethally reassuring presence of television in

American life, he seized the opening it offered, becoming a small-screen provocateur and *flâneur*, a troubling, charming, witness-bearing, truth-telling visitor from that singular world of his own making—the cinema of his mind.

* * * * *

The idea for this special section emerged from a roundtable at the Modern Language Association's conference in Seattle, which took place in January 2020, a few weeks before Covid precipitated our long isolation. That session, "Finding Work for the Devil: James Baldwin on Film," included the participation of Rich Blint, Justin A. Joyce, Quentin Miller, Karen Thorsen, and myself, and spurred a series of conversations among various attendees and ourselves in subsequent weeks and months. Over the course of an exceptionally tumultuous and difficult year, these articles were written.

Karen Thorsen's "The Disorder of Life: James Baldwin on My Shoulder, Part Two," is the second serialization of her memoir; "Part One" was published in volume 6 of *James Baldwin Review*. Thorsen directed *James Baldwin: The Price of the Ticket* (1990) after plans to collaborate on a film with Baldwin were interrupted by his terminal illness in 1987. This second part of her memoir offers an invaluable look at Baldwin's late-career views of his work, in print and in action, and also on film, since the civil rights era. It is also a portrait of Baldwin's interest in young people, their aspirations and ideals, as he aged and reflected on his own youth. Thorsen's own quest had taken her to France, to Vietnam, and, in a rather unlikely way, into the orbit of the great *cinéma vérité* filmmakers Albert and David Maysles, where she forged a filmmaking career of her own. Her account makes it clear that Baldwin, at the point of their meeting, valued her wide-ranging curiosity about the world, and her model of social commitment in the face of contemporary global affairs, at least as much as he cared about her background in film.

In "*The Devil Finds Work*: A Hollywood Love Story (as Written by James Baldwin)," D. Quentin Miller revisits this most vexing of Baldwin's books. Many readers have struggled to classify *The Devil Finds Work*, and have ended up comparing it, usually unfavorably, to earlier works—and particularly to *The Fire Next Time*, an extended essay that likewise combines memoir with other modes of storytelling and analysis in the service of larger claims regarding race, culture, and American citizenship. Miller breaks with this critical tradition, suggesting instead that a more apt comparison may be to Baldwin's fiction. The "love story" in Baldwin's long relationship with the movies, he finds, has striking parallels with the love story in *Giovanni's Room* (1956), Baldwin's second novel. In seeing *The Devil Finds Work* as the story of a failed love affair, Miller positions Baldwin's film criticism anew, and reads across Baldwin's multifaceted career a larger sense of coherence and integration.

In "Another Cinema: James Baldwin's Search for a New Film Form," Hayley O'Malley combines readings of archival documents, literature, film, and print culture to examine three distinct modes in Baldwin's ongoing quest to revolutionize film for his own purposes. Literature, she argues, served as a key site to practice being a filmmaker. Beginning as early as *Go Tell It on the Mountain* (1953), Baldwin adapted cinematic grammars in his fiction and portrayed moviegoing in such a way that he could, in effect, direct his own movies, turning the novel and the short story into alternative genres of filmmaking. In the 1960s, Baldwin took a more direct route to making movies, as he composed screenplays, formed several production companies, and attempted to work in both Hollywood and the independent film scene in Europe. Finally, O'Malley explores how Baldwin sought to change cinema not only by trying to work behind the camera, but also by performing in front of it, in particular during his collaboration on Dick Fontaine and Pat Hartley's documentary *I Heard It Through the Grapevine* (1982). This little-known film follows Baldwin as he revisits key sites from the civil rights movement and reconnects with activist friends as he endeavors to construct a revisionist history of race in America and to develop a media practice capable of honoring Black communities.

Peter Lurie's "Everybody's Protest Cinema: Baldwin, Racial Melancholy, and the Black Middle Ground" uses Baldwin's 1949 critique of the protest novel to consider its corollary in the 1990s New Black Cinema. Reading that tradition, and particularly Spike Lee's *Malcolm X* (1992), against more recent films by Barry Jenkins and the collaboration of Joe Talbot and Jimmy Fails, Lurie argues for the resurgent importance of Baldwin's critical model and its ethics as well as his aesthetics across the three decades since *Malcolm X* emerged as perhaps the most influential Black film of its time. Jenkins's adaption of *If Beale Street Could Talk* (2018) and Talbot and Fails's *The Last Black Man in San Francisco* (2019) offer a cinematic version of racial narrative at odds with the protest tradition Lurie associates with Lee and other earlier Black directors, a cinema we may see as both a direct and an indirect legacy of Baldwin's views on African American culture.

In one of his last television appearances, a December 1986 C-SPAN broadcast of Baldwin's speech at the National Press Club in Washington, DC, he was asked his opinion of a new film called *She's Gotta Have It*. The crowd, and Baldwin, giggled at the mention of the title—a moment of levity in the midst of hard questions about the Cold War, South Africa, and African American history. With a grin, Baldwin said he hadn't seen it. Nor would he live to see the enormous, rich tradition of African American cinema that has been produced since those early films of Spike Lee were released. It is a body of filmmaking that continues to reveal—perhaps more now than ever, as Peter Lurie senses—Baldwin's abiding influence upon the thought and expression of contemporary Black culture.

Baldwin did, however, call forth a vision of historical continuity in his speech, implicating the institutions of American film in an ignoble past that continued to shape the present:

We can see if we examine our legends that very shortly after I was discovered in Africa, where I was the sometimes noble savage, in the twinkling of an eye, after the Middle Passage, I am found on the Metro-Goldwyn-Mayer backlot, singing and dancing, the noble savage now transformed into the happy darky. No one quite knows how this happened. We are living with these myths until today. And it corrupts the view from here.[28]

His closing remarks that day, some of the last lines he delivered before a camera, considered these tired, racist images even as they hinted at other possible futures. Baldwin had survived the American century long enough to witness how disastrously white supremacy in domestic affairs, including those of Hollywood, had stunted American understanding of the rest of the world. He wanted to hope for something else:

> The reason it is important now is that, out of this endeavor, what we call the white American has created only the nigger he wants to see. The reason that's important and terrifying and corrupts the view from here is because when this same white man looks around the world, he sees only the nigger he wants to see. And that is mortally dangerous for the future of this country, for our present fortunes. The world is full of all kinds of people who live quite beyond the confines of the American imagination and who have nothing whatever to do with the guilt-ridden vision of the world which controls so much of our life and our thinking, and which paralyzes very nearly our moral sense. We are living in a world in which everybody and everything is interdependent. It is not white, this world. It is not black either. The future of this world depends on everyone in this room, and that future depends on to what extent and by what means we liberate ourselves from a vocabulary which now cannot bear the weight of reality. Thank you.[29]

I hope that *JBR* readers will receive this special section's scholarship in the Baldwinian spirit in which it has been produced: for even as it speaks in urgent ways to the problems of the present, it is hardly the last word in the conversation. The scale and complexity of Baldwin's relationship with film, and the as-yet-unproduced nature of the future, make it so. I know that there will be a great deal more for all of us, individually and collaboratively, to say and do, as we seek to bend these after times to good purpose, as we attempt, several decades late, to trade in the American century for something better.

Notes

1 James Baldwin, *The Devil Finds Work* (1976), in *Collected Essays*, ed. Toni Morrison (New York, Library of America, 1998), p. 483.

2 Caryl Phillips, "James Baldwin: The Lure of Hollywood," in *A New World Order* (New York, Vintage, 2002), p. 74.

3 See Rob Nixon, *Slow Violence and the Environmentalism of the Poor* (Cambridge, MA, Harvard University Press, 2013).

4 James Agee, *Agee on Film: Criticism and Comment on the Movies* (New York, Modern Library, 2000), p. 313.

5 Baldwin, *The Devil Finds Work*, p. 511.

6 Agee, *Agee on Film*, p. 153.
7 James Baldwin, *The Fire Next Time*, in Morrison (ed.), *Collected Essays*, p. 292.
8 Here I follow Eddie S. Glaude, Jr., who, contemplating Baldwin's moral imagination after the civil rights movement, borrows the phrase "after times" from Walt Whitman. See Eddie S. Glaude, Jr., *Begin Again: James Baldwin's America and Its Urgent Lessons for Our Own* (New York, Crown, 2020), pp. 16–17.
9 Agee, *Agee on Film*, p. 38.
10 *Ibid.*, p. 39.
11 *Ibid.*
12 *Ibid.*, p. 40.
13 *Ibid.*, p. 41.
14 For one of many such examples, see Baldwin, *The Devil Finds Work*, p. 500: "That the movie star is an 'escape' personality indicates one of the irreducible dangers to which the moviegoer is exposed: the danger of surrendering to the corroboration of one's fantasies as they are thrown back from the screen."
15 Baldwin, *The Devil Finds Work*, p. 571.
16 *Ibid.*, p. 482.
17 *Ibid.*, p. 483.
18 *Ibid.*, p. 522.
19 *Ibid.*, pp. 521, 522.
20 *Ibid.*, p. 521.
21 *Ibid.*, pp. 522–3.
22 See Karen Thorsen (dir.), *James Baldwin: The Price of the Ticket* (Maysles Films & PBS/American Masters, 1990).
23 James Baldwin, "Faulkner and Desegregation," in Morrison (ed.), *Collected Essays*, p. 214.
24 Alan Brinkley, *The Publisher: Henry Luce and His American Century* (New York, Vintage, 2010), p. 163.
25 James Agee, *Letters of James Agee to Father Flye* (New York, Ballantine, 2nd ed., 1971), p. 146.
26 Agee, *Agee on Film*, p. 313.
27 Agee, *Letters of James Agee to Father Flye*, pp. 141–2.
28 *The World I Never Made*, C-SPAN (10 December 1986), www.c-span.org/video/?150875-1/world-made (accessed 24 April 2021).
29 *Ibid.*

Works Cited

Agee, James, *Agee on Film: Criticism and Comment on the Movies* (New York, Modern Library, 2000).
_____ *Letters of James Agee to Father Flye* (New York, Ballantine, 2nd ed., 1971).
Baldwin, James, *The Devil Finds Work* (1976), in *Collected Essays*, ed. Toni Morrison (New York, Library of America, 1998), pp. 477–572.
_____ "Faulkner and Desegregation" (1956), in *Collected Essays*, ed. Toni Morrison (New York, Library of America, 1998), pp. 209–14.
_____ *The Fire Next Time* (1963), in *Collected Essays*, ed. Toni Morrison (New York, Library of America, 1998), pp. 287–347.

Brinkley, Alan, *The Publisher: Henry Luce and His American Century* (New York, Vintage, 2010).

Glaude, Jr., Eddie S., *Begin Again: James Baldwin's America and Its Urgent Lessons for Our Own* (New York, Crown, 2020).

Nixon, Rob, *Slow Violence and the Environmentalism of the Poor* (Cambridge, MA, Harvard University Press, 2013).

Phillips, Caryl, *A New World Order* (New York, Vintage, 2002).

Thorsen, Karen (dir.), *James Baldwin: The Price of the Ticket* (1990), Maysles Films & PBS/American Masters.

The World I Never Made, C-SPAN (10 December 1986), www.c-span.org/video/?150875-1/world-made (accessed 23 April 2021).

Contributor's Biography

Robert Jackson is the James G. Watson Professor of English at the University of Tulsa, where his work explores interdisciplinary connections among literature, film and media, and social history in the modern and contemporary United States. His most recent book, *Fade In, Crossroads: A History of the Southern Cinema* (Oxford University Press, 2017), considers the varied relations between Black and white southerners and the motion picture medium from the silent era to mid-century. He has edited special issues of *The Faulkner Journal* and *The Global South*, and has contributed articles and reviews to *Modernism/modernity, Modern Fiction Studies, James Baldwin Review, The Faulkner Journal, Southern Literary Journal, Journal of American History, Journal of Southern History, Virginia Quarterly Review, Mississippi Quarterly*, and other publications. Currently, he is at work on a book about James Baldwin's relationship with Robert F. Kennedy, particularly in the context of their infamous but mysterious May 1963 meeting to discuss the state of American race relations with a group of Baldwin's friends and associates.

ESSAY

The Disorder of Life: James Baldwin on My Shoulder, Part Two

Karen Thorsen

Abstract

Filmmaker Karen Thorsen gave us *James Baldwin: The Price of the Ticket*, the award-winning documentary that is now considered a classic. First broadcast on PBS/American Masters in August, 1989—just days after what would have been Baldwin's sixty-fifth birthday—the film premiered at the Sundance Film Festival in 1990. It was not the film Thorsen intended to make. Beginning in 1986, Baldwin and Thorsen had been collaborating on a very different film project: a "nonfiction feature" about the history, research, and writing of Baldwin's next book, "Remember This House." It was also going to be a film about progress: about how far we had come, how far we still have to go, before we learn to trust our common humanity. But that project ended abruptly. On 1 December 1987, James Baldwin died—and "Remember This House," book *and* film died with him. Suddenly, Thorsen's mission changed: the world needed to know what they had lost. Her alliance with Baldwin took on new meaning. The following memoir—the second of two serialized parts—explores how and why their collaboration began. The first installment appeared in the sixth volume of *James Baldwin Review*, in the fall of 2020; the next stage of their journey starts here.

Keywords: James Baldwin, "Remember This House," *The Price of the Ticket*, filmmaking, Vietnam, Algeria, film, *cinéma vérité*

James Baldwin Review, Volume 7, 2021, © The Authors. Published by Manchester University Press and The University of Manchester Library
http://dx.doi.org/10.7227/JBR.7.4

James Baldwin and I met only once. It's still stunning to me how much my life changed with just one physical meeting. There were many other exchanges with him over the course of my lifetime, but only one meeting. My whole "Part I" essay in volume 6 of *James Baldwin Review* is about the lead-up to that single encounter, and my reasons for trying to find him.[1]

I had a film to propose: a Direct Cinema portrait that aimed to explore what the civil rights activist and best-selling author was up to "today." I was to produce it; Albert and David Maysles, the famous *vérité* filmmakers, would be the directors of record; and the new PBS series, *American Masters*, had agreed to help fund it … *if* we could land a commitment from Baldwin.

Back in 1985, he was still a transatlantic commuter. It was hard to figure out how to reach him, going through publishers and the various people who knew him, then actually figuring out where he was on the planet. And then, how to get his attention. But I knew he'd been teaching in Massachusetts—and when I finally found him, it was through his colleagues at UMass.

He was, understandably, beset and besieged by too many proposals like mine. His first instinct was to say "yes" to everyone—but that left many hanging, hoping their turn would come. As for those he *did* see, he almost always gave more of himself than anyone on the receiving end ever expected—which almost always took longer than planned. That's part of why he was so often late (forty minutes in my case … and that was better than most). But finally, we connected.

Our exchanges took place in stages, over the winter of 1985–86: first a letter, then faxes, then phone calls … then in April at The Ginger Man, his midday New York City restaurant of choice. It was an extraordinary, long, wet lunch; it was everything I could have hoped for: suddenly, my months of planning a film about him and his current concerns became real. Yes, I'd done my research—but as I look back now, I realize I was so naïve about the whole undertaking at that point. I had such a superficial understanding of who he really was, what he'd been through, about the weight of his message and the social forces at stake. And I'm still learning. Even after decades of exploring his journey, my understanding keeps evolving, his words keep inspiring new notes in my margins.

I now know that that was one of his gifts: he could make people feel like kindred spirits. I say this with all humility. Our lunch went well in part because of who I am, who I was then—but far more because of his own ability to embrace the stranger, racially, socially, intellectually, spiritually. He was by nature warmhearted. Empathetic. And curious: he clearly liked to seed encounters with questions.

We touched on so many subjects. A lot of what I wrote in Part I of my *JBR* essay was drawn from that day, from the personal histories we shared over omelets, white wine, and his whiskey on refill. What we loved about France. What we saw in Jean Genet, Thomas Paine, a Vietnamese general. Adventures in Connecticut, Istanbul. Church. What his next book could be, and should be. What he hoped for his country, his students, for young people in general. And, most especially, filmmaking.

What strikes me now is that even though it was race, civil rights, which had brought us together as potential collaborators, that wasn't our primary topic. We talked across differences, not about them. We dove into ideas, what shaped our impressions, what might be achieved. The possibility of making a film that explored life as we saw it. And we laughed. A lot.

* * * * *

He was no stranger to film. He'd loved movies ever since he was a kid, he'd poured his heart into scripts that never made it to screen, he'd appeared on screen himself countless times—and, as I already knew from our prior exchanges, he was searching for something.

He had a project in mind, he called it "Remember This House"—or, as he sometimes wrote the title, "Re/Member This House"—that he envisioned as both a book and a film. It had been on and off his back burner since the late 1970s: it had almost become a *New Yorker* essay; it was a work-in-progress for which McGraw-Hill had paid a substantial advance; it had even been impetus for the 1982 documentary, *I Heard It Through the Grapevine.*[2] But it had yet to become what he believed it should be.

Like all his ideas, this one kept evolving. What he had first seen as a revisitation of civil rights in the sixties, a retracing of history and the three men who gave their lives to the movement—Medgar Evers, Malcolm X, and Martin Luther King, Jr.—now promised to be a more personal, more intimate memoir. This was still to be an assessment of then vs. now, a keen examination of progress and the lack thereof; but it would also be, he insisted, a far deeper exploration than his original vision: a first-person journey through friendship, family, and generational courage.

I could see in his face how much this project mattered.

As a necessary continuation of his own past work. As a tribute to his friends' lost lives. As salve for his still-open wounds.

As his own form of sorrow song: "so many of us, cut down, so soon."[3]

His eyes, those "big world-absorbing eyes" that had so deeply searched mine, looked aside, still in mourning, trying to fathom the pain.[4] For a moment, words failed him—and that, as he finally began to explain, was the problem with "Remember This House." Somewhere, in some un-nameable distance, he was sure there were answers; but it had become increasingly difficult to put thoughts on paper … especially when these three men were concerned. His expression turned vulnerable, almost pleading: he admitted that he'd already tossed several drafts—and that the phone discussions we had had were part of why he was meeting me now.

Maybe, just maybe, the mix of research and writing with filmmaking would help his narrative find its voice.

* * * * *

The more we talked, the more it seemed possible.

He was wary, of course, of outside intervention. He'd had his share of filmmakers who had tried to define him, indulging their own vision instead of his. And he had already flirted with *cinéma vérité*—or Direct Cinema, as the Maysles Brothers chose to call it—and discovered the pitfalls. In retrospect, he confessed, he'd been disappointed by the *vérité* aspects of past filmmaking efforts he had been part of because the films that resulted felt random, diffuse. Conversations lacked substance; encounters felt forced… What good was *vérité* if life "as it happened" was boring? Or fake? To his credit, he didn't just blame the filmmakers: he blamed himself for believing that his presence on screen would be enough to sustain an audience.

What he wanted was structure, a narrative plan that was shaped by more than the quirks of his schedule. And depth. He quoted Vincent Canby's review of *I Heard It Through the Grapevine*—"Something seems to be missing"—and laughed at its vagueness: "so polite!"[5] Then he leaned in, suddenly serious. "What's really missing in that film is hope."[6]

He wasn't denying the frustration he felt, the anger, the fear that gripped the souls of Black folk on a near-daily basis. He wasn't negating the obvious truth, that progress hailed by the white world was more fiction than fact, that lives were still being crushed on what he called "Freedom Road." But he still believed that progress was possible, and he wanted people to know that.

He had faith in potential, in our innate need for love—and that had been his conviction for most of his life. I know this, but not just from his writings. I heard it then in his words, in the pained insistence that shaped them; I confirmed it later after his death, while combing through hundreds of hours of archival material during research for my own film, *The Price of the Ticket* (1990). This man was consistent: I could intercut the first half of a statement he made in his thirties with the end of a statement he made at age sixty without changing the message. Whether at the height of his fame or no longer admired, he never wavered. Love was the solution. And hope was essential.

Even so, the public reaction to *Grapevine* still rankled. He regretted its darkness—and he wanted "Remember This House" to reflect the light that he saw, both in his three friends and in "some" human beings. Why "some"? As he counseled his teenage nephew in *The Fire Next Time* (1963), "Destruction and death … is what most of mankind has been best at since we have heard of man. But remember: most of mankind is not *all* of mankind."[7]

Medgar, Malcolm, Martin… Their presence—their absence—consumed him. Each one of these men held a complex place in history, each one of them held a complex place in his heart. All three had struggled with the pull of public life, the constant demands of the cause; all three had welcomed him into their homes, their families. All three had had children, infants whom he had held, kids about whom he still cared, sons and daughters who were now in their twenties.

As he stated on British television, just months after our lunch, "You can't tell the children there's no hope."[8]

* * * * *

This project was far more complex than I'd dared to imagine.

It was to be both a book and a film. It was to examine three famous men who'd been killed—*assassinated*—through the lens of a man who loved them. It was to be about the civil rights movement on a very personal level, about a search for the past and what that means to the present. It was still to be about progress—but on a national, global, even spiritual level, in terms of the human soul. He knew it would be painful, that this kind of probing would come at great cost to himself; he knew that was why it was so damn hard to write. But he was determined.

He quizzed me intently on process, on how the Maysles Brothers and I might approach this shared journey. I had already sent him a brief proposal; it described Direct Cinema, the brothers' impressive history and how the three of us hoped to follow him with our camera and sound gear, gradually crafting a nuanced portrait. For fundraising purposes, we'd called our project "James Baldwin Today," but that was way too generic for this conversation.

Based on what he'd told me thus far, I dove in. While the remains of my omelet got cold, I suggested that a film version of "Remember This House" might resemble his approach to the Atlanta child murders: a search without foregone conclusions; a search, not for gruesome facts, but for larger ideas found in intimate details. He had just published *The Evidence of Things Not Seen* about brutal killings in the city "too busy to hate," first as an essay in *Playboy* that won the magazine's 1981 Best Nonfiction Award, then as a 1985 book that received tepid reviews.[9] "Far too much sermonizing," said the *New York Times*—a comment he shrugged off as predictable.[10] He warned me against reading reviews—"They can kill your initiative"—but I could tell he was pleased that I was paying attention. He waved for a refill. "The truth is hard to take, but that's what I'm searching for. Or as some call it, *vérité*." He smiled, but we both knew he had issued a challenge. He wanted to hear what "our" word meant to us.

I took a deep breath: *this* was why we were having lunch.

I described our approach as a form of faith in humanity, a decision to explore a particular individual, a conviction that there was a story worth telling. A way of using real-life interactions to reveal central truth. I explained how we always began with a framework, an initial focus which would tell us where to start filming: in his case, it was likely to be a mix of research in the South, teaching in the North, and time spent with the families he wanted to write about. We would travel together, and then, as our journey evolved, the four of us would decide what to film next. Other than the presence of film crews, our only intervention in the "truth" that we captured would be in the edit room, where the real storytelling takes shape—and where he would be welcome to participate in our progress.

He nodded. "But what about the children?" he asked. "What role would they play?" I wasn't prepared for that question.

As we debated the possibilities, the themes he hoped to address and various narrative arcs that might be able to carry his themes, two ideas took hold: "Remember This House" would be his message to the next generation—and three young people would help him shape it. The eldest son of Martin Luther King, Jr., the eldest daughter of Malcolm X, and the youngest son of Medgar Evers would be his through-line.

He had watched all three of them lose their fathers.

*****

Jimmy loved children, he always had—far beyond the fact that they represented the future. (I forgot to mention: somewhere in the course of our life-changing lunch, he insisted that I call him Jimmy.) First of all, he had raised his own siblings, almost as a parent. As the eldest of nine, he knew what it was to hold a book in one hand and bounce kids on his knee with the other. Second, as a gay man, he didn't have his own children, but he cared deeply about his nieces and nephews. And third—a surprise that arrived later in life, once he began teaching—he loved his students. Not only did they offer hope, but they also "kept him honest." He cared enormously about what they thought. In many regards, he felt as if they were teaching him.

He was currently a professor at the University of Massachusetts, shuttling between classes at five different colleges. He was notoriously erratic; he'd zoom in, late for class, or miss classes entirely because he was traveling—then make up for it later both on and off campus, during afternoon office hours and, even better, after hours, when he'd take groups of students out for drinks or to his home in Pelham for late-night discussions. This was not run-of-the-mill teaching; it was how he interacted with most human beings. Students adored him.

And he revered them. It was their honesty, their curiosity, their eagerness to learn and evolve that got him. Their unfiltered innocence.

He told me how on his very first day of teaching as a Writer-in-Residence at Bowling Green State University in Ohio, in the fall of 1979, a white student had asked him point-blank "Why does the white boy hate the nigger?" He laughed, eyes widened, reliving the moment: the class was racially mixed, there was no way he'd expected to dive in that deep on day one, but he had little choice—and his students ran with it.

"I underestimated those children."

He knew what they would have to face once they were out in the world, that they would soon be "forced to be strangers"—but not yet, not now.[11] The rest of that first class—and the entire semester—flew by in candid discussion, each one taking gradual measure of the "other" lives in the room and the baggage they carried.

He wrote about that experience, about those "innocent" students, a year later in *Esquire*: "They were trying to become whole. They were trying to put themselves and their country together."[12] A lofty goal. It was what he'd been trying to do for most of his life; it was what he wanted to do with "Remember This House."

And it began with a question.

*****

Questions were a constant in James Baldwin's life. They were central to his search for identity, to his role as a writer, a teacher, to his frustration with the pace of "progress." For him, asking questions, tough questions, was a given: it came with the territory of being human.

He wrote about this repeatedly, underscoring our need for self-discovery—which, he believed, would lead to a better understanding of others. His experience in Ohio had confirmed this. At first, I laughed with him as he described that first class, feeling the shock that he'd felt, dismissing his student's question as clueless. But then I realized—I wasn't so different from that kid, just more polite. My own copies of his books were proof: pages full of underlined questions—later starred multiple times in various colored inks—that showed how uncertain I was.

I, too, was searching for answers. And his questions helped:

"Isn't love more important than color?"[13]
"What, under heaven ... could cause any people to act as white people acted?"[14]
"Who is it for and who is paying for it? And why isn't it for you?"[15]
"If you think I'm a nigger, it means you need it. Why?"[16]
"What, exactly, is the 'good' of society?"[17]

These were questions he lived with, questions he had spent a lifetime trying to answer—questions that we all, as Americans, need to ask ourselves. Not just need to ask, but *must* ask, he insisted: "the future of the country depends on that."[18]

So why do people, white people, find Baldwin's questions so hard to tackle? He blames fear: fear of guilt, fear of pain, fear of difference. Fear of losing the identity that we're convinced we deserve. According to him, we've been stuck in a trap of our own making: "the sunlit prison of the American dream," "the place where questions are not asked."[19] Instead of curiosity, empathy, we've chosen indifference. Instead of questioning and evolving, we've chosen denial. Willful ignorance: anything to help us feel safe and keep illusion intact.

No wonder we feel so divided.

"Alienation from oneself and one's people is, in sum, the American experience."[20]

I told Jimmy I'd encountered that statement at Vassar, when I was the same age as his students at Bowling Green. It was in my assigned reading, in *Notes of a Native Son*, the essay titled "Encounter on the Seine." It's near the end of the book, but of course I read that one first: I was just back from Paris, a junior year abroad that, like Baldwin's questions, rocked my perspective.

Alienated? I felt more than alienated. I felt ashamed. And driven.

"Why?" His eyes were so focused, I almost felt swallowed. "Why did you feel that way?"

I looked across at him, hesitant—who was I to explain alienation to *him*—but he reassured me.

"That's why I love teaching: I get to connect with the next generation."

Once again, I dove in. I confessed that I'd felt out-of-place, stuck in a system I didn't agree with, even before I read *Notes*. I was part of the counter-culture, one of those flower children whom Baldwin called "idealistic, fragmented … impotent."[21] I'd felt that way as a student in Paris, when I tried to pretend I was Danish, just to avoid constant reminders of my nation's exploitation of others. I'd felt that way later, post-graduation, once I'd become a journalist: just as he had squirmed as a young book reviewer, expected to write about one subject only—"all those post-war 'Be kind to colored people,' 'Be kind to Jews' books," as he put it—I was Time Inc.'s token hippie, expected to satisfy what they called the "youth market."[22]

On top of that, I was female.

Most white men don't know how it feels to be less than. Even my own father, who went out of his way to emphasize my ability, my equality, didn't know how many times I felt obliged to dumb down, just to fit in. How many times I had to fight off self-doubt, wondering whether an achievement was due to talent … or looks. How many men I had to handle with care, deflecting advances without exploding their ego. Yes, I was privileged, by my whiteness and all that came with it; the battles I fought were minor compared to those fought by women of color. But even so, I felt diminished, devalued.

Was it simply that I wasn't as good as Jane Howard—the *LIFE* magazine reporter who, way back in May 1963, had written so articulately about Baldwin—or the few other female reporters whom Time Inc. had deemed worthy of bylines?[23] I teetered between self-doubt and determination.

I had to fight for the right to write about "adult" topics, male topics, like crime and war. And when I did crack that door open, I had to fight for the right to express my "female" perspective: one that tended toward a more empathetic, more personal take. I'm still proud of the few times I broke through, pieces on living in fear and anti-war protests that became *LIFE* cover stories—but I'm also well aware that those minor triumphs could never have happened without the help of two men: my superior Richard Stolley and his boss Philip Kunhardt, two exceptional editors who heard my frustration and let me try.[24]

A lot like my filmmaking mentor, Albert Maysles, a full decade later. He not only let me try, he made my Jimmy film *possible.*

That said, I never once wanted to be male—any more than Baldwin wanted to be white. Who could possibly want, as he so pointedly asked in *The Fire Next Time*, "to be integrated into a burning house?"[25] I simply wanted, like him, to enjoy equal opportunity, recognition. The right to define myself.

"Not *what* I was, but *who*."[26]

That phrase came straight out of *Notes*. It felt weird, quoting Baldwin to Baldwin, but I couldn't resist.

Jimmy smiled. "I'm still trying to answer that question myself."

*****

My struggles as a twenty-something beginner led to publishing memories of his own. I had already read the preface he wrote for the 1984 re-release of *Notes of a Native Son,* so I knew part of the story: that his close friend from high school, Sol Stein—who by the mid-1950s had become an editor at Beacon Press—had suggested that Jimmy publish a collection of essays, and that Jimmy resisted. At age 29, he declared, he was "too young to publish" his "memoirs."[27] I also knew that despite those misgivings, he'd finally agreed to author *Notes of a Native Son* (1955) because he was broke, and that he'd written its titular essay—widely regarded as one of his best—in a rush, desperate to earn a fee from *Harper's* magazine before Beacon Press published the book.

What I didn't know until we traded tales over lunch was how much energy he'd put into revising those early essays, not just rewriting but reinstating passages that had been cut by his editors. Most egregious was *Harper's*: to avoid alienating white "liberal" readers, they had changed the essay's title from "Notes of a Native Son"—dropping his reference to Richard Wright's inflammatory protest novel, *Native Son* (1940)—to the less confrontational "Me and My House," a biblical phrase which had been one of his original titles.[28] And, even worse, they had cut the description of his stepfather's funeral service, the eulogy that evoked American racism, reminding him not to judge the departed too harshly: "the man who had gone down under an impossible burden."[29]

"What? Not the section with that line about preparing the child?"

I was shocked. That passage contained one of the questions I'd underlined: "How to prepare the child for the day when the child would be despised?"[30] Not only was this quintessential Baldwin, it was also an impossible question to answer … and close to unbearable. I guess that's why they cut it.

Jimmy helped me connect the dots.

In the fall of 1953, *Harper's* had already published one of his essays, "Stranger in the Village," about his time in a Swiss village whose inhabitants had never seen a Negro. They had featured the article on their cover, with the contents intact; after all, that piece was less threatening, it looked at race from a distance. But then the South began to reach critical mass. In May 1954, the US Supreme Court overruled the 1896 *Plessy v. Ferguson* "separate but equal" decision, stating in *Brown v. Board of Education* that racial segregation in public schools was unconstitutional—and that was just the beginning. In May 1955, the Court issued a second decree, further enforcing school integration. In August 1955, 14-year-old Emmett Till was brutally murdered, lynched in Mississippi after "disrespecting" a white shopkeeper's wife. In September 1955, once Till's mutilated body was found, his mother chose to have an open-casket funeral "so the world could see." America was on edge. As was the young Baldwin: he had been pouring his energy into two uphill efforts, both unlikely to see publication—*The Amen Corner* (1968), a play that pitted church against family, and *Giovanni's Room* (1956), a novel that explored homosexual love—and he needed money.

"So I let it happen."

Harper's published "Me and My House" on 1 November 1955. His editors had also cut other, less significant segments, supposedly in the interest of "adjusting for page length"—but as Jimmy recalled it, what bothered him most was that they had excised specific emotional triggers, his more speculative passages about "bitterness." "Rage." "Another me trapped in my skull."[31] They'd even cut one of the lines that has since become so well known: "Hatred, which could destroy so much, never failed to destroy the man who hated."[32]

We stared at each other, contemplating the loss.

"It feels like a violation. Not as overt as others I've suffered, but still … It stings." He told me how outraged he'd been at age 12, when a Pentecostal church bulletin censored his first work in print. "By the time I found out, it was too late to object."

At least he was able to publish the full text of his essay in the book version of *Notes*—and though the book didn't sell well initially, his fee from *Harper's* plus the advance from Beacon was enough for him to return to France.

And the dots kept connecting.

"That summer with Emmett Till: I didn't know it back then, but that's when 'Remember This House' really took on a mind of its own."

The way Jimmy saw it now, he had been sidling up to this exploration of Southern roots—"his inescapable identity"—for most of his life.[33] Beyond all the "books and headlines and music" that sang of the South there was this unspoken sense of *community* that stretched all the way North to his childhood in Harlem: love and religion and warmth mixed with bloodshed and unspeakable suffering.[34] Plus the conundrum of history: the unavoidable fact that his "ancestors were both white and black," that he was "bone of their bone, flesh of their flesh."[35]

The American South is part of Baldwin's DNA. It runs through his writing in a torrent of conflicting emotions—fictionalized, dramatized, interpreted, eulogized—but it wasn't until 1957, haunted by Emmett Till, by the traumas of desegregation, that he actually went there. Then again. And again. It was during his first trip that he met Martin Luther King, Jr.; it was during his 1963 lecture tour, the one covered by Jane Howard for *LIFE* magazine, that he met Medgar Evers. His exploration of "what Negroes sometimes call the Old Country"—the deeply personal dive that began with *Go Tell It*, with "Notes of a Native Son" (aka "Me and My House") and so much of his writing since then—was once again demanding attention in "Remember This House."[36]

I asked him whether the "House" in both titles were one and the same.

He nodded, almost rueful. "When I left for Paris, I thought I was running away—but I've been running toward this all of my life."

* * * * *

Jimmy leveled his gaze.

"Know whence you came."[37] Now it was his turn to quote himself, this one from *The Fire Next Time*. "That advice wasn't just for my nephew, it's for all of us. Including me. Even when it's painful."

Know whence you came. Or, as he once told Studs Terkel in a radio interview, "If you don't know what happened behind you, you've got no idea of what is happening around you."[38] For Baldwin, this had become another "immutable law": in order to shape the future, we have to understand the history behind us.[39]

"History is not the past. It is the present. We carry our history with us. We *are* our history."[40]

But that doesn't mean we have to perpetuate it.

My history suggested that after dabbling with a career, I was expected to marry, have kids, be a patriotic American. Baldwin's history alleged that expectations were useless, that he would be lucky if he survived at all.

His solution: examine lies; explore truth; expand potential.

He expressed this more fully in the introduction to his 1961 collection of essays, *Nobody Knows My Name*:

> It would seem, unless one looks more deeply at the phenomenon, that most people are able to delude themselves and get through their lives quite happily. But I still believe that the unexamined life is not worth living; and I know that self-delusion, in the service of no matter what lofty cause, is a price no writer can afford. His subject is himself and the world and it requires every ounce of stamina he can summon to attempt to look on himself and the world as they are.[41]

I first read that when I was still in my twenties. Baldwin was born over two decades before me, but when he wrote about his world it felt as if he were speaking directly to mine. Not just because I had left home in search of myself, not just because I was questioning thoughts that once felt like givens, but because I saw more wrong than right with my country. As if endless assassinations weren't enough, the Nixon years were living proof that the majority of my voting-age countrymen were deluded. I was a child of the sixties and seventies, I had written about Vietnam as a journalist, I had driven down to DC to protest the war, I had linked arms with my Viet-vet friend when he threw his Purple Heart at the Capitol—and when I read Baldwin's critiques of French Indochina and colonial exploitation "for the good of the natives" in *No Name in the Street*, it was 1974 and I had just returned from Saigon myself.[42]

The dangers of self-delusion became an important part of our Ginger Man ramblings. When I told him that based on his writings, my determination to live a more closely "examined life" had led to a month in Vietnam, he laughed—but in true Jimmy form, he wanted more.

"Was this before or after the peace agreement?"

"After."

We both knew what that meant.

In May 1973, after quitting my job in Paris as a foreign correspondent for *Time* (the assignment I'd taken on when *LIFE* ceased publication), I hitchhiked to Cannes, planning to cover the Festival as a freelancer—but then I met a French team prepping a film shoot in Asia, and they asked me to join them. We spent the rest of the year filming in Sri Lanka, India, and, on a second trip, Bali; when we finally wrapped, they flew back to France while I headed East. By the time I arrived in Vietnam, it was early 1974—warm on the coast with snow in the highlands—and the war was ostensibly over. The Paris Peace Accords had been signed, most

US troops had withdrawn, Congress had cut promised funding… The struggle, at least on the surface, was now exclusively Vietnamese, North v. South: in retrospect, an illusion with a predictable ending. For many Americans, it felt almost like victory, they couldn't wait to forget—but for me, it was unfinished business.

As Jimmy said about his need to leave Paris and join the civil rights struggle in person back in the late 1950s, "I simply had to go."

I had history to deal with. I went because I had so many questions, because I'd been so bombarded by government disinformation that I wanted to see for myself—and because so many had died there. As an American, I felt I owed them … something.

Acknowledgment. An apology. And selfishly, absolution: I wanted to let the Vietnamese people know that I was *not*, as Jimmy wrote about his own fractured identity, "to be confused with the Marshall Plan, Hollywood, the Yankee dollar, television, or Senator McCarthy"—or, for that matter, with the Tonkin Gulf Resolution, the My Lai massacre, Agent Orange, or Kent State.[43]

All those things had been done by Americans for "the 'good' of society" … or so they tried to tell us.[44] Self-delusion? The irony hung between us: here we were, two Americans, enjoying the comforts of capitalism while exploring past shame.

* * * * *

When I told Jimmy about General Thi, he was fascinated—as I hoped he would be.

General Lam Quang Thi—whose surname was Lam, but whom I soon came to call Thi, or, more respectfully, General Thi—was Commander in Chief, Forward Command for ARVN, the US-supported Army of the Republic of Vietnam. I first met the general because of photographer Larry Burrows. Back in 1971 when I was still with *LIFE*, Burrows had died on assignment, his helicopter shot down over Laos; I steeped myself in his photos, eight years of exquisitely framed wartime pain and compassion. Two of them left me in tears: one, a wounded Black soldier, reaching out to his wounded white comrade; the other, a young Vietnamese woman, grieving over the body bag holding her husband. Both of those images came from the DMZ, the no-man's land between North and South Vietnam. They summed up why I was so fervently anti-war … and why, once I'd explored Saigon, I felt compelled to fly north.

On the plane up to Hue, fate sat me next to a young South Vietnamese government official. The fact that I was a former foreign correspondent for *Time*, now freelance, led to a meeting with General Thi—in a room thick with white male "advisors," heads bent over maps. This was the era of post-Peace Accord Vietnamization, when Americans no longer wore uniforms but still called the shots. They looked at me askance. My take? I think the general brought me there as a form of defiance: an offense small enough for the suits to tolerate.

The encounter expanded from there. Beyond my Time Inc. credentials, the fact that I was fluent in French, that I had studied French culture, created a special bond. We spoke more French than English; he asked me to call him Thi. "*Ça me rappelle mes années d'étudiant à Paris*," he told me. "This brings back my years as a student in Paris."[45] When I told him I had a room in a local hotel, more affordable than respectable, he invited me to be his houseguest; his family was down south in Saigon, he had plenty of room. "*Je vous donnerai de quoi écrire*," he assured me. "I will give you something to write about."

I was too intrigued to say no.

After a tour of Hue's war-damaged Citadel, the eighteenth-century Imperial City where Nguyen Lords once ruled a unified Vietnam, we turned into a cobblestone courtyard next an impressive villa, more Western than Asian, with a view of the Perfume River. I had a suite of my own; dinners were formal, served by uniformed staff; the cuisine was international, and superb. (The general was a foodie.) I was his pampered guest for five days: organized excursions each morning, most of them in his personal helicopter; free time in Hue each afternoon.

Day #1: A scenic trip up and down river via Swift Boat—basically, a souped-up water taxi with gun turrets—while the general explained regional history and pointed out landmarks. We visited floating markets; we pulled up beside sampans to buy local treats. It was hard to believe this was a country at war.

Day #2: A return to Hue's airport, Phu Bai, the region's support base for armed South Vietnamese forces—which, I was astounded to learn, had just reopened after being damaged in combat. It was a contest for the hills, ARVN v. PAVN, still ongoing: whoever held the crests decimated the opposition below.[46] We visited the hospital at one end of the runway; wounded soldiers were airlifted in while we watched.

Day #3: A trip north to the notorious 17th parallel, the "temporary" DMZ established by the 1954 Geneva Accords, extending three miles on each side of the border. We spent most of our time underground, exploring tunnels recently captured and "cleansed" by the general's army. Carved out of limestone by the Viet Cong, they were part shelter, part supply route, part booby trap: pits lined with sharp punji sticks were still a hazard.

Day #4: A trip west, toward Laos: we landed in a valley near a bombed-out building, a two-story schoolhouse with a huge hole in the center and walls still intact. Stairs led to what was left of the second floor, where American soldiers had taken refuge, trying to fend off attackers. The white walls were covered with messages scrawled in English: last words of love addressed to girlfriends, wives, mothers. "101st Airborne," the general told me. "*C'étaient des héros*." "They were heroes."

Day #5: It began with *Taekwan-Do*. When I came down for breakfast, Thi was in full regalia, the sole Vietnamese general with a black belt in martial arts. While I sat on his front staircase, not sure what to expect, aides placed wooden planks on two pedestals; he broke them, one after another, each one increasing in size, with his bare hand. Over croissants and coffee, he explained the science ... and then ushered me to his chopper for our final excursion.

We flew south until we reached a clearing, an elegantly tiled terrace surrounded by weather-worn statues and a moss-covered temple: partially hidden by vines, this once majestic tomb of Emperor Gia Long had fought off the jungle for over

150 years.[47] It was Gia Long who had unified Việt Nam after centuries of feudal warfare, moved its capital from Hanoi to Hue, begun building the Citadel as a tribute to Confucian wisdom. Under the gaze of stone warriors, we picnicked on the shrine steps—another sumptuous feast—while Thi linked the Emperor's many achievements to a 22-year alliance with a French Jesuit priest. "In return for help from the French," he explained, "Gia Long allowed the Church to expand in Southeast Asia." For Thi, this justified his own jumbled embrace of Confucian tradition, French culture, Catholic faith, and democratic ideals.

It was this history that captured Jimmy's attention. Spanning nations and centuries, it was a world view of oppressed and oppressors, a mix of conflicting selfhoods condensed into Thi's personal search for meaning. Identity. Like so many people of color, Thi had been educated by and for his oppressor—"*Nous, les Gaulois,*" he had been taught to say, "We, the Gauls"—but as he learned far too late, when empires crumble, when power is threatened, maps are redrawn without thought for the people.

"It is power, not justice, which keeps rearranging the map."[48]

Baldwin wrote that sentence in *No Name in the Street* because he had lived it himself. In 1948, he left the US for Paris in order to save his own life; in 1954, he was in Paris when the French lost Indochina; in the late 1950s, early 1960s, he was there when the French lost Algeria; from the late 1950s on, he witnessed similar struggles for freedom in the American South. He saw what those conflicts cost, not just in lives but in minds and in hearts—and he understood the contradictions embodied by General Thi. Economic, religious, social, cultural. Personal.

Near the end of our picnic, Thi stood up, straightened his uniform. "You know the French poet, Lamartine?" He moved to the step just above me, cleared his throat:

Que me fait le coteau, le toit, la vigne aride ?
Que me ferait le ciel, si le ciel était vide ?
Je ne vois en ces lieux que ceux qui n'y sont pas !
Pourquoi ramènes-tu mes regrets sur leur trace ?
Des bonheurs disparus se rappeler la place,
C'est rouvrir des cercueils pour revoir des trépas ![49]

Alphonse de Lamartine was a nineteenth-century poet and statesman, an idealistic Romantic; he and the general had a lot in common. Both were men of provincial nobility who dedicated their lives to a republican cause—and both saw their republics defeated.

What does this vineyard mean to me, the roof, the dry vine?
What would heaven mean to me if heaven were empty?
I see in these places only those who are not here!
Why do you bring my regrets back to where they began?
To remember the place of vanished happiness
is to reopen coffins in order to see the remains.[50]

As I listened to Thi's recitation, I heard his lament—not just for the Emperor buried nearby, not just for the republic about to be lost, but for the person he wasn't, the potential denied. Later that day, he escorted me to the airport, back again to Phu Bai where the wounded were still arriving on stretchers. When I boarded my plane, waving a final goodbye, he saluted.

I cried.

*****

"Your General Thi is my Madame Faure." Jimmy's voice was suddenly tender. "The past was taken from both of them. And their present. And future."

"Madame Faure?"

"She's my … She's my Algerian friend, my French—She sold me my house in Saint-Paul."

He knew: the cry of pain that I'd witnessed on the steps of that temple wasn't just for a conflicted Vietnamese general. It was for the uprooted, for all oppressed people, for the "many thousands gone" and for all those still fighting.[51]

"She was as violated by her past as he was by his." The lines in his face deepened. "That's what most people don't realize: the oppressor winds up as wounded as the oppressed. Maybe more so."

Why don't people get this? The answer tracks back to "self-delusion" and Baldwin's 1961 intro to *Nobody Knows My Name*.[52]

One of the roadblocks to self-awareness, to understanding identity, is that an oppressor rarely sees himself as unjust—and these two were no exception. Jeanne Faure was Jimmy's friend, yes, but she was also, like Thi, on the wrong side of war (if that oxymoron is even possible). Both she and Thi had been born far from France and yet they both were "*la vieille France*" incarnate: both had been raised "by and for France" to support a colonial empire that was "visibly and swiftly crumbling"; both had been "stripped of their birthrights" by rebels willing to die, and kill, for what they hoped would be freedom. And both she and Thi were loath to let go of the indoctrination that formed them.[53]

As Jimmy states on the last page of *No Name in the Street*, words he told me he'd written "down in my *donjon*," his dungeon, the ground floor of the home that he shared with Jeanne Faure, "It is terrible to watch people cling to their captivity."[54]

Mlle. Faure—or *Madame* as Jimmy sometimes called her, a form of respect that replaced *Mademoiselle*, the appropriate title for an unmarried French female—was his landlady in Saint-Paul de Vence. A proper, high-cheekboned woman with firmly stated convictions, she was known to less respectful neighbors as a *pied-noir*, a French citizen who was Algerian-born and whose feet had been blackened by time on African soil. For the first sixty-seven years of her life, she had lived in Oran, an ancient port on the north coast of Africa that had been an outpost of the Ottoman empire for well over a century—until 1830, when attacks by French warships plus years of targeted genocide turned the region into a resource-rich colony: *l'Algérie française*.

The Faure family had been there for generations. Jeanne was proud to be a Faure, it was a familiar name in French history: her distant relatives back on the mainland had been noblemen, ministers, even president (President Félix Faure was known for his refusal to pardon the falsely accused Dreyfus, and for having died while in mid-intercourse with his mistress). And she was proud of her Algerian birthplace, a city washed by sun, wind, and sea where members of the Faure clan had helped rebuild the harbor and she had played on the beach as a child. Yes, there was violence, Muslim Arabs and Berbers had been trying to oust their oppressors for years; and yes, ever since 1 November 1954, when the bloody All Saints Day attacks took the world by surprise, the colony was officially at war. But even so, Jeanne and most of the people she knew never expected real change. In the 1960 census, her French-ruled home boasted over one million non-Muslim civilians, most of them European, most of them Catholic—and most of them longtime residents of Oran. They tried to lead normal lives ... until 1962, when President Charles de Gaulle signed a ceasefire with the Algerian FLN (*Front de Libération Nationale*), promising independence from France, and some irate citizens refused to yield. Shots were fired; a mob massacred thousands of colonial loyalists. In less than three months, Oran lost half its population—and with little more than a suitcase, Jeanne and her brother, Louis, fled their native land.

It was Dien Bien Phu all over again.

The two Faure siblings were outcasts, both in their sixties and forced to start over. As Jeanne later told Jimmy, and he told me, they chose Saint-Paul de Vence in part because relatives lived in the region, in part because of its limestone, the rocky crags high above the Mediterranean that reminded them of the hills overlooking Oran. Using the last of their cash from the *Banque d'Algérie*, they turned an eighteenth-century farm just outside of Saint-Paul into a much-needed source of income: keeping one wing for themselves, they rented the rest out to boarders and raised produce for city markets down on the coast. By the time Jimmy met them, they were living two lives. *Français repatriés*, repatriated French citizens, standing tall as if they had always belonged on the mainland—and *Algériens aliénés*, alienated Algerians, resented because of lives lost in war, ostracized because of "black-feet" roots ... mourning a life that no longer existed.

A lot like General Lam Quang Thi: another identity fractured. Split between France and Asia, driven from Vietnam when Saigon fell, my fallen war hero faced the fate of most displaced people. His past was erased, his life irrevocably changed. This was true for Jimmy's ancestors; it was true for the Faures. As for Thi, he finally found haven in Fremont, California—forced to start over in a land that cared little for him or his history.

*****

"And they wonder why so many feel broken."

Jimmy stared into his drink. He too had been split: between Black and white, between oppressed and oppressor, between those who accused him of abandoning his own people and those who praised him for embracing theirs. Our silence weighed heavy; I worried. Had I derailed our discussions? Who was I to compare my problems to his, why had I felt so free to fill his time with my own self-indulgence… Maybe I had misread him.

He looked up.

"You know what gives me hope? The fact that those two refused to give up. The fact that we're sitting here feeling bad for them, even though they're our polar opposites." I exhaled; he laughed. "Did your general know you were an anti-war protester?"

I hesitated. "We never really—" I must have looked worried, because he jumped back in.

"That's my point. I've been consorting with the enemy for most of my life, it goes way back to sixth grade and my teacher, Bill Miller: she taught me how much we all have in common."

What a rebound. I suddenly flashed on an observation that Jimmy made back in the 1960s, a quote about our common humanity that I still turn to for sustenance. (I've already cited it in Part I of this essay—and included it in my film *The Price of the Ticket*, as a voiceover recorded by Baldwin.)[55] It's the quote that first appeared in Jane Howard's profile of the world-famous author, the one she wrote for *LIFE* magazine where she intercut her impressions with a long monologue of his own:

> You think your pain and your heartbreak are unprecedented in the history of the world, but then you read. It was Dostoyevsky and Dickens who taught me that the things that tormented me most were the very things that connected me with all the people who were alive, or who ever had been alive.[56]

Those were the authors he'd read with his beloved Bill Miller. The discussions they'd had, the adventures they'd shared, were still with him. It had been years since he'd seen Bill, years since I'd looked at that magazine profile, but I could still see its headline—pure essence-of-Baldwin in eighteen-point type:

"The doom and glory of knowing who you are."

I asked him if he remembered that phrase.

"I do now." He paused, revisiting his own words, weighing their meaning. "*That's* what I want to achieve with 'Remember This House': helping those three kids—and the world—understand who they are."

I was impressed. We'd just spent two hours ranging all over the map, but he never lost focus—and now here we sat, right back on topic. Examine your life. Know whence you came. Understand where you are. Figure out what needs to be changed and face it. Only then, only when you've set out to do that, can you say yes to love and explore your connections to others.

That's the message I was receiving, that's the message I believe Jimmy hoped to deliver. Our film was beginning to take shape in my mind: one third *vérité* footage of Baldwin, down South with the families and up North in his classrooms; one third first-person truth-telling, with Baldwin and his "witnesses" speaking straight to the camera; one third archival history, images drawn from Baldwin's past to illuminate present and future. A three-legged stool where no single segment would stand without support from the others—and where all three would be intercut with each other.

He agreed.

"But the main point of all this is the kids."

Jimmy called them kids, but they were actually young adults: at the time of our lunch, Medgar Evers's son James, aka "Van," was 25; Malcolm X's daughter Attallah Shabazz was 26; Martin Luther King, Jr.'s son Martin III was 27. There were other brothers and sisters, but these were the ones he knew best.

"They're just the right age: no longer naïve, not yet cynical. Still unbridled." He grinned, enthusiasm building. "Remember, I left the country at age 24; I would've had plenty to say if someone had asked me. And besides, these kids know me. They'll trust me."

For Jimmy, these three young adults—and their fathers—epitomized "doom and glory."[57] He'd been searching for a way into the memoir he was trying to write; he'd scrapped draft after draft, unable to solve it. I sat there, humbled, as his thoughts kept evolving. But this felt like the key: making a film while he wrote would help him structure his story; this wounded trio, their pain, their fate, the way they chose to deal with the conflicts they faced, the hope they held for our future would be the fulcrum on which his story would pivot. Their fathers were activists who made history happen. They were recipients of both progress and loss. Like his nieces and nephews, like his students, they had a perspective that was beyond his reach: they could teach him and, even better, reach the next generation. Whatever it was they were thinking. That was the exciting part, he had no way of knowing how they might respond. He just had to figure out which questions to ask.

Once again, there it was: the importance of questions. Back and forth we went, suggesting ideas, debating reactions, trying to imagine the conversation he wanted to have. And then one possibility gave us both chills.

"Was it worth it that your father was assassinated?"

I repeat:

"Was it worth it that your father was assassinated?"

We stared at each other. Was this too strong for an opener? Too insensitive, given their personal history? Jimmy was silent a moment, then shook his head, no.

"I know these kids, they can take it. They're smart, they're tough—They've faced far worse. And you know what?" His face softened. "I think they need this."

We had our first question.

If those young souls could face this—if we *all* were able to face it, unpack it, explore what it might mean if their lives were our lives—"Remember This House" might make a difference.

As Baldwin wrote in a 1962 essay, a phrase that was to guide us in the journey ahead, "Not everything that is faced can be changed. But nothing can be changed until it is faced."[58]

Notes

1 Karen Thorsen, "The Disorder of Life: James Baldwin on My Shoulder," *James Baldwin Review*, 6 (2020), pp. 140–54.
2 Dick Fontaine and Pat Hartley (dirs.), *I Heard It Through the Grapevine* (USA, 1982).
3 James Baldwin, *No Name in the Street* (New York, Dial Press, 1972), p. 156.
4 Amiri Baraka, qtd. in Karen Thorsen (prod./dir.), *James Baldwin: The Price of the Ticket* (USA, 1990).
5 Vincent Canby, "Film: Revisiting Civil-Rights South," *New York Times*, 3 March 1982; "so polite" was Baldwin's remark about Canby's review.
6 Karen Thorsen conversation with James Baldwin at The Ginger Man in New York City, April 1986. All subsequent quotations are taken from this conversation unless otherwise indicated.
7 James Baldwin, *The Fire Next Time* (New York, Dial Press, 1963), p. 19.
8 James Baldwin, qtd. in Thorsen film, *The Price of the Ticket*.
9 James Baldwin, *The Evidence of Things Not Seen* (New York, Henry Holt, 1986), p. 4.
10 John Fleming, "In Short: Nonfiction," *New York Times*, 24 November 1985.
11 James Baldwin, "Dark Days," *Esquire Magazine*, October 1980, p. 46.
12 *Ibid.*
13 Baldwin, *Fire Next Time*, p. 98.
14 James Baldwin, *The Devil Finds Work* (New York, Dial Press, 1976), p. 6.
15 James Baldwin, "A Talk to Teachers" (1963), in *The Price of the Ticket, Collected Nonfiction* (New York, St. Martin's/Marek, 1985), p. 327.
16 James Baldwin, qtd. in Kenneth B. Clark, "A Conversation with James Baldwin," *Freedomways*, 3 (summer 1963), p. 368.
17 James Baldwin, "Everybody's Protest Novel" (1949), in *Notes of a Native Son* (New York, Beacon Press, 1990), p. 19.
18 Baldwin, qtd. in Clark, "A Conversation with James Baldwin," p. 368.
19 Baldwin, "Everybody's Protest Novel," p. 19; James Baldwin, "A Question of Identity" (1954), in *Notes of a Native Son*, p. 130.
20 James Baldwin, "Encounter on the Seine: Black Meets Brown" (1950), in *Notes of a Native Son*, p. 123.
21 Baldwin, *No Name*, p. 184.
22 Baldwin, qtd. in Thorsen film, *The Price of the Ticket*.
23 Jane Howard, "The Doom and Glory of Knowing Who You Are," *LIFE Magazine*, 24 May 1963, pp. 81–90.
24 Karen Thorsen, "The Cities Lock Up: Fortress on 78th Street," *LIFE Magazine*, 19 November 1971; Karen Thorsen, "POW Wife," *LIFE Magazine*, 29 September 1972.
25 Baldwin, *Fire Next Time*, p. 108.
26 James Baldwin, "Equal in Paris" (1955), in *Notes of a Native Son*, p. 146.
27 James Baldwin, Preface, in *Notes of a Native Son*, p. xxix.
28 Josh. 24:15.
29 James Baldwin, "Notes of a Native Son" (1955), in *Notes of a Native Son*, p. 106.

30 *Ibid.*
31 *Ibid.*, pp. 89, 90, 102.
32 *Ibid.*, p. 113.
33 James Baldwin, "Nobody Knows My Name: A Letter from the South" (1959), in *Nobody Knows My Name: More Notes of a Native Son* (New York, Dell, 1986), p. 87.
34 James Baldwin, "A Fly in Buttermilk" (1958), in *Nobody Knows My Name*, p. 76.
35 Baldwin, "Nobody Knows My Name," p. 86; Baldwin, "Encounter on the Seine," p. 123.
36 Baldwin, "Notes of a Native Son," p. 86.
37 Baldwin, *Fire Next Time*, p. 22.
38 James Baldwin, qtd. in Studs Terkel, "An Interview with James Baldwin" (1961), in *James Baldwin: The Last Interview and Other Conversations* (New York, Melville House, 2014), p. 30.
39 Baldwin, "Notes of a Native Son," p.113.
40 James Baldwin, "Black English: A Dishonest Argument" (1980), in *The Cross of Redemption: Uncollected Writings*, ed. Randall Kenan (New York, Vintage, 2011), p. 154.
41 Baldwin, *Nobody Knows My Name*, p. 12.
42 Baldwin, *No Name in the Street*, p. 26.
43 Baldwin, "A Question of Identity," p. 129.
44 Baldwin, "Everybody's Protest Novel," p. 19.
45 Karen Thorsen conversations with General Lam Quang Thi in the Republic of Vietnam, 1974. Subsequent quotations from General Lam are taken from these conversations unless otherwise indicated.
46 PAVN: People's Army of Viet Nam.
47 Emperor Gia Long (1762–1820), the first Emperor of the Nguyễn dynasty of Vietnam.
48 Baldwin, *No Name in the Street*, p. 44.
49 *Alphonse de Lamartine, "La vigne et la maison (III)," Cours familiers de littérature (1856–69).*
50 Karen Thorsen *translation of "La vigne et la maison" by Alphonse de Lamartine.*
51 Baldwin, "Encounter on the Seine," p. 123.
52 Baldwin, *Nobody Knows My Name*, p. 12.
53 Baldwin, *No Name in the Street*, pp. 48, 25.
54 *Ibid.*, p. 195.
55 Baldwin, qtd. in Thorsen, "Disorder of Life, Part I," p. 143; Baldwin, qtd. in Thorsen film, *The Price of the Ticket*.
56 Baldwin, qtd. in Howard, "Doom and Glory," p. 89.
57 *Ibid.*, p. 89.
58 James Baldwin, "As Much Truth as One Can Bear," *New York Times Book Review*, 14 January 1962, p. 38.

Works Cited

Baldwin, James, "As Much Truth as One Can Bear," *New York Times Book Review*, 14 January 1962, pp. 1, 38.
         "Black English: A Dishonest Argument" (1980), in *The Cross of Redemption: Uncollected Writings*, ed. Randall Kenan (New York, Vintage, 2011), pp. 154–60.
         "Dark Days," *Esquire Magazine*, October 1980, pp. 42–6.
         The Devil Finds Work (New York, Dial Press, 1976).

_____ "Encounter on the Seine: Black Meets Brown" (1950), in *Notes of a Native Son* (New York, Beacon Press, 1990), pp. 117–23.

_____ "Equal in Paris" (1955), in *Notes of a Native Son* (New York, Beacon Press, 1990), pp. 138–58.

_____ "Everybody's Protest Novel" (1949), in *Notes of a Native Son* (New York, Beacon Press, 1990), pp. 13–23.

_____ *The Evidence of Things Not Seen* (1985) (New York, Henry Holt, 1986).

_____ *The Fire Next Time* (New York, Dial Press, 1963).

_____ "A Fly in Buttermilk" (1958), in *Nobody Knows My Name: More Notes of a Native Son* (New York, Dell, 1986), pp. 75–85.

_____ *No Name in the Street* (New York, Dial Press, 1972).

_____ "Nobody Knows My Name: A Letter from the South" (1959), in *Nobody Knows My Name: More Notes of a Native Son* (New York, Dell, 1986), pp. 86–99.

_____ *Nobody Knows My Name: More Notes of a Native Son* (1961) (New York, Dell, 1986).

_____ *Notes of a Native Son* (1955) (New York, Beacon Press, 1990).

_____ *The Price of the Ticket, Collected Nonfiction* (New York, St. Martin's/Marek, 1985).

_____ "A Question of Identity" (1954), in *Notes of a Native Son* (New York, Beacon Press, 1990), pp. 124–37.

_____ "A Talk to Teachers" (1963), in *The Price of the Ticket, Collected Nonfiction* (New York, St. Martin's/Marek, 1985), pp. 325–32.

Canby, Vincent, "Film: Revisiting Civil-Rights South," *New York Times*, 3 March 1982.

Clark, Kenneth B, "A Conversation with James Baldwin," *Freedomways*, 3 (summer 1963), pp. 361–8.

Fleming, John, "In Short: Nonfiction," *New York Times*, 24 November 1985.

Howard, Jane, "The Doom and Glory of Knowing Who You Are," *LIFE Magazine*, 54:21, 24 May 1963, pp. 81–90.

Kenan, Randall (ed.), *The Cross of Redemption: Uncollected Writings* (New York, Vintage, 2011).

Terkel, Studs, "An Interview with James Baldwin" (1961), in *James Baldwin: The Last Interview and Other Conversations* (New York, Melville House, 2014), pp. 3–34.

Thorsen, Karen, "The Cities Lock Up: Fortress on 78th Street," *LIFE Magazine*, 19 November 1971, pp. pp. 26–36.

_____ "The Disorder of Life: James Baldwin on My Shoulder, Part I," *James Baldwin Review*, 6 (2020), pp. 140–54.

_____ "POW Wife," *LIFE Magazine*, 29 September 1972, pp. 32–42.

Thorsen, Karen (prod./dir.), *James Baldwin: The Price of the Ticket* (Maysles Films & PBS/American Masters, 1990).

Contributor's Biography

Karen Thorsen is an award-winning writer/filmmaker who finds inspiration at the intersection of art and social justice. Her heroes are game-changers, the artist/activists who shape history; her films tell stories without narration, weaving first-person narratives with archival treasures. Thorsen began as a writer. After graduating from Vassar with a year at the Sorbonne, she was an editor for Simon and Schuster, journalist for *LIFE* and foreign correspondent for *Time*. Screenwriting followed, then directing. Her first feature-length documentary was *James Baldwin: The Price of the Ticket* (1990), produced with Maysles Films and PBS/American Masters. Now considered a classic, it has been honored in twenty-five countries. Recently remastered in WideScreen 2KHD, the new 'Digital Baldwin' is a centerpiece of the James Baldwin Project's nationwide series of community forums on racism, discrimination, and the meaning of brotherhood. Supported by the Ford Foundation, NEA, and others, these film screenings and "talkbacks" have already reached tens of thousands. Beyond Baldwin, Thorsen's credits include broadcast productions, museum installations, documentary shorts, and interactive media—often in collaboration with DKDmedia's Douglas K. Dempsey. Their films have screened on six continents and in six museums on the National Mall; permanent installations include the Smithsonian Museum of American History, George Washington's Mount Vernon, Great Platte River Archway, and Pilgrim Hall Museum. Recognition ranges from multiple THEA and festival honors to Parents Choice and the Oscars short list. Thorsen's current projects include *The Disorder of Life: James Baldwin on My Shoulder* in book form (a continuation of the two essays published by *JBR*); *Keep It Lit!*, a digital design-your-own James Baldwin curriculum (with the National Writing Project); *Thomas Paine: Voice of Revolution*, a feature-length documentary and museum app (an NEH "We The People" project); *Inside the Glass House: Exploring Philip Johnson*, an interactive mix of long- and short-form documentaries (with the National Trust for Historic Preservation); and *Joe Papp in Five Acts*, a feature-length documentary codirected with Tracie Holder that premiered at the Tribeca Film Festival and will be broadcast by PBS/American Masters in 2022.

ESSAY

The Devil Finds Work: A Hollywood Love Story (as Written by James Baldwin)

D. Quentin Miller   Suffolk University

Abstract

Baldwin's *The Devil Finds Work* (1976) has proven challenging since its publication because readers and critics have trouble classifying it. The challenge may be related to a common feature of Baldwin criticism, namely a tendency to compare late career works to early ones and to find them lacking: the experimental nature of later works of nonfiction like *No Name in the Street* (1972), *The Devil Finds Work*, and *The Evidence of Things Not Seen* (1985) does not square easily with the more conventional essays that made Baldwin famous in his early years. I attempt to reframe *The Devil Finds Work* not through a comparison to other Baldwin essays, but rather through a comparison to his fiction, specifically the novel *Giovanni's Room*. I posit that a greater appreciation for *Devil* can result from thinking of it as a story, specifically the story of a failed love affair.

Keywords: *The Devil Finds Work*, James Baldwin, film, film criticism, history of American cinema, race, love, exile, expatriate

James Baldwin Review, Volume 7, 2021, © The Authors. Published by Manchester University Press and
The University of Manchester Library
http://dx.doi.org/10.7227/JBR.7.5

What exactly is *The Devil Finds Work* (1976)? This quirky, late-career book is not in the accepted pantheon of must-read Baldwin works despite recent efforts to excavate, recover, and honor those writings of his that had previously been overlooked or denigrated. Its obscurity has something to do with the fact that it is a genre-obliterating outlier, a work of film criticism, cultural critique, and personal history that is as unique as its creator. It's not a difficult book to read in the sense that it is accessible and firmly grounded, and Baldwin's voice is sharply analytical and, at times, entertainingly arch, but it is a difficult book to interpret because of its slippery context and unpredictable structure. Some critics see it as a precursor to modern film theory: Cassandra Ellis classifies it as a "prophetic text that offers fresh insights for re-imagining the critical dimensions of spectatorship and identification."[1] Others, including Alice Craven, regard it as a "critique" connected to Baldwin's early critiques of literature, and suggest that he applies similar standards to film that he once applied to the novels of Richard Wright and Harriet Beecher Stowe.[2] Jenny James calls it a "loose-form critical reflection on film, popular culture, and history," and Nicholas Boggs describes it broadly as Baldwin's "meditations on blacks and film."[3] William Dow sums up its reception this way: "The eclecticism and experimental form of *The Devil Finds Work*—including Baldwin's conflation of film history and memoir—continues to challenge critics."[4] I fully agree, and after nearly three decades of studying Baldwin from a number of different angles, I continue to feel challenged by *The Devil Finds Work*.

To be challenged by a Baldwin work, particularly after encountering it repeatedly and through different lenses, is largely the point. In a review of *Devil* in *The Nation*, Jerry H. Bryant arrives at a largely insightful, clear-eyed, and thorough synopsis of the book, but laments, "I should not have had to work as hard as I did."[5] The review is the very archetype of the response to Baldwin's post-1963 work: it compares *Devil* unfavorably to *The Fire Next Time* (1963), asserts that Baldwin has lost touch with changing times, that his "powers really have declined," and that he relies on his own experience rather than new ideas: "He has taken the old subject of race and made it more personal."[6] (One can easily picture Baldwin's eyebrows arching at that line.) Despite the fact that the reviewer has developed an "affection for [Baldwin] that [he has] never had before," he is ultimately "disappointed" because *Devil* "fails as a coherent piece."[7] It's possible that Bryant and other readers do not recognize the essay's structure as "coherence" because they are primarily using Baldwin's early essays as the model for how that word might be understood. Readers of his nonfiction expect him to build outward from personal experience to include observations about American cultural contradictions that lead to a hortatory conclusion about race relations like "This world is white no longer, and it will never be white again" or "No more water, the fire next time!"[8] Readers of his fiction, though, are much more comfortable with ambiguity and formal experimentation. The challenges of *The Devil Finds Work* may actually be less about formal conventions and more about readerly expectations: even though it is a book that defies classification, readers like Bryant label it an "essay" and, mapping it onto Baldwin's earlier and more "coherent" essays, they find it lacking.

Although I'm certainly not suggesting that the book is fiction, there may be some-thing to gain by thinking of it as a story.

In order to arrive at a fresh reading of it, I tried a radical experiment: namely, I set aside the idea that the book is primarily about American cinema, and consid-ered it rather as being about Baldwin's *relationship* to American cinema. If we regard the subject of *The Devil Finds Work* as James Baldwin, we are perhaps closer to understanding its through-line. As his dedicated readers well know, however, there is no meaningful way to formulate "James Baldwin" as a stable subject: his achievement is his capacity for constant change and expansive growth. If we go a step further and regard *Devil* as a reflection of Baldwin's psychological, intellec-tual, and emotional state in 1975, we are yet closer to a context that might produce a new reading.[9] David Leeming leads us in this direction in his biography of Bald-win, but still sees the book as contiguous with Baldwin's essays; he writes, "*Devil* is, in effect, a continuation of a long autobiographical essay, which he had begun with several pieces in *Notes of a Native Son* and in *Nobody Knows My Name*, fol-lowed by *The Fire Next Time* and *No Name in the Street* ... [it] is in one sense a fifty-year-old's evaluative reminiscence."[10] Movies are not the true subject of the book, in Leeming's estimation, but are rather "catalysts for an extensive discussion of the American psyche, his own life, and the sociopolitical climate in America."[11]

Yes, *and*, as I'm exploring here, movies provide the occasion for Baldwin to tell a story. Cinema was Baldwin's first love, and his mood in the mid-1970s is analo-gous to that of a furious ex-lover. Cinema seduced him when he was a child, dis-appointed him in young adulthood, and rejected him in middle age. Baldwin regards Hollywood, like America generally, as an entity that has failed to live up to its potential and has become criminally smug about its refusal to change. In 1975, just a decade before his premature death, Baldwin is fed up with his strained rela-tionship with both his country and its most prominent cultural export. *The Devil Finds Work* can be compared to a love affair that follows a narrative arc from infat-uation, to disillusionment, to impassioned argument, and finally to the big kiss-off. In this context, though it seems unlikely, the Baldwin text that might be the key to reevaluating *Devil* is *Giovanni's Room* (1956), a tragic tale of two lovers who could have had something great and lasting if one hadn't lacked courage and imagination. Baldwin is Giovanni in this analogy and Hollywood is David. David's realization at the end of that novel, of course, comes too late as he has lost Giovanni and essentially condemned him to death. In *The Devil Finds Work* the outcome is not quite so grim—no one faces the guillotine, although an entire film Baldwin wrote ends up on the cutting room floor—but Baldwin does tell both Hollywood and America in no uncertain terms that he's through with their abuse: if they are willing to change, fine, but he doesn't need them anymore. Once the love affair is over, he claims, "I learned something."[12] So, too, can the readers of this rich, enig-matic text, but a willingness to work at it is, unfortunately for Bryant and others who want a Hollywood ending, a requirement.

Baldwin's Hollywood romance begins in his childhood with a magical fantasy that takes the form of infatuation. Look again at the opening sentences of *The*

Devil Finds Work: "Joan Crawford's straight, narrow, and lonely back. We are following her through the corridors of a moving train."[13] Although the second sentence is meant to mimic the experience of watching a film, it indicates something much more immediate and intimate: Baldwin imagines himself and his fellow viewers as part of the film, actively on the screen along with Joan Crawford, "following her." He is so eager to connect to the world of the silver screen that he imagines he enters it. He follows Crawford *into* this movie, then he follows her *within* this movie, and despite his rational fears of the situation he finds himself in, he is at least initially unable to confine that experience to moviegoing:

> I certainly did not wish to be a fleeing fugitive on a moving train; and, also, with quite another part of my mind, I was aware that Joan Crawford was a white lady. Yet I remember being sent to the store sometime later, and a colored woman, who, to me, looked exactly like Joan Crawford, was buying something … when she paid the man and started out of the store, I started out behind her.[14]

His attraction to the screen starlet is so strong that he translates her racial identity to fit his own circumstances and actually does what he says he is doing while watching *Dance, Fools, Dance* (1931): he follows the woman who is the object of his desire.

The opening montage of *Devil* is a series of transferences that connect Black and white women and that connect the fantasy of the silver screen to the reality of Baldwin's humble world. The Black woman in the store is twice described as "beautiful" and, since she "looked exactly like Joan Crawford" in the young Baldwin's mind, the standard of beauty she represents originates in a Hollywood ideal.[15] On the next page he also proclaims the "young white schoolteacher" Orilla "Bill" Miller "a beautiful woman," and confesses, "I loved her, of course, and absolutely, with a child's love."[16] Soon after this proclamation he declares his child's love for another woman: "I loved my mother, and I knew that she loved me." This statement acts as a defense against his father, who called the young James "the ugliest boy he had ever seen," associating his denigrated physical features with his mother's, especially the shape of their eyes. Baldwin writes, "I thought that he must have been stricken blind … if he was unable to see that my mother was absolutely beyond any question the most beautiful woman in the world."[17] Movies help him recognize his father's insults as a kind of "infirmity" by allowing him to define female beauty and to love beautiful women, not sexually, but "with a child's love."[18] He sees Bette Davis onscreen and is astounded that she shares his and his mother's "pop-eyes" and that she is therefore "*ugly*" in his father's assessment, but also "a *movie star*," and therefore beautiful (emphases original).[19] He concludes that his father must be wrong. Movies represent, essentially, a higher power than the tyrannical David Baldwin. If Hollywood allows the young James Baldwin to love and to appreciate the beauty of five very different women—Joan Crawford, the woman from the grocery store who resembles her, Bill Miller, his mother, and Bette Davis—it also allows him to love himself, even if it is only in a childish way that enables him to escape his world and his father's oppressive judgment. Thus, the love affair begins.

In fact, in part one of *The Devil Finds Work*, Baldwin is charmed by Hollywood in a way that he would never be again and lured by its power to affect his emotions and his imagination. His resistant readings and glib dismissals from the later sections are almost absent from this first one as he focuses less on the films' content and more on how they made him feel. The film version of *A Tale of Two Cities* (1935) left him "tremendously stirred and frightened."[20] The film *They Won't Forget* (1937) is marked by an "icy brutality" that "both scared me and strengthened me."[21] He recognizes that some white film actresses like Sylvia Sidney "moved" him and that he "identified" with Henry Fonda.[22] These strong responses and connections, all of which happen prior to his violent religious conversion, are ways for Baldwin to follow the lead of a powerful and seductive set of narratives that can make him feel more deeply while helping him connect his limited world to a broader one. Significantly, movies can both allow him to escape his world and to interpret it. In the space of a page, Sylvia Sidney "reminded me of a colored girl, or woman," "reminded me of reality," and "reminded me of Bill [Miller]."[23] As the teachings of the church would later do, movies enable him to employ a pre-existing framework to interpret and validate his own experience. Throughout the first section he repeatedly utters variations of a phrase: "I understood *that*," "I had seen *that*," or "I knew something about that" (emphases original).[24] As a child, this corroboration is merely exciting. It is only later in life that he will understand "the danger of surrendering to the corroboration of one's fantasies as they are thrown back from the screen."[25]

The love affair between Giovanni and David in *Giovanni's Room* also begins with a yearning for connection. Though Giovanni is older, he is notably boyish. When he and David are finally fully alone on the morning after the night they meet, David says to him, "You look like a kid about five years old waking up on Christmas morning."[26] There is perhaps an echo here of John Grimes in *Go Tell It on the Mountain* (1953) who wakes up in that novel's first scene on his fourteenth birthday, and his mother gives him a present quite relevant to this essay: money to go to the movies. Giovanni then tells David how he first met Guillaume: "in a cinema!"—and David again notices a "childlike" note in Giovanni's voice as he describes this initial encounter.[27] When they are about to make love for the first time, David describes it this way: "He pulled me against him, putting himself into my arms as though he were giving me himself to carry."[28] Giovanni clearly trusts David as a child would and wants his care and his attention. David—cowardly, unimaginative, and self-involved—is no more up to the task than Hollywood is up to the task of sustaining the young James Baldwin's dreams.

The sweet, soft-edged glow of a honeymoon phase of a relationship inevitably leads to stress, strains, and arguments, filmed in a harsher light. Baldwin's perspective in the first section of *Devil* is that of a child, and I have highlighted Giovanni's childlike qualities from the early scenes of *Giovanni's Room*, yet it is important to point out that children in Baldwin's world aren't innocent: they are just more willing than adults are to believe in magic. In a key scene in the story "Sonny's Blues" (1957), the narrator recalls how children and family elders sit in a bright living room, keeping the darkness outside at bay. The child "hopes that the hand which strokes his forehead will never stop—will never die ... But something deep and watchful in the child knows that this is bound to end, is already ending."[29] Children know the truth, in short, about the ever-encroaching darkness of their existence. Innocence in Baldwin's work is a willed condition, one that is antithetical to true love. Even as Giovanni places his absolute trust and faith in David in the early scenes above, he also knows that David is a stereotypical American, innocent and smug, oblivious to "all the serious, dreadful things, like pain and death and love, in which you Americans do not believe."[30] When David replies, "What makes you think we don't?" Giovanni doesn't answer, but if he did, the answer could easily be "the movies." In Giovanni's linking love to "dreadful things, like pain and death," we get a glimpse of the Baldwinian definition of love, not as something schmaltzy and artificial, "not in the infantile American sense of being made happy but in the tough and universal sense of quest and daring and growth," as he says in *The Fire Next Time*, or as something even more grave in *No Name in the Street* (1972): "Love is a battle; love is a war; love is a growing up."[31] In the second section of *Devil*, then, Baldwin takes America and Hollywood to task for their refusal to grow up, and thus to love maturely, with all of the pain and awareness of death associated with love. Giovanni memorably tells David that he cannot accept "the stink of love."[32] Baldwin, essentially, says the same thing to Hollywood.

Section two of *The Devil Finds Work* is thus markedly different from section one in that Baldwin does not let his lover off the hook, as he did when he was a child and wanted so badly to believe, to express his "child's love." Mid-twentieth-century films that are supposedly liberal when it comes to race relations, almost always starring the magnificent Sidney Poitier, are the recurrent objects of Baldwin's scrutiny in this section, and he puts them in conversation with *The Birth of a Nation* (1915), an unabashedly racist "fable" from the silent film period that Baldwin acknowledges is regarded as "one of the great classics of American cinema."[33] The hypocrisy he calls out is essentially that American cinema of the civil rights era purports to show the love that exists between its Black and white citizens, but that what it actually reveals is, as Giovanni would say, a refusal to take a hard, honest look at "all the serious, dreadful things" that love involves. Thus, any supposedly enlightened cinematic Poitier vehicle just glosses over the racial nightmare of *The Birth of a Nation* with a thick layer of "polish."[34] After twice using that word to describe *Guess Who's Coming to Dinner* (1967), Baldwin again uses the same word he had used to describe *The Birth of a Nation*, calling *Guess Who* a "light and self-serving ... fable."[35] As any reader of Baldwin's work knows, he's only interested in fables when he wants to expose the dangers of mistaking them for reality, and when he sees something that appears polished, his urge is to scratch it to reveal the reality under the surface.

If love is "a growing up," part two of *Devil* shows Baldwin growing out of his love for movies as pure infatuation and growing into a lover who is secure enough to recognize shortcomings and to express them honestly. Since love is also a "battle" and a "war," this expression often takes the form of a lover's quarrel. One of Baldwin's frustrated lifelong ambitions was to contribute to the film industry as meaningfully as he contributed to the world of letters, but of course that did not happen, for reasons that will be explored in the next section. He was, after all, a literary writer, and one of his consistent points throughout the first two sections is that novels and plays are always better than films. The claim "the book is better than the movie" is a cliché, but Baldwin's contribution to this debate is more nuanced and more specific. Though he might believe that books constitute a superior art form, that is not his claim here; instead, he suggests that films refuse to live up to their potential due to a lack of courage and imagination, a tendency to play it safe like David in *Giovanni's Room*. The section begins with a somewhat lengthy consideration of a now obscure film, *I Shall Spit on Your Graves* (1959), based on a 1946 novel by Boris Vian. One of Baldwin's critiques of the adaptation is that it does not deal with the complex intersection of sex, social stratification, and existential angst: "This intersection, where life disputes with death, is very vivid in the book: and it does not, of course, exist in the film."[36] This critique sounds remarkably like Giovanni's accusation that Americans avoid the "serious, dreadful things, like pain and death and love." The snide "of course" in Baldwin's statement only makes sense when we understand his evolving perspective: essentially, Hollywood, like America more generally, simply cannot handle the troubling complexity that love involves. Hollywood replaces feeling with action: he describes a typical Hollywood scene that anchors the film version of *I Shall Spit on Your Graves*, complete with a loaded gun, a drunken southerner, and a car escape; he writes, parenthetically, "None of this paranoia is in Vian's book."[37]

The "paranoia" he speaks of is, essentially, Hollywood's reliance on stock footage that will cause its viewers' hearts to race, but not to feel. In addition to playing it safe, Hollywood also is guilty of taking shortcuts, and thus shortchanging human experience. Baldwin returns throughout this section to a critique of "plot" v. "story," which is an important if frequently overlooked dimension of his analysis in this work. It is the only way to make sense of the presence of McCarthyism and the FBI in this section that is otherwise focused on films. The "paranoid" aspects of American public/political life represented by McCarthyist red-baiting and FBI intimidation are also at the mercy of a plot. Here is Baldwin:

> A story is impelled by the necessity to reveal: the aim of the story is revelation, which means that a story can have nothing—at least not deliberately—to hide. This also means that a story resolves nothing. The resolution of a story must occur in us, with what we make of the questions with which the story leaves us. A plot, on the other hand, must come to a resolution, prove a point: a plot must answer all the questions which it pretends to pose.[38]

It is through this critique that Baldwin is able to build his surprising claim that an earnest if flawed civil rights era movie like *In the Heat of the Night* (1967) is the descendant of an overtly racist spectacle like *The Birth of a Nation*. As Alice Craven and others rightly claim, this rhetorical move is parallel to his critique of *Uncle Tom's Cabin* (1852) and *Native Son* (1940) along the same lines, but in this context, I would link Hollywood's preference for plot over story—or resolution over revelation—to Baldwin's definition of love. If love is "quest, daring, growth, growing up," it is never *resolved*: it is always in process. Hollywood's problem, in Baldwin's eyes, is not that it attempts to address America's racial woes, but that it attempts to *solve* them without being honest, nuanced, or bold. The conclusions of Baldwin's stories and novels—features of his fiction which don't get nearly enough attention or praise—are masterpieces of ambiguity: they force the reader to articulate or intuit what might be called the resolution. His emphasis on revelation might be deemed his art, but it also coincides with his understanding of love, which is the driving force behind art.

What bothers Baldwin about movies is parallel to what bothers Giovanni about David: they want everything to be clean. *In the Heat of the Night* leads to a resolution that is analogous, in Baldwin's memorable analysis, to "the obligatory fade-out kiss," a Hollywood staple that "did not really speak of love, and, still less, of sex: it spoke of reconciliation, of all things now becoming possible."[39] Such happy endings are problematic because of their "appalling distance from reality."[40] This particular film fails because it "helplessly conveys—without confronting—the anguish of people trapped in a legend. They cannot live within this legend: neither can they step out of it."[41] The cardinal American sin in Baldwin's eyes is to replace love with happiness. Happiness is a romantic fantasy whereas actual love is a mess, involving pain and confrontation as well as quest and daring and growth. It's not as though movies can't be messy, but they refuse to.

Enter Giovanni, who tries and fails to explain this principle to David, if only through example. Giovanni's room, the novel's richest symbol from the title on, is characterized by extreme disorder, even chaos. In a moment of clarity, David describes it as "Giovanni's regurgitated life."[42] In other words, it is his depth, his soul, his disorganized but ever questing mind. David, occasionally referred to as "monsieur l'américain," finds the surfaces of things much more captivating, just as Hollywood is reluctant to pursue the messy reality of lived experience, particularly the lived experience of African Americans.[43] As part two of *Giovanni's Room* begins, David says, "In the beginning, our life together held a joy and amazement which was newborn every day. Beneath the joy, of course, was anguish and beneath the amazement was fear."[44] David is aware of the difference between surface and depth even as he looks on his lover's face, and he is scared of the depth: "the wide and beautiful brow began to suggest the skull beneath. The sensual lips turned inward, busy with the sorrow overflowing from his heart."[45] David believes Giovanni's private room and the private sorrows of his heart and soul must be cleaned up or papered over. His personal mission is "to destroy this room and to give Giovanni a new and better life."[46] He goes about cleaning the room and disposing of the clutter, but since the room is Giovanni's regurgitated life, he is unconsciously attempting to destroy

Giovanni, or at least the part that disturbs David. This is not love, of course, but an attempt to control and sanitize reality. In contrast to Giovanni's room is the brightly lit and squeaky clean American Express office where David goes to get his mail, and to get away from Giovanni and his filthy room. He notices that the American men gathered there "smelled of soap, which seemed indeed to be their preservative against the dangers and exigencies of any more intimate odor."[47] Although he distances himself from his countrymen, he is guilty of the exact same thing, which Giovanni states clearly when he tells him he cannot accept "the stink of love."

To return to *Devil*, section two translates the dynamic of a love affair to the state of race relations in the United States. Baldwin has drawn this parallel before, including in the famous conclusion to *The Fire Next Time*: "If we—and now I mean the relatively conscious whites and the relatively conscious blacks, who must, *like lovers*, insist on, or create the consciousness of the others—do not falter in our duty now, we may be able … to end the racial nightmare, and achieve our country" (emphasis mine).[48] True lovers, in Baldwin's world, have to work hard, and suffer, and commit. In the above passages, David refuses to do so, preferring to cling to the infantile inception of love that is only "joy and amazement which was newborn every day." So too Hollywood. Baldwin writes, "in order for a person to bear his life, he needs a valid re-creation of that life, which is why, as Ray Charles might put it, blacks chose to sing the blues."[49] Hollywood, in Baldwin's view, doesn't have the courage to produce such a valid recreation and instead produces and reproduces a counter reality, or mythology, or "legend"; he writes, "Even the most thoughtless, even the most deluded black person knows more about his life than the image he is offered as the justification of it."[50] Whereas the young Baldwin introduced in section one saw things on the screen and claimed, "I knew something about *that*," in this section he discusses what Black men know of reality and how they are disgusted by the distortions as rendered on the screen, distortions born of "cowardice," "sentimentality," "American self-evasion," and ultimately "the brutally limited lexicon of those who think of themselves as white, and imagine, therefore, that they control reality and rule the world."[51] From the time of its publication, readers and critics of *Giovanni's Room* have been puzzled by the fact that it is not about American race relations, and it isn't, but these words make clear that it is about a similar social power dynamic. David doesn't run away from Giovanni just because he is conflicted about his own homosexual desire coupled with his ingrained homophobia: it is because he is cowardly and wants to cling to his facile, immature understanding of love as joyful and beautiful, without any pain, chaos, or "stink." Hollywood similarly constructs plots that resolve the sometimes painful and ugly struggle toward ending the racial nightmare without exploring the true depth of this struggle in the way the blues do.

And so, the lovers fight. Giovanni screams at David, "You do not … love anyone! You never have loved anyone, I am sure you never will! You love your purity, you love your mirror … You want to be *clean*."[52] Baldwin screams a little less loudly, but just as effectively, at the end of his analysis of *In the Heat of the Night*:

nothing, alas, has been made possible by this obligatory, fade-out kiss, this preposterous adventure: except that white Americans have been encouraged to continue dreaming, and black Americans have been alerted to the necessity of waking up ... a black man, in any case, had certainly best not believe everything he sees in the movies.[53]

The boy had been eager to believe it all; the man cautions about believing everything, but we sense that he is increasingly moving toward not believing anything he sees on the silver screen, not as long as Hollywood's motivations are like David's: self-serving, self-loving, and hopelessly distorted.

When love affairs end in Baldwin's work or his life, they tend to end with a blowout argument followed by permanent and painful separation. The spurned lover suffers and screams at the smug lover who refuses to change, and then he storms away. By 1976 Baldwin had settled into the only house he ever bought for himself, in Saint-Paul de Vence in southeastern France. His critics had long accused him of being out of touch with the volatile cultural changes in America, given his residence in Europe, and although he deflected such charges, his self-described "commutes" across the Atlantic were less frequent during the mid-1970s. He used the Joycean convention of concluding his published works with the cities in which they were composed. 1968's *Tell Me How Long the Train's Been Gone* ends "New York, San Francisco, Istanbul." The signature locations from 1972's *No Name in the Street* are "New York, San Francisco, Hollywood, London, Istanbul, St. Paul de Vence." But 1974's *If Beale Street Could Talk* and *The Devil Finds Work* both end with a single location abroad: Saint-Paul de Vence. His later works dispense with this publishing convention, though they were largely written in Saint-Paul. Beginning in the mid-1970s, for better or worse, he is declaring that he is an expatriate, perhaps even going so far as to identify as a European. It was a messy breakup, but he has once and for all left the American cities in which he partly composed his previous works, including one notable non-city, Hollywood, one of the listed locations where he wrote *No Name*.

The reason Baldwin breaks up with Hollywood and America is that he realizes Hollywood is too set in its ways to change even though he fights with all his energy to bring about such a change. He begins the third section of *Devil* by showing what happens when Hollywood attempts "controversial, courageous, revolutionary films" about the underground leaders Che Guevara and Malcolm X, which is an extension of what happens when it attempts films about race relations.[54] Because these films are "packaged for the consumer society," and thus more concerned with "action" and "entertainment" than with the truth, they lead Baldwin to conclude that he and the filmmaking industry have no future together: "I simply walked out."[55] Giovanni expresses the same sense of resignation during his final breakup scene with David: "'We will not fight any more,' he said. 'Fighting will not make you stay.'"[56] David steels himself to return to the heterosexual status quo of his life, and to return to America. When Giovanni prompts him about what he wants, he says, "I want to end this terrible scene."[57] And like his analog Hollywood, he'll do everything in his power to make sure it ends up buried in some unopened canister in a locked archive.

Baldwin's love affair with the movies is decidedly over when the screenplay of Malcolm X's life he has been asked to write is thoroughly coopted and debased, or, to adopt the term he uses repeatedly to describe this misadventure, "translated."[58] What he witnesses during his excursion into the lion's mouth is an exercise of power, the power to reshape reality. He intercepts a memo circulated among the studio executives that clearly indicates that the film should emphasize that Malcolm "had been mistreated, early, by some whites, and betrayed (later) by *many* blacks: emphasis in the original."[59] Such an attempt to rewrite Baldwin's vision of the complex and highly important figure of Malcolm X is essentially an act of violence. "Translation" is a euphemism for abuse. He recognizes and calls out this violence when he analyzes *Lady Sings the Blues* (1972), the story of another Black culture hero, Billie Holiday, whose life is mistranslated when portrayed on the screen:

> Now, obviously, the only way to translate the written word to the cinema involves doing considerable violence to the written word, to the extent, indeed, of forgetting the written word. A film is meant to be seen, and, ideally, the less a film talks, the better. The cinematic translation, nevertheless, however great and necessary the violence it is compelled to use on the original form, is obliged to remain faithful to the intention, and the vision, of the original form.[60]

Cinematic translation is neither "faithful" nor "honest" in the way Billie Holiday was honest in her book.[61] A lover who is neither faithful nor honest cannot be redeemed. But more: the silver screen has filtered out the essence of Holiday's "testimony," a word Baldwin chooses and emphasizes deliberately; he writes, "I repeat: her testimony, for that is what we are compelled to deal with, and respect, and whatever others may imagine themselves to know of these matters cannot compare with the testimony of the person who was there."[62] Or, as Giovanni would say, "You have never loved anyone. I am sure you never will!"[63] For Baldwinian love ultimately involves recognition, respect, understanding, and knowledge. The violence of cinematic "translation" is just the opposite, the work of the devil.

Having loved and lost, Baldwin realizes that the so-called magic of the movies is actually the will to "control reality and rule the world."[64] Now that he has paid attention to the proverbial man behind the curtain, or "seen this machinery at such close quarters," he no longer finds it alluring, and indeed, considers it dangerous.[65] Translation in the context of what he calls "the American looking-glass" is a distortion; the magic we see on screen is actually a means of lying about reality and calling it a myth.[66] But Baldwin does not simply walk away and throw up his hands; rather, he returns to the concept of "revelation" that he learned from his physically and spiritually exhausting conversion experience in the church: "This moment changes one forever."[67] Revelation (as opposed to cinematic resolution) gives one the strength to sing the blues, and "to engage Satan in a battle which we knew could never end."[68] We recall that "battle" is one of the words Baldwin uses to define "love," and we realize that the love battle with Hollywood he has been describing is meant to do precisely what he says revelation is to do: revelation is "the aim of the story," the resolution of which "must occur in us, with what we make of the questions with which the story leaves us." "Us"—readers of *The Devil Finds Work*—have just read a love story in the form of a Baldwin testimony rather than "pure bullshit Hollywood-American fable."[69] It is only once we have stripped away the fables, distortions, myths, translations, and legends that Hollywood fashions out of America's most damaging hierarchies that we can finally see self and other clearly, and here is Baldwin's ultimate revelation: "To encounter oneself is to encounter the other: and this is love."[70] The screen goes dark, the lights come up, the audience exhales. *Fin.*

Notes

1 Cassandra M. Ellis, "The Black Boy Looks at the Silver Screen," in D. Quentin Miller (ed.), *Re-Viewing James Baldwin: Things Not Seen* (Philadelphia, PA, Temple University Press, 2000), p. 192.

2 Alice Mikal Craven, "Black Bodies on Screen, White Privilege in Hollywood: James Baldwin on Lang and Preminger," in Alice Mikal Craven and William E. Dow (eds.), *Of Latitudes Unknown: James Baldwin's Radical Imagination* (London, Bloomsbury Academic, 2019), pp. 15–31.

3 Jenny M. James, "A Long Way from Home: Baldwin in Provence," in D. Quentin Miller (ed.), *James Baldwin in Context* (Cambridge, Cambridge University Press, 2019), p. 72; Nicholas Boggs, "Of Mimicry and (Little Man, Little) Man," in Dwight McBride (ed.), *James Baldwin Now* (New York, New York University Press, 1999), p. 135.

4 William Dow, "Reviewers, Critics, and Cranks," in Miller (ed.), *James Baldwin in Context*, p. 296.

5 Jerry H. Bryant, "Review of *The Devil Finds Work* by James Baldwin," *The Nation*, 3 July 1976, p. 27.

6 *Ibid.*, pp. 26, 27.

7 *Ibid.*, pp. 25, 27.

8 James Baldwin, "Stranger in the Village" (1953), in *Collected Essays*, ed. Toni Morrison (New York, Library of America, 1998), p. 129; James Baldwin, *The Fire Next Time* (1963), in Morrison (ed.), *Collected Essays*, p. 347.

9 1975 is the year the text was completed, though it was published in 1976.

10 David Leeming, *James Baldwin* (New York, Knopf, 1994), p. 332.

11 *Ibid.*

12 James Baldwin, *The Devil Finds Work* (New York, Laurel/Dell, 1976), p. 115.

13 *Ibid.*, p. 3.

14 *Ibid.*, p. 4.

15 *Ibid.*

16 *Ibid.*, p. 5.

17 *Ibid.*, p. 7.

18 *Ibid.*

19 *Ibid.*, p. 8.

20 *Ibid.*, p. 14.

21 *Ibid.*, p. 24.

22 *Ibid.*, pp. 24, 25.

23 *Ibid.*

24 *Ibid.*, pp. 30, 31, 15.

25 *Ibid.*, p. 35.

26 James Baldwin, *Giovanni's Room* (1956) (New York, Vintage, 2013), p. 58.

27 *Ibid.*, pp. 60, 61.

28 *Ibid.*, p. 64.

29 James Baldwin, "Sonny's Blues" (1957), in *Early Novels and Stories*, ed. Toni Morrison (New York, Library of America, 1998), p. 841.

30 Baldwin, *Giovanni's Room*, p. 34.

31 Baldwin, *The Fire Next Time*, p. 341; James Baldwin, *No Name in the Street* (1972), in Morrison (ed.), *Collected Essays*, p. 467.

32 Baldwin, *Giovanni's Room*, p. 141.

33 Baldwin, *Devil*, p. 52.

34 *Ibid.*, pp. 88, 89.

35 *Ibid.*, p. 89.

36 *Ibid.*, pp. 50–1.

37 *Ibid.*, p. 50.

38 *Ibid.*, p. 53.

39 *Ibid.*, p. 67.

40 *Ibid.*

41 *Ibid.*

42 Baldwin, *Giovanni's Room*, p. 87.

43 *Ibid.*, p. 52.

44 *Ibid.*, p. 75.

45 *Ibid.*

46 *Ibid.*

47 *Ibid.*, p. 90.

48 Baldwin, *The Fire Next Time*, pp. 346–7.

49 Baldwin, *Devil*, p. 73.

50 *Ibid.*, pp. 71–2.

51 *Ibid.*, pp. 75, 90, 91.

52 Baldwin, *Giovanni's Room*, p. 141.

53 Baldwin, *Devil*, pp. 68–9.

54 *Ibid.*, p. 116.

55 *Ibid.*, pp. 116, 120.

56 *Ibid.*, p. 120; Baldwin, *Giovanni's Room*, p. 143.

57 Baldwin, *Giovanni's Room*, p. 142.

58 Baldwin, *Devil*, pp. 117, 118, 119.

59 *Ibid.*, p. 117.

60 *Ibid.*, p. 130.

61 *Ibid.*

62 *Ibid.*, p. 131.

63 Baldwin, *Giovanni's Room*, p. 141.

64 Baldwin, *Devil*, p. 91.

65 *Ibid.*, p. 117.

66 *Ibid.*, p. 120.

67 *Ibid.*, pp. 138, 139.

68 *Ibid.*, p. 140.

69 *Ibid.*, p. 133.
70 *Ibid.*, p. 148.

Works Cited

James Baldwin, *The Devil Finds Work* (New York, Laurel/Dell, 1976).

_____ *The Fire Next Time* (1963), in *Collected Essays*, ed. Toni Morrison (New York, Library of America, 1998), pp. 287–347.

_____ *Giovanni's Room* (1956) (New York, Vintage, 2013).

_____ *No Name in the Street* (1972), in *Collected Essays*, ed. Toni Morrison (New York, Library of America, 1998), pp. 349–476.

_____ "Sonny's Blues" (1957), in *Early Novels and Stories*, ed. Toni Morrison (New York, Library of America, 1998), pp. 831–64.

_____ "Stranger in the Village" (1953), in *Collected Essays*, ed. Toni Morrison (New York, Library of America, 1998), pp. 117–29.

Boggs, Nicholas, "Of Mimicry and (Little Man, Little) Man," in Dwight McBride (ed.), *James Baldwin Now* (New York, New York University Press, 1999), pp. 122–60.

Bryant, Jerry H.. "Review of *The Devil Finds Work* by James Baldwin," *The Nation*, 3 July 1976, p. 27.

Craven, Alice Mikal, "Black Bodies on Screen, White Privilege in Hollywood: James Baldwin on Lang and Preminger," in Alice Mikal Craven and William E. Dow (eds.), *Of Latitudes Unknown: James Baldwin's Radical Imagination* (London, Bloomsbury Academic, 2019), pp. 15–31.

Dow, William, "Reviewers, Critics, and Cranks," in D. Quentin Miller (ed.), *James Baldwin in Context* (Cambridge, Cambridge University Press, 2019), pp. 287–300.

Ellis, Cassandra M., "The Black Boy Looks at the Silver Screen," in D. Quentin Miller (ed.), *Re-Viewing James Baldwin: Things Not Seen* (Philadelphia, PA, Temple University Press, 2000), pp. 190–214.

James, Jenny M., "A Long Way from Home: Baldwin in Provence," in D. Quentin Miller (ed.), *James Baldwin in Context* (Cambridge, Cambridge University Press, 2019), pp. 66–75.

Leeming, David, *James Baldwin* (New York, Knopf, 1994).

Contributor's Biography

D. Quentin Miller is Professor of English at Suffolk University in Boston where he teaches courses on American literature, African American literature, and fiction writing. He is the author or editor of three books on James Baldwin, most recently *James Baldwin in Context* (Cambridge University Press, 2019). His most recent books are the co-edited textbooks *Literature to Go* (4th edition, Bedford/St. Martin's, 2019) and *The Compact Bedford Introduction to Literature* (12th edition, Bedford/St. Martin's, 2019).

Manchester University Press

ESSAY

Another Cinema: James Baldwin's Search for a New Film Form

Hayley O'Malley   University of Iowa

Abstract

James Baldwin was a vocal critic of Hollywood, but he was also a cinephile, and his critique of film was not so much of the medium itself, but of the uses to which it was put. Baldwin saw in film the chance to transform both politics and art—if only film could be transformed itself. This essay blends readings of archival materials, literature, film, and print culture to examine three distinct modes in Baldwin's ongoing quest to revolutionize film. First, I argue, literature served as a key site to practice being a filmmaker, as Baldwin adapted cinematic grammars in his fiction and frequently penned scenes of filmgoing in which he could, in effect, direct his own movies. Secondly, I show that starting in the 1960s, Baldwin took a more direct route to making movies, as he composed screenplays, formed several production companies, and attempted to work in both Hollywood and the independent film scene in Europe. Finally, I explore how Baldwin sought to change cinema as a performer himself, in particular during his collaboration on Dick Fontaine and Pat Hartley's documentary *I Heard It Through the Grapevine* (1982). This little-known film follows Baldwin as he revisits key sites from the civil rights movement and reconnects with activist friends as he endeavors to construct a revisionist history of race in America and to develop a media practice capable of honoring Black communities.

Keywords: James Baldwin, film, visual culture, archives, *I Heard It Through the Grapevine*

James Baldwin Review, Volume 7, 2021, © The Authors. Published by Manchester University Press and
The University of Manchester Library
http://dx.doi.org/10.7227/JBR.7.6

JAMES BALDWIN
will write and will direct
Miss DIANA SANDS
in "THE INHERITANCE"
for Kelly-Jordan Enterprises, Inc.
Fall 1972

Kelly-Jordan Enterprises, Inc., 342 Madison Avenue, New York, N.Y. (212) 682-1720

Figure 1   Baldwin in Paris. Kelly-Jordan advertisement, *Variety*, 1972

In May 1972, the production company Kelly-Jordan Enterprises placed a full-page ad in *Variety* announcing that James Baldwin would write and direct their next film, "The Inheritance."[1] It was to star Diana Sands, but the ad focused on Baldwin, featuring a photograph of him in Paris wearing trademark dark glasses and a scarf beside a bookstall by the Seine. He gazes directly at the camera, a slight smile playing on his lips—pleased, it seems, to be making his directorial debut in France, an ocean away from Hollywood. Baldwin dove into the project, setting aside his in-progress novel, *If Beale Street Could Talk* (1974), so he could concentrate on writing "The Inheritance."[2] The film, unfortunately, was never made, but it is an exemplary moment in a larger story about Baldwin's relentless efforts to be a film auteur.

Baldwin was, of course, a frequent and outspoken critic of Hollywood. From his early essays on Otto Preminger's *Carmen Jones* (1954) and *Porgy and Bess* (1959) to his 1976 memoir of moviegoing, *The Devil Finds Work*, Baldwin showed how the American film industry, through a combination of racist hiring practices and aesthetic choices, consistently buttressed white supremacist mythologies.[3] Baldwin didn't just catalog Hollywood's failings, though—he was a cinephile himself, and references to international cinema pepper his books and letters. His friend and biographer David Leeming reports that Baldwin "liked nothing better than talking and writing about the movies."[4] So it's crucial to recognize that Baldwin's searing critique of film was not of the medium itself, but of the uses to which it was put. Baldwin saw in film the chance to transform both politics and art—if only film itself could first be transformed.

Baldwin's own work was an attempt to do just that. As I show in this essay, he actively sought to be a filmmaker throughout his career. This pursuit manifested itself in both his explicit attempts to write, direct, and produce films and also in his fictional, critical, and autobiographical writings, which became an alternative literary space for filmmaking when he could not literally bring his vision to the screen. Drawing on new archival research, this essay pieces together Baldwin's many experiments with the moving image to analyze his deep and career-long belief in the aesthetic, moral, and political possibilities of film and to track his restless attempts, across a range of genres and artistic media, to reimagine what the movies could be.

I examine three distinct modes in Baldwin's ongoing quest to revolutionize film. First, I argue, literature served as a key site to practice being a filmmaker, as Baldwin adapted cinematic grammars in his fiction and frequently penned scenes of filmgoing in which he could, in effect, direct his own movies, turning the novel and the short story into alternative genres of filmmaking. I then show how, starting in the 1960s, Baldwin took a more direct route to making movies, as he composed screenplays, formed several production companies, and attempted to work in both Hollywood and the independent film scene in Europe. Finally, I explore how Baldwin sought to change cinema not only by trying to work behind the camera, but also by performing in front of it, in particular during his collaboration on Dick Fontaine and Pat Hartley's documentary *I Heard It Through the Grapevine* (1982). Baldwin described the film as "a personal endeavor on a public platform," an effort to use the mass medium of film to circulate intimate conversations in which he and his longtime activist friends reflected on the civil rights movement, constructed a revisionist history of race in America, and worked to develop a media practice capable of honoring Black communities.[5]

* * * * *

Baldwin always wanted to make movies. His 1955 essay collection *Notes of a Native Son* includes his scathing review of *Carmen Jones*, but it also features a different vision for film. In the opening essay, "Autobiographical Notes," Baldwin opines, "About my interests, I don't know if I have any, unless the morbid desire to own a sixteen-millimeter camera and make experimental movies."[6] Critics have cited this line to suggest how deeply Baldwin was invested in film spectatorship and how intensely he took his work as a budding film theorist.[7] But I want to take Baldwin more literally, as articulating a fundamental desire to *create films*, and I want to argue that this "interest" deeply structured his work as an author. Filmmaking may have been a "morbid desire"—a perhaps impossibly uphill battle—but seeing Baldwin as an aspiring filmmaker allows us to read his literary fiction as a form of "experimental movies." In *The Devil Finds Work*, Baldwin mused that "It is said that the camera cannot lie, but rarely do we allow it to do anything else, since the camera sees what you point it at: the camera sees what you want it to see. The language of the camera is the language of our dreams."[8] In his fiction, Baldwin made the camera see what *he* wanted it to see, penning film sequences in *Go Tell It on the Mountain* (1953), *Another Country* (1962), and *Little Man, Little Man* (1976) that use cinema to tell a different kind of truth than Hollywood allowed.

The filmgoing scene in *Go Tell It*, Baldwin's autobiographical first novel, has long attracted critical attention, in part because of its clear connection with *The Devil Finds Work*, but it also reveals Baldwin's furtive hopes for film as a medium for interpersonal connection.[9] Early in the novel, Baldwin's avatar, John Grimes, spends an afternoon wandering New York City alone. He longs to go into a candy store and climb the steps of the New York Public Library, but he mainly keeps to the sidewalks, having internalized the fact that "this world was not for him."[10] The open expanse of Central Park is more welcoming, yet as John runs down a snow-covered hill, he almost knocks over an elderly passerby. To John's surprise, rather than reacting in anger, "the old man smiled. John smiled back. It was as though he and the old man had between them a great secret."[11] Encouraged by the encounter, John returns to the streetscape and continues his quest for human connection. Tellingly, he decides to go to the movies.

John chooses the film carefully, studying the movie posters and selecting the one that feels closest to his own experience: "he felt identified with the blond young man, the fool of his family, and he wished to know more about his so blatantly unkind fate."[12] Baldwin never names the film, but the narrative he describes matches *Of Human Bondage* (1934), the film that made Bette Davis a star. In the theater, instead of identifying with the young man on the movie poster, John is pulled into rooting passionately for the doomed prostitute played by Davis. The image of her dying face inspires soul-searching by John, with cinema facilitating the kind of interpersonal connection that otherwise remains ineffable. Yet when John returns home, "real life" reasserts itself: his younger brother has been stabbed. With such sequencing, Baldwin seemingly asks whether the interpersonal intimacies John feels in the movie theater are a necessary antidote to a violent world, or part of the problem, cheap imitations of the bonds that matter.

If Baldwin is ultimately ambivalent about the ethical possibilities of film spectatorship, though, he readily adapts cinematic vocabularies as a narrative tool and as a means to interrogate how we know others. In the first scene of *Go Tell It*, John, having slept in, stumbles into the kitchen. As he gazes at his mother and younger brother, he "saw them for a moment like figures on a screen, an effect that the yellow light intensified."[13] This gives him a new perspective on his daily life, as "the windows gleamed like beaten gold or silver, but now John saw, in the yellow light, how fine dust veiled their doubtful glory."[14] His mother's face, too, takes on different dimensions on the "screen" of his mind's eye: "the room shifted, the light of the sun darkened, and his mother's face changed. Her face became the face that he gave her in his dreams."[15] If, as Baldwin later said in *The Devil Finds Work*, "the camera is the language of our dreams," then John has internalized a cinematic logic for experiencing and inhabiting his world.[16]

Baldwin's complex relationship with film is even more foundational for his 1962 novel *Another Country*. The book opens bleakly, casting cinema as complicit in the malaise of modernity: "He [Rufus Scott] was facing Seventh Avenue, at Times Square. It was past midnight and he had been sitting in the movies, in the top row of the balcony, since two o'clock in the afternoon."[17] Another character, Cass, later deems the cinema "a hideous place of worship"—as she watches the screen, "she thought, irrelevantly, *I never should come to movies, I can't stand them*, and then she began to cry."[18] Movies are a powerful form of entrapment in these scenes, both the cause and effect of isolation.

Yet *Another Country* also, more hopefully, explores film's capacity to change people's perspectives and inspire sociality. In a scene late in the novel, Baldwin invents and narrates a film, allowing him to direct it like an auteur on the page. Vivaldo, Cass, Eric, and Ida decide to go to a French movie in which Eric has a bit part. Tensions between the characters are simmering: Ida and Vivaldo, an interracial couple, are bickering, and Vivaldo and Eric's relationship has been strained, partly because they were both in love with Rufus. Going to the movies, though, temporarily unites the group. They "came, laughing, through the doors just as the French film began."[19] The darkened theater mends bonds and enables new intimacies:

> Ida grabbed Vivaldo's hand in the darkness, and clung to it as though she were a child, mutely begging for reassurance and forgiveness. He pressed his shoulder very close to hers, and they leaned against one another. The film unrolled. Cass whispered to Eric, Eric whispered to Cass. Cass turned towards them, whispering, "Here he comes!" and the camera trucked into a crowded café, resting finally on a group of students. "That's

our boy!" cried Ida, disturbing the people around them—who sounded, for a second, like the weirdest cloud of insects.[20]

The theater fosters a rare instance of un-anxious togetherness, even if it remains precarious and structured by gendered and raced hierarchies, such as Ida's child-like submission.

Baldwin lovingly details the scene in which Eric appears, attending to film framing and its possibilities. He focuses in particular on the effect of cinematic realism and the minimalism of Eric's performance: Eric "was compelled to be still during this entire brief scene," but his presence, as planned by the director, "held the scene together, and emphasized the futility of the passionate talkers."[21] If *Go Tell It* raises a question about the power of faces on film, *Another Country* offers an answer: "the director had surely placed Eric where he had because this face operated, in effect, as a footnote to the twentieth-century torment ... It was a face which suggested, resonantly, in the depths, the truth about our natures."[22] Baldwin here fantasizes about genuine collaboration between a director and a performer—something he argued Otto Preminger could never cultivate with Black actors.[23] The result deeply moves Vivaldo, who believes (somewhat naively) that he has finally glimpsed the real Eric on screen, catalyzing their subsequent affair. Baldwin thus suggests that film, at its best, could enable the kinds of intimate explorations of interiority that he aspired to in his novels.

Indeed, film played a pivotal role in the composition of *Another Country*. In 1959, on assignment for *Esquire*, Baldwin interviewed Ingmar Bergman in Stockholm. In the resulting essay, Baldwin recalls that after their first interview, he was so "struck by what seemed to be our similarities" that he "amused [himself], on the ride back into town, by projecting a movie."[24] He imagines a historical drama, then reflects on the burdens of personal history and the possibilities for representing it: "It did not seem likely, after all, that I would ever be able to make of my past, on film, what Bergman had been able to make of his."[25] "What was lacking in my movie," Baldwin writes, "was the American despair, the search, in our country for authority ... What would a Bergman make of the American confusion? How would he handle a love story occurring in New York?"[26] With these questions swirling, Baldwin returned to Paris and resumed work on *Another Country*, his New York love story. He found that the novel "was flowing again."[27]

If film helped Baldwin finish *Another Country*, he also, appropriately, tried repeatedly to adapt it for the screen. Elia Kazan read *Another Country* in galleys, and by the spring of 1962, before it was published, he urged Baldwin to return to New York to discuss a screen adaptation.[28] Then, in 1964, the British director Tony Richardson acquired the film rights, with the understanding that Baldwin would write the screenplay.[29] Baldwin traveled to Los Angeles and began composing the script, confident that in the era of Sidney Poitier and interracial films, he and Richardson would find studio backing.[30] But that didn't happen, and Baldwin's collaboration with Richardson became one in a long line of failed film projects. Baldwin, though, never stopped pursuing his cinematic dreams, and as he worked back and forth between his literary and filmic projects, the two media dialogically informed each other.

Baldwin's 1976 illustrated children's book *Little Man, Little Man*, an often overlooked entry in his canon, showcases that cross-media dialogue. The book's young narrator, TJ, envisions his block in Harlem as a film.[31] "This street long," he says, "It real long. It a little like the street in the movies or the TV."[32] TJ then riffs on the genre of the police procedural, conjuring a chase scene and zooming in and out on the action, cutting between characters' perspectives. The illustrations, by Yoran Cazac, keep pace, portraying the events as a sequence of shots on a film reel. But unlike most cop dramas, TJ refuses to reify the surveilling gaze of the police and instead privileges the felt experiences of the man being pursued and the local residents, who can only watch and "get real uptight" as "the cops keep coming real slow and careful down this long street."[33] The result is an imagined film in TJ's mind that does much more than simply reproduce what he has watched on popular screens.

In control of the camera, as it were, TJ makes a home movie of his local community, tracking the impact of state violence even as he lovingly films his block from his own child's-eye perspective, defined by his favorite places—the church, the ice-cream parlor, his friend Blinky's house. And as TJ explores the imaginative possibilities of film for understanding his home, the literary space of *Little Man, Little Man* allows Baldwin to experiment with the affordances of film, speculating about what an alternative cinematic depiction of Harlem—his Harlem—might look like. Blending literary fiction with hand-drawn illustrations to create a cinematic scene, Baldwin mobilizes a range of different arts to push the boundaries of what film can do and the stories it can tell. As TJ describes his block in Harlem, recreating it, to borrow a phrase from *The Devil Finds Work*, in a "cinema of [the] mind," Baldwin repurposes a filmic medium that had long been used to malign Blackness, creating a new cinematic space for Black aesthetic innovation and communal empowerment.[34]

*****

None of Baldwin's works actually reached the silver screen during his lifetime. But not for lack of trying. Besides *Another Country*, he wrote adaptations of *Giovanni's Room* (1956) and *Blues for Mister Charlie* (1964), at least three original screenplays, and countless film treatments. Why? "Cinema is an art in the hands of an artist," he said in 1968, "and I am an artist."[35] His best-known film project is his screenplay about Malcolm X, later published as *One Day When I Was Lost* (1972), but following Baldwin's own lead, critics typically frame that as a singular dalliance with film—and one that Baldwin was keen to leave behind.[36] In truth, Baldwin's cinematic dreams were far more expansive: As I trace in this section, he turned intensely to film in the 1960s and 1970s, seeking to script, produce, and direct films from *One Day When I Was Lost* to "The Inheritance." What this shows is that Baldwin wasn't just committed to critiquing Hollywood, he was determined to develop an alternative to it, in the form of transnational Black independent film.

In late 1967, Columbia Pictures asked Baldwin to write a screenplay about Malcolm X. It was the offer he had been waiting for. But he was also skeptical that any Hollywood production would be equal to the subject. Deeply conflicted, Baldwin bought a plane ticket to Geneva—his only luggage was a copy of Alex Haley's *The Autobiography of Malcolm X*—and spent a weekend in a hotel room "reading and re-reading—or, rather, endlessly traversing—the great jungle of Malcolm's book."[37] It wasn't the first time Baldwin had thought about a Malcolm script: he had been planning a stage production with Haley and Kazan. And with that work as a foundation, he ultimately resolved to bring Malcolm's life to the screen.[38]

What followed has been much rehearsed, by both Baldwin and his critics. His Hollywood sojourn "was, by all accounts, a disaster."[39] Columbia paired him with a white screenwriter, Arnold Perl, who rewrote many of his scenes, and the studio instructed him to depoliticize Malcolm, a task he found unconscionable—not to mention impossible.[40] In 1969, Baldwin fled Hollywood, telling Louise Meriwether,

> I don't think Mrs. Baldwin's little boy should fall so far beneath himself as to be found dead or mad in Hollywood and so I shook the dust of that city—my God—from off my feet. There was absolutely nothing left to discuss: I was not going to make their movie … It was ghastly.[41]

And, indeed, Baldwin's Malcolm film was never made. In *The Devil Finds Work*, he proclaims, "I would rather be horsewhipped, or incarcerated in the forthright bedlam of Bellevue, than repeat the adventure."[42]

Such harsh rhetoric, however, obscures Baldwin's deep investment in the film. At least initially, he had seen it as a means to reimagine American cinema. No naïf, Baldwin had "been to Hollywood before," he told reporter C. Robert Jennings in 1968, and he only agreed to the project on the "very abnormal terms" that he "approve director, cast, and final cut."[43] The FBI, for one, was nervous about what Baldwin might accomplish: William J. Maxwell says that "FBI newspaper clippers got busy documenting Baldwin's work on [the] movie," and FBI agents tried to discover his address in California so they could keep tabs on the film.[44] Baldwin, in turn, reported to Eugene Lerner, a film agent and friend, that he was hard at work on the script, a project which was doing "strange things to [his] nights and days."[45]

Baldwin's writing process was always torturous, but his ambitions for this project were particularly high: he was trying to invent something new. As he explained to Lerner, "I don't see many movies that I like; even those I like don't seem, rally [*sic*], to address themselves to anything I really want to do."[46] He was especially "avoiding foreign films" because, he said,

> my subject being so atrociously American—to say nothing of myself—I can't really, at the moment, learn anything from them, except the very last thing I need to learn, that

is effects. But the effect, or effects, made by a European movie come out of the European mind. No, I must find my own vocabulary.[47]

Baldwin was no newcomer to cinema, and for that very reason, he was well positioned to recognize the necessity of creating a new American film language for Malcolm X. He ended his letter, though, with a wink: "Enough. I will probably have a Malcolm X beard by the time you see me again. Grey. I never believed that shit before about living your role. Home soon."[48]

More than the "effects," though, it was the people that made a movie for Baldwin, and as the filmmaker Sedat Pakay would recall, "Everybody wanted to play Malcolm X and everybody wanted to do the film."[49] Gordon Parks launched a campaign to direct, showing Baldwin a rough cut of *The Learning Tree* (1969), while the studio proposed everyone from Charlton Heston to Jim Brown as Malcolm; Baldwin wanted Billy Dee Williams.[50] Columbia also pushed Poitier— clearly hoping for a repeat of *Guess Who's Coming to Dinner* (1967)—but Baldwin refused: "I said Sidney could *never* do it and they could either have him or me. It's *got* to be right. Otherwise it's the end of *me*. Sidney would sink the movie and he knows it."[51] Baldwin was similarly decisive in his approach to the narrative: "The whole effort is to do it from the inside; otherwise, you only have a propaganda poster."[52]

Perhaps to avoid the flattening of propaganda, the beginning of Baldwin's script embraces a filmic grammar designed to narrate complicated histories. The sideview mirror of a car becomes a portal to Malcolm's past, and Baldwin calls for "Inexplicable images, swift, overlapping, blurred."[53] Those images soon become legible as both Malcolm's memories and icons of a longer history of racial violence: hooded men destroying his house, with his pregnant mother standing outside; his father laid across train tracks seen from an oncoming streetcar.[54] While the montaged memories are to be "swift," Baldwin also insists on visual pauses and aural silences, creating a melancholy ambience.[55] His script reads as both an adaptation of Haley's *Autobiography* and an extension of Gordon Parks's iconic photographs of Malcolm in *LIFE* magazine. Film thus serves as an omnivorous medium where Baldwin can bring together the multilayered narrative of a biography with the arresting indexicality of a photograph and the soulfulness of sound, all in a manner that's accessible for a mass audience. But that was not the kind of film Columbia wanted, and when the studio refused to hire Parks, citing his supposed "inexperience," Baldwin had had enough.[56] He packed his bags and left, taking his copyrighted script, too.

As he had before, Baldwin turned to Europe, specifically Turkey, to regroup. In Istanbul, he made his directorial debut on the stage with *Fortune and Men's Eyes*.[57] Its success, and his intimate rapport with the actors, whom he deemed his "Turkish children," gave him confidence in his directorial abilities.[58] He also starred in his friend Sedat Pakay's black-and-white film *From Another Place* (1970), an intimate, *cinéma vérité* production. In one of the first scenes, Baldwin lies sprawled in bed. Willing himself to rise, he opens the curtain, letting in the light, and walks toward the camera, unabashedly wearing only briefs. As Magdalena Zaborowska notes, "This is not how we are used to seeing famous writers."[59] In other sequences, Pakay's camera accompanies Baldwin as he wanders the city. That a film could be such an intimate affair—both in its production and its aesthetics—may well have restored Baldwin's faith in the artform.

In the fall of 1970, Baldwin also launched his own production company, Berdis Films, presumably named for his mother. Newspapers in the United States took note. Ollie Stewart, a columnist for the *Afro-American*, devoted his weekly "Report from Europe" to Baldwin's new venture, under the headline "James Baldwin Turns to Movies," and *Variety* ran a front-page story, explaining that Baldwin "wants to be able to have the say in the adaptation of any of his works … However major distrib [sic] would not be eschewed once the film was finished or even before, provided there was no interference."[60] The initial projects were to include a film version of *Another Country* directed by Joseph Losey, which had been in the works since the mid-1960s, and an adaptation of "This Morning, This Evening, So Soon," a short story about film culture and artistic collaboration. Baldwin would write the scripts for both. And his film company would be thoroughly transnational: *Variety* said that French-language films "would also be considered" and that Baldwin wanted to work with Constantin Costa-Gavras and Alan Resnais, while Stewart remarked on Baldwin's choice of Paris as his base of operations and speculated that "Hollywood is becoming an also-ran."[61] Having found Hollywood wanting, Baldwin turned to foreign film and the independent scene.

Baldwin had long valued independent film. In 1962, he sold "This Morning" to an independent producer, who planned to have Edward Albee or Ossie Davis write the screenplay, and Baldwin had been cautiously optimistic: "It might turn out quite well—no stars, low budget, foreign market, prizes at Cannes, all that jazz."[62] Aside from the prizes at Cannes, by the 1970s, Baldwin also saw independent film as a way to unite art and politics. In 1971, he and Costa-Gavras planned a film entitled "Soledad Brother," but even more pressing political demands interrupted their plans: soon after Baldwin finished the film treatment, George Jackson was murdered and Baldwin "had to go on the road, for Angela Davis."[63] That same year, Baldwin also wanted to resurrect his Malcolm film, as he had initially intended it.[64] Failing that, he published his script as *One Day When I Was Lost*, and he wrote about his Hollywood experience in *No Name in the Street*. The two texts, both published in 1972, marked Baldwin's break from Hollywood, but they also added to his growing film portfolio—his concerted attempt to declare his place in the world of film.

Berdis Films never produced any pictures, but by the spring of 1972, Baldwin had agreed to do a film called "The Inheritance" with Kelly-Jordan Enterprises.[65] Kelly-Jordan's roster of writer-directors also included Maya Angelou and Bill Gunn, and Baldwin himself had previously partnered with Jack Jordan, one of the few Black producers in the business, though with no results. That spring, however, Kelly-Jordan had released *Georgia, Georgia*, starring Diana Sands and scripted by Angelou, and in Leeming's words, Baldwin felt that "If Jordan could do it for Maya, why not for him?"[66] So Baldwin signed on to write "The Inheritance"—and to direct. That summer, as he wrestled with his screenplay, he told his friend the actor David Moses that it was "far more complex than I'd expected it to be, I don't yet know enough about the people, and, in short, I'm sweating my balls off."[67] The plot of "The Inheritance" follows Brigid Bryant, a bi-racial dancer to be played by Sands, who travels from Birmingham to Berlin to confront her white German father, whom she has never met, and to claim her "inheritance." In the script, Brigid's German family assumes her quest is materialistic, but Baldwin was after much larger questions of identity, complicity, and memory, charting a multi-generational family saga that weaves together scenes from America and Germany to interrogate forty years of history—and white supremacy—on two continents.

There are clear stylistic connections between "The Inheritance" and *One Day When I Was Lost*, but "The Inheritance" comes closer to a shooting script. The opening, like *One Day*, is emotionally saturated with the past: "In silence: a black woman's hand, regal, heavily-burdened with pride, ornate with spangles at the wrist, splendid with rings, moves across and within a kind of private space: a dance elaborately private, the key-note of which is, nevertheless, farewell."[68] As the narrative progresses, Baldwin remains dedicated to his characters' emotional terrain, but he is also more attentive to cinematography than in his other scripts, consciously orchestrating close-ups and point-of-view shots. He does, though, leave some direction for the set. In a montage introducing 1929 Berlin, for example, a staccato list suffices: "Bread-lines; Soup kitchens; Riots; Whores, female; Whores, males."[69] As the film's planned director, Baldwin would be able to film that montage exactly as he wanted.

"The Inheritance" also treats film as a technology of memory. In an early scene in Istanbul, Brigid visits a fortune teller, a "medium," who functions as an obvious stand-in for the medium of film. Rather than illuminate the future, the fortune teller focuses on the past. A series of flashbacks show her visions, and throughout the screenplay Baldwin embraces the opportunity to leap between time periods and across oceans with a simple cut. So, when Brigid responds to a query about why she came to Germany, "Well, time and space have altered. Both are smaller than they were before, and so one can do more with them," the line immediately signifies as a meta-cinematic comment on what a camera can do.[70]

Baldwin uses this filmic ability to compress time and space to explore the resonances between America and Germany, but without asserting any easy moral equivalency. Brigid's father Wilfred, for instance, wants to aid Germany's drive toward industrial autonomy as an engineer but then becomes complicit in Hitler's rise. Baldwin likewise analyzes contemporary Germany, describing the Berlin Wall as an "excessive border," before calling for an overhead shot that shows "Cars crawling East: cars crawling West."[71] By interweaving these German vignettes with scenes from Birmingham, Baldwin makes the political connections clear, not least with a scene in which Brigid's husband is murdered by an Alabama police officer.[72] Baldwin never shies away from depicting the national nightmares of both countries, but he also, not unlike *Go Tell It*, retains some hope that interpersonal connections, particularly a friendship between Brigid and her blond-haired German nephew, can bridge differences.

"The Inheritance," however, was never made: Kelly-Jordan Enterprises went bankrupt, and in 1973 Baldwin had to sue to retain the rights to the film.[73] Even amid that legal battle, Baldwin didn't give up on cinema. He attended the Cannes Film Festival, where Bill Gunn's avant-garde vampire film *Ganja & Hess* (1973) was the only American movie to screen at Critics' Week, and later that summer he finished writing "The Inheritance." With the screenplay complete, Baldwin tried to start another new film company. He wrote to Moses and detailed his casting plans, which were to include Simone Signoret. He also shared his ambition "to create a nucleus of people who will continue working together" and rattled off ideas for location shooting.[74] "I'm very excited and very frightened," he concluded, "but the reaction to the script has been extraordinary."[75]

By 1974, popular films like Parks's *Shaft* (1971) and Melvin Van Peebles's *Sweet Sweetback's Baadasssss Song* (1971) had ushered in a boom in Black cinema, and *Esquire* commissioned Baldwin to write about the phenomenon. Two years earlier, when George Goodman, Jr. of the *New York Times* had asked Baldwin about mainstream Black films, Baldwin responded, "Are they in fact black?"[76] And his tune had not changed in 1974: he told Moses that he was "doing research for a long essay <u>Esquire</u> asked me to do on Black films (Lord) and was therefore trapped in projection rooms in Paris."[77] Baldwin saw his own filmmaking endeavors as fundamentally different—an artistic rather than a commercial project—and it's an unfortunate irony that he seems to have disregarded many of the Black independent films of the period.[78]

Baldwin, though, was still forging ahead with "The Inheritance." His intended lead, Diana Sands, had died of cancer the year before, but Baldwin told Moses that he had recently pitched the script to Ingo Preminger, whom Baldwin deemed a friend and "a very different cat" from his brother Otto.[79] Baldwin also had new casting plans, including Diana Ross for the lead (or if not her then Rosalind Cash), Thommy Berggren, and Sylvia Sidney. There were also parts for David Baldwin and Abbey Lincoln, as well as Moses, newcomer Ivan Nikolov, and Richard Attenborough, whom Baldwin had recently met. "Not a bad package," he concluded, "and I think we'll get most of it: we might get it all."[80] Baldwin had carefully plotted camera angles in his script, but his conception of filmmaking was ultimately less about cinematography and more about bringing different artists—and the different arts—together. "To guide my poor self through" as director, he wrote to Moses, "I have the nucleus of the technical crew. Have the set designer. Will get Quincy Jones to do the music. I <u>don't</u> have a cameraman, but I expect him to present himself shortly."[81]

Baldwin's last long discussion of "The Inheritance" with Moses comes in a 1976 letter. He begins by apologizing for being "distant," explaining that he was afraid he had become a "jinx on actors," particularly ones he was close to: "I wrote <u>The Inheritance</u> for you, and my beloved Diana [Sands]. You saw how the producer (Jack Jordan) fucked <u>that</u> up."[82] Then, seeming to forget his 1974 letter about new casting possibilities, he asserted that "when Diana died, I had no heart to go any further."[83] But Baldwin was newly resolved to see the project through, and he eagerly outlined other film ventures, too, noting that Third World Cinema might do *If Beale Street Could Talk* with Michael Schultz directing and Baldwin writing the screenplay. He was in high spirits about the work. He had realized that he would have to "do it myself" if he wanted any project to reach the screen, and he felt that he could, finally, focus entirely on film.[84] "Actually," he mused, "with two books coming out in a single year, and with <u>Beale Street</u> still working, I don't <u>want</u> to bring out another book for awhile. Which means that I may, at last, have bought the time I needed to work in films."[85]

Baldwin likely wrote *Beale Street* itself with the intention of bringing it to the screen, but at the very least, he saw the novel as an enabler: "It's funny, but it would appear that <u>Beale Street</u> will make it possible for us to do a lot of the things we wished to do long before I wrote that least 'controversial' of my novels."[86] In 2018, Barry Jenkins belatedly proved this true when his adaptation of *Beale Street* became the first of Baldwin's novels to reach the big screen.[87]

*****

Perhaps Baldwin's most explicit connection to visual mass media was as a subject. From his 1965 Cambridge University debate with William F. Buckley, Jr. to his regular appearances on television talk-shows, Baldwin became a media icon. So although he struggled to get behind the camera, he could at least share his perspective from in front of it. In documentary films from Pierre Koralnik's *Un étranger dans le village* (1962) to Richard O. Moore's *Take This Hammer* (1963) and Horace Ové's debut *Baldwin's Nigger* (1968), Baldwin collaborated with directors and appeared onscreen himself to explain, examine, and critique his world.

Of all the documentaries Baldwin collaborated on, *I Heard It Through the Grapevine* (1982) is both the most ambitious and the closest to Baldwin's own vision for film: using the medium to tell intimate stories with serious political stakes, in ways not typically seen in mainstream media. I therefore close this essay by narrating the making of *Grapevine* and reading both the film and additional interviews Baldwin conducted for it in order to show how Baldwin crafted a counter-media project and a revisionist history of civil rights through independent film.

In 1980, as Ronald Reagan and Jimmy Carter hit the campaign trail, Baldwin began his own road trip. Ostensibly on assignment for *The New Yorker*, and planning to write a book, too, Baldwin traversed the South to reflect on the gains and the stagnation of the civil rights movement.[88] He revisited key sites from Atlanta to Selma and reconnected with friends and activists, including Jerome Smith, Sterling Brown, and John Lewis. The husband-and-wife team of Dick Fontaine and Pat Hartley accompanied him with a small film crew, recording Baldwin's six-week journey and the hours of conversations he had along the way. *Grapevine* was the result.

Inspired by *No Name in the Street*, Fontaine envisioned *Grapevine* as a "Baldwin essay on film."[89] The film's thesis is, essentially, that only superficial changes have occurred. Baldwin calls Atlanta the world's best "make-up job," for example, and in New Orleans, he says that "Everything has changed on the surface, but nothing else has been touched. In a way, the state is more powerful than ever because it has given us so many tokens." Time and again, Baldwin expresses the feeling that he's only been gone from the South for a few minutes and has reentered the same conversations he was having in the 1960s. At one point, he reflects that "It is very bitter to have fought so hard for the vote only to enter the system and realize there is nothing to vote for," a stinging critique given the television footage of Carter's and Reagan's campaigns that we see Baldwin watching periodically throughout the film. In Eddie Glaude's words, Baldwin is preoccupied with "the complex relationship between history and memory ... as he witnessed the country's zealous embrace of Reaganism. So much was being willfully forgotten at a breathtaking pace, and just as much was being relived."[90] Fontaine initially pitched the film to Baldwin as a funded research trip, but it soon became much more, as Baldwin realized the power of telling this story in moving images.[91]

The film's historical consciousness develops through a series of visual juxtapositions, tacking between 1960s documentary footage, contemporary 1980s scenes, and intimate conversations between Baldwin and his longtime friends. Sometimes, the historical footage is intentionally jarring, as when a white sheriff calmly describes to television audiences the use of electric cattle prods on protestors. At other times, *Grapevine*'s editing emphasizes the seamless transitions between time periods, for example cutting, mid-sentence, from the activist Oretha Castle Haley speaking in 1980 to finish her thought with a speech she delivered in the 1960s as president of the New Orleans chapter of the Congress of Racial Equality (CORE). Similarly, when Baldwin crosses the Edmund Pettus Bridge into Selma, the site of Bloody Sunday, the film cuts between contemporary and historical footage of the city to suggest how the past still haunts the present. These visual effects and the film's elegiac lyricism are tightly tied to Baldwin's own running commentary and his bodily performance: it is very much his film. As Baldwin emphasized in a conversation with James Meredith, contrasting *Grapevine* with his Malcolm film, this time "the whole thing has been done from my point of view."[92]

Indeed, *Grapevine* is an intensely personal film, and it experiments with how to use such personal experiences to interpret history. It opens with Baldwin at his desk, paging through a book of documentary photographs, and as Glaude writes, "One can see the slight smile on Baldwin's face or the furrow of his brow as he pauses to look at a photo. He *feels* the images."[93] Then Baldwin reflects, in voiceover:

It was 1957 when I left Paris for Little Rock. 1957. This is 1980, and how many years is that? Nearly a quarter of a century. And what has happened to all those people, children I knew then, and what has happened to this country, and what does this mean for the world? What does this mean for me?

Baldwin's reflection on his photo album is metonymic of *Grapevine* as a whole: the film effectively sets those photographs in motion, treating them as a bridge between times rather than as remnants of a fundamentally different past.

Grapevine was also a family affair. Fontaine's close friendship with Baldwin's brother David "made a difference" for the author, who was initially "a bit reluctant" to trust a white British filmmaker, and once on the road, Baldwin found a kindred spirit in Fontaine's wife Hartley, a Black New Yorker. "He cared about us," Fontaine recalled. "Whether or not we were going to survive [as an interracial couple]."[94] And in the film itself, Baldwin visits Bunkie, Louisiana, his stepfather's birthplace, where he encounters, apparently for the first time, a photograph of his stepfather's half-brother, whose father was the white master of the house. "It was strange to see, in effect, your father in whiteface," Baldwin tells David. The camera slowly zooms in on the photograph, then cuts to a picture of Baldwin's stepfather, letting the first image linger. The slow dissolve produces a ghostly double-image, like a daguerreotype, creating a striking visual of the fundamental entanglement of white and Black America.

The heart of the film, though, is the bond between James and David Baldwin. David appears in most of the film's non-Southern scenes, which must have pleased his older brother, who always wanted to cast him in his movies, and over drinks at Mikell's in Harlem they reflect on Baldwin's trip South. Portions of their conversation at Mikell's appear throughout, forming the film's "spine," in Fontaine's words, and providing a narrative and expository framework.[95] Their easy rapport and

Figure 2   Screenshot from *I Heard It Through the Grapevine* (dir. Dick Fontaine, 1982) (Courtesy of the Dick Fontaine Paper and Film Outtakes Collection, 1960–1990, Harvard Film Archive, Harvard College Library)

sometimes elliptical discussions evoke the ambience of a home movie, and indeed, the intimate, semi-narrative style of *Grapevine* is itself a politics: a commitment to contesting the stereotypical images of Black life circulated by mainstream media and using the camera to record both the explicit and the subtle ways that America's history of racist violence continues to shape everyday life.

Weaving together personal and national memory, *Grapevine* seeks to inspire historical literacy in a period at risk of political quiescence. Hoyt Fuller, for example, tells an incredulous Baldwin about a recent exchange with one of his students at Cornell who had left a question on a quiz blank: when Fuller asked her to read it aloud, she admitted she had never heard of "Malcolm ten." But rather than offer a parade of facts, *Grapevine* advocates a more fundamental shift in perspective. In one scene on the road to Selma, for example, shot from inside a car, as the camera captures the rural highway scenery, Baldwin says, in voiceover, "When I first went South, I felt, I felt I had come home," and then, pausing, he continues, "You are aware of the trees. You are aware of how many of your brothers hung from those trees. In that landscape. Under that sky. And the people in that landscape have been doing that for generations. And may now do it to you." Sun streams through the window as he speaks, a juxtaposition that demands that viewers recognize the saturation of the landscape with racist violence. The film's interviewees share Baldwin's sense of urgency for circulating alternative perspectives on American history. Oretha Castle Haley, for example, says Baldwin's project has the potential to "teach and enable people to understand why things have happened" and to provide "a sense of renewal, a sense of re-dedication to the struggle that we are engaged in."[96] With its limited release, *Grapevine* probably wasn't quite so transformative, but the film, and Baldwin's oral histories for it, still represent an invaluable archive of political history and Black radical thought.

It's important to recognize, though, that only a fraction of Baldwin's recorded interviews made it into the film.[97] Some of the most searing political critiques were left on the cutting-room floor, including Baldwin's conversation with Ben Chavis, who had just been released from prison, the last of the Wilmington Ten. Archived transcripts reveal that Baldwin often spoke in terms of state-sanctioned "genocide" against Black Americans, rather than "racism," and that he argued that the civil rights movement was best categorized as the "latest slave rebellion," for "as Malcolm pointed out a long time ago, if you're a citizen you have your civil rights. If you don't have your civil rights, what are you … a slave."[98] Baldwin's criticism of politicians is similarly sharper in the archived transcripts: during his conversation with Chavis, for example, Baldwin repeatedly notes that Nixon was president during Chavis's unjust trial, and at one point he interjects, "I want to say one thing, about Mr. Nixon, I want to say, do not cut this out, Nixon was a kind of amateur Hitler."[99] The line, however, was cut. Fontaine later told Leeming that he had enough material for a four-hour film and that the final cut for British television was "too compressed,"[100] but even in its edited version, Baldwin was shocked that they let it air.[101]

The threat of racist violence wasn't only in the past, however. During Baldwin's opening remarks at a conference on African literature in St. Augustine, Florida, at the start of his trip for *Grapevine*, a man's voice interrupts over a loudspeaker, demanding, "You're going to have to cut it out Mr. Baldwin, we can't stand for this kind of going on."[102] Some of the audience members giggle in disbelief, while others look aghast, seemingly more from the impropriety of it than any real sense of danger. But Baldwin quickly grasps the lethal possibilities of the threat. Standing at the front of the conference room, utterly exposed, he refuses to step down, and with extemporaneous force, he declares,

> Mr. Baldwin is nevertheless going to finish his statement. And I will tell you now, whoever you are, that if you assassinate me in the next two minutes, I'm telling you this: it no longer matters *what* you think! The doctrine of white supremacy on which the Western world is based has had its hour—has had its day. It's over!

The audience then breaks into thunderous applause and leaps to its feet, at least sonically and symbolically sheltering Baldwin in an act of solidarity against a very present white supremacist menace.

In fact, a crucial feature of film, for Baldwin, was its capacity to carry political critiques to a global audience and thereby build solidarity. When Chavis details his unjust incarceration, for instance, Baldwin interjects: "I want you to explain on what legal pretext this could happen. We are talking to Tehran, we are talking to another country."[103] Similarly, in his conversation with Oretha Castle Haley, Baldwin emphasizes that "Malcolm and Martin were murdered at the point where they connected the black situation in this country with the non-white situation around the world. That was a terrible menace to the entire Western world."[104] And at the conference in St. Augustine, Baldwin meets the Nigerian novelist Chinua Achebe for the first time, leading to a moving picture of diasporic solidarity. Baldwin and Achebe visit a former slave market that later served as a Ku Klux Klan meeting place, and as they enter the open-air structure, Baldwin grasps Achebe's hand and proclaims that this was where they met four hundred years ago: "You were chained to me," Baldwin says, "And I was chained to you." Reflecting on the experience later with David, Baldwin explains, "There we were—together. It defeated a conspiracy that meant we should never be able to speak." For the writer and filmmaker Toni Cade Bambara, film was perfectly suited to forging such connections. "How shall a diasporized people communicate?" Bambara asked rhetorically. "Answer: independent films."[105] *Grapevine* suggests that Baldwin would have agreed.

Indeed, the finished film and Baldwin's archived interviews emphasize his commitment to making *Grapevine* a counter-media project, designed to circulate alternative images and narratives about Blackness in America and to equip audiences with a critical media literacy. In a scene in Oretha Castle Haley's living room, for example, Haley shows Baldwin the front page of the local newspaper, which features a sketch of a young Black man pointing a gun directly out at the

Figure 3   Screenshot from *I Heard It Through the Grapevine* (dir. Dick Fontaine, 1982) (Courtesy of the Dick Fontaine Paper and Film Outtakes Collection, 1960–1990, Harvard Film Archive, Harvard College Library)

reader. In his pupils, the artist has drawn skulls. The film then cuts from a close-up on the newspaper to a shot of Haley's young son, who is Black, and his white friend. The two boys peer around the doorway as Haley's son, with a mischievous grin, asks when dinner will be ready. Haley's expression in response is a complex mixture of amusement, weariness, and love that raises the question: what kind of world will her son be able to grow up in? And how can a media landscape that demonizes and endangers Black life be challenged and remade?

We get a sense of Baldwin's own answer to that latter question in his conversation with James Meredith, another interview that was cut from the film. The last time Baldwin had seen Meredith was when Baldwin was planning a film collaboration with Warren Beatty, and reflecting back on that project, Baldwin tells Meredith that "Warren is all right but Hollywood is a strait jacket. There's very little I can do in that framework."[106] Their conversation then turns to the popular television miniseries *Roots* (1977), based on Alex Haley's novel. They agree that the series has been oriented toward white audiences, and they are both "frightened" by its particular framing of Blackness and Black history. In a statement about TV that echoes his early film reviews, Baldwin then proclaims, "the phenomenon of television can distort everything, and it is really, I've begun to think more and more and more, one of the most effective ways ever devised to destroy history, to make everything unreal."[107] *Grapevine*, which was made for TV and centers on the recovery of familial and national history, aimed to accomplish just the opposite.

Throughout his career, Baldwin saw film as a powerful tool for forging connections and collectivity. In one scene in *Grapevine*, Oretha Castle Haley says, of her New Orleans community, "Many of us have lost contact with each other and within the past year, we were forced to recognize that we have got to come together to recognize what's going on." *Grapevine* implicitly argues that her sentiment applies to the Black community in the 1980s nationwide. So it's important that the very process of making the film became a way to build community: as Baldwin crisscrossed the country, reconnecting with activist friends, he recreated the grapevine, reestablishing many of their ties with each other. The film's initial screening was a similarly communal affair, held at Mikell's, where some of the film was shot, and attended by Baldwin's family and close friends, including Toni Morrison, Ossie Davis, and Max Roach.[108] *Grapevine* was then shown at the Film Forum Festival in New York and appeared on television in Britain and the United States. Today, though, it is extraordinarily difficult to see the film—it has become an archival object. But Harvard Film Archive is working to restore and re-release it.[109] If *Grapevine* was, in some ways, a realization of many of Baldwin's dreams for film, hopefully its re-release will build new communities. Such a project remains necessary today.

Acknowledgment

My thanks to Robert Jackson, Justin A. Joyce, Ed Pavlić, and Andrew Lanham for their very helpful comments on earlier drafts.

Notes

1 "James Baldwin will write and direct Miss Diana Sands in 'The Inheritance,'" advertisement, *Variety*, 17 May 1972, p. 23.

2 David Leeming, *James Baldwin: A Biography* (New York, Simon and Schuster, 2015), p. 316. Leeming is, to my knowledge, the only critic who has discussed "The Inheritance." His treatment is brief; he is primarily interested in possible connections between Baldwin's life and the screenplay's plot. For contemporaneous reporting, see Richard Lingeman, "American Notebook: Baldwin," *The New York Times*, 11 October 1970.

3 James Baldwin, "On the Horizon: On Catfish Row," *Commentary*, September 1959; James Baldwin, "Carmen Jones: The Dark is Light Enough" (1955), in *Notes of a Native Son* (Boston, Beacon Press, 2012), pp. 47–55.

4 Leeming, *James Baldwin*, p. 165.

5 James Baldwin and Hoyt Fuller, interview transcript, Box 15, Dick Fontaine Collection, Harvard Film Archive, Fine Arts Library, Harvard University.

6 Baldwin, *Notes of a Native Son*, p. 9.

7 Cassandra M. Ellis, "The Black Boy Looks at the Silver Screen: Baldwin as Moviegoer," in D. Quentin Miller (ed.), *Re-viewing James Baldwin: Things Not Seen* (Philadelphia, PA, Temple University Press, 2000), p. 190.

8 James Baldwin, *The Devil Finds Work* (1976) (New York, Vintage, 2011), p. 35.

9 For example, see Ellis, "The Black Boy Looks at the Silver Screen"; Ian Balfour, "The Force of Black and White: James Baldwin's Reflections in/on his Early Experience of

Film," *Critical Philosophy of Race*, 3:2 (2015), pp. 180–202; Ryan Jay Friedman, "'Enough Force to Shatter the Tale to Fragments': Ethics and Textual Analysis in James Baldwin's Film Theory," *ELH*, 77:2 (2010), pp. 385–411; Baldwin's hopes for film are also mentioned explicitly in Leeming, *James Baldwin*, p. 17.

10 James Baldwin, *Go Tell It on the Mountain* (1953) (New York, Vintage, 2013), p. 35.

11 *Ibid.*, p. 33.

12 *Ibid.*, p. 36.

13 *Ibid.*, p. 18.

14 *Ibid.*, p. 19.

15 *Ibid.*

16 There is an affinity between Baldwin's relationship to cinema and that of Virginia Woolf, who railed against the imitative dullness of the medium while also speculating about its yet-to-be-realized possibilities. Virginia Woolf, "The Cinema," *The Nation and Athenaeum*, 3 July 1926.

17 James Baldwin, *Another Country* (1962) (New York, Vintage, 1993), p. 3.

18 *Ibid.*, p. 283.

19 *Ibid.*, p. 328.

20 *Ibid.*, p. 329.

21 *Ibid.*

22 *Ibid.*, p. 330.

23 Baldwin was also writing "This Morning, This Evening, So Soon," a short story published in 1960, which details the collaboration between a film actor and his director. James Baldwin, "This Morning, This Evening, So Soon," in *Going to Meet the Man* (New York, Vintage, 1995).

24 James Baldwin, "The Northern Protestant," in *Nobody Knows My Name: More Notes of a Native Son* (1961) (New York, Vintage, 1993), p. 178.

25 *Ibid.*, p. 180.

26 *Ibid.* As novelist Randall Kenan notes, the film that Baldwin conjures at the end of his Bergman essay borrows from the plot of a novel he was working on. Kenan, "The Good Ship 'Jesus': Baldwin, Bergman, and the Protestant Imagination; or, Baldwin's Bitter Taste," *African American Review*, 46:4 (2013), pp. 701–14.

27 Leeming, *James Baldwin*, p. 167.

28 Letter from James Baldwin to Mary Painter, 10 May 1962, Box 2, Folder 7, Walter O. Evans Collection of James Baldwin. James Weldon Johnson Collection in the Yale Collection of American Literature, Beinecke Rare Book and Manuscript Library.

29 Peter Bart, "Baldwin Making Novel into Film; Author of 'Another Country' Signs to do Screenplay," *The New York Times*, 10 October 1964.

30 *Ibid.*

31 James Baldwin, *Little Man, Little Man: A Story of Childhood*, illustrations by Yoran Cuzac, ed. Nicholas Boggs and Jennifer Devere Brody (Durham, NC, Duke University Press, 2018), p. 40.

32 *Ibid.*, p. 12.

33 *Ibid.*, pp. 14, 13.

34 Baldwin, *The Devil Finds Work*, p. 9.

35 C. Robert Jennings, "Warning for Mr. Charlie," *Los Angeles Times*, 7 July 1968.

36 See, for example, D. Quentin Miller, "Lost and … Found? James Baldwin's Script and Spike Lee's Malcolm X," *African American Review*, 46:4 (2013), pp. 671–85.

37 James Baldwin, *No Name in the Street* (1972) (New York, Vintage, 2007), p. 99.

38 Leeming, *James Baldwin*, pp. 284, 288.

39 Miller, "Lost and ... Found?," p. 671.

40 *Ibid.*; Baldwin, *The Devil Finds Work*, pp. 99–103.

41 Letter from James Baldwin to Louise Meriwether, 22 September 1969, Box 1, Louise Meriwether papers, Emory University.

42 Baldwin, *The Devil Finds Work*, p. 99.

43 Jennings, "Warning for Mr. Charlie."

44 William J. Maxwell (ed.), *James Baldwin: The FBI File* (New York, Arcade, 2017), p. 311.

45 Letter from James Baldwin to Eugene Lerner, 13 January 1968, Box 2, Folder 9, Walter O. Evans Collection of James Baldwin, Beinecke Rare Book and Manuscript Library.

46 *Ibid.*

47 *Ibid.*

48 *Ibid.*

49 Interview with David Leeming and Sedat Pakay, May 1992, David Leeming Collection of James Baldwin Research. James Weldon Johnson Collection in the Yale Collection of American Literature, Beinecke Rare Book and Manuscript Library.

50 *Ibid.* Interview with David Leeming and David and Sharon Moses, 21 February 1989, David Leeming Collection, Beinecke Rare Book and Manuscript Library.

51 Jennings, "Warning for Mr. Charlie." A month previously, Baldwin published a profile on Sidney Poitier for *Look* magazine. Newly enmeshed in the Hollywood system, Baldwin uses his discussion of Poitier to work through his complex attitude toward his own similar position. He comments, for instance: "It takes a long time in this business, if you survive it at all, to reach the eminence that will give you the power to change things. Sidney has that power now, to the limited extent that *anyone* in this business has. It will be very interesting to see what he does with it." James Baldwin, "Sidney Poitier," *Look*, 32:15, 23 July 1968, p. 58.

52 Jennings, "Warning for Mr. Charlie."

53 James Baldwin, *One Day When I Was Lost* (1972) (New York, Knopf Doubleday, 2013), p. 5.

54 *Ibid.*

55 *Ibid.*

56 "God knows what they consider experience to be," Baldwin complained to Meriwether. Letter from James Baldwin to Louise Meriwether, 22 September 1969, Box 1, Louise Meriwether papers, Emory University.

57 Leeming, *James Baldwin*, p. 306.

58 Letter from James Baldwin to David Moses, 20 February [likely 1971], Box 1, Folder 2, James Baldwin, Letters to David Moses, Stuart A. Rose Manuscript, Archives, and Rare Book Library, Emory University. Access to much of Baldwin's correspondence is restricted, so his letters to Moses are especially important for piecing together this film history.

59 Magdalena J. Zaborowska, *James Baldwin's Turkish Decade: Erotics of Exile* (Durham, NC, Duke University Press, 2009), p. 33.

60 "James Baldwin's Own Paris Pix Co," *Variety*, 260:9, 14 October 1970, p. 1.

61 "James Baldwin's Own Paris Pix Co," p. 68; Ollie Stewart, "Report from Europe: James Baldwin turns to Movies," *Afro-American*, 24 October 1970.

62 Letter from James Baldwin to Mary Painter, 10 May 1962. Walker O. Evans Collection, Beinecke Rare Book and Manuscript Library.

63 Letter from James Baldwin to David Moses, 27 September 1981, Box 1, Folder 22, Emory University.

64 Letter from James Baldwin to David Moses, 20 February [likely 1971], Box 1, Folder 2, Emory University.

65 George Goodman, Jr., "For James Baldwin, a Rap on Baldwin," *The New York Times*, 26 June 1972.

66 Leeming, *James Baldwin*, p. 316.

67 Letter from James Baldwin to David Moses, [summer 1972], Box 1, Folder 4, Emory University.

68 James Baldwin, "In the Cross, A Trembling Soul: The Inheritance," screenplay, Box 14, Dick Fontaine Collection, Harvard University, p. 1.

69 *Ibid.*, p. 18.

70 *Ibid.*, p. 116.

71 *Ibid.*, p. 74.

72 Brigid is an international performer who uses that position as a platform for activism, representing a clear departure from the apolitical character Sands played in *Georgia, Georgia* (1972).

73 Letter from James Baldwin to David Moses, 27 September [1974], Box 1, Folder 16, Emory University.

74 *Ibid.*

75 *Ibid.*

76 Goodman, Jr., "A Rap on Baldwin."

77 Letter from James Baldwin to David Moses, 27 September [1974], Emory University.

78 *Ibid.* Baldwin did not, for example, appear familiar with *The Spook who Sat by the Door* (1973). In both his published work and correspondence, Baldwin's references are generally to Hollywood movies.

79 Letter from James Baldwin to David Moses, 27 September [1974], Emory University.

80 *Ibid.*

81 *Ibid.*

82 Letter from James Baldwin to David Moses, 4 January 1976, Box 1, Folder 19, Emory University.

83 *Ibid.*

84 *Ibid.*

85 *Ibid.*

86 *Ibid.*

87 In 1984, Stan Lathan directed a made-for-television film adaptation of *Go Tell It on the Mountain*.

88 The book was to be called *Remember This House*. The fact that Baldwin never finished it forms the premise for Raoul Peck's film *I Am Not Your Negro* (2016). Fontaine initially proposed a different kind of collaboration: he wanted to write a play that would "consist of images, scenes and narrative from all parts of [Baldwin's] work" and then film the production process. Dick Fontaine, "Tomorrow Brought Us Rain (treatment)," Box 28, Folder 1, Dick Fontaine Collection, Harvard University. Baldwin was initially intrigued by the idea, but when he saw the script in 1979, he took offense, apparently shouting at Fontaine, "I am *not* going to let you define me." Leeming, *James Baldwin*, p. 353. Baldwin did, however, trust Fontaine to make *Grapevine*.

89 Dick Fontaine, interview with David Leeming, undated, David Leeming Collection, Beinecke Rare Book and Manuscript Library.

90 Eddie S. Glaude, Jr., *Begin Again: James Baldwin's America and Its Urgent Lessons for Our Own* (New York, Crown, 2020), p. 152.

91 Dick Fontaine, interview with author, 12 February 2021; Fontaine interview with Leeming.

92 James Baldwin and James Meredith, interview transcript, Box 15, Folder 21, Dick Fontaine Collection, Harvard University. Fontaine told me that he generally avoided discussing Baldwin's previous film endeavors, since he "didn't want [them] to sour our experience" and instead wanted *Grapevine* "to have its own integrity." Fontaine interview with author, 12 February 2021.

93 Glaude, *Begin Again*, pp. 154–5.

94 Fontaine interview with author, 12 February 2021; Fontaine interview with Leeming.

95 *Ibid.*; Fontaine interview with author, 12 February 2021.

96 Oretha Castle Haley and filmmakers (Baldwin is not present), interview transcript, Box 15, Dick Fontaine Collection, Harvard University.

97 Fontaine had wanted Baldwin to talk with Rap Brown—to have a conversation with someone who wasn't necessarily his friend—but Baldwin was reticent, likely remembering earlier hostility toward him by Black radicals. Fontaine interview with Leeming.

98 New Orleans, Oretha meeting, interview transcript, Box 15, Folder 14, Dick Fontaine Collection, Harvard University.

99 James Baldwin and Ben Chavis, interview transcript, Box 15, Folder 4, Dick Fontaine Collection, Harvard University.

100 Fontaine interview with Leeming.

101 *Ibid.*

102 For more on this scene, see Ed Pavlić, *Who Can Afford to Improvise? James Baldwin and Black Music, the Lyric and the Listeners* (New York, Fordham University Press, 2016). Pavlić is one of the few scholars to have written on *Grapevine*; I am grateful for his encouragement to view the Dick Fontaine Collection.

103 James Baldwin and Ben Chavis, interview transcript, Box 15, Folder 4, Dick Fontaine Collection, Harvard University.

104 Baldwin in conversation with Oretha Castle Haley and Richard Haley, interview transcript, Box 15, Folder 16, Dick Fontaine Collection, Harvard University.

105 Toni Cade Bambara, "Reading the Signs, Empowering the Eye: *Daughters of the Dust* and the Black Independent Cinema Movement," in *Deep Sightings and Rescue Missions: Fiction, Essays, and Conversations*, ed. Toni Morrison (New York, Pantheon, 1996), p. 118.

106 James Baldwin and James Meredith interview, Box 15, Folder 21, Dick Fontaine Collection, Harvard University.

107 *Ibid.*

108 Leeming, *James Baldwin*, p. 353. D. A. Pennebaker ran the projector. Fontaine interview with Leeming.

109 "When James Baldwin Went South," *The New Yorker*, 17 September 2020, www.newyorker.com/culture/video-dept/when-james-baldwin-went-south.

Works Cited

Baldwin, James, *Another Country* (1962) (New York, Vintage, 1993).

_____ "Carmen Jones: The Dark is Light Enough" (1955), in *Notes of a Native Son* (Boston, Beacon Press, 2012), pp. 47–55.

_____ *The Devil Finds Work* (1976) (New York, Vintage, 2011).

_____ *Go Tell It on the Mountain* (1953) (New York, Vintage, 2013).

_____ *Going to Meet the Man* (1965) (New York, Vintage, 1995).

_____ *Little Man, Little Man: A Story of Childhood* (1976), illustrations by Yoran Cazac, ed. Nicholas Boggs and Jennifer Devere Brody (Durham, NC, Duke University Press, 2018).

_____ *No Name in the Street* (1972) (New York, Vintage, 2007).

_____ *Nobody Knows My Name: More Notes of a Native Son* (1961) (New York, Vintage, 1993).

_____ "The Northern Protestant" (1959), in *Nobody Knows My Name: More Notes of a Native Son* (New York, Vintage, 1993), pp. 163–80.

_____ *Notes of a Native Son* (1955) (Boston, Beacon Press, 2012).

_____ "On the Horizon: On Catfish Row," *Commentary*, September 1959

_____ *One Day When I Was Lost* (1972) (New York, Knopf Doubleday, 2013).

_____ "Sidney Poitier," *Look*, 32:15, 23 July 1968, pp. 50–8.

_____ "This Morning, This Evening, So Soon" (1960), in *Going to Meet the Man* (New York, Vintage, 1995), pp. 145–93.

Balfour, Ian, "The Force of Black and White: James Baldwin's Reflections in/on his Early Experience of Film," *Critical Philosophy of Race*, 3:2 (2015), pp. 180–202.

Bambara, Toni Cade, "Reading the Signs, Empowering the Eye: *Daughters of the Dust* and the Black Independent Cinema Movement," in *Deep Sightings and Rescue Missions: Fiction, Essays, and Conversations*, ed. Toni Morrison (New York, Pantheon, 1996), pp. 89–138.

Bart, Peter, "Baldwin Making Novel into Film; Author of 'Another Country' Signs to do Screenplay," *The New York Times*, 10 October 1964.

Ellis, Cassandra M., "The Black Boy Looks at the Silver Screen: Baldwin as Moviegoer," in D. Quentin Miller (ed.), *Re-viewing James Baldwin: Things Not Seen* (Philadelphia, PA, Temple University Press, 2000), pp. 190–214.

Fontaine, Dick, and Pat Hartley (dirs.), *I Heard It Through the Grapevine* (1982).

Friedman, Ryan Jay, "'Enough Force to Shatter the Tale to Fragments': Ethics and Textual Analysis in James Baldwin's Film Theory," *ELH*, 77:2 (2010), pp. 385–411.

Glaude, Jr., Eddie S., *Begin Again: James Baldwin's America and Its Urgent Lessons for Our Own* (New York, Crown, 2020).

Goodman, Jr., George, "For James Baldwin, a Rap on Baldwin," *The New York Times*, 26 June 1972.

"James Baldwin's Own Paris Pix Co," *Variety*, 260:9, 14 October 1970, pp. 1, 68.

"James Baldwin will write and direct Miss Diana Sands in 'The Inheritance,'" advertisement, *Variety*, 17 May 1972.

Jennings, C. Robert, "Warning for Mr. Charlie," *Los Angeles Times*, 7 July 1968.

Kenan, Randall, "The Good Ship 'Jesus': Baldwin, Bergman, and the Protestant Imagination; or, Baldwin's Bitter Taste," *African American Review*, 46:4 (2013), pp. 701–14.

Leeming, David, *James Baldwin: A Biography* (New York, Simon and Schuster, 2015).

Lingeman, Richard, "American Notebook: Baldwin," *The New York Times*, 11 October 1970.

Maxwell, William J. (ed.), *James Baldwin: The FBI File* (New York, Arcade, 2017).

Miller, D. Quentin, "Lost and … Found? James Baldwin's Script and Spike Lee's *Malcolm X*," *African American Review*, 46:4 (2013), pp. 671–85.

Pavlić, Ed, *Who Can Afford to Improvise? James Baldwin and Black Music, the Lyric and the Listeners* (New York, Fordham University Press, 2016).

Peck, Raoul, *I Am Not Your Negro* (New York, Vintage, 2017).

Stewart, Ollie, "Report from Europe: James Baldwin turns to Movies," *Afro-American*, 24 October 1970.

"When James Baldwin Went South," *The New Yorker*, 17 September 2020, www.newyorker.com/culture/video-dept/when-james-baldwin-went-south.

Woolf, Virginia. "The Cinema," *The Nation and Athenaeum*, 3 July 1926.

Zaborowska, Magdalena J., *James Baldwin's Turkish Decade: Erotics of Exile* (Durham, NC, Duke University Press, 2009).

Contributor's Biography

Hayley O'Malley is an Assistant Professor of Cinematic Arts at the University of Iowa. Before coming to Iowa, she was a Mellon postdoctoral fellow with the Black Arts Archive Sawyer Seminar at Northwestern University. She holds a PhD in English Literature and a certificate in African American and Diasporic Studies from the University of Michigan, and she holds a master's degree in Film Aesthetics from Oxford University. Her research and teaching focus broadly on African American literature, film, and visual culture, with a particular emphasis on Black feminist art and political thought. Her current book project, *Dreams of a Black Cinema*, is an archival history of the rich cross-pollination between African American literature and Black independent cinema since the 1960s. Her writing has been published or is forthcoming in *Black Camera*, *ASAP/J*, and the *Cambridge Companion to Contemporary African American Literature*.

ESSAY

Everybody's Protest Cinema: Baldwin, Racial Melancholy, and the Black Middle Ground

Peter Lurie   University of Richmond

Abstract

This article uses Baldwin's 1949 essay "Everybody's Protest Novel" to consider that literary mode's corollary in the 1990s New Black Cinema. It argues that recent African American movies posit an alternative to the politics and aesthetics of films by a director such as Spike Lee, one that evinces a set of qualities Baldwin calls for in his essay about Black literature. Among these are what recent scholars such as Ann Anlin Cheng have called racial melancholy or what Kevin Quashie describes as Black "quiet," as well as variations on Yogita Goyal's diaspora romance. Films such as Barry Jenkins's adaptation of *If Beale Street Could Talk* (2018) and Joe Talbot and Jimmy Fails's *The Last Black Man in San Francisco* (2019) offer a cinematic version of racial narrative at odds with the protest tradition I associate with earlier Black directors, a newly resonant cinema that we might see as both a direct and an indirect legacy of Baldwin's views on African American culture and politics.

Keywords: protest novel, New Black Cinema, melancholy, romance, "cinema of attractions," African American film

James Baldwin Review, Volume 7, 2021, © The Authors. Published by Manchester University Press and The University of Manchester Library
http://dx.doi.org/10.7227/JBR.7.7

The "protest" novel, so far from being disturbing, is an accepted and comforting aspect of the American scene ... Whatever unsettling questions are
raised are evanescent, titillating; remote, for this has nothing to do with us,
it is safely ensconced in the social arena, where, indeed, it has nothing to do
with anyone, so that finally we receive a very definite thrill of virtue from the
fact that we are reading such a book at all.

James Baldwin, "Everybody's Protest Novel"[1]

Spike Lee's films have a penchant for powerful opening and closing sequences.
While we likely expect this of any provocative or purposeful director, Lee's pictures show this tendency in particularly vivid ways, often as a result of his utilizing
found footage of events that he understands to have an unsettling effect. He
opened his 1992 *Malcolm X* with George Holiday's video of the Rodney King beating by the LAPD that had occurred the year before. During the final minutes of his
2019 *BlacKkKlansman* appears digital media coverage of the "Unite the Right"
rally that occurred in Charlottesville, Virginia, in 2017, including the impact of
the car that killed Heather Heyer.

The reasons for Lee including this material are clear. In the case of his biopic, he
sought to remind viewers that the biases surrounding Malcolm X's life, and that of
Martin Luther King, Jr., which resulted in both men's assassination, were still prev-
alent in 1992. Nearly thirty years later, telling the story of Ron Stallworth infiltrat-
ing the Ku Klux Klan, Lee telescopes from his protagonist in 1978 to the same
white supremacists' return to the contemporary political landscape—including
former Klan Grand Wizard David Duke, who is portrayed fictionally in the movie
but who appears in the Charlottesville footage at its end.

The opening of Lee's breakout feature, *Do the Right Thing* (1989), is different in
that nowhere in the film does he avail himself of the public digital archive (other
than the glancing appearance at the film's close of the famous photo of Martin
Luther King and Malcolm X together). Notwithstanding the fact that in 2014 Lee
rightly claimed that the picture's ending anticipated the death of Eric Garner in a
police chokehold, the film's account of Radio Raheem's murder and its other events
are staged.[2] The particular stylization of the film's *mise-en-scène*, like that of Lee's
movies generally, is important to this discussion, and I return to it below. At the
outset I mean to note only that Rosie Perez's duly celebrated appearance in the
opening titles dancing to Public Enemy's "Fight the Power" is of a piece with Lee's
urge toward engaging audiences with urgency and, as here, with a direct, frontal
challenge to their political awareness.

This is not to say that Lee's films in any way lack artistry. Indeed, his cinema
includes filmic images as powerfully rendered as those of any practicing director
and as aesthetically accomplished as the classical *auteurs*.[3] As is well known, Lee's
appeal is different from some of his earlier contemporaries in the New Black
Cinema, the 1990s movement that included directors like the late John Singleton,

the Hughes brothers, Mario Van Peebles, and Gary Gray. Singleton's *Boyz N' the Hood* (1991), released two years after *Do the Right Thing*, was notable for its direct account of violence, police surveillance, drug use, and loss in the Black community of South-Central LA. Both films were considered part of a then-vanguard of what critics dubbed "hood cinema" that showed viewers Black urban life in ways US film never had before. Yet unlike Lee, Singleton's style was not self-conscious or overtly artful, possessing a realism that impressed contemporary reviewers and influenced other directors who followed him.

To note that a filmmaker can be both political, even strident, while at the same time pursuing such aims with artistic subtlety is not a particularly new observation. Yet as my title means to imply, and as James Baldwin's observations about protest fiction help me argue, something important happens in the example of Spike Lee's films by way of this combination. Or rather, something *appears* to happen on the surface of the viewers' encounter with the film that agitates her or him, but that ultimately, Baldwin would suggest, leaves viewers with less than what Lee hopes to offer them, or even what some scholarly defenders see as his films' value.

I take up particular aspects and assertions from Baldwin's 1949 essay "Everybody's Protest Novel" below. At the outset, I mean these remarks to highlight the humanist, but always political, element of his thinking. Baldwin urges readers to see the striking, in his view often lurid, appeal of works that, however important or necessary their moral argument, appeal to a sense of outrage that renders their narratives, characterization, or even their language alien to what Baldwin calls "that truth, as used here, [which] is meant to imply devotion to the human being, his freedom and fulfillment."[4] Lest we confuse this with a bland, increasingly discredited classical or Enlightenment tradition defined by virtue of its whiteness, I point to Baldwin's own clarification of his terms. His argument "is not to be confused with a devotion to Humanity which is too easily equated with a devotion to a Cause; and Causes, as we know, are notoriously blood-thirsty." Baldwin points to the elusive figure (what literary theory might posit as the subject) he means us to seek as writers as well as readers of fiction: "He is … something resolutely indefinable, unpredictable. In overlooking, denying, evading his complexity," as Baldwin claimed the writers of the protest tradition did, "we are diminished and we perish; only within this web of ambiguity, paradox, this hunger, danger, darkness, can we find at once ourselves and the power that will free us."[5] It is this blend of the political, imaginative, and decidedly lower-case humanism Baldwin extols that I see more recent African American film demonstrate.

My consideration of Lee's films relates to the ongoing role of Baldwin in our broader understanding of Black-themed and -produced art. I offer Lee's particular example of an aspect of Black cinema that I associate with Baldwin's critique of the protest tradition because it helps me describe a quality that Lee's films lack, but that Baldwin's enormously sensitive thinking helps me identify as an element of other recent Black films. Of particular note is Barry Jenkins's 2018 adaption of Baldwin's *If Beale Street Could Talk* (1974), which I treat at length. I close my discussion with a turn to 2019's *The Last Black Man in San Francisco*, a film that, with

Figure 1   Screenshot from *Malcolm X* (dir. Spike Lee, USA 1992)

Jenkins's *Beale Street* and other recent pictures, shows a vital dimension in the contemporary cultural landscape of race that I trace to Baldwin's ethos.

Two moments from Lee's films serve to make my ancillary point. Oddly, they each involve the presence of a phenomenon that marks the Southern landscape and its history by which Lee is understandably troubled but which, as these examples suggest, holds a powerful visual fascination for him. Two of the most ravishing images in Lee's corpus involve the Ku Klux Klan. The earlier appears in the early section of *Malcolm X*, the flashback to Malcolm Little's childhood when he narrates the scene of the attack on his family. After an invading Klan set fire to the family's home and threaten Malcolm's father, a scene Denzel Washington narrates in flashback, the marauders flee on horseback "into the moonlight as suddenly as they had come." Accompanying this voiceover is the shot shown in Figure 1. Enveloped by the haunting choral voices on the soundtrack, this image is arresting, and its visual and aural splendor, appearing at the end of the Klan's violent attack, come as something of a surprise.

A later instance of this same kind of imagery is even more striking. It appears at the end of *BlacKkKlansman*, when Ron and Patrice are interrupted in Ron's apartment by an ominous knock on his door at night. Transitioning by way of one of Lee's signature rear-projection tracks, with the motionless couple appearing to move through space toward the viewer with their guns drawn, the sequence ends with a closeup on one of the Klansman contemplating his and his fellows' symbolic burning cross. Lee's camera lingers on the shot of the Klansman conspicuously, and the meticulous constructedness of its image compels our attention, as does the shot's duration. Seeing the detail of the burning cross reflected in the Klansman's eye, viewers are as mesmerized by this image as is he by the swirling conflagration. An image of pure hate, it is also groundless, in that we don't know

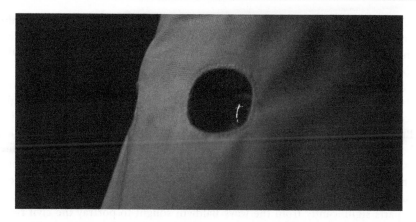

Figure 2   Screenshot from *BlacKkKlansman* (dir. Spike Lee, USA 2019)

where exactly the Klan gathering is taking place. Not purely fantastical, as we have encountered the Klan's activities earlier in the film, it is unclear what actual spatial or temporal link this image and the sequence of the cross burning has to the action of the film at this point. Such a free-floating image thus further captivates viewers who are encouraged to invest, we might even say cathect, in its reifying of white supremacist evil.

We might say that these shots exemplify what Todd McGowan, following 1970s and 1980s film theory, calls Lee's "cinema of excess" in his book-length study of the director. McGowan refers explicitly to the work of Stephen Heath, Roland Barthes, and Kristin Thompson.[6] Allowing for differences in their approaches, he nevertheless sums up their ways of conceiving filmic semiosis. "For each of them, filmic excess opposes itself to narrative and to signification; it is what doesn't have a clear function in the filmic narrative or a clear meaning for the film's signification."[7] While the Klansmen's action is part of the diegesis, Lee's rendering of it as a highly aesthetic spectacle is, indeed, in excess of its narrative function. As Baldwin wrote about the protest novel, the "dazzling pyrotechnics of these current operas" keep them from engaging with humanity in the terms he valued.[8] Though he writes about literature, such terminology is relevant to moments like these and others in Lee's cinema. At issue with them is, indeed, their momentary quality. Highly wrought and strikingly pictorial, they in fact extend their temporal moment and impede the film's narrative flow. Tom Gunning's early but widely influential model of the cinema of attractions described this spectatorial quality of early film, and other scholars have shown how it persists in particular genres or aesthetic gestures. Supercharged with the director's energy and Lee's visual flourish, such moments and the general mood of outrage they subtend are galvanizing. They are not, however, to again borrow from Baldwin, what he considers fully engaged in "devotion to the human being," either that of the work's characters or the reader/viewer's response to them.[9] As Baldwin says in "Everybody's Protest Novel," the "fulfillment" of a character, as of our response to them, depends on their "freedom" in becoming or change. Divested of narrative temporality as many moments in Lee's films are, they lock their images—and their subjects—into a languorous stasis, inhibiting the unfolding or developing self Baldwin sees as key to narrative art.

In this sense it is important to note that for *Malcolm X*, Lee worked from Baldwin's own original screenplay for Columbia Pictures about the civil rights icon. He credited Baldwin at certain points (though not at others), but when Baldwin's family saw the finished film years after the author's death, they asked Lee to remove any reference to him.[10] And this fact furnishes ground for other ways to distinguish Lee's filmmaking from Baldwin's ideas about Black culture and the protest tradition. Among other points I suggest below is the irony surrounding the fact that, despite Lee working from a Baldwin property, he departs significantly from the ways Baldwin sought to portray the civil rights leader. While there is little surprise in the fact of any screenwriter altering a script to her or his own creative vision, it is worth noting the ways that vision is at variance with the particular aspects of Malcolm that Baldwin worked hard to emphasize in his working script and, as he describes in his nonfiction, that he sought in general in his art.[11]

Baldwin wrote of his frustration with his Hollywood experience and his protracted and acrimonious conflict with the studio; it was a time he regretted bitterly. He refers to this singularly frustrating experience in *The Devil Finds Work* (1976) as "a gamble which I knew I might lose, and which I lost—a very bad day at the races: but I learned something."[12] The gamble Baldwin made was that he could depict Malcolm in the ways he wished and in a screenplay that was complicated, nuanced, and true to his vision of the civil rights icon. What he learned was that the studios then, as perhaps even now, were not interested in such an approach to narrating a Black subject.

Several critics have described Baldwin's work in Hollywood as well. Erica Edwards succinctly describes the nature of Baldwin's and Columbia's tensions, saying, "The source of conflict during what Baldwin calls his 'Hollywood sentence' was the incompatibility between Baldwin's fidelity to a multifarious, multilayered vision of Malcolm's life and [the studio's] desire for the sensationalistic story of charismatic leadership and interracial betrayal," and she refers to Baldwin's Hollywood clash as the

> conflict ... between the demands of realism and Baldwin's kaleidoscopic depiction of Malcolm's life. Baldwin mobilizes the flashback and the placement of mirrors throughout the script to produce a narrative that attempts to render Malcolm out of linear representation, disrupting the reader's—or viewer's—expectations for political leadership or cinematic closure.[13]

D. Quentin Miller makes similar observations about the differences between Baldwin's script and Lee's version of Malcolm's story. He shares Edwards's view, but he goes further, making some of the points I offer above about the tendentiousness of Lee's film and the ways they are at variance with Baldwin's whole approach to the screenplay.

In ways that Miller elaborates, Lee's film, produced and released twenty years after Baldwin published his Malcolm screenplay as *One Day When I Was Lost*, in fact realized the studio ambition. Miller relies heavily on Baldwin's description of his Malcolm script as a "confession," citing David Leeming's 1994 biography for this declaration.[14] Contrasting Lee's and Baldwin's sensibilities, Miller states, "Baldwin's use of the word 'confession' signals something crucial in his vision that cannot be accommodated by Lee's, or by any film. Confessions are public declarations of personal insights. Lee speaks of the Malcolm he *sees*, but Baldwin's Malcolm is *felt* as well as seen."[15] These claims echo my emphases above on Lee's cinema's supreme visuality, notable perhaps most troublingly in his elaborately constructed images of the Klan as part of his extended "vision" of Malcolm's life, indeed of the civil rights and Southern history Lee recounts across several films. Miller describes Baldwin's script in the ways Edwards does, contrasting "Baldwin's temporal experimentation" with the script against "Lee's relatively straightforward three-stage structure" and claiming, piquantly, that "Baldwin's inability to function within the Hollywood context and Lee's resistance to making a film true to Baldwin's vision are two sides of the same coin."[16] As Miller implies, that coin has Lee on one side, more closely aligned with the commercial imperative for a highly dramatic, forward-thrusting film with high production values and, on the other, an approach like Baldwin's, which we would more readily associate with the experimental or art cinema or even the essay film. Elsewhere Miller refers to Lee's film's "polemical excess" versus the way Baldwin's approach to Malcolm "is insistent, critical, and powerful, [but] without resorting to shouting" in the ways Lee's films so often do—recall Baldwin's account of the protest novel's "dazzling pyrotechnics."[17]

Recent approaches to racial narrative and Black-produced texts help illuminate this difference with an eye on Baldwin's relevance for our contemporary context. What my discussion will emphasize next is a tone that we find in Baldwin's thinking about Hollywood and the protest novel that also animates recent African American cinema, one that offers a decidedly different—but no less powerful— claim on Black agency than did the New Black Cinema. If the tone of such films is at odds with Lee's or others' more overt politics, there is still much to gain by attending to the ways these films register the concerns Baldwin raised in his "Protest Novel" essay as well as his fiction. Above all what they proffer is a version of African American subjecthood and experience that is no less insistent than Lee's, but they do so in a manner that acknowledges loss and longing as well as love in a timbre that differs from New Black Cinema in its vanguard.

As we've noted, Lee's movies and the imagery in them are disturbing. But this is true in ways that insist on their political meaning, or their political as well as aesthetic "positioning" with a stridency that prevents what Anne Anlin Cheng, in her book *The Melancholy of Race*, calls an "ethics" of response. Cheng is at pains to delineate politics and ethics. She opens her book by asking readers to ponder the question, "How does an individual go from being a subject of grief to being a subject of grievance?"[18] Availing herself of examples from two very different artists, Cheng meditates on Whitman's 1851 'Crossing Brooklyn Ferry' and Anna Deavere Smith's 1993 *Twilight: Los Angeles 1992*, and claims that they each pursue rhetorical modes that are exploratory and questioning about the premise of American conflict and union.[19] They both

> reveal from two historical vantages the fundamental history of loss and retention that finds and continues to sustain America. Smith's concluding urban vision … delineates a momentary negotiation, rather than erasure, of the past and future ravages of racial antipathy. In a world defined by sides, where everyone speaks in the vocabulary of 'them' vs. 'us,' not to take a side means to exist in an insistent, resistant middle ground that is also nowhere.[20]

Cheng's sense of a "resistant middle ground" is not an anodyne, timid non-position vis-à-vis the racial landscape. In her account of it as a "negotiation," she recalls Baldwin's insistence in "Everybody's Protest Novel" on the "void" from which "our unknown selves, demanding, forever, a new act of creation" as that "which can save us."[21] Lee's image of the Klan or his use of the most incendiary images from the racial archive—Rodney King's beating, the Charlottesville riot—present the "ravages of racial antipathy," as Cheng puts it in the passage above, in their baldest form. There is no negotiating with such images or with those in which Lee embeds them. Particularly in their aestheticized, spectacular aspect, they construct a rigidly demarcated space of separation between their content and the viewer. There is nothing "unknown" about this imagery and our relation to it or anything in it that would relate, as Baldwin avers, to "our unknown selves." Nor can such a cinema "save us" or allow or what Cheng calls an ethical response to a racially concerned art.

Cheng's question about grief versus grievance is important, and it allows me to turn to the recent adaptation of Baldwin's *If Beale Street Could Talk* and to other examples of racial melancholy they offer. Cheng avers that this shift

> from suffering injury to speaking out against that injury, has always provoked profound questions about the meaning of hurt and its impact. Although it may seem that the existence of racial injury in this country is hardly debatable, it is precisely at such moments when racial injury is most publicly pronounced that its substance and tangibility come into question.[22]

What Cheng and Baldwin's earlier challenge to the protest tradition suggests is that the "ravages of racial antipathy"—such as Baldwin saw in the protest novel and I describe in Lee's films—do not proffer a view of ourselves in relation to the larger world, one that includes seeing ourselves as (racial) subjects differently or in a way that we did not already.

Barry Jenkins's *Beale Street* operates differently from films like Lee's. The film is frankly, unapologetically romantic, opening on a lush overhead shot of a pastoral-seeming New York while Fonny and Tish walk hand in hand and kiss, a memory of hers from earlier in their life that segues by way of her voiceover to a contemporary scene when she tells Fonny of her pregnancy while he's in jail. Fonny's expression of concern at the news conveys the most elemental truths of his predicament, the simplest human fact of the challenges of impending fatherhood. That this fact is compounded by his circumstances—wrongly incarcerated due to his race—is the film's central concern, as it is the novel's. Yet Jenkins's manner of initiating the story does not create space between his characters and the viewer, but rather seeks a ground for them to share, "an insistent, resistant middle ground" in Cheng's formulation.

Among the ways Jenkins does this is by creating a particular kind of cinematic encounter for viewers. One way to describe this would be to say that, unlike Lee, who offers provocations and images before which viewers stand at a distance (and in awe), Jenkins's cinema draws viewers in. This is a banal-seeming observation and one that admittedly does not allow for the vast differences between subject matter or genre—the fact that Lee's epic biopic of Malcolm X or his dramatizing of Ron Stallworth's undercover infiltration of the Klan do not purport to offer intimacy with their protagonists. Yet Jenkins's choice, not only to present romance across a range of pictures including the *Beale Street* adaptation but also in *Medicine for Melancholy* (2008) and, in a different but no less plaintive way, in *Moonlight* (2016), is entirely to the point. Like other contemporary Black film artists—as well as many scholars working in critical race studies—Jenkins tarries with the elegiac or mournful in ways that 1990s Black directors wouldn't let themselves.

My account of *Beale Street* follows from the evocations and implications of Jenkins's use of cinematic time. For example, in an early scene of the couple's lovemaking, Jenkins offers a two-minute long single take of them in Fonny's apartment. The shyness and vulnerability they both feel is supported or "held" by this scrupulous editing, as Jenkins offers an intimacy and humanity that is the opposite of Lee's spectacular optical constructions. In a cinematic language that expresses one of Baldwin's precepts in his essay, Jenkins's film in these ways shows how "our humanity is our burden, our life; we need not battle for it; we need only to do what is infinitely more difficult—that is, accept it."[23] Jenkins "does" very little in such depictions of his characters; he accepts them and their life as lovers. In so doing he does what Baldwin does for his characters in his novel.

The extended take of the lovers' gentle touching is redolent of much. In the shot's duration and its closeness to the characters, it enacts what film theory calls "haptic" cinema, a practice that solicits viewers' full sensory engagement with the medium.[24] There is no nudity or anything exploitative or prurient; we don't exactly, or merely, "watch" the scene voyeuristically. In ways that are respectful as well as intimate, Jenkins allows viewers to share a spatiotemporal experience with his characters, to encounter their vulnerability and perhaps relive our own.

This quality of Jenkins's film is evident in other moments. The sequences of Fonny in his studio naturally seek to convey his engagement with his medium as a sculptor. In another extended take while he works on one of his pieces, we see

Fonny work on the woodblock from a camera angle that encompasses the entire space of the studio while he chisels. True to the period of the story's events, Fonny, like other characters throughout the film, smokes, and the wispy clouds he exhales, along with the sawdust he blows, suffuse the shot with another sensory element; we can practically touch or smell the atmosphere—or be touched by it.[25]

Baldwin himself refers to such a mode indirectly in his commentary on film in *The Devil Finds Work*, focusing on the matter of touch and its impact within film viewing that I emphasize here. He does so while speaking about an earlier picture, Lawrence Kramer's *The Defiant Ones* (1958), which starred Sidney Poitier and Tony Curtis as escaped convicts who must overcome their mutual racial enmity as they escape from prison. The film has long vexed scholars owing to its shallow liberalism and its strained ending, when Poitier's Noah gives up a chance to escape the sheriff's posse in order to help his ailing, newly embraced white "buddy." The film's muted account of what gender scholars would call its evident homosocial subtext prompted Baldwin to remark of the film, "I doubt that Americans will ever be able to face the fact that the word, homosexual, is not a noun. The root of this word, as Americans use it—or, as the word uses Americans—simply involves a term of any human touch, since any human touch can change you."[26]

Baldwin's focus is on the close of *The Defiant Ones*, which depicts the white and Black men in a literal embrace that is as sentimental as it was soothing to a burgeoning civil rights era audience. More recently Michael Boyce Gillespie comments on Baldwin's remarks about the film and refers to his claim for "the connotative capacity of touch" and the "mutuality and change that Baldwin" sees in it.[27] In the ways I've described *Beale Street*, in the long take of Tish and Fonny's lovemaking or of Fonny in his studio, in our encounter with the film as a form of touch—these aspects of it allow for a "mutuality" between its spectator and for change that, I use Baldwin to suggest, the visual adamancy of a director like Lee cannot.

Lee's visual acuity is among his art's accomplishments. And far be it from any scholar to impugn a cinema of powerful, evocative imagery. All films are supremely, if not above all, visual in their appeal, of course. And Jenkins's picture is no exception. His particular visual *mode*, however, including key elements of *mise-en-scène*, differs meaningfully from those examples in Lee I've cited. In my reference above to the quality of mutuality between viewer and film that defines *Beale Street*, I mean to refer to the combination of the personal, the "human," and the political—what Cheng might term "ethical"—that defines Baldwin's thinking about writing and race. This is Cheng's "middle ground" as well as that "something resolutely indefinable" that Baldwin posited against the surety of the protest novel and that, in Lee's example, I see in a cinema that proffers great beauty, but which often does so in the service of a strict separating of the viewer from the horror as well as grandeur of what is viewed. This is not a function of Baldwin's queerness, per se, or of Jenkins's sexuality as a cis director. Critics have, in fact, referred to Baldwin's "intersectional imagination" and to Jenkins's sensibility in rendering it onscreen. It is what Tre'vell Anderson, writing in *Out*, attributes to the filmmaker. He quotes Tarall Alvin McCraney, the author of the play *In Moonlight Black Boys*

Look Blue (the source for Jenkins's *Moonlight*), describing as an aspect of Jenkins's approach:

> It's profound how much [directors] don't pay attention to what's on the page ... but Barry pays attention to what's there, to what the feelings are of how the words come together to make a thing happen. He does deep dives into the nuance of language and that, in truth, is where the queer imagination lies. Because everything is how one sees the black and the white, but also the purple and the green.[28]

As Anderson goes on to say about Jenkins's ability to convey a queer subject, identity, or aesthetic, "It's this attention to detail that allows Jenkins to capture the essence of an experience unlike his own and transpose it in a way still authentic to its source."[29]

One way of defining Jenkins's "cinema of nuance" is by attention to color. Chromatic density varies across film stocks, including the many variations that a constantly evolving digital landscape includes. Jenkins's "palette" for *Moonlight*, for example, which he developed with his cinematographer James Laxton—who also shot *Beale Street*—and his colorist Alex Bickel, was decidedly diaphanous and shimmering, as critics have noted. Some of this undoubtedly owed to the film's approach to its subject, its novel account of Black masculinity on screen expressed in its title and in one character's memorable line (the source of the title of McCraney's play), "In moonlight black boys look blue." Jenkins's and Laxton's approach to *Beale Street* was different. There they used the digital intermediate (DI) process of restoring to their footage some of the properties of the Technicolor celluloid stock used in the 1950s melodramas that the movie emulates. The film's creators' enormous sensitivity to such modulations is evident in every shot, particularly in the dense chromatic richness of costuming, location, and the film's overall pictorialism. The matching yellow of Tish's dress with the autumn leaves in the opening and its reappearance standing out in subsequent dark, evening sequences; the teal green of Fonny's sweater; the predominance of a pattern like paisley; the deep red of the vinyl seats at the Greenwich Village restaurants where the couple and, later, Tish and her sister eat—these surfaces, textures, and materials of dress or décor are rendered in extraordinary depth and tacticity by the film's material workings. Telling Tish and Fonny's story, Jenkins does so in a manner similar to other directors such as David Lynch, whose own films' *mise-en-scène* has been described as effecting neuro-emotive responses in viewers that are like the sensations one feels upon falling in love.[30]

Scholars have commented on the uniqueness of Black screen romance. And their remarks are helpful to thinking through the particular aesthetic properties of Jenkins's film in relation to Baldwin's young lovers. Yogita Goyal writes in *Romance, Diaspora, and Black Atlantic Literature* about the dislocations of transnationalism but also the ways in which "the sign of Africa," whether referenced directly or proffered as a utopian "phantasm" of a racial future, features in Black art.[31] Her focus on the romance genre allows her to claim for it a quality that, I suggest,

Jenkins expresses in his film. She refers to romance as "a form that … helps black Atlantic writers collapse distances of time and space to imagine a simultaneity of experience."[32] Elsewhere, Goyal cites Baldwin directly as evidence of the writer's felt need to overcome isolation and the search for a sense of home. She refers to his essay "Encounter on the Seine" and "this depthless alienation from oneself and one's people [that] is, in sum, the American experience."[33]

The "whole" of what Goyal terms diasporic romance appears in the love scene with Tish and Fonny and in Fonny's studio in the means by which Jenkins renders them: the long take, the 360-degree spatial rotation.[34] In ways Goyal outlines about time, the novel and the film's displaced temporality allow Baldwin's narrative its "progressive history read backwards from a future point of redemption."[35] That futurity is intimated in the film's ending. Set in a prison visiting room, with Fonny having accepted a plea bargain and still incarcerated, the final scene might seem to undermine hope. Yet its tone is otherwise. Alonzo Jr. is drawing happily, his parents' love is still strong, and the Black family, which the film has exalted throughout its story by way of the Rivers' deep commitment to one another and to Fonny, will clearly flourish. Appearing at the end of a disjointed, often desperate narrative, this ultimately hopeful ending comports with Goyal's account of Black and diaspora romance. *Beale Street* may not recall the Middle Passage in the particular ways Goyal implies about African American literary romance. But the film's temporal breaks and discontinuities are, if anything, more dislocating of typical narrative "progress" than even those of the novel. And Goyal's reference to the Jubilee is implied in Jenkins's singularly bright outlook for his young couple.[36]

The nuclear family is not often the focus of African American film. Nor was it, we know, the specific subject of the protest tradition Baldwin questioned in his essay. But it is among the points of Baldwin's novel that Jenkins emphasizes. Tish ends her narration in the book lamenting the endless crying of her new baby. Here the writer seeks and finds a common humanist ground. The film's plot and its ending, especially, replay the novel's focus on generational ties, the "Jubilee" of its main characters' future life together after Fonny's release from prison— Jenkins's nod to contemporary enslavement in the prison-industrial complex. The prison sequence that ends the film plays out quietly, with the family saying grace together over the snacks Tish brought and Fonny teasing his son affectionately about the job he has so as to pay for them. If it is notable that Jenkins shows such regard for the characters Baldwin conceived, that is because it is only now that he finds himself able to do so. The success of *Moonlight* clearly played a role here, allowing the director to turn to material and to ways of presenting it to viewers that he might not have been as free to do prior to his film receiving the Academy Award for Best Picture in 2017. But to be able to adapt Baldwin's novel for the screen in the ways he does says much about changes in Black film in the most recent years.

One of those ways includes another notable break from not only other Black cinema, but from Baldwin's novel itself. Reviews of the picture were often strong. Some, however, took issue with Jenkins's notable departures from his source.

These critics felt that the director softened the novel's realism in several ways, including omitting Fonny's father's suicide and his friend Daniel's story of having been raped in prison. These are fair objections. Yet some of the same reviewers who pointed them out allowed that, notwithstanding these omissions, Jenkins's film offered something important in their stead.[37] I suggest that that something can be found in Jenkins's film and in a release that followed it, one that shares the political value of what Kevin Quashie calls Black "quiet," and whose thinking helps me draw the lines of my discussion together.

I turn in closing to another recent film, one released after Jenkins's *Beale Street* that bears no direct link to Baldwin. Yet its manner and its tone are close to aspects of Jenkins's film and to the questions I've sought to raise about the place in contemporary Black cinema for the nature of Baldwin's temperament as evident in some of the works I've mentioned. In particular it extends the note of melancholy and reflectiveness I've meant to stress in Baldwin's art and his legacy for recent African American cinema.

The film I refer to is Joe Talbot's *The Last Black Man in San Francisco*. Released in 2019, it received far less fanfare than Jenkins's *Beale Street*, his Oscar-winning *Moonlight*, and certainly than Lee's 1992 *Malcolm X* or most of Lee's films since. Talbot, who is white, wrote the screenplay based on a story by his Black childhood friend Jimmy Fails, with whom he grew up in San Francisco and who plays the lead character of the same name. Clearly the finished film is a collaboration between the two and is based on their shared experiences. And while there are no interracial relationships in the all-Black story, the fact of Talbot and Fails's shared investment in the film's story and its production allows a version of what some scholars have recently called for in defining African American film. Michael Gillespie, for example, calls for an entire redefinition of what he calls "film blackness" rather than Black film. In particular, he urges a turn toward the aesthetic and formal properties of film art that he describes as following, not from direct accounts of the Black "lifeworld," but from the variations in approaches to narrative, medium, image-making, and the film industry (with an eye on independent production) that have determined notions of "cinema" since its advent.[38] Gillespie's approach is enormously capacious while also extremely rigorous, and he offers the most compelling account for an approach to scholarship about African American cinema and art that we have. To do justice to his subtle yet vigorous recasting of a term such as "Black film" is beyond the scope of this discussion. Yet some of his key assertions are salient to Talbot and Fails's film as a legacy of Baldwin's call for an alternative to protest writing.

One way Gillespie orients his discussion is by way of earlier attempts at just such a reframing as his. Referring to Mark Reid's *Redefining Black Film* (1993), Gillespie sees great value in Reid's own call for a "guiding attention to polyphony" as well as to films made outside the commercial mainstream.[39] Yet he distinguishes his own approach from what he terms Reid's "prescriptive prerogative," asking, "Does any good really come from refusing to let art exceed your expectations?"[40] Gillespie's apostrophe, as I take it, addresses an interlocutor like Reid and other

Black scholars who define Black cinema by way of strict attention to its creators' race as determinative of a work's value. As he puts it,

> Black film offers a vast array of possibilities for conceiving race in creative terms, and film blackness follows through on that promise without devaluing a lifeworld or over-valuing an art. Film blackness restages the conceptual casting of blackness as equal parts thought, élan, aesthetic, and inheritance. This is not a simple matter, nor should it be.[41]

If we allow that Lee's artistry is formidable in his treatment of certain tropes—like the Klan—we can also say that such examples demonstrate "overvaluing an art" in his lavish, extravagant productions.

In something of a felicitous turn, Talbot and Fails, neither of whom had any filmmaking experience before the movie, got their start on making the picture after soliciting advice from Jenkins, who they knew had shot *Medicine for Melancholy* in San Francisco.[42] What specific input he offered is not known. What is clear is that the younger artists found something in Jenkins's approach to his filmmaking that imbues their own picture.

Gillespie does not discuss this affinity or Talbot and Fails's exchange with Jenkins. He does, however, refer to the city as Black *topos* in ways that describe elements of *The Last Black Man* that I mean to extol as an avatar of Baldwin's artistic and political ethos. He speaks, first, about San Francisco as a place in which the characters in *Medicine for Melancholy* experience "the rhythmic traces of histories and cultures" and "that produce the city as an affective phenomenon."[43] *The Last Black Man* is expressly about the city's histories: Jimmy spends the film trying to restore the home he believes his father built and where he grew up, but from which gentrification has displaced him. Gillespie's use of de Certeau's account of urbanism as a narrative space speaks directly to Talbot and Fails's story of Jimmy's displacement. De Certeau's musings on perambulation, loss, and urbanism offer terms that are suggestive of the dislocations Talbot and Fails trace in their film.

> [T]he geometrical space of urbanists and architects seems to have the "proper meaning" constructed by grammarians and linguistics in order to have a normal and normative level to which they can compare the drifting of "figurative" language. In reality, this faceless "proper" meaning … cannot be found in current use, whether verbal or pedestrian.[44]

Elsewhere de Certeau puts it concisely in ways that apply clearly to Fails's character: "To walk is to lack a place. It is the indefinite process of being absent and in search of a proper."[45]

Talbot and Fails open the film with its two main characters waiting for the bus after witnessing a young Black girl confront a white sanitation worker in a HazMat suit, then a local speechifier holding forth about racial inequity. They then effort-lessly glide to a neighborhood miles away, traversing well-known parts of San Francisco and encountering the range of ethnic, class, racial, and mental health conditions of the city's denizens. (Seeing the two men riding a skateboard together, one addled former hippie chases them while undressing and says, "Take me with you!") The San Francisco we see at the outset foregrounds what the dispossessed Jimmy has already experienced as what de Certeau calls "an immense social expe-rience of lacking a place," a fact that his hostile encounters with the white occu-pants of his former home later in the film make clear.[46] The film's sorrowful, tuba-accompanied rearrangement of Scott McKenzie's 1960s anthem "Are You Going to San Francisco?" further layers the city's history into Talbot and Fails's depiction of its wandering protagonist.[47]

Perhaps more important is the role in the story of Kevin Quashie's notion of "quiet." In his *The Sovereignty of Quiet: Beyond Resistance in Black Culture*, Quashie begins by urging readers to see the inexpressed interiority of iconic moments of Black resistance that are often overlooked. Referring to the endless repetition of the photo of Tommie Smith's and John Carlos's raised fists at the 1968 Olympics, Quashie asks us to note the fact that both men are also at the same time praying. "In truth the beauty of the protest is enhanced by noting the intimacy, in reading Smith and Carlos not only as soldiers in a larger war against oppression but also as two people in a moment of deep spirituality, in prayer, as vulnerable as they are aggressive."[48] Echoing the tone and very nearly the language of Baldwin's "Protest Novel" essay, Quashie writes of the athletes, "what is compelling is their humanity on display, the unexpected glimpse we get of the inner dimensions of their public bravery."[49] Most relevant to my earlier discussion of Spike Lee, and in ways that point a way forward to my final observations about Baldwin's legacy in contempo-rary film, Quashie asserts:

> As an identity, blackness is always supposed to tell us something about race or racism, or about America, or violence and struggle and triumph over poverty and hopeful-ness. The determination to see blackness only through a social public lens, as if there were no inner life, is racist ... But it has also been adopted by black culture ... it creeps into the consciousness of the black subject, especially the artist, as the imperative to represent. Such expectation is part of the inclination to understand black culture through the lens of resistance.[50]

If such views seem apt for thinking about Lee in the ways I have suggested, they also clear a path for the heretofore anomalous character of Jimmy Fails in his and Talbot's film. Such quiet "vagary" as Quashie calls for defines Jimmy throughout. He rarely raises his voice; often scenes reveal him looking at his surroundings rather than acting on them or with others. His very name carries the sense of mel-ancholy or disappointment that seems etched in, not only his face, but his move-ments and an unspoken, but nonetheless movingly conveyed interiority.

Yet Jimmy's quiet should not be mistaken for quietude, as least not in a political sense. His performance and the film's understated mood are the opposite of Spike Lee's or other protest directors' version of "public Blackness," fully formed positions and subjectivities that they pit against forces of oppression or specific white or same-race antagonists (as in the "hood" pictures). Very little happens in his and Talbot's film. It includes scenes of Jimmy and his friend Monte, an artist and aspiring playwright, watching movies with Jimmy's blind father, and its "climax" is Monte's late mounting of his long-gestating play, staged in Jimmy's old Victorian house. It is here, finally, in Jimmy's striving, his state of "becoming" rather than an active, decisive, oppositional *being* that he offers what Baldwin sought long ago in questioning the long protest tradition that extended from *Uncle Tom's Cabin* through *Native Son* and, I suggest, Spike Lee's early films, including his "breakout" picture *Do the Right Thing*. Jimmy Fails, Monte, and the forlorn scene they inhabit in San Francisco conjure what in the protest essay Baldwin calls the "void, our unknown selves, demanding, forever, a new act of creation."[51] That new act includes the making and collective viewing of Talbot and Fails's and Jenkins's films, as well as those of many others who furnish glimpses of Black melancholy or becoming: Jordan Peele with *Get Out* (2017), Lee Daniels with *Precious* (2009), Jenkins's earlier films, including *Medicine for Melancholy* as well as *Moonlight*, and Regina King's *One Night in Miami* (2020). This is a cinematic tradition at odds with earlier films such as those that defined New Black Cinema but one which, I suggest, emerges from Baldwin's example and his work.

Talbot and Fails made a deeply personal movie. Despite Talbot's role, it can hardly be accused of "devaluing [the] lifeworld" of its Black characters, including Fails, playing a version of himself as a displaced, wistful young man confronting gentrification in one of the world's most expensive cities. In addition to his friend Monte, there are other characters present on the film's—but not the city's—margins, notably a group of young men who have appeared as seminal types in cycles like the 1990s films of the New Black Cinema. In one of the movie's many willful subversions of Black film and its capacity to "let art exceed your expectations," these tertiary figures appear initially as they have in other representations: menacing, sullen, confrontational. Jimmy interacts with them at points throughout the movie. They are familiar with one another, and he and Monte communicate in both the group's street vernacular and in their own uninflected, standard locution. At one moment, we see Monte in an exchange with the nameless men he and Jimmy encounter periodically on the street. "You're doing marvelous work," he tells them, commenting on the performative nature of their "street theater" personae. "Remember Stanislavski, Gratowski," he urges. "I believe you. But we can go deeper."

In an astonishing sequence late in the film, the two friends come upon the group as described above. And in it, they and the film "go deeper" indeed. They gang-like members are silently milling; something bad has clearly happened. When Jimmy queries them with a powerful demand that they explain what's going on, we glean the cause of their sullenness: one of their members has been shot and

Figure 3   Screenshot from *The Last Black Man in San Francisco* (dir. Joe Talbot, USA 2019)

killed. What ensues is what appears initially as a standard male challenge, one the filmmakers structure deliberately to elicit foreboding and suggest incipient violence. When Jimmy calls out angrily that it was "your fault" that their mutual friend died, one of the group's members approaches him while Monte looks on uneasily. While each character directs vitriol and the n-word at the other, with the gang intoning off-screen "You going to let him say that?," Jimmy confronts his antagonist in close up. The next moment in the sequence stuns. Recalling Anne Cheng's question, "How does an individual go from being a subject of grief to being a subject of grievance?", the film here reverses the question, as Jimmy's challenger suddenly collapses on his shoulder, weeping. The subject of grievance (or anger or of demanding redress) becomes a subject of grief, a mournful, weeping intimate.

Embracing the sobbing man, with the others in the group emoting and Monte bowing his head, Jimmy's position and the sequence are ultimately more faithful to the Black "lifeworld" than we had been led to expect by the editing, the content, and the backdrop of what I began this essay calling a kind of protest movie in the New Black Cinema and the films of Spike Lee. These characters change before our eyes in that they defy convention and what we—or they themselves—expect of certain screen personae or types. This is also the *temporal* becoming and what in the essay Baldwin calls a human "fulfillment" that a cinema of spectacle or protest would deny.

This moment is not the ending of the film. I close with it, however, because it offers a way to see *The Last Black Man* revise aspects of race relations and racial solidarity that in Baldwin's work remained vexed—such as his meeting the French Algerian man in "Encounter on the Seine" or his troubled time in

Hollywood working on the Malcolm X script. An important element of this sequence, and part of the Baldwinian echoes of Talbot and Fails's film, is what it allows for mutuality, for recognition, for what Baldwin in the "Protest Novel" essay called characters' as well as our "freedom." The "gangsters" in the film are not bound by their partial resemblance to similar characters in earlier movies or their counterparts in US cities. And unlike what Tom Gunning might call Spike Lee's use of a cinema of "attractions" in his films' reliance on spectacle, Talbot and Fails offer a film that, in moments like this, literally relies on the sense of touch, on a conjoining of its characters and, with them, the spectator who partakes of their physical and spatial intimacy. Like the interracial male bonding at the end of *The Defiant Ones*, this moment shows a reconciliation. Unlike in *The Defiant Ones*, the intraracial moment of unity here is plausible—if we follow Baldwin's call for an art that renders its subjects in their most basic human state. Jimmy's anger at the start of the scene that led to the seeming confrontation is evident, and it is the only moment in the movie when he expresses a "grievance." But it is not one based only on a racial subjectivity. As he declares, asking for an answer to what happened, "He was my friend too!" That claim demands a response. And the reaction he gets involves a moment of Black sympathy and affection rather than outrage.

That response involves our own encounter with a moment of affect and mutual support. Finding ourselves again in intense proximity to the characters, as we were in Tish and Fonny's love scene in *Beale Street*, lingering with them as they absorb and respond to the other's presence, we become imbricated into the characters' spatial awareness in San Francisco, the scene of so much displacement in the film's diegesis and in Talbot and Fails's experience—like that of so many of the city's denizens. The scene in *The Last Black Man* essays a unity between its characters, who arrive in the diegetic space from very different backgrounds. Yet through the film's workings, they manage a profound connection, despite other than racial differences (here class and, potentially, education). They strike, that is, a positive diasporic note that was missing in *Beale Street*. When Sharon travels to Puerto Rico to confront Victoria Rogers about her false accusation against Fonny, she fails; cross-racial unity in Baldwin's vision for his novel world was not fully possible.[52] While the scene in *The Last Black Man* is not interracial, its evidence of overcoming class and educational distinctions allows it a meaningful hope. The diaspora romance Baldwin imagined for the novel version of *Beale Street* extended into Jenkins's adaptation, as we noted. It also recurs here, though, in the later film's vision of Black connectedness. At the close of "Everybody's Protest Novel," Baldwin writes, "The failure of the protest novel lies in its rejection of life, the human being, dread, power, in its insistence that it is his categorization alone which is real and which cannot be transcended."[53] Baldwin's fiction showed such a transcendence for his Black women and men. So too do examples like Jenkins's and other recent films, including *The Last Black Man* and its tarrying with both grief and grievance. In the work of film artists who followed Baldwin, both those who were directly influenced by his work as well as others who shared his convictions, we see what is real about the Black lifeworld and what aspects of it—and of its earlier representation in film—can be transcended, both within the worlds of the films and, with Baldwin's urging in mind, possibly without.

Notes

1 James Baldwin, "Everybody's Protest Novel," in *Notes of a Native Son* (Clinton, MA, The Colonial Press, 1955), p. 19.

2 Lee made this claim in a 2019 interview in the *New York Daily News*, among other places. See Leonard Greene, "'We Had the Crystal Ball': 30 Years Later, Spike Lee's *Do the Right Thing* Stands the Test of Time," *New York Daily News*, 23 June 2019, www.nydailynews.com/new-york/ny-spike-movie-anniversary-20190623-sa5ocpsmgfht-de4nnnuzx7wzqm-story.html (accessed 4 April 2021). Following the death of George Floyd in 2020 he also released a 94-second video titled "Will History Stop Repeating Itself" that splices footage of Garner's and Floyd's deaths into the sequence of Radio Raheem being killed from his film.

3 Paula Massood describes this aspect of Lee's films, saying, "This formal experimentation, influenced by global cinema movements, remains one of the characteristics of the director's filmmaking and explicitly marks some of his films, such as *Summer of Sam*, which is just as much about Scorsese's New York from the 1970s as it is about the Son of Sam murders from 1977." Massood, "Introduction," in Paula Massood (ed.), *The Spike Lee Reader* (Philadelphia, PA, Temple University Press, 2007), p. xvii.

4 Baldwin, "Everybody's Protest Novel," p. 15.

5 *Ibid.*

6 Others have written insightfully about film spectacle and theorized its impact on viewers' encounter with narrative content. See Yvonne Trasker, *Action and Adventure Cinema* (Malden, MA, Wiley-Blackwell, 2015), including her remarks about the various kinds of spectacle that appear in different genres such as the war film or the musical. Carol Clover's considerations of victimhood in horror films relevant to viewers' positionality and the "politics of displacement" in *Men, Women, and Chain Saws: Gender in the Modern Horror Film* (Princeton, NJ, Princeton University Press, 2015) are apposite here, as are Linda Williams's observations about the Lumiérè brothers' *actualités* evoking a spectacle "bordering on terror" in *Viewing Positions: Ways of Seeing* (New Brunswick, NJ, Rutgers University Press, 1995).

7 Todd McGowan, *Spike Lee* (Champaign, IL, University of Illinois Press, 2012), p. 4. Mary Ann Doane, too, in her theorizing of spectatorship, emphasizes moments such as this that draw specific attention to themselves as imagery in ways that arrest/suspend narrative temporality. See Doane, *Femmes Fatales: Feminism, Film Theory, Psychoanalysis* (London, Routledge, 1991), particularly her chapter on G. W. Pabst's *Pandora's Box*, "The Erotic Barter."

8 Baldwin, "Everybody's Protest Novel," p. 19.

9 *Ibid.*, p. 15.

10 Ashley Clark, "The Devil Finds Work: James Baldwin on Film," *Film Comment*, 11 September 2015, www.filmcomment.com/blog/the-devil-finds-work-james-baldwin-on-film/ (accessed 4 April 2021).

11 Reginia King's *One Night in Miami* (2020), from Kemp Powers's play of the same name, offers a portrait of Malcolm X that allows excesses and genuine vulnerability in his

personality and interactions (emphasized movingly in Kingsley Ben-Adir's performance), elements of the film that Baldwin might have admired. I am thankful to this special issue's editor, Robert Jackson, for urging me to highlight the ironies attending Lee's use of Baldwin's script.

12 James Baldwin, *The Devil Finds Work* (1976) (New York, Vintage, 2011), p. 99.

13 Erica Edwards, "Baldwin and Black Leadership," in Michele Elam (ed.), *The Cambridge Companion to James Baldwin* (Cambridge, Cambridge University Press, 2015), p. 160.

14 Quentin D. Miller, "Lost and … Found?: James Baldwin's Script and Spike Lee's *Malcolm X*," *African American Review*, 46:4 (2013), p. 672.

15 *Ibid.*

16 *Ibid.*

17 *Ibid.*, pp. 673, 672.

18 Ann Anlin Cheng, *The Melancholy of Race: Psychoanalysis, Assimilation, and Hidden Grief* (Oxford, Oxford University Press, 2000), p. 3.

19 It is worth noting that Deavere Smith's play opened the year after the Rodney King beating. Yet, unlike Lee's *Malcolm X*, it is closer in tone or approach to what I mean to attribute to Baldwin's Malcolm script or to later African American cinema that, I suggest, more closely evinces Baldwin's ethos.

20 Cheng, *The Melancholy of Race*, p. 194.

21 Baldwin, "Everybody's Protest Novel," pp. 20–1.

22 Cheng, *The Melancholy of Race*, p. 3.

23 Baldwin, "Everybody's Protest Novel," p. 23.

24 See Vivian Sobchack, "What My Fingers Knew: The Cinesthetic Subject, or Vision in the Flesh," in her *Carnal Thoughts: Embodiment and Moving Image Culture* (Berkeley, CA, University of California Press, 2004), and Laura U. Marks, *The Skin of the Film: Intercultural Cinema, Embodiment, and the Senses* (Durham, NC, Duke University Press, 1999).

25 An inveterate smoker himself, Baldwin flourished his cigarette as part of his own artful rhetoric in his appearance on the *Dick Cavett Show* in May of 1969 and in many other public arenas in the same period as the film and his novel's events. In these ways his presence may be said to infuse Jenkins's highly sensuous movie.

26 Baldwin, *The Devil Finds Work*, p. 69.

27 Michael Boyce Gillespie, *Film Blackness: American Cinema and the Idea of Black Film* (Durham, NC, Duke University Press), p. 113.

28 See Tre'vell Anderson, "How a Straight Man is Telling Well-Rounded Queer Stories in Hollywood," *Out*, 14 December 2008, www.out.com/entertainment/2018/12/14/how-straight-man-telling-queer-stories-hollywood (accessed 15 June 2021).

29 *Ibid.*

30 The chromatic intensity of Lynch's *mise-en-scène* in films such as *Mulholland Drive*, as well as his films' emotional intensity, has also been seen as the director's debt to 1950s cinema, a point of contact or affinity, then, between Lynch and Jenkins's work on *Beale Street*. For more on the emotive visual design at work, see Justus Nieland, *David Lynch* (Champaign, IL, University of Illinois Press, 2012), p. 96.

31 Yogita Goyal, *Romance, History, and Black American Literature* (Cambridge, Cambridge University Press, 2010), p. 8.

32 *Ibid.*, p. 9.

33 James Baldwin, "Encounter on the Seine: Black Meets Brown," in *Collected Essays*, ed. Toni Morrison (New York, Library of America, 1998), p. 89, quoted in Yogita Goyal,

"Introduction: The Transnational Turn," in Yogita Goyal (ed.), *The Cambridge Companion to Transnational American Literature* (Cambridge, Cambridge University Press, 2017), p. 3.

34 Goyal, *Romance, History, and Black American Literature*, p. 10.

35 *Ibid.*, p. 10.

36 Brian Norman describes Baldwin's effort in *Beale Street* to restore "an African American family destroyed by the practices of the US judicial system," an aspect of the novel I see Jenkins take up in particular ways. See "James Baldwin's Confrontation with U.S. Imperialism," *MELUS*, 32:1 (2007), p. 132. Michael Gillespie cites Goyal in terms that are relevant to the temporal disjunctions of *Beale Street* and to my point about the film's end (*Film Blackness*, pp. 134–5).

37 Doreen St. Felix asks whether including a scene relaying Fonny's father's suicide would have made it a "vastly different, and perhaps, better film," and says that Jenkins might have "shave[d] away the spikes of the original text." Yet she allows that even Baldwin himself wrote that the adaptations were necessary in *The Devil Finds Work* and sees Jenkins convey the novel's darker details while not inflicting "more of the pain we've already endured." Doreen St. Felix, "Can We Trust the Beauty of Barry Jenkins's *If Beale Street Could Talk*?," *The New Yorker*, 21 December 2018, https://www.newyorker.com/culture/cultural-comment/can-we-trust-the-beauty-of-barry-jenkinss-if-beale-street-could-talk (accessed 4 April 2021).

38 See Gillespie, *Film Blackness*, introduction and *passim*.

39 *Ibid.*, p. 10. Reid's book was contemporaneous with the New Black Cinema of Lee, Singleton, and the Hughes brothers, and it shared with some films of the movement a limited approach to gender, evident in Black feminists' ire over Lee's treatment of women in his early films.

40 *Ibid.*, p. 10.

41 *Ibid.*, p. 11.

42 See Lindsey Bahr, "The Newcomers Behind *The Last Black Man in San Francisco*," *AP News*, 13 June 2019, https://apnews.com/article/24f15b705fb84e8da325868c96045311 (accessed 4 April 2021).

43 Gillespie, *Film Blackness*, p. 120.

44 Michel de Certeau, *The Practice of Everyday Life*, trans. Steven Rendall (Berkeley, CA, University of California Press, 1984), p. 100.

45 *Ibid.*, p. 103.

46 *Ibid.*

47 Talbot solicited the singer Michael Marshall to perform the vocals and, in a particularly purposeful addition, commissioned the Norwegian jazz musician Daniel Herkedal to play the tuba in a manner that resembled the foghorns on San Francisco Bay near the Black Hunters Point neighborhood, where Talbot and Fails spent time together growing up and where many of the film's events take place. See Eric Ducker, "How *The Last Black Man in San Francisco* Soundtrack Reshapes the City's Hippie Nostalgia," *Pitchfork*, 17 June 2019, https://pitchfork.com/thepitch/the-last-black-man-in-san-francisco-soundtrack-reshapes-the-citys-hippie-nostalgia-joe-talbot-interview/ (accessed 4 April 2021).

48 Kevin Quashie, *The Sovereignty of Quiet: Beyond Resistance in Black Culture* (New Brunswick, NJ, Rutgers University Press, 2012), p. 3.

49 *Ibid.*, p. 3.

50 *Ibid.*, p. 4.

51 Baldwin, "Everybody's Protest Novel," p. 20.

52 Norman notes that Tish does experience something of this aim on her prison visits, where she encounters Puerto Rican mothers of inmates who are quite warm to her and call her "Daughter" (Norman, "James Baldwin's Confrontation with U.S. Imperialism," pp. 123–6).
53 Baldwin, "Everybody's Protest Novel," p. 23.

Works Cited

Anderson, Tre'vell, "How a Straight Man is Telling Well-Rounded Queer Stories in Hollywood," *Out*, 14 December 2008, www.out.com/entertainment/2018/12/14/how-straight-man-telling-queer-stories-hollywood (accessed 15 June 2021).

Bahr, Lindsey, "The Newcomers Behind *The Last Black Man in San Francisco*," *AP News*, June 2019, https://apnews.com/article/24f15b705fb84e8da325868c96045311 (accessed 4 April 2021).

Baldwin, James, *The Devil Finds Work* (1976) (New York, Vintage, 2011).

_____ "Encounter on the Seine: Black Meets Brown," in *Collected Essays*, ed. Toni Morrison (New York, Library of America, 1998), pp. 85–90.

_____ "Everybody's Protest Novel" (1949), in *Notes of a Native Son* (Clinton, MA, The Colonial Press, 1955), pp. 13–23.

Cheng, Ann Anlin, *The Melancholy of Race: Psychoanalysis, Assimilation, and Hidden Grief* (Oxford, Oxford University Press, 2000).

Clark, Ashley, "The Devil Finds Work: James Baldwin on Film," *Film Comment*, 11 September 2015, www.filmcomment.com/blog/the-devil-finds-work-james-baldwin-on-film/ (accessed 4 April 2021).

Clover, Carol, *Men, Women, and Chain Saws: Gender in the Modern Horror Film* (Princeton, NJ, Princeton University Press, 2015).

de Certeau, Michel, *The Practice of Everyday Life*, trans. Steven Rendall (Berkeley, CA, University of California Press, 1984).

Doane, Mary Ann, *Femmes Fatales: Feminism, Film Theory, Psychoanalysis* (London, Routledge, 1991).

Ducker, Eric, "How *The Last Black Man in San Francisco* Soundtrack Reshapes the City's Hippie Nostalgia," *Pitchfork*, 17 June 2019, https://pitchfork.com/thepitch/the-last-black-man-in-san-francisco-soundtrack-reshapes-the-citys-hippie-nostalgia-joe-talbot-interview/ (accessed 4 April 2021).

Edwards, Erica, "Baldwin and Black Leadership," in Michele Elam (ed.), *The Cambridge Companion to James Baldwin* (Cambridge, Cambridge University Press, 2015), pp. 150–63.

Gillespie, Michael Boyce, *Film Blackness: American Cinema and the Idea of Black Film* (Durham, NC, Duke University Press, 2016).

Goyal, Yogita, "Introduction: The Transnational Turn," in Yogita Goyal (ed.), *The Cambridge Companion to Transnational American Literature* (Cambridge, Cambridge University Press, 2017), pp. 1–16.

_____ *Romance, History, and Black American Literature* (Cambridge, Cambridge University Press, 2010).

Greene, Leonard, "'We Had the Crystal Ball': 30 Years Later, Spike Lee's *Do the Right Thing* Stands the Test of Time," *New York Daily News*, 23 June, 2019, www.nydailynews.com/new-york/ny-spike-movie-anniversary-20190623-sa5ocpsmgfhtde4nnnuzx7w-zqm-story.html (accessed 4 April 2021).

Marks, Laura U., *The Skin of the Film: Intercultural Cinema, Embodiment, and the Senses* (Durham, NC, Duke University Press, 2000).

Massood, Paula, "Introduction," in Paula Massood (ed.), *The Spike Lee Reader* (Philadelphia, PA, Temple University Press, 2007), pp. xv–xxviii.

McGowan, Todd, *Spike Lee* (Champaign, IL, University of Illinois Press, 2007).

Miller, D. Quentin, "Lost and … Found? James Baldwin's Script and Spike Lee's *Malcolm X*," *African American Review*, 46:4 (2013), pp. 671–85.

Nieland, Justus, *David Lynch* (Champaign, IL, University of Illinois Press, 2012).

Norman, Brian, "James Baldwin's Confrontation with US Imperialism in *If Beale Street Could Talk*," *MELUS*, 32:1 (2007), pp. 119–38.

Quashie, Kevin, *The Sovereignty of Quiet: Beyond Resistance in Black Culture* (New Brunswick, NJ, Rutgers University Press, 2012).

Sobchack, Vivian, *Carnal Thoughts: Embodiment and Moving Image Culture* (Berkeley, CA, University of California Press, 2004).

St. Félix, Doreen, "Can We Trust the Beauty of Barry Jenkins's *If Beale Street Could Talk?*," *The New Yorker*, 21 December 2018, https://www.newyorker.com/culture/cultural-comment/can-we-trust-the-beauty-of-barry-jenkinss-if-beale-street-could-talk (accessed 4 April 2021).

Trasker, Yvonne, *Action and Adventure Cinema* (Malden, MA, Wiley-Blackwell, 2015).

Williams, Linda, *Viewing Positions: Ways of Seeing* (New Brunswick, NJ, Rutgers University Press, 1995).

Contributor's Biography

Peter Lurie is Associate Professor of English and Film Studies at the University of Richmond. He is the author of *American Obscurantism: History and the Visual in U.S. Literature and Film* (Oxford University Press, 2018) and *Vision's Immanence: Faulkner, Film, and the Popular Imagination* (Johns Hopkins University Press, 2014). He is the editor, with Ann J. Abadie, of *Faulkner and Film: Faulkner and Yoknapatawpha 2010* (University Press of Mississippi, 2014) and the Editor of the *Faulkner Journal*. His current research project is titled *Black Evanescence: Seeing Racial Difference from the Slave Narrative to Digital Media*.

GRADUATE STUDENT ESSAY AWARD WINNER

"In the Name of Love": Black Queer Feminism and the Sexual Politics of *Another Country*

Matty Hemming   University of Pennsylvania

Abstract

This essay explores Black queer feminist readings of the sexual politics of James Baldwin's *Another Country*. Recent work at the intersection of queer of color critique and Black feminism allows us to newly appreciate Baldwin's prescient theorization of the workings of racialized and gendered power within the erotic. Previous interpretations of *Another Country* have focused on what is perceived as a liberal idealization of white gay male intimacy. I argue that this approach requires a selective reading of the novel that occludes its more complex portrayal of a web of racially fraught, power-stricken, and often violent sexual relationships. When we de-prioritize white gay male eroticism and pursue analyses of a broader range of erotic scenes, a different vision of Baldwin's sexual imaginary emerges. I argue that far from idealizing, *Another Country* presents sex within a racist, homophobic, and sexist world to be a messy terrain of pleasure, pain, and political urgency. An unsettling vision, to be sure, but one that, if we as readers are to seek more equitable erotic imaginaries, must be reckoned with.

Keywords: Black queer feminism, James Baldwin, *Another Country*, the erotic, sexual politics

James Baldwin Review, Volume 7, 2021, © The Authors. Published by Manchester University Press and
The University of Manchester Library
http://dx.doi.org/10.7227/JBR.7.8

"They tear you limb from limb, in the name of love," muses Ida Scott, the Black female character at the center of James Baldwin's third novel, *Another Country* (1962).[1] Ida's diagnosis of desire's selfish and destructive potential illuminates this novel's ambivalence about the capacity of romantic bonds to overcome political strife. Describing how her deceased brother was exploited by lovers under the guise of this grand emotion, Ida offers a theory of specifically romantic and erotic love that is borne out by the novel. Love, *Another Country* posits, is no panacea for the imbalances of power. Indeed, love can itself host the very antagonisms we trust it to resolve. At times shockingly violent and consistently tense with the navigation of gender- and race-based power dynamics, the novel details to visceral effect the psychic impact of anti-Black racism upon gay and straight interracial couples in Jim Crow era Manhattan. With its plot structured around a series of fraught erotic couplings, *Another Country* depicts a network of romantic and sexual relationships riven by the workings of power. But while the imbrication of racial and gendered hierarches in erotic "love" leaves no one untouched, the novel considers the heightened burden of emotional labor shouldered by its sole Black female character.

This description of Baldwin's attention to the uneven effects of gendered and racial power on all romantic and erotic dynamics cuts against the grain of the novel's critical reception. Indeed, this reassessment of the novel's formal structure challenges readings that position *Another Country* as a liberal progress narrative. Written for a largely white readership and mostly narrated from the perspective of white middle-class characters, the novel seems to leave little room for imagining the interior lives of its Black characters, and its sole Black female character in particular. Regarding Baldwin as himself reproducing a liberal vision of political change at the level of the white individual, critics such as Matt Brim, William Cohen, and Robert Reid-Pharr have analyzed the link between *Another Country*'s lack of Black representation and its seeming fascination with white male homoeroticism. Centering their analyses around a single scene of erotic encounter between two characters, Eric Jones and Vivaldo Moore, these critics claim that the novel presents a disturbingly liberal vision of gay sex as a source of idealized transcendent self-revelation for its white male protagonists.

In this essay, I argue that *Another Country* does not confidently promote a vision of the erotic as the autonomous site of transcendent and politically utopian "love." Departing from critiques of Baldwin's rose-tinted representation of white gay male sexuality, I explore the possibilities for Black queer feminist and queer of color critique readings of sex in *Another Country*. In particular, I suggest that the work of Kadji Amin, Sharon Patricia Holland, and Jennifer Nash presents generative tools for reassessing Baldwin's unsettling novel. These scholars offer useful critical frameworks for analyzing the political implications of *Another Country*'s web of erotic relationships. They also allow us to reconsider certain assumptions at work within the novel's critical reception. As I will discuss below, queer critics have focused on Baldwin's supposed idealization of white gay male eroticism, exposing a potentially disturbing element of the novel. But this focus itself occludes the novel's depiction of other sexual arrangements, and risks reproducing the very overrepresentation of white male subjects in queer theorizing that such scholars rightly decry.

I pursue instead a more expansive reading of *Another Country* that accentuates its portrayal of a web of racially fraught, power-stricken, and often violent sexual relationships. In order to appreciate how *Another Country* theorizes sexual intimacy, we need to look beyond its depiction of supposedly redemptive white gay male sex. When we focus instead on the novel's web of interconnected erotic experiences and prioritize among these, we can perceive how its structure formally approximates this expansive racial imaginary, complicating a reading of *Another Country* as a white male *Bildungsroman*. In turning to the descriptive language of the little-addressed interracial relationship between Ida and Vivaldo, I suggest that the novel's web of messy relations culminates not in interracial harmony but in an image of the exhaustion wrought by the emotional labor expected of Black women in white spaces.

This reassessment of the sexual politics of *Another Country* enriches our understanding of Baldwin as a prescient queer theorist. Claiming Baldwin's novels as key texts of queer theory, and not just queer fiction, has been part of the long-standing project of challenging and surpassing the whiteness of queer theory's concepts, assumed subjects, and authorized genealogies.[2] Indeed, the twenty-first-century resurgence of scholarship appraising Baldwin's radical political voice affirms that his corpus contributes rich material to a Black and queer of color centered queer studies. Yet while much attention has been paid to the racial politics of *Giovanni's Room* (1956), and the Black male homoeroticism of *Go Tell It on the Mountain* (1953) and *Just Above My Head* (1979), less recognized is the extent to which *Another Country* offers foundational insights into the inseparability of racial and gendered hierarchies from erotic desire.[3]

Another Country would seem to offer little to Black queer studies and queer of color critique committed to Black queer feminist scholarship. As E. Patrick Johnson and Sharon Holland note, much recent work in these fields hails Black queer feminists' longstanding attention to Black female sexual subjectivities.[4] Turning to Baldwin's novels as a potential site for such feminist theorizing might seem counterintuitive at best and counterproductive at worst. Baldwin's career-wide portrayal of Black women's eroticism would not seem to sit easily with the political sensibilities of Black queer feminist theory. And this is especially true of his contentious third novel. As the critiques of *Another Country*'s depiction of white gay male sex would suggest, the novel seems to reproduce an understanding of the queer, and even the erotic, subject as white and male. However, this essay proposes that the novel's sexual politics are precisely best read through a Black queer feminist lens. Utilizing key thinkers in and adjacent to this field, I posit that what is theoretically significant about the novel is its imperfect and unsettling depiction of Black female eroticism within an anti-Black environment.

In the opening pages of *The Erotic Life of Racism* (2012), Holland argues that, overall, queer studies has not lived up to its intent to theorize the place of racism in the erotic. Holland asks the deceptively simple questions: "Can work on 'desire' be antiracist work? Can antiracist work *think* 'desire'?"[5] These questions are simple in the sense that the inextricability of pleasure, sexuality, and sexual choice from the workings of racial ideologies has long been articulated by Black feminist theorists. And yet they are deceptively simple because, for Holland, queer studies' investment in uncovering the politics of desire has, over the years, made desire "autonomous," a realm of individual experience and even a form of asocial escape.[6] In dominant and conceptually white strains of queer theorizing, the erotic is imagined to transport one outside of the constraints of the racist ordinary. As I will outline, this is precisely what critics who have analyzed *Another Country* accuse Baldwin of doing in his depiction of white gay male sex. However, I argue that Holland asks us to read the novel differently. Her key claim, that "there is no raceless course of desire," animates my essay.[7] Holland's observation that erotic relations cannot be free of racial power compels us to approach *Another Country* as a text that inhabits rather than escapes from the uncomfortable workings of racialized desire. Furthermore, Holland is particularly critical of a tendency in queer studies to unwittingly imagine that, in the US context, Black women's sexuality is singularly and overly determined by the nation's racist past.[8] While arguing for an overdue engagement with the complexity of Black queer feminist discourses about Black female sexuality, Holland also underscores how *all* forms of sexuality are impacted by the history of slavery. I consider *Another Country* as a text that stages these dynamics. It firmly positions each erotic encounter within an anti-Black environment. But, in highlighting the white desire for Black female transparency, it poses productive challenges for the reader who seeks to affirm, without further burdening, Ida's sexual subjectivity.

Recent work in queer of color critique has taken up Holland's articulation of the place of racial and gendered power in all things erotic to reapproach key queer theoretical depictions of sexual practice. Kadji Amin builds upon Holland's thought to question why, how, and to what effect queer theory continues to idealize its objects. Also locating an uneasy idealization of queer sexual practice in certain "dominant strains" of queer theory, Amin calls upon the field to more carefully locate the place of damage, racialization, and power within the queer histories and cultural objects from which it draws energy.[9] Amin's methodological approach informs my reading of *Another Country*. He seeks to resist the polarizing tendencies of queer reading practices, which, when faced with problematic queer objects, tend either to reject through critique, or to idealize to obfuscating effect. Amin offers a model for exploring Baldwin's imperfect vision of sexual politics: one that neither idealizes his work—which would involve ignoring the difficult-to-read depictions of violent sexual encounters—nor simply critiques it, as has been the tendency, for its failure to adhere to readers' political sensibilities. Rather, we might see the novel as anticipating Amin's reminder that queer desire, like all desire, is always shot through with racial power. Thinking with Holland, he writes, "racialized erotic life foils the queer theoretical desire to equate queer sexuality with liberation, political resistance, or a movement beyond the social order all together."[10] This assertion invites a reframing of *Another Country* as a text which attempts to grapple with this reality, even while it has formerly been regarded as a partially escapist text that sets white queer sex on a liberatory pedestal.

The tendency to read the novel's depiction of romantic relationships as an ideological commentary on twentieth-century American social politics is due in no small part to the fact that *Another Country* was published a year before *The Fire Next Time* (1963). In this widely read collection of two essays, Baldwin argues for the importance of self-reckoning, writing of the imbrication of white American racism with a fantasy of innocence. Speaking directly to his nephew James in "My Dungeon Shook," Baldwin declares, "we, with love, shall force our brothers to see themselves as they are, to cease fleeing from reality and begin to change it," a theory of love that seems to offer a secular alternative to the nonviolent concept of "agape" forwarded by Martin Luther King, Jr.[11] Reading these two books together, it is hard to imagine their simultaneous generation. One eloquently theorizes both a state of Black disenfranchisement and the potentiality of integrationist politics. The other fictionally depicts the messy internal violence of racism's effects, portraying a world in which "love" is imagined not through the communal politics of the essays, but through the turbulent form of the eroticized couple. If *The Fire Next Time* holds out for the antiracist potential of interracial—and not necessarily romantic—relationships, then, as Dagmawi Woubshet has suggested, *Another Country* seems to virulently assert the difficulty of achieving such intimacy within a world of quotidian, psychic, and materially impactful racism.[12]

With its fraught relationships and unlikeable or unknowable characters, *Another Country* has inspired strong responses, to say the least. As one contemporaneous critic noted, it offers "something for everyone—in this instance, something offensive for everyone."[13] Famously, Black Panther leader Eldridge Cleaver described the novel as exemplifying the "Negro homosexual's … racial death-wish" to "have a baby by a white man."[14] Cleaver's framing of characters' sexual choices as irreducibly political might seem a reductive reading of this capacious literary text, but this cannot be chalked up to an overemphasis on the place of sex in the novel. Indeed, while much of the queer scholarship addressing the novel's social vision repudiates Cleaver's homophobic conclusions, this scholarship nonetheless shares his sense that gay male sex is central to the politics of *Another Country*. William A. Cohen critiques what he sees as Baldwin's "liberal faith" in the power of the individual to overcome social inequality. Cohen detects this belief in Baldwin's portrayal of gay male eroticism, and especially in Vivaldo's achievement of "a heightened consciousness" which "enters him through the sexual act" with Eric.[15] Central to Cohen's argument is the claim that Baldwin's liberal agenda of "love" is strategically funneled through the site of "sexuality" rather than "race." Cohen writes that during the Black Power moment it would have seemed "disingenuous for Baldwin to claim that individual love could conquer racial discord," whereas pre-Stonewall, "love" could more easily be imagined through the "more readily privatized terms of sexuality."[16] For Cohen then, "love" finds expression as romantic love, a suturing of Baldwin's language of self-reflexivity with homoerotic sexual connection that runs throughout the scholarship. My own reading of *Another Country* through Black queer feminism addresses the limitation of Cohen's analytic categories. I argue that "sexuality," "race," and "love" in fact coalesce; that the novel problematizes a public/private divide; and that Baldwin engages in political theorizing through his depiction of *interracial and heterosexual* sex.

A more recent strain of queer criticism looks beyond the novel's investment in white gay male sexuality and attends more fully to *Another Country*'s related limited depiction of Black interior life. Matt Brim frames this lack as a failure of Baldwin's "queer imagination," one limited by the historical constraints of homophobia and racism.[17] What is absent for Brim from *Another Country* is, in particular, an ability to imagine Black queer male experience—let alone that of Black queer women—as anything other than a "specter," narratively important only to the extent that intimacy between Black and white men facilitates the "straight" Vivaldo's achievement of self-revelatory enlightenment through a sexual encounter with the white Eric.[18] I agree with Brim that "Baldwin gives queer thinkers a lot of work to do."[19] With its language of "love," "transformation," and "revelation" mired in the violence of structural racism and white liberalism, this difficult novel calls for further treatment of these uneasy entanglements. But while Brim's book is dedicated to occupying "the space of Baldwin's own absent critique," and imagines correcting the "underlying immobility" of social relations in the novel, my own approach is to attend to *how* Baldwin produces this sense of immobility through his descriptive language.[20] Indeed, I consider Baldwin's "incoherent" and "unsettling" depiction of relationships as a site generative for scholarship, not as something to be hypothetically resolved within the world of the novel, but as a difficulty which the novel genre can productively, though perhaps not optimistically, explore.[21] Indeed, thinking with Amin and Holland suggests that to embrace Baldwin as a key figure of queer theory is to grapple with *all* of him, potential idealization of white gay sex *alongside* an impoverished depiction of Black female interiority, as a way of reckoning with the field's own internal tensions. A task of current queer theorizing might then be to attend to what Baldwin's fictional worlds can continue to teach, and to consider what resonances with current queer and feminist frameworks might emerge when we sit with, rather than imagine that we have moved past, what is "disturbing" about those worlds.

Before turning to the descriptive passages that will take up the majority of this analysis, it is worth asking, what kind of world are we in when reading *Another Country*? What are its structuring principles, its dominant affects? *Another Country* depicts a 1950s Manhattan not unlike Manhattan today: it is both laced with white liberal sentiment and shaped by structural racism. The novel's ambient ambivalence and anxiety appear in its iconic opening section, which establishes many of the tonal and thematic elements that will be developed throughout. *Another Country* commences with a long section narrated from the point of view of Rufus Scott, a young Black musician whose turbulent relationship with the white southerner Leona is one of many factors leading to his suicide, an act that haunts the rest of the novel, permeating the relationships between his sister Ida, friend Vivaldo, and ex-lover Eric. Depicting the "disintegration of a black boy," this section underlines in often piercing terms the extent to which race- and gender-based power structures Rufus's everyday life, and, in particular, his erotic encounters.[22]

Indeed, the first sex act of the novel is shaped both by a misogynist disregard for consent and, simultaneously, by Rufus's experience of the psychic effects of racism, specifically interracial intimacy. During the consummation of Leona and Rufus's relationship, sex is described as the "violence of the deep," with Leona's face "trans-figured with agony," and Rufus's penis a "weapon," his semen "venom," "enough for a hundred black-white babies."[23] In imagining Rufus through such racist terms, we might see Baldwin writing through what W. E. B. Du Bois called "double con-sciousness." This awareness of the white gaze is later scaled up in Rufus's percep-tion of the response to his and Leona's relationship in their home in the West Village. Walking alone with Leona, Rufus is painfully aware of their subjection to racist interpellation: "Villagers, both bound and free, looked them over as though where they stood were an auction block or a stud farm."[24] We might imagine this encounter as a metonym for those taking place in the city at large, for this pre-Civil Rights Act novel presents a city infused with the social, if not the legal, effects of the Jim Crow era.

Within this hostile environment, the presence of queer desire is far from redemptive. In addition to the vitriol directed outward toward implicitly lesbian figures, and the depiction of coerced gay male sex work in a moment of despera-tion, I note an ambivalence to Rufus's memories of Eric, the white southerner with whom he had a relationship.[25] Though looking back from a place of regret, wishing he had been kinder to Eric, Rufus's recollection of his own experiences of desire and affection are textured with a simultaneous antagonism. This affective disposi-tion registers the entanglement of imbalanced racial power with the mechanics of queer shame: "Rufus had despised him because he came from Alabama; perhaps he allowed Eric to make love to him in order to despise him more completely."[26] The conflicting sensations are uneasily enmeshed: "affection, power and curiosity all knotted together in him—with a hidden unforeseen violence which frightened him a little."[27] With desire and violence bound together and embodied as an "intol-erable pressure in his chest," the experience of male–male intimacy in the novel, much less of politically redemptive love, is ambivalent from the start.[28]

Rufus's section establishes the inextricability of racialization, the effects of structural racism, and erotic drive. Here, Baldwin anticipates Holland's claim that there "is no raceless course of desire."[29] This attention to structural racism also appears in the novel's formal structure: We move next to the point of view of the white middle-class Cass Silenski, the novel's events never again filtered through the perspective of a character of color. Despite both this prioritization of white voices, *and* the haunting presence of Rufus throughout *Another Country*, it is Ida who appears to have been, for Baldwin, the figure at the center of the novel.[30] This, despite the fact that among the text's other main characters—Rufus, Vivaldo, Eric, and Cass—Ida is the only one without a section narrated from her point of view. As Trudier Harris wrote in 1985, and as a reading of more recent engagements with the novel would support, "[f]ew critics have considered Ida worthy of extensive commentary in her own right; they usually comment on her only passingly in relation to other characters' development and fulfillment."[31] Considering what it would mean to take seriously Ida's importance to what critics have regarded as the novel's political messaging, Harris points to the difficulty of definitively accessing Ida's point of view, writing that "she is just as elusive narrationally as she is personally to the white protagonists in the novel."[32] For Harris, Ida's relative opacity—we only see her through "several cloudy lenses"—speaks to the burden she bears, representing "Black woman" for the white characters.[33]

Wary of further burdening Ida with the weight of representing Black female sexuality in a novel easily reduced to a depiction of social types, my choice to focus primarily on the sex scenes limits what can be said of Ida in a manner that a longer treatment would complicate. But to take seriously the project of analyzing both Baldwin's persistent and often disturbing descriptions of sexual acts, as well as their reception in queer theoretical readings of the novel, requires carefully addressing the depiction of Ida's sexual relationship with Vivaldo. Ida is first introduced to readers as Rufus's concerned younger sister, who comes looking for him at Cass and Richard's apartment. Soon becoming romantically involved with Rufus's friend Vivaldo, it is his narrative perspective through which we not only meet Ida, but which also shapes our perception of her eroticization. Vivaldo's attraction to Ida, Baldwin seems to warn readers, is inextricable from a history of heterosexist and racist conditions shaping romantic and economic bonds between Black women and white men in the mid-twentieth century. Previous to their relationship Vivaldo would travel to Harlem in the pursuit of his own virility. He believed that with Black sex workers he was "snatching his manhood from the lukewarm waters of mediocrity and testing it in the fire."[34] We see how Vivaldo's perception of Ida is shaped by internalized racist and heterosexist logics in his language of "violation," his fantasy of Ida as "virgin" awaiting a loss of innocence, and also by his desire for full transparency.[35]

In Vivaldo's apartment after a night spent together, the two are presented as tentatively unsure of one another. Simultaneously recognizing Ida's right to privacy and wanting to "strike deeper into that incredible country in which … she paced her secret round of secret days," the language of penetration is never far from Vivaldo's narrative vocabulary.[36] This is a problematic toward which the novel's title might call our attention. Is Ida's "incredible country" the "another" alluded to, a clue to her significance in the novel? Ida's own behavior in this scene is perceived by Vivaldo as similarly conflicted. She at once looks like a "virgin," and speaks in a "tone that mixed hostility with wonder."[37] After Ida asks him if he has slept with other Black women, Vivaldo replies in the affirmative, stating silently to himself: "*I paid them.*"[38] Notably, this italicized internal second declaration is available to readers and not to Ida, a reminder of Vivaldo's narratorial control.

Vivaldo's desire for psychic penetration is visualized metaphorically as well as bodily. With Ida's "surrendering" sigh in the next sentence, we move into the erotic scene described below and framed tellingly with the words, "the struggle began":[39]

> She opened up before him, yet fell back before him, too, he felt that he was travelling up a savage, jungle river, looking for the source which remained hidden just beyond the black, dangerous, dripping foliage. Then, for a moment, they seemed to be breaking through. Her hands broke free, her thighs inexorably loosened, their bellies ground cruelly together, and a curious, low whistle forced itself up through her throat, past her bared teeth … He had never been so patient, so determined, so cruel before.[40]

It is hard not to read the eventual "breaking through" of orgasm that comes moments after this section as a penetration of the "incredible country" discussed above, one that is highly racialized with the language of the "jungle" and its "black, dangerous, dripping foliage." The rhythmic language of falling, opening, and grinding might not be unusual to descriptions of bodies in the throes of desire. But what is striking about Baldwin's language is the combination of affects in this quote and in the passage more broadly. In Baldwin's descriptive world, sex emerges as a fraught process: a "struggle," "dangerous," and seeming to require patience, determination, but also cruelty. When the exchange of fluids releases emotions, the language of love enters Vivaldo's consciousness: "all the love in him rushed down, rushed down, and poured itself into her."[41] Fern Marja Eckman described the sex scenes in *Another Country* as "sentimentalized," its interracial couplings "glorified as the apotheosis of love."[42] But what are we to do with this "love" couched in the section's broader language of power? Vivaldo's sense that Ida's body now "belonged" to him emphasizes that, though the scene might lead to a form of emotional transformation, this transformation is most immediately available through white male eyes.[43] Vivaldo's gender- and race-based power manifest in his narrative dominance: he controls what we can know of Ida's "incredible country."

In Robert Reid-Pharr's reading of *Another Country*, the queer of color critic suggests that Baldwin has "worked" to tell us "what white men, particularly white queer men, think when they fuck."[44] While describing Vivaldo's relationship with Eric, Reid-Pharr's words can also be applied to his experiences with Ida. Indeed, Reid-Pharr writes that Ida and Vivaldo are presented as being most concretely racialized during sex: "The two are most sealed in their whiteness and blackness … at precisely the moment of their 'joining.'"[45] But if Vivaldo's point of view allows Baldwin to effectively theorize white masculinity, how do we attend to the politics of Ida's absent narration? Is Ida's presence wholly determined by Vivaldo's perspective, by the racial scripts that Reid-Pharr sees their sexual relationship as only exacerbating? Is it possible to locate a reading of Ida's own experience of desire in a passage so easily reducible to a racist sexual fantasy? Or should we take Vivaldo's pursuit of Black women, and later his pleasurable submission to the white gay Eric, as a kind of sexual tourism from which nothing of critical value can be extracted? What are the frameworks available for reading this scene that do not simply involve wishing Baldwin had written a different novel, one more carefully attentive to the experiences of its female characters?

I might go some way toward addressing these questions by turning to the work of Black feminist thinker Jennifer Nash, who explores potential methods for reading Black women's pleasure within problematic texts. She provocatively challenges readers to see desire and agency in the most unlikely of places, namely, in racialized hardcore pornography. Nash's project is deeply indebted to Black feminist interpretations of the visual. As she puts it, given dominant representations of Black women as a site of historically ongoing injury, pornography is an extreme, but not singular, example of violent objectification. However, in a potentially counterintuitive departure from this framework, Nash proposes a re-engagement with the visual, asking, "What would it mean to read racialized pornography not for evidence of the wounds it inflicts on black women's flesh, but for moments of racialized excitement, for instances of surprising pleasures in racialization, and for hyperbolic performances of race that poke fun at the very project of race?"[46] Nash's analysis performs an "aggressive counter-reading" of pornographic iconography, namely, of the *performances* of Black female characters within racially stereotypical films.[47] To the viewer who cannot see the possibility of locating any politically viable sources of pleasure in these images, Nash introduces an alternative framework, one that "contains a utopian wish for black feminist theory" to make space for the presence of a Black female ecstasy that, though messy and contradictory, is irreducible to woundedness.[48] Importantly, Nash's is not a redemptive framework, one that would suppress or even decentralize the imbalances of power within the representations analyzed. Hers is a project that, like Amin's, problematizes critical approaches to troubling objects that entail either wholesale rejection or idealizing recuperation. Indeed, in imagining the erotic as a site of both potentiality and harm for racialized subjects, Nash's work resonates with that of both Amin and Holland, offering another framework for tracing "the intimate connections between sexual subjectivity and racial subjectivity" as they emerge in less than perfect but potentially generative cultural objects.[49]

Of course, *Another Country* is not pornography, and neither is the novel committed to producing a pleasurable experience on the part of the reader. Indeed, Baldwin's intention seems to have been to produce the opposite effect, what Ernesto Javier Martínez calls an "unsettling" reading experience, in particular for readers resistant to having a Black female character's sexuality reduced to the role of facilitating a white man's sexual and emotional transformation. Baldwin is certainly not best known for his depictions of Black women's experiences of pleasure and pain. While the lack of complexity ascribed to Black female characters in this novel might be somewhat redressed in the characterization of Julia in *Just Above My Head* or the protagonist Tish in *If Beale Street Could Talk* (1973), we could conclude that the simple fact of a lack of narrative perspective overly curtails Ida's presence. Nash's framework allows us to see this as an overdetermination of the power of both author and narrator. Indeed, the authority that free indirect discourse lends Vivaldo's perspective in this erotic passage can be tempered by focusing on the few moments in which Ida's own point of view seems to break through to the reader. One such instance is Ida's coital utterance "*Vivaldo, Vivaldo, Vivaldo*," given in the italicized text that often denotes interior thought rather than speech, a textual anomaly that seems to trouble Vivaldo's hold on the descriptive language of sex.[50] Internally vocalized in the throes of desire, could we think of this utterance as an expression of interior ecstasy?

For Nash, Black female ecstasy is specifically articulated when female characters in pornographic films actively perform and therefore expose racial fictions. Here we only see such racial fictions figured through Vivaldo's perception of Ida. Her own response to this fetishization is opaque to readers, and perhaps strategically so. What is clear, though, is that Ida too experiences the encounter as one of heightened pleasure and self-transformation. Furthermore, in a rare departure from Vivaldo's point of view, Baldwin turns to Ida's perspective for a single sentence as they are about to have sex: "She touched him for the first time with wonder and terror, realizing that she did not know how to caress him."[51] In spotlighting Ida's sense of "wonder and terror," as well as her unexpected realization, Baldwin seems to suggest that Vivaldo is as much a mystery to her as she is to him. He signals the complexity of her own interiority, one that has been present all along, even if it has been withheld from the reader. Finally, with the audible expressions of pleasure depicted through sound—Ida emits a "curious, low whistle" and says "It never happened to me before—not like this, never"—an intensity of erotic experience is established.[52] Employing a diversity of forms such as interior thought, speech, and nonverbal utterance, Baldwin seems to undermine Vivaldo's narrative hold, asserting that Ida is not simply a victim of Vivaldo's fetishization, but actively desirous of his touch.

I read this compromised scene for Ida's pleasure by drawing on Black queer feminist understandings of pleasure's involvement in the social. Although she recognizes that "hierarchy often wears the guise of pleasure," Nash also cautions that the inevitable existence of hierarchy within all sexual dynamics can overdetermine our ability to read pleasure within the supposedly subordinated subject-position.[53] While we cannot speak to how Ida's desire is experienced in relation to the power dynamics explicitly presented through Vivaldo's racializing gaze, to focus solely on the language of his pleasure and not hers would be to run roughshod over these moments of Ida's self-expression. To misrecognize or pity Ida's desire risks demanding that pleasure only count as such when it is free of, or legibly subverting, the uncomfortable language of power.

Baldwin's short-lived insistence on giving voice to Ida's perspective is vital to the novel's broader political vision. Though Ida does not have her own section of free indirect discourse, this interjection of her point of view exposes the limitations of the white male narrative voice. Thinking with Nash's practice of reading agency into the performances of Black female actors within spaces that are seemingly inhospitable to their self-expression reveals that Ida—no less than the men whose formal and narrative prominence nearly crowd her out—is a fully conscious actor within the world of the novel. As explored in my opening paragraph, her wariness of romantic love impedes a too-easy critical alignment of that term with Baldwin's so-called liberal vision. Baldwin may withhold from Ida a full section of narration, perhaps doing so to thwart his white characters', and readers', desire for Black interior transparency. Through moments of dialogue and narrative interruption, he necessitates her place in any analysis of the novel's sexual politics. Baldwin thereby also reminds us that we must listen to Ida without demanding that she speak with full transparency.

Before arriving at the scene of homoeroticism most associated with Baldwin's vision of sexual politics, then, we have encountered a depiction of the ostensibly private sphere of "sexuality" that complicates a reading of the novel's liberal and utopian sexual politics. If Vivaldo and Ida's erotic relationship has prompted few critical readings, the opposite can be said for the single and seemingly revelatory encounter between Vivaldo and Eric. And while the fraught intimacies between Rufus, Leona, Vivaldo, and Ida would suggest that romance is hardly a source of political optimism in the world of *Another Country*, readings of this scene of homoeroticism suggest otherwise. It is striking, indeed, that within a novel so cognizant of power's imbrication in eroticism, Eric and Vivaldo's night together is presented through a seemingly easeful and yet jarring use of the language of love and revelation. Their bond is forged during a late-night conversation in which Eric is open about both his attraction to men, and the "torment" that confusion about his sexuality has caused, while Vivaldo confesses the intimate and almost sexual encounter he had with Rufus the last time they saw each other.[54] After thus opening up to one another, the two men fall asleep, and upon waking, begin what Vivaldo experiences as the "monstrous endeavor" of having sex.[55] The four-page passage that this erotic scene takes up offers an at times bewildering array of descriptive terms, significantly hard to pin down to a single meaning. In certain moments Vivaldo experiences his own "lust" as "unaccustomedly arrogant and cruel and irresponsible."[56] This language of cruelty recalls his experience with Ida, and the repetition of terms compels us to ask whether this sadism is unusual for Vivaldo. In other moments, Vivaldo sees sex with Eric as somehow both wholly new and comfortingly familiar, "far removed from the necessary war one underwent with women."[57] The potential implications of this encounter for his own sexuality arise only to be rejected when Vivaldo wonders "What was it like to be a man, condemned to men? He could not imagine it and he felt a quick revulsion, quickly banished for it threatened his ease."[58] And significantly, while being penetrated by Eric, Vivaldo thinks of Rufus. Baldwin records Vivaldo's longing in italics that strikingly recall Ida's "*Vivaldo, Vivaldo, Vivaldo*": "*Rufus. Rufus.* Had it been like this for him? ... Had he murmured at last, in a strange voice, as he now heard himself murmur. *Oh Eric. Eric.*"[59] This moment recalls Ida's utterances. The visual and syntactic echo stretches the limits not only of Vivaldo's perspective but also, more broadly, of any critical practice that assumes that Baldwin uniformly privileges the white male voice.

The scene ends with the two declaring their mutual love, a feeling that for Vivaldo constitutes a "great revelation," making him feel "fantastically protected, liberated."[60] It is this language of sexual transcendence, and specifically its placement in the plot of the novel, coming as it does before much of the building tension reaches its climax, that has elicited so many critiques. Arguing that Baldwin constructs a fantasy of "homosexual sacrifice disguised as revolutionary love," Brim goes so far as to call Baldwin a "gay trader," since, for the "straight" Vivaldo, the "loving transformation" offered by sex with Eric "prepares him to confront what is represented as the related yet more impenetrable border of interracial desire."[61] What is most disturbing about this narrative trope is the way in which white homoerotic potentiality seems to rely on the spectral role of Black gay male friends and lovers, exemplified by the haunting absences of Rufus and Eric's childhood friend, LeRoy.[62]

The prioritization of white and usually male narratives within the ensemble structure of *Another Country* clearly limits the extent to which this novel can be said to share the investment of Baldwin's wider corpus in depicting Black queer interiority and historical experience. However, the casual claim that Rufus's and LeRoy's haunting absences facilitate a healing experience for Eric and Vivaldo, which in turn solves the conflicts of the heterosexual interracial couple, heuristically centers white, male eroticism at the cost of a more sustained analysis of the novel's broader range of erotic encounters. This is what reading the novel as an *idealizing* text entails. But what might regarding *Another Country* as a novel that precisely challenges the idealization of gay male sex allow us to see about its plot structure and narratorial choices? I have been suggesting that we can begin to answer this question by centering Ida's racist sexualization by Vivaldo, as well as the fraught textual glimmers of her own pleasure. Once we see the narrative of *Another Country* as a recursive web with Ida at its center, rather than a progressive line culminating in white male redemption, we can begin to reassess its vision of sexual politics, and, in particular, its resonances with Black queer feminism.

We might therefore reconsider Baldwin's depiction of the interconnectedness of differently power-riven couplings as critically descriptive rather than only complicit. For just as Vivaldo's racialization of Ida during sex resonates with his previous encounters with Black female sex workers, so do previous encounters with men inform the ways in which we read the experience of male–male desire for both Vivaldo and Eric. Two events precede Vivaldo's experience of "revelation" with Eric: his youthful participation in a violent group attack on a gay man, and his highly racialized homoerotic display of masculine virility with a fellow soldier while in service. The memory of such incidents textures the reader's understanding of the present-day scene. For Eric, who more recognizably inhabits a gay identity position, sexual awakening comes at a young age, when, in a much-analyzed scene, an attraction to his friend LeRoy develops into a formative sexual encounter with life-changing effects. Throughout *Another Country*, Baldwin explicitly and implicitly suggests that sexual acts in the present are sutured to those of the past. This entanglement of past and present foregrounds the embeddedness of memory, shame, and the fungibility of Black bodies for his white characters. Notably, Black queer male figures are written out of the text almost as soon as they appear, with Rufus's and LeRoy's haunting absences implying an agency limited to their effect upon white memory. But rather than simply critiquing this as a failure of Baldwin's queer imagination, we can read *Another Country* as deliberately illuminating on a formal level—through its own over-representation of white male interiority—a political and social landscape in which some lives are consistently prioritized over others. This is a risky claim to make, though. In suggesting that what is disturbing may also be what is most revealing of historical experience, I might skirt too close to a recuperation of aspects of the text that are deeply troubling and hard to read.

An alternative approach to reading *Another Country* as a meditation on, rather than a condonement of, the imbrication of racism, power, and eroticism might reorient focus toward those characters whose presence has been read as facilitating white male self-knowledge. This would involve reading LeRoy as one figure in a constellation made up of Eric, Ida, Vivaldo, Rufus, Leone, and many others: a character in his own right, and not simply part of a causal chain. What might this reframing reveal about the supposed queer optimism of the encounter between LeRoy and Eric? As with Vivaldo's perception of Ida, the narratorial privilege held by Eric in this moment of remembering means that LeRoy's own experience of the act is, at least in terms of his lack of access to free indirect discourse, markedly absent. Perhaps one way to read against this troubling effect of the novel is to give LeRoy's words greater significance than their proportional word count might imply, therefore giving less airtime to the causal narrative within which his relationship with Eric has been read. For while Baldwin does not record LeRoy's perspective, he does incorporate his verbal reminders of the more urgent dangers of exposure for himself, compared to the risks for Eric, whose "Daddy *owns* half the folks in this town."[63] Here, the patronymic accentuates the specifically gendered as well as racialized nature of the patriarchal context in which LeRoy, Rufus, and Ida all interact with white men. When LeRoy, looking "exasperated," urges Eric with the words "you got to stop coming to see me," Baldwin asserts the uneasy place of racial power within eroticism.[64] Even if they go unmarked by the novel's white characters, such moments are powerful reminders that race and gender are *central to*, and not lacking from, *Another Country*'s vision of queer desire.

Finally, in addition to focusing on LeRoy's own words, further attention to the language of this scene invites a rethinking of the extent to which the sexual act actually can be read as transformative. One the one hand, Eric's memory of LeRoy's touch does seem to suggest a transporting experience: "He was frightened and in pain and the boy who held him so relentlessly was suddenly a stranger; and yet this stranger worked in Eric an eternal, a healing transformation."[65] And yet, moments later, when the language of revelation enters Eric's description of the experience, the future implications of this word are left strikingly uncertain: "For the meaning of revelation is that what is revealed is true and must be borne," Eric thinks to himself from the vantage point of adult hindsight, but he wonders without an answer, "how to bear it?"[66] With this open question, one that might describe the self-questioning experienced by the novel's characters more broadly, Baldwin seems to imagine that understanding one's position within a regime of sexuality-based knowledge does not necessarily lead to a more livable, or more ethical, life.[67] What emerges from this scene, then, is a far from an idealizing vision of homoeroticism. Rather, the risks of queerness are unevenly dealt, and the attainment of self-awareness is constrained within a landscape of shame and uncertainty.

Foregrounding a web of sexual bonds between Leone, Rufus, Ida, Vivaldo, Eric, and LeRoy, I do not seek to downplay the striking difference in tone between the seeming ease of white gay male sex and the fraught language of every other erotic dynamic in *Another Country*. This difference is exemplified in the passages contrasting depictions of that most Baldwinian of terms, innocence. While Vivaldo's intimacy with Eric brings him "back to his innocence," suggesting an escape from the realities of the present, Ida is later described as "stroking the innocence out of him" in their scene of vulnerable reconciliation.[68] It is in this moment, arguably the climax of the novel, that Brim reads Vivaldo and Ida's relationship finally beginning the "long and painful endeavor" of "racial intersubjectivity."[69] For Brim, importantly, it is the liberatory skin-shedding experience of intimacy with Eric that makes possible for Vivaldo the self-reflexive "love" imagined in *The Fire Next Time*, a love for which in its final moments the novel seems to hold out hope.

A linear narrative of progression, however, is not the only framework through which to read this scene. Instead, we can shift the focus away from the couple's potential futurity, looking backward instead to the unsettling complexity of sexual connection established by Rufus's point of view in the novel's first pages, and developed in Ida's and LeRoy's encounters with white men. By decentering the relationship between Eric and Vivaldo and looking to a broader range of sexual encounters presented through often racist and sexist descriptive language, I challenge a uniformly optimistic reading of the novel's conclusion. Moments before her allegorical act of stroking, Ida is the object of Vivaldo's suspicion and contempt. Learning of her affair with television producer Steve Ellis mere sentences before he will re-declare his love for her, Vivaldo thinks, "She too, was a whore; how bitterly he had been betrayed."[70] This charge raises the question, how much has Vivaldo really learnt? With mutual anger meeting tenderness, the pair cling together: "There was nothing erotic about it; they were like two weary children."[71] In a scene in which exhaustion, rather than hope, seems to be the dominant affect, Ida and Vivaldo's "love" is hardly transformed by, as Brim would have it, the "love of a good gay man."[72] It is rather a messy, unresolved culmination of the "straight" woman's vulnerable outpouring of her interior "secret round of secret days" that Vivaldo has longed for.[73] If Vivaldo has indeed reached a state of political self-awareness, ready for the shedding of innocence that Baldwin considers to be central to white America's ability truly to be free of racism and the fiction of white supremacy, then it is not Eric, but Ida, who facilitates his growth. By centering Ida, we are compelled to see that it is—all too predictably—the Black woman whose emotional labor raises the political consciousness of the white man.

As I have sought to demonstrate, reading *Another Country* alongside queer of color critique and Black queer feminist theorizing allows for the emergence of new interpretations of a text whose troubling vision of sexual politics would seem to be at odds with celebrations of Baldwin's queer theoretical prescience. In its uneasy depiction of the psychic hold of oppressive regimes upon a range of characters, *Another Country* demands that theorists problematize the subject-positions through which sexual knowledge is produced. As my focus on the connections between differently power-inflected erotic scenes suggests, the politics of Baldwin's depiction of white gay male sex is necessarily informed not only by the under-narrated depiction of Black gay figures, but also by that of heterosexual interracial sex. Far from idealizing gay male sex, Baldwin situates even intimacy between two white men as actively imbricated within a racist, homophobic, and sexist world. In staging an unlikely dialogue between Nash's Black feminist theories of pleasure and Baldwin's depiction of Black female eroticization *and* erotic interiority, I have argued that a fuller understanding of the novel's sexual imaginary can be achieved when we listen for Ida's compromised but meaningful presence. In fact, the novel's theory of sexual politics responds to Ida's observation of desire's destructive potential: it can leave you torn, at least psychically, "limb from limb." Rather than a balm to resolve conflict, acting "in the name of love" leads Baldwin's characters into a messy terrain of pleasure, pain, and political urgency. An unsettling vision, to be sure, but one that, if we as readers are to seek more equitable erotic imaginaries, must be reckoned with.

A potential fallout of this essay is that its engagement with *Another Country* might run the risk of an overly optimistic recuperation of the text, even if it does so by attending to Baldwin's pessimism. Could my choice to center the novel's most violent moments lead to a counterintuitive valuing of those elements above others? I hope, instead, that in framing *Another Country* as unflinchingly and imperfectly exploring the lived psychic conditions of race, gender, and sexuality in the American mid-century, we might sit with the lessons the novel offers to sexuality studies in the present. As such, *Another Country* might be considered a reminder from the past that attending to the political potentialities of non-normative sexuality must go hand in hand with a recognition of the place of racial power in even the queerest—or indeed straightest—of relations.

Acknowledgment

I would like to thank Melissa Sanchez and Dagmawi Woubshet for their useful and generous feedback on various drafts of this essay.

Notes

1 James Baldwin, *Another Country* (1962) (New York, Vintage, 1993), p. 265.

2 For some key critiques of the whiteness of queer theory, see José Esteban Muñoz, *Cruising Utopia: The Then and There of Queer Futurity* (New York, New York University Press, 2009); Roderick Ferguson, *Aberrations in Black: Toward a Queer of Color Critique* (Minneapolis, MN, University of Minnesota Press, 2004); Amber Jamilla Musser, *Sensual Excess: Queer Femininity and Brown Jouissance* (New York, New York University Press, 2018). For the positioning of Baldwin as a queer theorist, see Michael Hames-García, "Can Queer Theory Be Critical Theory?", in Jeffrey Paris and William S. Wilkerson (eds.), *New Critical Theory: Essays on Liberation* (Lanham, MD, Rowman and Littlefield, 2001), p. 180.

3 See Margo Crawford, "The Reclamation of the Homoerotic as Spiritual in *Go Tell It on the Mountain*," in Carol E. Henderson (ed.) *James Baldwin's Go Tell It on the Mountain: Historical and Critical Essays* (New York, Lang, 2006), pp. 75–86; Mae G. Henderson, "James Baldwin's *Giovanni's Room*: Expatriation, 'Racial Drag,' and Homosexual Panic," in Mae G. Henderson and E. Patrick Johnson (eds.), *Black Queer Studies: A Critical Anthology* (Durham, NC, Duke University Press, 2005), pp. 298–322; Justin A. Joyce and Dwight A. McBride, "James Baldwin and Sexuality: *Lieux de Mémoire* and a Usable Past," in Douglas Field (ed.), *A Historical Guide to James Baldwin* (Oxford, Oxford University Press, 2009), pp. 111–39; Dwight A. McBride, "Straight Black Studies: On African American Studies, James Baldwin, and Black Queer Studies," in Henderson and Johnson (eds.), *Black Queer Studies*, pp. 68–89.

4 Sharon Holland argues that while queer of color critique and Black queer studies gesture toward the foundational insights of Black feminism, and often figure Black women at the "vanguard of sexual liberation," this positioning is rarely reflected in the citational engagement with the diversity of Black feminist thought. She asks, "Now that S.H.E is in the center, will the landscape of queer theorizing shift to acknowledge her presence?" See Sharon Holland, *The Erotic Life of Racism* (Durham, NC, Duke University Press, 2012), p. 77. Four years later, E. Patrick Johnson describes the increase in Black queer feminist scholarship considering Black women's sexuality, narrated as a response to Hortense Spillers' call for the theorization of Black women's symbolic position as a "different social subject." See E. Patrick Johnson, "Introduction," in E. Patrick Johnson (ed.), *No Tea No Shade: New Writings in Black Queer Studies* (Durham, NC, Duke University Press, 2016), pp. 11–14; Hortense Spillers, "Mama's Baby, Papa's Maybe: An American Grammar Book," *Diacritics*, 17:1 (1987), p. 80.

5 Holland, *Erotic Life*, p. 3.

6 *Ibid.*, p. 47.

7 *Ibid.*, p. 43.

8 Holland writes that all scholars of sexuality have "an *intellectual* responsibility to take seriously how the transatlantic trade altered the very shape of sexuality in the Americas for *everyone*." *Ibid.*, p. 56.

9 Kadji Amin, *Disturbing Attachments: Genet, Modern Pederasty, and Queer History* (Durham, NC, Duke University Press, 2017), p. 79.

10 *Ibid.*, p. 106.

11 James Baldwin, *The Fire Next Time* (1963), in *Collected Essays*, ed. Toni Morrison (New York, Library of America, 1998), p. 294. Outlining his theory of nonviolence, King writes, "When we speak of loving those who oppose us, we refer neither to *eros* nor

philia; we speak of a love which is expressed in the Greek word *agape*. *Agape* means understanding, redeeming good will for all men." See Martin Luther King, Jr., "An Experiment in Love," in *A Testament of Hope: The Essential Writings and Speeches of Martin Luther King, Jr*, ed. James Melvin Washington (San Francisco, Harper San Francisco, 1986), p. 19.

12 Woubshet writes that in *The Fire Next Time*, "Baldwin conjured up interracial love as a national ideal," and suggests that in *Another Country*, the author fictionalizes the difficulties entailed for those in interracial *romantic* partnerships in particular. See Dagmawi Woubshet, "How James Baldwin's Writings About Love Evolved," *The Atlantic*, 9 January 2019, www.theatlantic.com/entertainment/archive/2019/01/james-baldwin-idea-of-love-fire-next-time-if-beale-street-could-talk/579829/ (accessed 1 October 2020).

13 Qtd. in Matt Brim, *James Baldwin and the Queer Imagination* (Ann Arbor, MI, University of Michigan Press, 2014), p. 118.

14 Eldridge Cleaver, *Soul on Ice* (New York, McGraw-Hill, 1968), p. 102. The problem with this citation is that its popularity within scholarship on the novel (including my own) risks seeming to assume a blanket homophobia within the Black Power movement, an issue addressed by Matt Brim, who calls attention to Huey P. Newton's essay "The Women's Liberation and Gay Liberation Movements" (1970) which "argues for the necessary linkages among those fighting race, gender, and sexual oppression." I choose to cite Cleaver, however, to call attention to the central place ascribed to Baldwin's depiction of sexual desire within readings of the novel across divergent sites of political investment. See Brim, *Queer Imagination*, p. 187.

15 William A. Cohen, "Liberalism, Libido, Liberation: Baldwin's *Another Country*," in Patricia Juliana Smith (ed.), *The Queer Sixties* (Abingdon, Routledge, 1999), p. 212.

16 *Ibid.*, p. 216.

17 Brim, *Queer Imagination*, p. 97.

18 *Ibid.*, pp. 94, 98.

19 *Ibid.*, p. 15

20 *Ibid.*, pp. 15, 122.

21 Ernesto Javier Martínez, *On Making Sense: Queer Race Narratives of Intelligibility* (Stanford, CA, Stanford University Press, 2013), p. 45.

22 Baldwin once described *Another Country* as a depiction of the "disintegration of a black boy" that, like much of his own experience, had "never been seen in the English language before." See Magdalena J. Zaborowska, *James Baldwin's Turkish Decade: Erotics of Exile* (Durham, NC, Duke University Press, 2009), p. 11.

23 Baldwin, *Another Country*, p. 22.

24 *Ibid.*, p. 29.

25 I read as implicitly lesbian the "shapeless filthy women" in the bar to which Jane takes Vivaldo and Rufus. I note, also, Rufus's description of Jane, who "dresses like a goddam bull dagger," and who herself directs a racist remark toward Rufus. Later, on the brink of starvation, Rufus accepts a meal from an older white man who expects sexual favors in return, an exchange-based interaction which I read as one of many contributing to the novel's multifaceted portrayal of sexual dynamics. *Ibid.*, pp. 31–2, 41–5.

26 *Ibid.*, p. 45.

27 *Ibid.*, p. 46.

28 *Ibid.*

29 Holland, *Erotic Life*, p. 2.

30 Trudier Harris, *Black Women in the Fiction of James Baldwin* (Knoxville, TN, University of Tennessee Press, 1985), p. 100.
31 *Ibid.*, p. 99.
32 *Ibid.*, p. 108.
33 *Ibid.*, pp. 108, 206.
34 Baldwin, *Another Country*, p. 132.
35 *Ibid.*, p. 175.
36 *Ibid.*, p. 173.
37 *Ibid.*, p. 175.
38 *Ibid.*
39 *Ibid.*, p. 176.
40 *Ibid.*, p. 177.
41 *Ibid.*, p. 178.
42 Qtd., in Harris, *Black Women*, p. 127.
43 Baldwin, *Another Country*, p. 179.
44 Robert F. Reid-Pharr, *Black Gay Man: Essays* (New York, New York University Press, 2001), p. 91.
45 *Ibid.*, p. 94.
46 Jennifer C. Nash, *The Black Body in Ecstasy: Reading Race, Reading Pornography* (Durham, NC, Duke University Press, 2014), p. 1.
47 *Ibid.*, p. 2.
48 *Ibid.*, p. 3.
49 *Ibid.*, p. 4.
50 Baldwin, *Another Country*, p. 178.
51 *Ibid.*, p. 176.
52 *Ibid.*, pp. 177–8.
53 Nash, *The Black Body in Ecstasy*, p. 14.
54 Baldwin, *Another Country*, p. 336.
55 *Ibid.*, p. 383.
56 *Ibid.*, p. 384.
57 *Ibid.*, p. 389.
58 *Ibid.*, p. 385.
59 *Ibid.*, p. 386.
60 *Ibid.*, p. 387.
61 Brim, *Queer Imagination*, pp. 97, 93.
62 *Ibid.*, pp. 97, 121.
63 Baldwin, *Another Country*, p. 206.
64 *Ibid.*, p. 205.
65 *Ibid.*, p. 206.
66 *Ibid.*
67 For further discussion of this moment, see Brim, *Queer Imagination*, pp. 107–8. See also Kevin Ohi, "I'm Not the Boy You Want: Sexuality, 'Race,' and Thwarted Revelation in James Baldwin's *Another Country*," *African American Review*, 33:2 (1999), pp. 273–6.
68 Baldwin, *Another Country*, pp. 387, 342.
69 Brim, *Queer Imagination*, p. 103.
70 Baldwin, *Another Country*, p. 430.
71 *Ibid.*, p. 431.

72 Brim, *Queer Imagination*, p. 94.

73 Baldwin, *Another Country*, p. 173.

Works Cited

Amin, Kadji, *Disturbing Attachments: Genet, Modern Pederasty, and Queer History* (Durham, NC, Duke University Press, 2017).

Baldwin, James, *Another Country* (1962) (New York, Vintage, 1993).

_____ *The Fire Next Time* (1963), in *Collected Essays*, ed. Toni Morrison (New York, Library of America, 1998), pp. 291–348.

Brim, Matt, *James Baldwin and the Queer Imagination* (Ann Arbor, MI, University of Michigan Press, 2014).

Cleaver, Eldridge, *Soul on Ice* (New York, McGraw-Hill, 1968).

Cohen, William A., "Liberalism, Libido, Liberation: Baldwin's *Another Country*," in Patricia Juliana Smith (ed.), *The Queer Sixties* (Abingdon, Routledge, 1999), pp. 201–22.

Crawford, Margo, "The Reclamation of the Homoerotic as Spiritual in *Go Tell It on the Mountain*," in Carol E. Henderson (ed.), *James Baldwin's Go Tell It on the Mountain: Historical and Critical Essays* (New York, Lang, 2006), pp. 75–86.

Ferguson, Roderick, *Aberrations in Black: Toward a Queer of Color Critique* (Minneapolis, MN, University of Minnesota Press, 2004).

Hames-García, Michael, "Can Queer Theory Be Critical Theory?", in Jeffrey Paris and William S. Wilkerson (eds.), *New Critical Theory: Essays on Liberation* (Lanham, MD, Rowman and Littlefield, 2001), pp. 171–87.

Harris, Trudier, *Black Women in the Fiction of James Baldwin* (Knoxville, TN, University of Tennessee Press, 1985).

Henderson, Mae G., "James Baldwin's *Giovanni's Room*: Expatriation, 'Racial Drag,' and Homosexual Panic," in Mae G. Henderson and E. Patrick Johnson (eds.), *Black Queer Studies: A Critical Anthology* (Durham, NC, Duke University Press, 2005), pp. 298–322.

Holland, Sharon Patricia, *The Erotic Life of Racism* (Durham, NC, Duke University Press, 2012).

Johnson, E. Patrick, "Introduction," in E. Patrick Johnson (ed.), *No Tea No Shade: New Writings in Black Queer Studies* (Durham, NC, Duke University Press, 2016), pp. 1–26.

Joyce, Justin A., and Dwight A. McBride, "James Baldwin and Sexuality: *Lieux de Mémoire* and a Usable Past," in Douglas Field (ed.), *A Historical Guide to James Baldwin* (Oxford, Oxford University Press, 2009), pp. 111–39.

King, Jr., Martin Luther, "An Experiment in Love," in *A Testament of Hope: The Essential Writings and Speeches of Martin Luther King, Jr*, ed. James Melvin Washington (San Francisco, Harper San Francisco, 1986) pp. 16–20.

Martínez, Ernesto Javier, *On Making Sense: Queer Race Narratives of Intelligibility* (Stanford, CA, Stanford University Press, 2013).

McBride, Dwight A, "Straight Black Studies: On African American Studies, James Baldwin, and Black Queer Studies," in Mae G. Henderson and E. Patrick Johnson (eds.), *Black Queer Studies: A Critical Anthology* (Durham, NC, Duke University Press, 2005), pp. 68–89.

Muñoz, José Esteban, *Cruising Utopia: The Then and There of Queer Futurity* (New York, New York University Press, 2009).

Musser, Amber Jamilla, *Sensual Excess: Queer Femininity and Brown Jouissance* (New York, New York University Press, 2018).

Nash, Jennifer C., *The Black Body in Ecstasy: Reading Race, Reading Pornography*. (Durham, NC, Duke University Press, 2014).

Ohi, Kevin, "I'm Not the Boy You Want: Sexuality, 'Race,' and Thwarted Revelation in James Baldwin's *Another Country,*" *African American Review*, 33:2 (1999), pp. 261–81.

Perry, Imani, *Vexy Thing: On Gender and Liberation* (Durham, NC, Duke University Press, 2018).

Reid-Pharr, Robert F., *Black Gay Man: Essays* (New York, New York University Press, 2001).

Spillers, Hortense, "Mama's Baby, Papa's Maybe: An American Grammar Book," *Diacritics*, 17:1 (1987), pp. 64–81.

Woubshet, Dagmawi, "How James Baldwin's Writings About Love Evolved," *The Atlantic*, 9 January 2019, www.theatlantic.com/entertainment/archive/2019/01/james-baldwin-idea-of-love-fire-next-time-if-beale-street-could-talk/579829/ (accessed 1 October 2020).

Zaborowska, Magdalena J., *James Baldwin's Turkish Decade: Erotics of Exile* (Durham, NC, Duke University Press, 2009).

Contributor's Biography

Matty Hemming is a PhD Student in the Department of English at the University of Pennsylvania. She holds a BA in English Literature from Goldsmiths College, University of London, and an MA in Cultural Analysis from the University of Amsterdam. Her research traces connections between twentieth-century US counternarratives to the domestic novel, Black and woman of color feminisms, and the narration of queer and feminist genealogies.

DISPATCH

James Baldwin in the Fire This Time: A Conversation with Bill V. Mullen, the author of *James Baldwin: Living in Fire*

William J. Maxwell   Washington University in St. Louis
Bill V. Mullen   Purdue University

Abstract

William J. Maxwell, editor of *James Baldwin: The FBI File* (2017), interviews Bill V. Mullen on his 2019 biography, *James Baldwin: Living in Fire*, along the way touching on both Baldwin's early internationalism and his relevance to the current wave of racial discord and interracial possibility in the United States.

Keywords: James Baldwin, civil rights movement, *James Baldwin: The FBI File*, *James Baldwin: Living in Fire*, Afropessimism, Black Lives Matter, police

James Baldwin Review, Volume 7, 2021, © The Authors. Published by Manchester University Press and
The University of Manchester Library
http://dx.doi.org/10.7227/JBR.7.9

William J. Maxwell (WJM): To begin with, Bill, an orienting question about your 2019 biography of James Baldwin, *Living in Fire*, before we plow into Baldwin's extraordinary presence now in the summer of 2020. It's safe to say that the rediscovered twenty-first-century Baldwin is an overtly political as well as literary figure, not just an icon within the culture of Black Lives Matter but a major source of movement thought and perhaps even strategy. More than the significant Baldwin biographies before it, *Living in Fire* delves deeply into Baldwin's specifically political activities during his own lifetime—his party memberships and fellow traveling, his on-the-ground and on-the-stage experiences as a civil rights protestor and anti-imperialist activist, etc. What does your focus on his political life as such add to our contemporary impression of Baldwin as "woke" far ahead of the curve?

Bill V. Mullen (BVM): The focus on the activist or "woke" Baldwin emerged organically from my research. The more I read, the more I came to understand that almost every word Baldwin wrote had a material connection to a political problem he was trying to solve. For example, the motivation for the novel *If Beale Street Could Talk* (1974) came at least in part from his personal and financial defense of his dear friend Tony Maynard, who was falsely accused of murder and spent six years in jail. I make the argument that the rhetoric and to some extent the primary audience—his young nephew—for *The Fire Next Time* (1963) derived from his 1962 speaking tour for CORE (Congress of Racial Equality), when he went to college campuses to speak to young people and raise funds for the group. We like to say that Baldwin's *writings* were woke. To my mind, it was the political practices and commitments that informed the consciousness of the writing.

Stepping back a bit, I think the most provocative way to understand Baldwin as ahead of the curve is to appreciate his prescient internationalism. If Baldwin were alive today, I think he would understand Black Lives Matter as a global movement against global capitalism. We often forget that he was drawn into anticolonialism by serving as a witness to the Algerian struggle while in Paris; that in the 1950s he formed his politics out of careful consideration of the shape of Stalin's Soviet Union (which he hated); and in the 1960s and 1970s in response to events in Cuba, Chile, Vietnam, and South Africa. Somehow, Baldwin's support for Palestinian liberation has been lost in the flood of his other political commitments, but it is a powerful through line in his life and work as evinced by his struggle against Zionism and his attempts to analogize the Black and Arab world. I mean, all of the terms that we use today to describe something like a global consciousness—diasporic thinking, transnationalism, internationalism, etc.—were present in Baldwin's thought from the moment he left the US in 1948 and briefly considered moving to Israel, pausing to worry "which side" would he live on, Arab or Jew. So it seems to me that many of the major political questions we struggle with here and now, in our integrated world system, were faced directly by Baldwin. I find that thrilling and essential to remember and celebrate.

WJM: Almost from the start, at least as early as the famous 1955 essay "Notes of a Native Son," Baldwin's prose is elegantly but remarkably frank about police violence against African Americans. In comparison, Baldwin's somewhat older literary peer, Ralph Ellison, showed up for his freshman year at Tuskegee with a knot on his head from a railroad cop's billy club, but rarely returned to the subject without surreal irony after his first short story, "Hymie's Bull," published in 1996, but composed in the late 1930s. In the 1960 essay "Fifth Avenue, Uptown," written at the beginning of the decade when the "Long Hot Summers" got hot, Baldwin began comparing white policemen in Harlem to "occupying soldier[s] in a bitterly hostile country."[1] Does Baldwin's unusually deep, sharp, and consistent treatment of racialized policing amount to something like an early theory of systemic police brutality? Can it illuminate the transition from Baldwin the African American exceptionalist to Baldwin the anticolonial internationalist—a transition close to the heart of your *Living in Fire*?

BVM: Yes! It's important that Baldwin said that one of his first political traumas of racial identity was being knocked to the ground by two policemen when he was just ten years old. And that he lived through both the 1935 and 1943 race riots in Harlem, episodes triggered directly or indirectly by police violence and occupation. Baldwin was obsessed with the police presence in Black communities not just because they terrorized and subordinated the population, but also because they symbolized white fear, control, and violence against Black people. When he was in the South, he feared the sheriffs. When he was in Paris—as he famously recorded in the essay "Equal in Paris" (1955)—it was the experience of being sent to jail, and seeing so many North Africans there, that made him understand global policing as a maker of "Blackness." Then of course he went head-to-head with the FBI, as you well know; he defended Angela Davis when she was in jail; defended Tony Maynard; wrote *Beale Street*, and so on.

What is Baldwin's theory of systemic policy brutality? That, as he put it in "A Report from Occupied Territory" (1966), the police "are present to keep the Negro in his place and to protect white business interests, and they have no other function."[2] That is a fundamentally abolitionist position. Baldwin understood that to do away with the police you'd have to do away with capitalism—private property. He understood that reordering society to allow Black people to flourish—to be cared for, and loved, and given the resources to live—would mean abolishing the police as an obstacle to those things.

How does Baldwin's analysis of policing explain his transition to anticolonial internationalism? I think it was the combination of his personal experience of the police, as I described earlier, and his political education through groups like the Black Panther Party, that allowed Baldwin to see the police as part of the Western militarization of the planet: during the Vietnam War he often analogized the presence of the US military in the jungles of Southeast Asia and the killing of Black people at home by police. The essay I mentioned earlier, "Equal in Paris," was really a foreshadowing of all this. By the time he wrote the memoir *No Name in the*

Street in 1972, Baldwin was remembering the 1960s mainly as a decade of military violence and police violence against Black people in America and as a linchpin of US imperialism. In this respect, I argue that *No Name in the Street* is a kind of anti-imperialist sequel to *The Fire Next Time*. The hard lessons that Baldwin learned about what scholar Micol Seigel calls the "violence work" of policing between 1963 and 1972 help to explain its sequel status.

WJM: Speaking of Baldwin as an early or proto-theorist, what does he tell us about the historical habit of white American backlash and massive resistance—among other things, the antagonistic subject of his semi-Afropessimistic memoir *No Name in the Street*. What, in particular, does he tell us about this habit that 2020 needs to hear?

BVM: Well, it's been noted before that Baldwin in a way invented "whiteness studies." He famously said that being Black gave him the advantage of knowing more about white people than they knew about him, because he had to watch them so carefully in order to stay alive. But he also argued that whiteness was constructed, was ideological: "as long as you think you're white," he instructed, "there is no hope for you."[3] What we need to hear from Baldwin in 2020 are two things, I think. First, that white supremacy is a constituent part of capitalism. Whiteness, he said, is simply a metaphor for Chase Bank. I think that current anti-policing protests and calls for police reform have come to a similar conclusion: that the police are here to protect white business interests and keep Black people down.

Second, what we also need to hear, though, and we can actually see in the moment we are living in, is that white consciousness can change. That's the subtext and emphasis of "as long as you *think* you're white." Baldwin said that his experience of having a loving teacher in Bill Miller convinced him that he could never hate white people, even though he wanted to kill some of them. I think Baldwin so often targeted white audiences as a writer because he simply did the math, and knew that until the majority consciousness had shifted, nothing would change. In 2020, it feels like we are getting closer to something like that moment of change: even casual polls show that about 70 percent of Americans support the protests against police violence, and that more than half the people in the streets since George Floyd's murder in Minneapolis have been white, or non-black. This would have made Baldwin very happy, but I also think it's something he analytically concluded was fundamental to real change. I think that when we go back and read Baldwin, we need to remember his cautious optimism of the will, his faith that one day, though God knows it wasn't going to be easy, white Americans might themselves get woke.

WJM: A very different question on the political content of Baldwin's literary form, so to speak—one I've asked myself several times, but never answered to my own satisfaction. Isn't there something uncanny about Baldwin's anticipation, in the personal-to-prophetic voice of his nonfiction, of our own socially mediated remaking of progressive politics as a public theater of the self? In other words, isn't it strange—meaningfully so—that the blend of social prophecy and theatrical self-exposure in nearly all of Baldwin's best essays anticipates the very twenty-first-century job description of the freedom fighter/social media star? What does the tweet-friendly and constantly retweeted Baldwin tell us about both him and us?

BVM: I thought the Raoul Peck film *I Am Not Your Negro* (2016) was very clever in using so many film clips to both narrate and illustrate Baldwin's life. I believe that Peck understood that Baldwin's words, Baldwin's ideas, existed in conversation with the mass media sensorium that shaped him and to which he constantly reacted. *The Devil Finds Work* (1976) is really the autobiography of a Black consciousness made in movie theaters. But, at a deeper level, I think that Baldwin understood self-narration, or what we might call autoethnography, as a quintessentially twentieth-century (and now twenty-first-century) form. Baldwin said he was a "witness," intending the old church sense of someone who sees spiritual pain and suffering and reports on it. But I also hear in this self-description Baldwin the media theorist responding to the spectacular world of television, film, and advertising. John Wayne explained Ronald Reagan to Baldwin as much as the other way around. In tandem, the representation on the screen of, say, Sidney Poitier in *The Defiant Ones* (1958) held an ominous mirror up to Baldwin that demanded commentary and, pardon the pun, reflection.

I wanted to write a whole chapter about Baldwin on television—the Dick Cavett appearances, the debates with Malcolm X—because it seemed as if Baldwin was inventing radical Black political media performativity at the same time he was inventing Black public intellectual life. It's hard not to see Baldwin's media presence, peaking with the 1963 *Time* magazine cover, in the same frame as the spectacularly watched life of a figure like Muhammad Ali. And then there was his mastery of the new media itself—Baldwin's training in theater, his frustrated aspirations to act, manifesting as the production of a performative persona that was as powerful and effective as his literary presence. His 1965 debate with William F. Buckley at Cambridge fused these moments into the highest form of political theater: it was Baldwin's *Tempest*! And lastly, I think that Baldwin's persistent self-exposure and self-consciousness led to its own form of exposure exhaustion. The retreats to Istanbul, Saint-Paul de Vence, and Puerto Rico were necessary self-care expeditions, I think, to escape the geopolitical paparazzi that hunted and wore him down. These trips were returns not just to privacy but to the restoration of an evolving private self that was the genesis of his genius.

At the same time, Baldwin's essays are—you're right—something like letters from the self: long-form literary Instagrams, or tweets, highly self-conscious of their audience, gunning for the widest number of readers. There is always an implied "you" in Baldwin's writings—this reminds me of Toni Morrison's work— meaning that he was aware that his writing was only finished by the reader. I made a case for the need for a new biography of Baldwin not just because of his rediscovery by the Black Lives Matter movement but also because of blogs like Son of Baldwin, and Baldwin's endless citationality in places like Black Twitter—the reader coming home to roost. I think that Eddie Glaude, Jr. said it really well in 2016—"James Baldwin is everywhere"—as his face and words seemed to acquire a second or third afterlife in the mediasphere that he had helped to predict and create.[4]

WJM: Finally, Bill, as much as I admire Baldwin—and I know you do as well!—and think of him as a major social analyst and literary master, the best, most revealing, and most representative American essayist, as Glaude suggests, after Emerson, I'm suspicious of the impulse to canonize him as a patron saint or spirit guide. Baldwin and Baldwinism has been out in force in the remarkable wave of protest following the killing of George Floyd, his face pictured in hundreds of posters and his words quoted in thousands of posts. In a spirit of enlightening iconoclasm, however, could you give us a sense of the ways in which Baldwin's work does *not* jibe with or clarify our present? Could you speculate on What Baldwin Wouldn't See—or Wouldn't Do—about the ongoing movement for Black Lives?

BVM: I think that Baldwin would have struggled with the concept of anti-Blackness or Afropessimism. His thinking was too two-sided for it: the deeper that white supremacy and state power got, the more he swam in the direction of hope. Now, hope is not a flattened out concept in Baldwin. It depends on resistance: the fight both to make something happen in the world, and to make meaning of it. I'm also not sure where Baldwin would have come down on LGBTQ liberation in our time. His suspicions about queer-first politics in the 1980s might have gone in several directions, though I don't think he would ever have opposed or rejected the idea that sexual liberation was a cornerstone of world remaking. I think that Matt Brim's recent work on Baldwin raises interesting questions of that sort, including about Baldwin and feminism: I think he would have been thrilled to see Black queer women leading BLM, but I don't know exactly how he would have celebrated it. I believe that ongoing movements to reclaim Baldwin need to interrogate his ambiguities and contradictions. They need to remember that he too was never static, was always evolving, and in some ways never fully "arrived" at positions we might want to project onto him. I think that Baldwin would have loved to see statues of slave traders and Confederates tossed into the harbor, but I'm not sure he would want to replace them with monuments to himself. I think he preferred that history itself be iconoclastic. That meant it could still be dangerous.

Notes

1 James Baldwin, "Fifth Avenue, Uptown: A Letter From Harlem" (1960), in *Collected Essays*, ed. Toni Morrison (New York, Library of America, 1998), p. 176.

2 James Baldwin, "A Report From Occupied Territory" (1966), in Morrison (ed.), *Collected Essays*, p. 734.
3 James Baldwin, qtd. in *James Baldwin: The Price of the Ticket* (1989), dir. Karen Thorsen.
4 Eddie S. Glaude, Jr., "James Baldwin and the Trap of Our History," *Time*, 18 August 2016, https://time.com/4457112/james-baldwin-eddie-glaude/ (accessed 14 September 2020).

Works Cited

Baldwin, James, "Fifth Avenue, Uptown: A Letter from Harlem" (1960), in *Collected Essays*, ed. Toni Morrison (New York, Library of America, 1998), pp. 170–9.

_____ "A Report from Occupied Territory" (1966), in *Collected Essays*, ed. Toni Morrison (New York, Library of America, 1998), pp. 728–38.
Glaude, Jr., Eddie S., "James Baldwin and the Trap of Our History," *Time*, 18 August 2016, https://time.com/4457112/james-baldwin-eddie-glaude/ (accessed 14 September 2020).
Thorsen, Karen (dir.), *James Baldwin: The Price of the Ticket* (1989, USA).

Contributors' Biographies

William J. Maxwell is Professor of English and African and African American Studies at Washington University in St. Louis. He is the author of *F.B. Eyes: How J. Edgar Hoover's Ghostreaders Framed African American Literature* (Princeton University Press, 2015), which won an American Book Award in 2016, and *New Negro, Old Left: African American Writing and Communism between the Wars* (Columbia University Press, 1999). He is the editor of the collection *James Baldwin: The FBI File* (Arcade, 2017); of Claude McKay's *Complete Poems* (University of Illinois Press, 2004, 2008, 2013); and, along with Gary Edward Holcomb, of Claude McKay's previously unpublished novel *Romance in Marseille* (Penguin, 2020).

Bill V. Mullen is Professor Emeritus of American Studies at Purdue University. He is the author, most recently, of *James Baldwin: Living in Fire* (Pluto Press, 2019). His other books include *W.E.B. Du Bois: Revolutionary Across the Color Line* (Pluto Press, 2016), *Un-American: W.E.B. Du Bois and the Century of World Revolution* (Temple University Press, 2004), *Popular Fronts: Chicago and African-American Cultural Politics, 1935–1946* (University of Illinois Press, 1999). He is also co-editor, with Ashley Dawson, of *Against Apartheid: The Case for Boycotting Israeli Universities* (Haymarket Books, 2015), and has edited five other books in collaboration with Sherry Lee Linkon, James Smethurst, and Fred Ho. His articles have appeared in *Social Text*, *African-American Review*, *American Quarterly*, *Modern Fiction Studies*, *Electronic Intifada*, *Truthout*, *Mondoweiss*, *Jacobin*, and elsewhere.

Manchester University Press

DISPATCH

How Long Blues: An Interview with James Campbell

Douglas Field   University of Manchester
Justin A. Joyce   The New School

Abstract

James Baldwin Review editors Douglas Field and Justin A. Joyce interview author and Baldwin biographer James Campbell on the occasion of the reissue of his book *Talking at the Gates* (Polygon and University of California Press, 2021).

Keywords: James Campbell, *Talking at the Gates*, James Baldwin, biography, *New Edinburgh Review*, Norman Mailer, literary criticism, reviews

James Baldwin Review, Volume 7, 2021, © The Authors. Published by Manchester University Press and The University of Manchester Library
http://dx.doi.org/10.7227/JBR.7.10

James Campbell was born in Glasgow in 1951. He left school to take up a printer's apprenticeship, before going on to study at Edinburgh University. Between 1978 and 1982, he was the editor of the quarterly *New Edinburgh Review*, and later worked part-time as an editor at the *Times Literary Supplement* (*TLS*). For many years, as J.C., he wrote the NB column in the *TLS*. His books include *Gate Fever: Voices from a Prison* (1986), *Paris Interzone* (1994; published in the US as *Exiled in Paris*), *This is the Beat Generation* (1999), and a collection of essays, *Syncopations* (2007). He is the editor of the *Picador Book of Blues and Jazz* (1995). His memoir, *Just Go Down to the Road*, will be published in Britain and the US in 2022.

In anticipation of the reissue of *Talking at the Gates* on both sides of the Atlantic earlier this year, *James Baldwin Review* editors Douglas Field and Justin A. Joyce interviewed Mr. Campbell via email, the method being determined by travel restrictions and the various limitations of 2020. We are grateful to Mr. Campbell for his engaging responses and delighted to share them here with our readers.

James Baldwin Review (JBR): Can you begin by telling us how you came to write *Talking at the Gates*?

James Campbell (JC): I had no intention of writing a book about James Baldwin during the years I knew him, though I'm not quite sure why that should be so. I had written articles about him, after all, and had already published two books on other subjects by the time he died. So I ought to have been on the lookout for a good subject. Maybe I just thought he would never die.

The suggestion to write "a life," as we called it, came directly from Caryl Phillips, on behalf of Faber and Faber. He had read the obituary I wrote of Baldwin in the *Independent*. Faber might have suggested first that he write the book, but if so he passed the baton to me. He and I flew to New York together to attend the funeral at the Cathedral of St. John the Divine. We were present at the wake, in Mikell's on 97th Street and Columbus Avenue, where David Baldwin used to work behind the bar. We drank Bloody Marys all the way home on the daytime flight and I felt I was traveling through space at a higher altitude than the plane. On getting back, I started work more or less right away.

JBR: What was it like to work with Baldwin? And what was it like to socialize with him?

JC: In both cases, great. Baldwin liked collaboration, and so it was flattering to hear him say to others at a party or the like that we had "worked together." It also got me out of looking like the latest hanger-on. The work itself was modest: mainly on his essay "Of the Sorrow Songs: The Cross of Redemption," published in the autumn 1979 issue of the *New Edinburgh Review*, of which I was editor. The hardest task was prising the piece from him. When I was introduced to Victor Navasky,

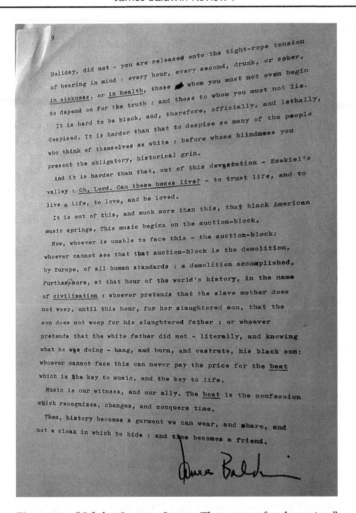

9

Holiday, did not - you are released onto the tight-rope tension
of bearing in mind : every hour, every second, drunk, or sober,
in sickness, or in health, those ⚫ whom you must not even begin
to depend on for the truth : and those to whom you must not lie.
    It is hard to be black, and, therefore, officially, and lethally,
despised. It is harder than that to despise so many of the people
who think of themselves as white : before whose blindness you
present the obligatory, historical grin.
    And it is harder than that, out of this devastation - Ezekiel's
valley : Oh, Lord. Can these bones live? - to trust life, and to
live a life, to love, and be loved.
    It is out of this, and much more than this, that black American
music springs. This music begins on the auction-block.
    Now, whoever is unable to face this - the auction-block:
whoever cannot see that that auction-block is the demolition,
by Europe, of all human standards : a demolition accomplished,
furthermore, at that hour of the world's history, in the name
of civilization : whoever pretends that the slave mother does
not weep, until this hour, for her slaughtered son, that the
son does not weep for his slaughtered father : or whoever
pretends that the white father did not - literally, and knowing
what he was doing - hang, and burn, and castrate, his black son:
whoever cannot face this can never pay the price for the beat
which is the key to music, and the key to life.
    Music is our witness, and our ally. The beat is the confession
which recognizes, changes, and conquers time.
    Then, history becomes a garment we can wear, and share, and
not a cloak in which to hide : and time becomes a friend.

Figure 1   "Of the Sorrow Songs: The cross of redemption,"
manuscript with Baldwin's signature

editor of *The Nation*, not long afterwards, it was with the words: "Meet someone else who succeeded in getting a piece out of James Baldwin." He was always gracious when we spoke on the phone—Edinburgh to Saint-Paul de Vence two or three times a week, no small thing in 1979—as well as funny and friendly. You could feel the charisma down the line. He sent me telegrams to keep me in touch about deadlines, and on the phone said, "I'm working on it, baby," but he wasn't. Only when I told him the cover was ready, with his picture, did he say: "I'm on the cover!? Oh, baby. I'd better get to work."

In Saint-Paul I read some things, including the then unpublished texts of *The Evidence of Things Not Seen* and several poems, and talked to him about them in

Figure 2   *New Edinburgh Review*, autumn 1979

the role of editor to writer. I think he liked this arrangement, and would have liked more of it (he needed more of it), but I was young, and not sufficiently assured in my part in the drama to press my points. I had the sense that I could have stuck around there and found a role, as a secretary or something, which would eventually have evolved into the role of hanger-on. I wish I had done more editing on "Of the Sorrow Songs." Not much. But an editor's principal task is to take a good piece and make it better. And I could have done that.

Jimmy was so sociable I'd almost say it was an affliction. An example: one day at Saint-Paul, we finished lunch (at about 4 p.m.), then sat around until he said he had to retreat downstairs and get to work. He had various things on the go, including a novel, "No Papers for Muhammad." He told his housekeeper Valérie this, making typing motions while saying, "*à la machine à écrire.*" When I said I would walk up to the village meanwhile and have a beer, Jimmy immediately changed his mind. "I'll come with you."

As we walked the quarter mile uphill to the Colombe d'Or together, he began to sing "How Long Blues." It is a precious memory—but he should have been working.

Otherwise, I accompanied him to parties and we had late-night drinking sessions. He was always the center of attention, and the stories—about being told by his publisher to change the sex of Giovanni and call the novel "Giovanna's Room", for example—were repeated and enhanced. You were always conscious of being in the presence of something great—it wasn't just your Uncle Jimmy. Not for me anyway, though we liked to say we had Calvinism in common. He could be introverted or extroverted, agreeable or tempestuous. I was the target of one of his rages only once (recounted in *Talking at the Gates*). On another occasion, after he had delivered a tirade against "white" people, I must have looked dismayed for he placed a hand on my knee and said, gently, "I'm not talking about you, baby. I'm talking about *the people who think they are white.*" That was a typical remark—which I've never ceased to resort to—and they came one after another.

JBR: Why did you decide to revise *Talking at the Gates* and what's different from the original Faber edition?

JC: The idea of a new edition came from Neville Moir at the Edinburgh publisher Polygon. He wanted a complete rewrite and update. It was tempting, but after thinking about it and taking advice from some experienced biographers, I decided against. A book billed as "the revised edition" has the immediate effect of making the copy on your shelf seem redundant. The revisions in this case are largely cosmetic, but there is a 5,000 word introduction, a brief afterword on the subject of conducting interviews, and a substantial Q&A interview about Baldwin with Norman Mailer, conducted in the bar of the Algonquin in 1988 but scarcely used. That's the new stuff, together with some improvements in the text.

JBR: You mention in the first section an early collaboration of Baldwin's with a friend—Theodore Pelatowski—on a photo and nonfiction essay book about Harlem, "Unto the Dying Lamb," that never came to fruition. Does the text or a draft of it survive somewhere?

JC: The first I ever heard of the Baldwin–Pelatowski collaboration was when David Baldwin sat me down at the Café de la Place in Saint-Paul de Vence, shortly after his brother's death, and produced a folio of black-and-white photographs. Pelatowski's main interest was in painting, apparently, but he and Baldwin—both in their early twenties—set out to record Harlem churches and dance halls, in image and word. I believe this was in late 1946. The book disappeared from the record, but an excerpt published in the New York daily newspaper *PM* in April 1947 has recently come to light. Other than that, nothing.

It would make a wonderful book, as I suggested to David at the time (1988). He said he had the text in his apartment in New York, but if it does exist it is not in the New York Public Library's holdings, as far as I have been able to determine. They do have some photographs, yet the sheaf of images they sent me in 2020 does not include those shown to me by David back then. At the time, I was very eager to get a look at the text, and to make a closer examination of the photographs, but nothing doing. They remained in David's grip. It was nevertheless good of him to volunteer to show them to me. One day it will come out. With an introduction by Hilton Als, probably. I can visualize it now.

JBR: *Talking at the Gates* is replete with interviews with Baldwin's friends and associates from across the globe. You tackled his friends and family. Can you tell us a bit about the process of writing the biography? And can you reflect on the differences between working on a biography now, compared to thirty years ago?

JC: In writing that book, and others before and after, I began with a pen and a notebook, into which I put observations, notes on interviews (I rarely used a tape recorder), simple ideas for structural arrangement, thoughts emerging from a reading of new materials and re-readings of old, including the primary texts. You can put anything in, and let it struggle to nose its way towards the finishing line. Much of what you include travels nowhere, of course, but the notebooks pile up and by the time you're ready to begin writing in earnest you already have a crude first draft.

All through the time of writing of *Talking at the Gates*—and the books on Paris and the Beats that came after—I was working as an editor at the *TLS*, but only for two days a week, and under a rather easy-going administration. So I was able to slip away from the office to go to New York, for example, and slip back in a fortnight later, without attracting much attention.

In the new introduction, I reflect on the process of making connections with Baldwin's friends and associates—some of them from way, way back—before the age of email. International Directory Enquiries was a great friend to me. Sometimes I had only a name and a possible city. If it was an unusual name—this was how I found Mrs. Pelatowski—the telephonist at the other end might be inveigled into giving up two or three listings, and maybe an address as well. You could then ring each number in turn, until—if lucky—you reached the person you were looking for. Directory Enquiries were ideal research assistants.

In the introduction I also mention traveling to libraries before the dawn of the internet. It could be laborious and time-consuming and expensive, but there is a lot to be gained in this pursuit. Serendipity is my other favorite research assistant. Just as one magazine or book leads to another, one interviewee does so, too. I like this way of working, because the unexpected is a good stimulant. A day out on Long Island to meet someone from the 1950s crowd can lead to the Actors Studio in Manhattan next morning, to talk about *Blues for Mr. Charlie*, then on to the Café de Flore when back in Europe. In many cases I just called up from the corner telephone booth. "Come on over." People brought me sheafs of letters from Baldwin—I'm thinking of Gordon Heath and Leslie Schenk in Paris, both friends from the 1950s—and said: Take them away and make copies; bring them back when you're ready. In both these cases, and in many others, friendships were formed. That wouldn't have happened if we'd been restricted to email.

I wrote letters and got letters in return. Engin Cezzar: "Come to Turkey. We are waiting for you." Fantastic! Engin took me to Yashar Kemal, a wonderful man, and acted as interpreter. We sat in a triangular arrangement in his living room, just outside Istanbul. Yashar made his points pithily. "Jimmy would say to me, 'Yashar, I feel free in Turkey.' I would say, 'Jimmy, that's because you are an American.'" Kemal had been imprisoned for his political activities more than once.

JBR: And you also took on the FBI.

JC: I tackled the FBI under the guidance of Anthony Summers, an investigative journalist. It was more difficult in those days. He told me how to go about gaining access to a file under the US Freedom of Information Act. But, he said, you'll need a lawyer. Of course, one's hair stands on end at the very idea, but James Lesar is the most reasonable lawyer in Washington. He sued the FBI under my name, though I paid just a nominal fee. The case went on for years and ended up in the US Court of Appeals, the second highest in the land: *James Campbell, plaintiff v. US Department of Justice, defendant*. It still gives me a kick to type it. Later on, I went to visit Lesar in his tiny office in Washington DC and wrote a piece about it all for *Granta*. Now you can get the files on the internet.

JBR: Forgive us for calling for a bit of armchair psychological speculation here, but you note several times the outsized influence Baldwin's stepfather, David, had on his life, and you've portrayed several people—Richard Wright, Beauford Delaney, and a few others—as surrogate fathers. Certainly Baldwin himself referred to them in this way. We wonder if you've given any thought to what sort of man or artist Baldwin might have become had his father not been so merciless and menacing?

JC: I think that's what is called a counterfactual. Impossible to say, and perhaps impertinent to try. If his father had been a kind and attentive "new man," would we be living without the author of *Go Tell It on the Mountain*? We wouldn't have that novel, certainly, since it's largely about life with father. We would be without "Notes of a Native Son" and "Down at the Cross," too. We don't choose what we're born into, and this branch of that particular family life is a domestic outpost of what Baldwin called "the nightmare called history"—in his *New Edinburgh Review* essay, as it happens. We wouldn't have had that piece either. A bit of private disturbance can result in an abundance of universally appreciated art. What else is one to say? It's the way the world turns, and we can't get back to the Garden.

JBR: The dust jacket for the 1991 hardcover edition of *Talking at the Gates* has a blurb from Arnold Rampersad who calls your approach to Baldwin's life "without reverence, though not quite irreverent." That seems rather apt, as you clearly have a great deal of respect and admiration for the man, but you also don't pull punches, and you have come in for a fair amount of, sometimes biting, critiques. All this, we think, is for the good and makes *Talking at the Gates* a wonderful resource.

However, one omission that seems striking is that you don't explicitly discuss Baldwin's multiple suicide attempts. Can you say a bit about that choice?

JC: Baldwin was the most magnetic and fascinating man I've ever met. That's a punch I'm happy not to pull. But I also happen to be burdened by a literary-critical tendency. If someone tells me that *Tell Me How Long the Train's Been Gone* and *If Beale Street Could Talk* are good novels, *qua* novels, I'll know where I stand in relation to that person's critical faculty. It didn't even occur to me to hide my responses while writing the book, which I'll agree seems surprisingly severe in places—even to me, when I reread it recently in preparation for the new edition. But if I couldn't be honest about what I don't like, how could the reader trust me when it comes to what I admire?

As for "biting critiques," by which I take it you mean harsh criticism … Has there been much of that? People should feel free to disagree. I don't enjoy bad reviews any more than anyone else, especially when they are lazy, but I don't mind a good, gloves-off slugging match, in which a reviewer really has it out with the book. A book should know at the end of the bout that it's been reviewed—that's the ideal sort.

The only odd situation I can think of involved Michael Thelwell, who barracked and harassed me in front of a crowd at Amherst College in 1991, where Caryl Phillips had invited me to give a talk. Then he went on to praise *Talking at the Gates* so profusely in the *Boston Globe* that Penguin took some of his no doubt carefully chosen words for the cover of the paperback. A couple of years year later, he started attacking me in public again—on this occasion in front of a crowd at Lincoln Center. In an interview a little later with Herb Boyd, he appeared to deny that he had even written the review in the *Boston Globe*.

A review shouldn't be too harsh. You can be honest without being cruel. It's usually people who haven't written anything of value themselves who feel the need to punish authors.

As for Baldwin's suicide attempts, that's simple: I knew nothing about them. If I had come into possession of some intimate information, would I have used it? I'm not sure. The same goes for detailed discussion of his mostly unhappy love affairs. Is it any of my business? Is it yours? Some things ought to remain private after death—especially a death so recent as Baldwin's was then.

If certain details could be used to quicken the narrative in a way that I wanted, then I might overrule my own squeamishness. One principle trumps all others in the writing of a book such as this: Don't be boring. But don't try to keep the reader's attention with a parade of salacious detail. Call me old fashioned.

JBR: *Talking at the Gates* is wonderfully detailed with the contextual moments of Baldwin's life—how he lived and moved and the ways travel, fame, etc., shaped and pressured his life. You mention in the introduction to the 2021 edition how profoundly these and other things have changed since the late 1980s, and you even note explicitly that one of your impressions was that Baldwin was of a "faded era" and that the dramatic arc of his life and fame was of a "different time." We think this is absolutely true, that Baldwin represents the high modernist sense of a literary artist, a sense very much no longer coherent. We wonder if you have any sense of how much the recuperation of Baldwin is a longing for the relative clarity of the sense and role of the artist from that earlier heyday that compares favorably to the notion of "artist" that is so much more diffuse now. In short, is it Baldwin himself that's so much in vogue, or is it the sense of literary genius that is being recuperated?

JC: Well, that's a very interesting question, which is what interviewees say when they can't immediately think of an answer. But let me try from my own perspective.

When Baldwin was first in vogue, in the early 1960s, there was a certain settled idea of what America was and what it promised, carried over from the postwar years. It was victorious in spirit and mostly beneficent. Hollywood movies reflected a positive image of national life, lived within a classic comedic structure: muddle leading to discontent, struggling toward truth and clarity, with sacrifice along the way, ending in happiness. Life could be like World War II in miniature. America will always see you through. The image was mostly white, and the style Anglocentric. Yet there was an underlying sense in the minds even of people who enjoyed this form of entertainment that it wasn't all there was, that another current ran darkly beneath the surface. We all know it, yet choose not to mention it. It isn't necessarily racial. "There's a lot of shit under the world," in the words of Allen Ginsberg's "Kaddish."

The role of a certain sort of serious writer is to dig under the surface, to challenge the notions that society has about itself. Baldwin wasn't the only one in the postwar era, of course. Mailer was subversive, so were Gore Vidal and John Cheever and Saul Bellow, all in different ways; Henry Miller and William Burroughs; later, Philip Roth, and so on. Literary form itself can be rebellious, and literature is often at its most subversive when we see this in action: think of *The Waste Land*, *Naked Lunch*, or, to bring it back to Harlem, *Invisible Man*. I don't think Baldwin had the chops to achieve a shake-up in form of this type, though he wanted to—the evidence is there in his talk about reshaping the English language to fit his experience (see the essay "Why I Stopped Hating Shakespeare"). His subversiveness lay in making his own Uptown New York experience clear and tangible to those who hadn't come within a mile of it in reality. That and his facility for saying significant things in a straightforward and charitable way.

There are doubtless those among the younger generation of novelists who are doing similar work in their turn. I'm not as well informed as I might be, but I don't think it's controversial, or even original, to say that the dimensions of the novel have shrunk since that great generation of the 1950s and 1960s, many of whom are disapproved of now for being insufficiently "correct" in their opinions, actions, characters. What's radical, when everyone who reads books is in accordance with received ideas about race, class, and gender? Shake things up! Say something shocking! That's where Mailer and Vidal and Baldwin would have come in. But when teachers in class are afraid to use the word "nigger," even when quoting from *The Fire Next Time*, literary expression is in deep trouble. How can people teach the work of Faulkner? You'll get challenged for it, suspended, and possibly sacked. This is a disastrous situation where freedom of the imagination is concerned. Censorship has become institutionalized all over again, and the new censors come mostly from the student ranks—traditionally the rebels. The so-called radical ideas of our present moment seem to someone like me to be in pursuit of constraint. Why aren't established writers speaking out against it? For fear of being on the wrong side, or of losing their university positions. Tell me I'm wrong.

In short, if there is a "sense of literary genius" abroad today, of the sort that Baldwin and others paraded, often noisily, ostentatiously, obnoxiously, I appear to have missed it.

JBR: One more on this. So much of the recuperation of Baldwin outside academic circles is happening through social media. Much of it in hashtags and the circulation of Baldwin's image or quotes that are taken out of context, which results, unfortunately, either in a rather one-dimensional portrait of a complex person— something Baldwin himself surely would have railed against—or is, in short, just wrong. There are a number of quotes attributed to him that simply came from elsewhere, though they are utilized a lot because they fill a certain sentiment and they often *sound* like something Baldwin would have said or wrote. How much damage do you think this inaccuracy is doing to the greater understanding of Baldwin and his legacy? Is there anything that can be done about it?

JC: I live in happy ignorance of the world of hashtags, but I understand what you're saying. Baldwin has greater presence as an icon than as a writer. Yes, there is something that can be done about it, and it's elementary: read his books. Then read other books. Reading *Invisible Man*, for example, you reach a certain understanding about Baldwin, which is that he could never have written a novel of that stature. He didn't share Ellison's deep relationship to the literature of the past. He did, however, write other things—he wrote twenty books, while in a considerably longer life Ellison produced three (not counting those published posthumously). Baldwin affected readers in ways that Ellison did not. Is that of greater value? Just thinking about these things leads to the formation of a critical faculty and the development of taste.

JBR: In addition to his presence on social media, there's been quite a flourishing of Baldwin imagery in terms of artistic portraits in recent years. We wonder if you've any thoughts about how his image—that of his face alone—circulates apart from his written work?

JC: We're back to where we were in 1965, aren't we? Baldwin as spokesman, a role he never really welcomed. Now it's gone further, if the spokesman is credited with things he never said. I imagine that this is how saints are created. No writer should be made into a saint.

JBR: What's your sense of how scholarship on Baldwin has changed since you wrote *Talking at the Gates*? Is it heading in the right direction?

JC: The most remarkable change is in the amount of it. And in the particularity. When I began writing my book, the full-length bibliography on Baldwin amounted to three or four items. There was a short critical study by Stanley Macebuh, Fern Marja Eckman's lively portrait, and maybe one or two collections of critical essays. Weatherby's book hadn't yet come out, though he had written *Squaring Off: Mailer vs. Baldwin*, which is good journalistic fun. Leeming's biography appeared after mine.

In the past twenty years or so, there has been an explosion—some but not all powered by queer studies. There are books about his time in Istanbul and Saint-Paul, books about his FBI file, a study of Baldwin and the law, another of Baldwin in the Reagan years, with more to come for sure. Some of the more predictably academic stuff would have baffled him—predictably incomprehensible, I mean— but on the whole I'm sure he would have been proud of the attention.

Is it headed in the right direction? Who can say? But more people are paying attention than they were when *Talking at the Gates* first appeared.

JBR: In writing on James Baldwin people refer to him as "Jimmy" a lot, presumably to signal some sort of affinity or closeness to him, though many never met the man. He comes across in nearly every account as a warm, genial person who could charm nearly everyone and was indeed often referred to by friends as "Jimmy." But we've not read anyone writing about Shakespeare refer to him as "Billy," nor to Hemingway as "Ernie" or even his own nickname "Papa." We are wondering if there's something about either Baldwin's writing, public image, or speaking style that seems to engender this supposed familiarity? Any thoughts on this?

JC: Billy Shakespeare I'm not sure about. One or two biographers have referred to Hemingway, in places, as Papa. Michael Reynolds, in his five-volume affair, calls him Ernest throughout, as I recall. It's fine in its proper place. Like so much in writing, it's all a matter of tone.

I generally disapprove of a biographer going straight for the first name. You can reserve it for areas where familiarity seems natural. It's impolite to address somebody senior by first name anyway, when you don't know them well. I do remember being in a television studio on the South Bank with Jimmy (there I go), waiting for him to go on some youthful Channel 4 program. A young man—a child, really—kept entering the green room to bark out instructions to "James." We had a laugh over it. "Is there anything I can get you, James?" "Some whisky wouldn't be bad." And he produced it! I'll mind my manners when I encounter Mr. Shakespeare.

JBR: Baldwin is certainly discussed a lot, but so much of the scholarship talks very little about his style, about his voice, about his technical skills and artistry with the written and spoken word. One of the things we appreciated most about *Talking at the Gates* is that you do a good deal of old-fashioned "close reading" and discuss in detail Baldwin's rhetorical style—part Henry James, part King James Bible, part Hemingway. Why do you think that's gone out of fashion in so much of the critical literature? Should it come back? If so, how would we accomplish that?

JC: It is surprising that as the amount of scholarship has grown, the focus on artistry has diminished. It's a function of relativism. Funny how literary critics appear to be uneasy with literary criticism. You get more mileage out of the labyrinth of sexual and racial identity, the bottomless pit of oppression.

I see it happening all over. In an issue of *The New Yorker*, recently, I read long reviews of new books about Adrienne Rich and William Faulkner, both by reputable critics. In each case, treatment of the writer's work was made secondary, almost to vanishing point, while discussion of the politics hogged the foreground. I might have wanted to know if Adrienne Rich was a poet worth my attention, or the attention of the general reader. But the stuff quoted was dull-as-ditchwater, feminist agitprop. Maybe she did some lovely work besides. I may never know. That she was a political pioneer was all that interested the reviewer. As for Faulkner, who said in a drunken interview with the *Reporter* in 1956 that he would fight for Mississippi, "even if it meant going out into the streets and shooting Negroes"— well, need we say more?

We do need to, actually. Trust the tale, not the teller. As Mailer remarked, "Faulkner said more asinine things than any other major American writer." To put it differently: genius is not fussy where it takes up residence. And no genius served twentieth-century American fiction better than William Faulkner. His novels are sometimes hard work, but are infinitely rewarding. His political mumblings (he promptly disowned that particular one, by the way) can't hurt them.

Should close reading come back now? I wish it would, and not only because it is "good for you." I feel truly sorry for people who don't read. They miss so much. They're mired in cultural poverty. That type of poverty isn't talked about as much as it ought to be.

JBR: In the 2021 edition you reprint the Norman Mailer interview you did for this book, and Mailer says of Baldwin's essays—coming from his critique of them in Mailer's own *Advertisements for Myself*, that Baldwin's essays weren't biting enough: "Well, he was too nice to the reader for a long time." In *Talking at the Gates*, though, you are very explicit several times that you thought Baldwin's strength lay in the essays. We wonder if you feel the same as Mailer about Baldwin's essays being "too nice" to the reader?

Figure 3   James Baldwin and James Campbell in Saint-Paul de Vence in 1984 (Photograph courtesy of Fanny Dubes)

JC: No, I don't think that at all. I find them to be models of literary eloquence. They are courteous toward the reader, which is different from "nice." What Mailer actually said in *Advertisements* was that Baldwin was "too charming to be major." Mailer was seeing it from his own point of view: he saw it as his job to offend, to provoke, to scratch. That's okay—I have great admiration for Mailer—but Baldwin at his best wasn't like that.

The main problem with Baldwin's essays derives from the fact that he didn't think highly enough of them himself. He didn't really see himself as an essayist. After 1963, the year of book publication of *The Fire Next Time*, he ceased to write ambitious essays. He did pieces for magazines, usually on request; he drafted statements and open letters; he wrote affectionate portraits of Lorraine Hansberry and Beauford Delaney. But nothing on the scale of "Down at the Cross" or "The Black Boy Looks at the White Boy" or "Notes of a Native Son." He did, of course, write three book-length works of nonfiction (*No Name in the Street, The Devil Finds Work, The Evidence of Things Not Seen*) but no more of the compact little master-pieces of his pre-superstar days.

When I first met Baldwin, in Saint-Paul in 1981, my gambit, as what he called "one of my editors," was to suggest a new gathering of essays, issued at the same time as a collected edition of the existing works. That would get a lot of attention, I said (he was in need of attention at the time). I think I even said I would like to edit it. He went quiet for a moment, then said: "You're ahead of me there." I suspect he was just being polite. The new collection never appeared in his lifetime, but *The Price of the Ticket* came in 1985. Forgive me for saying it's not as well edited as it might be—not edited at all, really.

JBR: A bit of a reach, we realize, as he'd be 96 now, but if Baldwin were still alive, what would you ask him if you could? After thirty years, is there a gap in your sense of the man, or in the way his image and legacy has developed, that you wish you could get Baldwin's own sense of? Or, alternately, is there anything in the paradigmatic changes since his death that you'd love to get Baldwin's take on?

JC: Another counterfactual. I don't feel that Baldwin's instinctive grasp of reality in his mature years was as powerful as it had been in earlier times. There had been breakdowns; there were the suicide attempts you mention; there were, above all, the deaths of his three heroes, Medgar Evers, Malcolm X, and Martin Luther King. These things attacked his nervous system, not surprisingly, and damaged his perception. *The Evidence of Things Not Seen*, written when he was under sixty, is not a mature flowering. There are scant grounds for believing that Baldwin at seventy or eighty would have astonished us with a "late period," like Philip Roth or, in another realm, Picasso, though he would have gone on enchanting those who encountered him.

I don't ponder any unfulfilled wishes or have any regrets. Being a count-your-blessings kinda guy, I do just that in relation to James Baldwin—what fantastic luck I had.

On a light note, I do have two small regrets. One is that he never had the opportunity to get to know Vera, my wife, though they did meet fleetingly at an opening of *The Amen Corner*. Jimmy loved women and he would have loved her.

The other is that when I was steering him round London radio stations at the time of the publication of *Evidence*, he said he was hungry in the middle of the afternoon and maybe we could have some fish and chips—which was amusing in itself. We found something, but at the time we were not far from a little restaurant in Bloomsbury called Giovanni's Room. It would have been fun to walk in and get the reaction of the proprietor. I believe it's gone now.

JBR: In *Begin Again: James Baldwin's America and its Urgent Lessons for Our Own* (2020), Eddie S. Glaude, Jr., wrote that he disagreed with the notion of Baldwin's decline as a writer from the 1960s, which is something you chart in *Talking at the Gates*. Can you say a bit more about this?

JC: This is something on which Mr. Glaude and I will just have to disagree. I've heard a good many defenses of the "late style," but I'm sorry to say most strike me as meretricious. Just as do the arguments that "the critics" turned against Baldwin—as if the critics ever formed a single, clubbable group—because at a late stage he ceased to write for white people and began addressing himself to Black people.

I wanted to believe in his late style myself at one point—his "Why I stopped hating Shakespeare" style—and was thrilled beyond measure when he wrote "Of the Sorrow Songs" for my magazine. I resisted those who found it sloppy. Like everything he ever wrote, it contains passages of brilliance, but the genius has to work every bit as hard as the common journeyman to get his pieces into shape, and Baldwin simply wasn't capable of that kind of hard labor any more—hadn't been, in fact, since before *Tell Me How Long the Train's Been Gone*.

His last book, *The Evidence of Things Not Seen*, is from one point of view lazy— but from a kinder perspective he simply didn't have the energy, nor the experience, to do the type of reporting job that the subject required. The book almost went unpublished in America. Why? Jimmy consoled himself with conspiracy theories. That was sad, too. Publishers aren't like that. They love controversy—it sells books—but it has to be well grounded. They're not hand in glove with the "authorities," whoever they are.

Something similar struck me in his talk about the failure of his play, "The Welcome Table," to be produced. "I want my brother to take the leading role, and no theater in America will *permit that*." This was said with a memorable challenging look in the eyes—as if people on Broadway were saying: "We've got to stop the Baldwin Brothers." (David Baldwin liked to use this phrase.) He really wanted to believe that he was still operating at the edge of risk. The idea that his brother simply couldn't act was too painful to contemplate.

JBR: You draw on a lot of Baldwin's correspondence, much of which isn't available to researchers. In writing about Baldwin's letters, released only in Turkish in 2007 by Engin Cezzar, you note that:

> All the aspects of Baldwin's character are exposed in these letters. He was magnetic, compulsively sociable, elaborately extrovert, darkly introverted, depressive, magnificently generous, self-absorbed, incorrigibly self-dramatizing, funny, furious, bubbling with good intentions, seldom hesitating over a breach of promise—and capable of exhibiting all of those traits between lunch and dinner, and again between dinner and the final Johnnie Walker Black Label at 4 a.m.

This is a compelling portrait for sure, but it's one inaccessible to so many because there is no collection of his letters in English. There are letters to and from him in several library archives, but nothing collected in an accessible way. How would Baldwin's letters give us a better understanding of the writer, and why do you think the letters haven't been published? Do you think they ever will be?

JC: They haven't been published because the Baldwin Estate withholds permission whenever the subject arises. David Leeming was assigned by Baldwin himself to edit a collection of letters, as well as to write a biography, but it came to nothing. It's rather quaint that permission should have been given for a collection in Turkish, but at the same time exasperating. The letters were written in English, after all.

A good-sized book, properly edited by someone experienced in that particular task, with informative notes and appendices, would be a wonderful thing to have. Letters are the closest you get to private conversation preserved in time. Baldwin writing to Leslie Schenk about the background to *Giovanni's Room*—and Schenk's replies, of which I have copies—offers a fundamentally different experience from reading the novel. They are secondary materials, sometimes just talk on paper—but informative, entertaining, instructive talk. Imagine if we had the letters of Shakespeare. No one would put forth an argument for closing them down. The Baldwin Estate has its own reasons for acting as it does, but it's a sad omission.

JBR: A follow-up on extant Baldwin materials in the archive. The Baldwin Estate has long had a position something akin to: "if it wasn't published in his lifetime, it won't get published." Yet there are at least two things of definite interest to scholarship on Baldwin—the play "The Welcome Table," and his script for the collaboration with Ray Charles, *The Hallelujah Chorus*. Do you have any thoughts on the Estate's position? Do you think it will ever change? If you had a magic wand, reprint wise, would you rather the letters come out or "The Welcome Table"?

JC: In answer to the last question, the letters for sure. "The Welcome Table" is a curiosity, as is the Pelatowski project, "Unto the Dying Lamb." *The Hallelujah Chorus* I'm less sure about. It might be better in a magazine. It's not easy for publishers to sell such things. The likes of you and me would love to have them—but how true that would be for the reading public at large is uncertain. It would be a risk. As things stand with the Estate, it's not a risk anyone is allowed to take.

JBR: Since Toni Morrison's endorsement of Ta-Nehisi Coates, a lot of speculation has occurred regarding who the "next Baldwin" is. In your opinion, who could carry that mantle? In fiction? In the essay?

JC: I don't much care for these comparisons. Baldwin was *sui generis*. Not everything he put out was worthy of his immense talent, but there was no one like him. That's why he continues to hold our fascination.

I read Ta-Nehisi Coates's first two nonfiction books with interest. But the repeated comparison with Baldwin is mostly publishers' hype. He's doing his own thing. The section I read of Coates's novel *The Water Dancer* (in *The New Yorker*) struck me as less original. I haven't read any reviews of it, but I wouldn't expect it to be reviewed honestly. Literary criticism has been corrupted by identity politics. "Identity approval trumps critical approval every time"—that was said by my comrade J.C. in the *TLS* six or seven years ago, when that particular virus was just settling in. Now we're living through a victimological pandemic. Why the fear of being offended? And, on the other hand, of appearing to offend? I find it baffling. The reviewer of a book should ask: How did it feel to read this book? Then attempt an honest report on his or her feelings. Anything else is a literary crime. In fact, it's an existentialist crime. It's *mauvaise foi*. There's a lot of it about.

That's not what you asked about, but I beg your indulgence.

JBR: Many of the things people liked about the recent film version of *If Beale Street Could Talk*—its lyricism in terms of sweeping camera moves and lingering close-ups, a perhaps overly sentimental romanticism, marshaling Baldwin as a protest against the carceral system—are some of the very critiques you have in *Talking at the Gates* about Baldwin's later novels, *Beale Street* included. I wonder how you felt about the film? About Raoul Peck's documentary?

JC: The most prominent imagery in recent times comes from the film *I Am Not Your Negro*, which I enjoyed, despite certain reservations, starting with the title, which is anachronistic. Baldwin never said that—"Negro" was his preferred usage until quite late in life. What he did say, in variations, was "I was never going to be anybody's nigger again." What thrilled audiences was Baldwin's magnetism before the camera. He had the unusual gift of being himself in the television studio. The camera loved him. Did people leave the cinema and head for the nearest book-shop? And close the doors and turn off the phones and disconnect the computers and spend days on end reading the books they purchased? Wouldn't it be nice to think so?

As for the film of *Beale Street* … oh boy. Must I? I'll only get into trouble. Enough to say that it makes use of every romantic cinematic cliché it can lay its hands on. That music! Those soulful looks! Such impeccable saintliness! The topic at the heart of the story, Black men incarcerated unjustly, is deadly serious; the style of the drama lacks any surprise or originality.

JBR: You note that the writers of Baldwin's generation sought to be bestsellers, Baldwin in particular. But they also had this high modernist sense of, as you put it, "writing on behalf of the energy of literature itself." Can you say more about this dichotomy? Is there any sense of this still today in literature?

JC: There are a few novelists today who would straddle the territories. One of them has recently died—Toni Morrison. Kazuo Ishiguro is of that stature. Hilary Mantel, Zadie Smith, Ian McEwan, William Boyd, Julian Barnes. I'm talking only about their professional standing. They are writers I think of as following in the tradition of Graham Greene, perhaps the very model of the novelist and man of letters, working in books, magazines, and film, one who could appeal to high and low taste at the same time. They command a readership: people wait impatiently for the next book. It's a great thing for a writer to have, and a rare one.

Others are burdened with the "literary fiction" yoke. When me and my pals were first gathering in Glasgow and Edinburgh, all fiction was literary, except the part that was trash, and that was unworthy of notice. But trash gradually gained the ascendancy. The process wasn't fully achieved by the end of the 1960s, the era of Baldwin, Vidal, Bellow, Styron, Vonnegut, early Roth, prime Updike—all likely to appeal to your ordinary book-buyer, all mid-table bestsellers, but all now stig-matized as "literary fiction," as if it's a special taste. The unstoppable rise of popular culture in the academy, which started in the late 1970s, the corresponding con-tempt for so-called high culture, the distrust of élitism—including élites in talent— the application of relativism in critical appreciation, the merciless condemnation of anything with even a micro-suggestion of racism or sexism, the contempt for concepts such as "the formation of taste," the demise of reading. If you do away with reading, you don't have to bother about taste and judgment. Images serve the purpose, as you suggested above.

These are a few of the factors at the root of it.

JBR: Finally, can you tell us what you've been reading lately, and what has gripped you?

JC: Going by what is on my book table right now? Volume 5 of *A Dance to the Music of Time* by Anthony Powell—enchanting, droll, and miraculously observant of human interaction. *The Last Assassin* by Peter Stothard, about "the hunt for the killers of Julius Caesar." Peter was my editor at the *TLS* for twelve years. A collection of film scripts by the French New Wave director Eric Rohmer, from his *Comédies et proverbes* sequence. I read the scripts in French, then try to watch the films (for the third or fourth time) without the subtitles. It's hard, so I need to read again and watch for a fifth time, which only increases the pleasure. And I like magazines: *Beat Scene*, *About Larkin*, the *Gissing Journal* and, needless to say, *James Baldwin Review*.

Contributors' Biographies

Douglas Field is a founding co-editor of *James Baldwin Review* and the author, most recently, of *All Those Strangers: The Art and Lives of James Baldwin* (Oxford University Press, 2015). He has written over twenty articles on Baldwin in publications such as the *Guardian* and the *Times Literary Supplement*, where he is a regular contributor. Field has also published numerous chapters on Baldwin and articles in top-tiered academic journals, among them *African American Review* and *English Literary History*. He was the expert on Radio 4's *Great Lives* in 2015 when Alvin Hall chose Baldwin, and he was the consultant on Raoul Peck's Oscar-nominated documentary, *I Am Not Your Negro*.

Justin A. Joyce is a founding co-editor of *James Baldwin Review* and Research Director for President McBride at The New School. An interdisciplinary scholar of American literature and film, his first monograph was *Gunslinging Justice: The American Culture of Gun Violence in Westerns and the Law* (Manchester University Press, 2018). He has featured in interviews and discussions on *The Humanities on the High Plains* podcast, the University of Leeds' PhD seminar "Quilting Points," and on *RadioWest*. Joyce's writings have also appeared in *James Baldwin Review*, *A Historical Guide to James Baldwin*, *James Baldwin in Context*, *Western American Literature*, *Pacific Northwest Quarterly*, *Great Plains Quarterly*, and *Public Seminar*.

Manchester University Press

DISPATCH

White Lies Matter: *Begin Again*, A Review Essay

Herb Boyd

Abstract

This review essay examines Eddie Glaude, Jr.'s new book *Begin Again: James Baldwin's America and Its Urgent Lessons for Our Own* against several other recent works on Baldwin such as Bill Mullen's *James Baldwin: Living in Fire* and Nicholas Buccola's *The Fire Is Upon Us*.

Keywords: James Baldwin, Eddie S. Glaude, Jr., Nicholas Buccola, Raoul Peck, Bill Mullen, *No Name in the Street*

James Baldwin Review, Volume 7, 2021, © The Authors. Published by Manchester University Press and The University of Manchester Library
http://dx.doi.org/10.7227/JBR.7.11

Several months after the publication of his book *Begin Again: James Baldwin's America and Its Urgent Lessons for Our Own* (2020), Eddie Glaude, Jr. was given a two-hour interview on C-SPAN's "In Depth." An appearance here—nearly as good as an endorsement by Oprah—is a good indication of a book's importance and popularity, and Glaude was peppered with questions from the host and callers.

"When you think about Du Bois, Martin Luther King, Stokely Carmichael, Malcolm X," the host Peter Slen asks Glaude, "where do you place yourself in that spectrum?"[1] Glaude begins by saying that he has never been asked that question before. "I'm always dealing with my rage," he says, "always on the verge of spilling over in some ways. And then there's this love. I guess this why I'm so attracted to Baldwin as a figure because he seems to stand in that space where rage and love exist simultaneously."[2]

Navigating that space between love and rage figures prominently in Glaude's book, but reconciling Baldwin's love and rage is not an easy endeavor in light of his famous quote that "To be a Negro in this country and to be relatively conscious is to be in a *rage* almost all the time."[3] It's a situation Glaude grapples with in the early pages of the book, noting that when he read *The Fire Next Time* (1963), "I could not reconcile his rage with his talk of love. It was like Dr. King meets Henry James meets Malcolm X meets Freud. Baldwin was *too* personal."[4]

That intimacy, however, that closeness to Baldwin, is exactly what Glaude adopts, a nearness that has been harnessed by a coterie of writers, activists, biographers, and filmmakers such as Hilton Als, Jesmyn Ward, and Raoul Peck. Like Peck, he has undertaken a deep dive into the Baldwin oeuvre, excavating and thoughtfully mining the most precious jewels of his thinking. To this end Glaude thinks along with Baldwin, weaving his way through a "complex bundle of evasions, denials, and hatreds that made up the American project, and point a pathway forward to becoming new, different human beings," emulating the moves of his esteemed predecessor.[5]

Confession is good for the soul it is often stated, and Glaude unloads on his evasion of Baldwin before allowing his invasive ideas.

> My classmates wrote dissertations on him, one of which eventually became an important scholarly book. I hesitated because I knew that, if I let him inside my head—inside of me—he would force me to look at myself honestly as the precondition for saying anything about the world. I was right. I finally found the courage to read him seriously, and in his work I found a way of thinking and a language to express what was happening inside of me and what I was seeing in my country.[6]

In summoning the genius of Baldwin, Glaude and Peck join a parade of luminaries who, far less extensively, have quoted or cited Baldwin to give their remarks additional gravitas. His works, in an almost biblical way, pop up daily in sundry disparate places, where his wisdom is used to amplify a moment or circumstance, and his words are particularly useful to summarize a production. A brief listing of some works released in 2020 alone bears this out: At the close of David Byrne's *America*

Utopia, his musical adapted for HBO by Spike Lee, Baldwin is summoned to drive home a message of hope and well-being; a closing statement from Baldwin appears in Ric Burns and Gretchen Sorin's engaging documentary *Driving While Black*; in the recent Netflix release *The Trial of the Chicago 7*, a young woman is removed from the jurors because she is reading a Baldwin book; and when Philip Gefter's biography of photographer Richard Avedon was published, mention of Baldwin was inevitable since they attended DeWitt Clinton High School and were contributors to the *Magpie*, the school's magazine. And it was expected that Baldwin would be featured in Alan Govenar's documentary *The Myth of a Colorblind France*.

At the outset of *Begin Again*, Glaude posits a caveat that "this is a strange book."[7] He declares that the book is not biography, not literary criticism, nor straightforward history, "but a combination of all three in an effort to say something meaningful about our current times."[8] This he does with all the clarity and insight of one who has thoroughly absorbed Baldwin's wisdom and vision, and he accomplishes this by moving backward and forward, vacillating, as he notes, between past and present, never losing sight or counsel of Baldwin's guidance. It's a very interesting and unique way to utilize Baldwin, using him as a co-conspirator as he interrogates the tenor of our times, mainly the fascistic-tending, pandemic dystopia created and overseen by Donald Trump.

Glaude is absolutely right when he says that in the book—seven tightly composed chapters and 239 pages is not a biography—it is not possible to access Baldwin's searing prose without discussing his "furious passage."[9] Even so, Glaude illustrates or underscores how the drama of Baldwin's life intersects with the American experience; or how his books are like literary milestones highlighting various episodic moments in the nation's history. His opening chapter, "The Lie," establishes a thematic tone that reverberates throughout the book. From the very creation of this nation, Glaude opines, there has been an inability to deal with the truth, which he insists is at the core of Baldwin's mission. Merging Baldwin with Black Lives Matter and unrest in the streets is deftly achieved when Glaude recounts an incident during the Freddie Gray demonstration in Maryland in 2015. One activist, he notes, had a sign quoting Baldwin that read: "Ignorance allied with power is the most ferocious enemy of justice."[10] This is further evidence of the extent to which Glaude has paid attention to the contemporary turbulence and how it often embodies Baldwin's motto to be a good writer and a witness.

To this end, Glaude is a keen observer, chronicling Baldwin's struggle to become a writer and a witness, whether in the South during the emerging civil rights movement, or alone in Paris, where the racism may have been less brutal, but nonetheless was everywhere evident, as so many other Baldwin authorities have written. Baldwin, who died in 1987, was not around to witness the confrontation in Charlottesville in the summer of 2017 when a neo-Nazi plunged his car into a crowd of activists, killing Heather Heyer. In his retelling of the incident, Glaude appropriates Baldwin's journalistic style, marinating it with historical information, some of which will be foreign to most Americans. Few writers and historians have the reach and insight to expound on W. E. B. Du Bois's *Black Reconstruction* (1935), leaning on the book's final chapter "exposing the lies of the historiography around Reconstruction."[11] This is Glaude's Baldwinesque pivot back to the book's basic theme about falsehoods that permeate the nation's history. It's an easy segue from here to the prevarications at the heart of any tweet from Trump.

There are thoughtful and heartfelt ruminations on Dr. King, Malcolm X, Medgar Evers, the Black Panthers, as well as Emmett Till, but the revelations here are gifted by Glaude's poetic turns and his perspective on Baldwin. "Through the 1960s, Baldwin turned his attention away from the gaze of white America and focused more directly on the well-being and future of Black people," Glaude writes.[12] That future was as troubled as ever, and by the early 1970s Baldwin was completing *No Name in the Street* (1972), which for him meant, as he told a reporter, "I'm beginning again."[13] These are the watchwords, so to speak, and riffs on this theme conclude each chapter of the book, a clear indication of the wide net Glaude has cast in his search for the essential Baldwin.

Of Baldwin's works, *No Name in the Street* gets the longest exposition, and for Glaude it is Baldwin's most "important work of social criticism." He places Baldwin's book of essays in the context of transcendentalist thinkers such as Ralph Waldo Emerson, and Glaude may have found a connection between them in a quote he cites from Emerson, who declared "Let me begin anew."[14] Often, beginning anew for Baldwin involved relocation, and this came with his journey to Istanbul. Glaude gives extensive coverage of this sojourn, much of which complements Magdalena Zaborowska's remembrance of Sedat Pakay in *James Baldwin Review*, a publication that Glaude mentions along with a number of other Baldwin scholars.[15] There was no need for him to forage into the territory they have fully plowed, but we are still awaiting a deeper dive into the CIA's surveillance of Baldwin, something Glaude touches on without going beyond a passing nod.

In this regard, more could have been said about Baldwin's article published in *Encounter* magazine, which was underwritten by the CIA, something neither Baldwin nor other writers were aware of at that time. Baldwin's submission was a review of the Negro-African Writers and Artists (*Le Congres des Ecrivains et Artistes Noirs*) that took place at the Sorbonne's Amphitheatre Descartes in Paris on 19 September 1956, entitled "Princes and Powers." Sixteen years later in *No Name in the Street*, which Glaude cites extensively, Baldwin observed that "In the fall of 1956, I was covering for *Encounter* (or for the CIA) the first international Conference of Black Writers and Artists."[16] Apparently, while living in London in an increasingly potent climate of radicalism, Baldwin felt the specter of the CIA. "Eventually, of course, Black Englishmen, Indians, students, conscientious objectors, and CIA infiltrators—no doubt—tracked me down, as we had known was inevitable," he wrote.[17]

Curiously, given the attention he devotes to *No Name in the Street*, more so than any of Baldwin's other books, there is no mention of *Encounter*, though Glaude does expend a lengthy paragraph on the essay "Princes and Powers," in which he sides with Eldridge Cleaver and notes that "the essay does leave much to be desired."[18] Moreover, he writes that "Baldwin's understanding of the geopolitics surrounding decolonization appears limited. He comes off as someone decidedly committed, despite his criticisms, to the exceptionalism of the American project."[19]

Some exception should be extended to the notion that Baldwin's "decolonization appears limited," especially if Glaude had more than a cursory chance to further examine Baldwin's unpublished novel "No Papers for Muhammad," which Bill Mullen discusses in his 2019 book *James Baldwin: Living in Fire*. Mullen writes that the

> paper trail around *No Papers* then serves as an ineffable coda to Baldwin's confession from *No Name in the Street* about his relationship as an African-American to the Arab world: "as I began to discern what their history had made of them, I began to suspect, somewhat painfully, what my history had made of me."[20]

The two authors may differ on Baldwin's perspective on decolonization, but they are seemingly in agreement about Baldwin's rejection of Négritude, according to Glaude, or his skepticism regarding the concept, according to Mullen. Neither go far enough in explaining Négritude and its historical connections, particularly to the Harlem Renaissance, though Mullen does cite the significance of Aimé Césaire's role in the movement.

An exegesis of Négritude would present a broad international tapestry and illustrate significant ties with authors from Africa and the Caribbean, who Baldwin encountered from a distance during the Congress in Paris in 1956. To be fair to Baldwin, Négritude was still in formation as a cultural and political outlook. Négritude as a term does not appear in his essay on the Congress, nor was the term mentioned—if Baldwin's article is taken as the source—by any of the major progenitors of the concept, including Diop, Césaire, Senghor, and others. Had he stayed a little longer at the Congress and heard Frantz Fanon's speech, Baldwin might have gathered a better understanding of Négritude from one of its most profound and revolutionary thinkers. Such a grasp of the concept would give recognition to the essentials that embody Négritude, of which there is no better definition than one issued by Senghor: "During the 1930s when we launched the Négritude movement from Paris, we drew our inspiration especially—and paradoxically—from 'Negro Americans' in the general sense of the word: from the Harlem Renaissance movement, but also from the 'indigenist' movement in Haiti."[21] He declared that all "the themes which were to be developed by the Négritude movement were already treated by [Edward] Blyden in the middle of the nineteenth century, both the virtues of Négritude and the proper mode of illustrating those virtues."[22] Baldwin's reluctance to embrace Négritude might have been the same impulse that made him stand apart from the Harlem Renaissance, since, as Senghor notes, they were inseparably linked. This break was insightfully discussed by John Drabinski in his essay "The Poetics of Beautiful Blackness: On Baldwin and Négritude" in *James Baldwin in Context* (2019), edited by Quentin Miller. At variance between Black Americans and their counterparts in the colonial world is the question of the place where oppression obtains. "Baldwin," Drabinski writes,

> breaks apart the racial identities at work in Négritude in order to reassemble those identities in the context of the United States. What we learn is that whiteness is

constructed in relation to blackness, blackness in relation to whiteness, and those constructions do not travel. A return to the cruel machinery that made such identities is a return to home. There is no need for an elsewhere. All the beauty of blackness is already in the poetics of this home.[23]

To completely understand the evolution of Négritude demands an interrogation of the conflict that simmered between African Americans and the immigrants from the Caribbean, and sometimes from Africa.

It is rather interesting that Glaude chose not to use the revelations from William J. Maxwell's *F.B. Eyes: How J. Edgar Hoover's Ghostreaders Framed African American Literature* (2015), which charts the surveillance of Baldwin begun by the CIA, and continued by the FBI, though that material remains either redacted or unavailable. This information is discussed in Glaude's "Author's Notes" without any explanation as to why he chose to leave it alone. When Mullen writes that Baldwin would begin "the slow process of tearing himself away from Western moorings, though not without an internal ideological struggle over the meaning of doing so," this notion converges with Glaude on Baldwin's gaining critical distance from America during his sojourn in Istanbul.[24] Freed from the "deadly dynamics of American life," Glaude continues, the silence enabled Baldwin "to hear his own language and, I suspect, feel his own grief more deeply. That distance gave him a different angle of vision not only on the United States but on himself apart from the lie that suffocated him and much of American life."[25]

Unlike Mullen, Glaude's pursuit of Baldwin the internationalist, save for his adventures in France, Switzerland, and Turkey, does not extend into the territory that Mullen has thoroughly investigated, especially his chapter entitled "Morbid Symptoms and Optimism of the Will: 1968–79." This decade or so in Baldwin's "furious passage" finds him deeply concerned about Black Power, anti-imperialism, the Vietnam War, and the Palestinian liberation struggle. The phrase "morbid symptoms" is taken from Antonio Gramsci's *Prison Notebooks*, and connects Baldwin with an unimpeachable political theorist. Noted author and activist Robin Kelley, in his blurb, wrote that "Mullen presents the James Baldwin we've been waiting for: the revolutionary, fierce internationalist, queer theorist, anti-imperialist, anti-Zionist, incisive dialectician, and perhaps the most dangerous thinking of the 20th century."[26] Baldwin's anticolonial stance may have taken some time to emerge, but he was soon convinced, as Mullen observes, "that the African-American, the Turk, the Arab, the Muslim, the African, the colonized everywhere, were one united 'wretched of the earth.'"[27]

While Mullen is unsparing in his denunciation of Zionism, Glaude veers away from any mention of Israel and its Baldwin associations. About the closest he comes to Israel is in his several references to the New Jerusalem, the Jewish idealized heaven, where for Baldwin, Glaude writes, "the idols of race and the shackles of obsolete categories that bound us to the ground were no more."[28] Baldwin, in *No Name in the Street*, recounts his visit to Israel, and how much he liked the country and the people.

But it was obvious why the Western world created the state of Israel, which is not really a Jewish state. The West needed a handle in the Middle East. And they created the state as a European pawn. When I was in Israel, it was as though I was in the middle of *The Fire Next Time*. I didn't dare go through Israel to Africa, so I went to Turkey, just across the road.[29]

Neither Mullen nor Glaude expends much insight on Baldwin's trip to Africa with his sister, Gloria, though Mullen does mention the countries they visited, including Ghana, Senegal, Sierra Leone, and Guinea. Nor do they devote much time or attention to Baldwin's voyage to London with his brother David and Carole Weinstein, and there is hardly any discussion of Baldwin's debate with William Buckley. In his 2019 book *The Fire Is Upon Us: James Baldwin, William F. Buckley Jr., and the Debate Over Race in America*, Nicholas Buccola revisits the famous debate held at Cambridge University in England in 1965. Mullen is not mentioned, but Glaude is acknowledged by Buccola since he attended a symposium at Linfield University in McMinnville, Oregon, to mark the fiftieth anniversary of the debate. Glaude is also credited by Buccola for answering a number of questions from the author. Buccola says that Glaude is a serious scholar, a principled thinker, and the same can be said of him. For more than 400 pages Buccola fully examines the hour-long debate, framing Baldwin and Buckley's exchanges within the vortex of the times. It was a war of words between an electrifying African American intellectual and a Brahmin-bred conservative, with no holds barred as they contested the question "The American dream is at the expense of the American Negro."

In his own review of *Begin Again*, Buccola compares Glaude to Baldwin, deeming both Jeremiahs, saying things that folks might not like to hear.[30] Some folks might not want to hear Glaude confess that he did not vote for Hillary Clinton, a decision he later explained, saying that it was done merely to push the Democratic Party to the left where his colleague Cornel West was ensconced. By taking such a stance, Glaude believed there was a chance to break the stranglehold of the corporate wing of the party:

The "carnival barker" nominated by the Republican Party offered a chance to upend the rules of the game, so I believed, because white America would never elect such a person to the highest office in the land. I was wrong, and given my lifelong reading of Baldwin, it was an egregious mistake.[31]

Buccola, in his review of *Begin Again*, welcomes Glaude's honesty, but finds a deeper problem at hand:

I appreciate Glaude's willingness to acknowledge the flaws in his political prognostication, but the wrongness that really matters here is that which was exhibited by the millions of voters whose journey to the polls was fueled by the delusion of the lie. And millions of American voters have proven, time and again, that the lie is a habit they just cannot kick. At the level of elite politics, then, we must stop pretending that these addicts can be saved. Instead, we must push elite politicians to stop just "playing it safe" and we must pressure elites to address structural inequality. But we must also sometimes recognize that we have to "buy more time" and set up safeguards that might protect innocent people from the wrath of those animated by the delusion of white supremacy.[32]

Buccola is spot on, and the world saw the terrible results of the lie when thousands, believing Trump was the victor and that the presidential election was rigged, rammed through doors and broke windows, resulting in the deaths of several people on Capitol Hill on 6 January 2021. White lies matter!

Glaude, in his praise for Buccola's book, said it "brilliantly describes our current malaise," and insists that it is a "must-read—especially as we are forced to choose between competing visions of who we take ourselves to be as Americans."[33] Given the nature of their projects, neither author devotes much time to homosexuality, and Glaude never mentions the word, though he does touch on the topic of sexuality when he notes how "this black queer man represented a different kind of radicalism than the masculinist politics of black male preachers."[34] It's a matter of speculation whether Glaude's deployment of queer theory would have sharpened and deepened his analysis, much in the manner of Matt Brim's *James Baldwin and the Queer Imagination* (2014). However, as Brim warns, such an endeavor might have brought in its wake further complications and "failures."

When Brim evokes Bayard Rustin, it's as if wishing he had joined in collaboration with Baldwin, and a similar wish might also be found in Glaude. Rustin, born in 1912, was twelve years older than Baldwin and was devoutly anchored in the civil rights movement, but beyond their common queerness they were both supremely gifted intellectuals with a deep, abiding affinity to Black music. Both died in 1987, Rustin in August and Baldwin in December. Except for noting his position in the civil rights movement, Glaude offers this comment from Rustin in relation to Baldwin: "People sometimes didn't understand Jimmy's intense identification with people in the Movement. He often came off a platform after speaking trembling with emotion. It's a wonder to me such intensity didn't wear out the frail body long ago."[35]

In his chapter entitled "The Dangerous Road," which is a gesture to Baldwin's "The Dangerous Road Before Martin Luther King," Glaude expends most of his time on King in 1968 in California, where Baldwin was asked to say a few words at a fundraiser for King. Glaude could have gleaned more from Baldwin's "Dangerous Road," composed in 1961, and his impressions of Rustin after he was dismissed from King's camp. Baldwin asserted that King's dismissal of Rustin was more than unwarranted:

[King] lost much moral credit, for example, especially in the eyes of the young, when he allowed Adam Clayton Powell to force the resignation of his [King's] extremely able organizer and lieutenant, Bayard Rustin. Rustin, also, has a long and honorable record as a fighter for Negro rights, and is one of the most penetrating and able men around. The techniques used by Powell—we will not speculate as to his motives— were far from sweet; but King was faced with the choice of defending his organizer, who was also his friend, or agreeing with Powell; and he chose the latter course.[36]

The struggle between Powell and King had been brewing ever since the minister from Atlanta emerged as the leader of the civil rights movement and displaced Powell as the spokesperson for Black America. Powell, angered that he had been excluded from a planned march outside the Democratic National Convention in Los Angeles in 1960, warned King that if he didn't dismiss Rustin from his retinue, Powell would call a press conference and expose them as lovers. King capitulated, called off the demonstration, and put social and political distance between himself and Rustin. But none of this dismayed Rustin who, with A. Philip Randolph's blessing, was more in the thick of things by 1963 when he was the architect of the historic March on Washington.

This could have been a perfect moment for Glaude to comment on the movement and homosexuality. An elaboration of this situation would also have fit comfortably in Brim's wheelhouse. Gay author Hilton Als has more than once voiced his delight and introspection regarding Baldwin's life and legacy, and has specifically addressed the topic of homosexuality. During an interview in 2019 with Lester Fabian Brathwaite, a former senior editor of *Out* magazine, Als responded to the question of why Baldwin never fully formed his ideas on queerness. "In doing research, I interviewed an editor of his and he was working on a novel that was specifically about that," Als recalled.[37]

> This is the era when people were arrested and careers were destroyed because of it [homosexuality], so I think if he could fictionalize it with a white person to distance himself as the protagonist, this was a way to speak but not be seen. So I think he did the best he could with the information he had and the times he had.[38]

An increasingly popular Black intellectual, Glaude often appears as a panelist on television news broadcasts, particularly on cable. He is even more on call in literary circles, where his opinions on the latest book are requested. When twenty-two prominent authors were asked by the *New York Times* to list a book they might suggest to President-elect Joe Biden, Glaude recommended *James Baldwin: Collected Essays*, the 1998 collection of nonfiction essays edited by the late Toni Morrison. "Given the moral reckoning we face in this country," Glaude wrote, "I would urge President Biden to spend some time with the nonfiction writings of James Baldwin. The book offers a cleareyed view of what rests at the heart of our national malaise, and he writes about it—bears witness to its effects—without a hint of sentimentality."[39]

Sadness and nostalgia surface a little when Glaude recounts the racist incident in Charlotte, North Carolina, when Dorothy Counts, a teen, was reviled and spat on by white protesters as she and others integrated an all-white school. It was a galvanizing moment in history and one Baldwin claimed convinced him to return to the US and get involved in the movement. But, as Glaude points out, this was not the case. "It could not have been the image of Dorothy Counts that spurred Baldwin to give up France. The ordeal at Harding High School happened in the fall of 1957, a year after the 1956 conference in Paris."[40] In effect, Baldwin's memory failed him on this occasion, and Glaude is not reluctant to correct his guide.

Instances abound when Glaude is on his own, exercising his agency without Baldwin's counsel, most vividly when he visits the Legacy Museum in Alabama or Ferncliff cemetery, where Baldwin is interred not too far from Paul Robeson, Malcolm X, and Dr. Betty Shabazz. "As I walked up and down the cemetery, I chuckled as I thought to myself that my refuge from the betrayal of the country and the craziness of Donald Trump was the storm of Jimmy's life. Made sense to me."[41]

No mention of Donald Trump is complete without the precedence and presidency of Barack Obama. Glaude is only eight pages into his book when Obama appears as he expounds on the American "lie": "The stories we often tell ourselves of the civil rights movement and social progress in this country, Rosa Parks's courage, Dr. King's moral vision, and the unreasonable venom of Black Power, culminating in the election of Barack Obama, are all too often lies."[42] Much later in the book, Glaude rightly pairs Obama with the Black Lives Matter movement that gradually inculcated Baldwin's visionary ideas.

Glaude quotes and defends numerous prominent authors along his route to Baldwin's insights for our current moment. On several occasions in the book Ralph Waldo Emerson is cited. Historian Nell Painter is one of a number of scholars who have written that Emerson was a racist. From one of Emerson's early musings, Painter provides this glimpse of a man who was often deemed an abolitionist:

> I think it cannot be maintained by any candid person that the African race have ever occupied or do promise to occupy any very high place in the human family. Their present condition is the strongest proof that they cannot. The Irish cannot; the American Indian cannot; Chinese cannot. Before the energy of the Caucasian race all the other races have quailed and done obeisance.[43]

You wonder how Baldwin would react to the notion that his writings, particularly *No Name in the Street,* by Glaude's estimation stand in the tradition of American writing that dates back to Emerson.

Glaude is not alone, though, in reading Baldwin and Emerson together. Prentiss Clark, in her essay for *James Baldwin Review,* "What 'No Chart Can Tell Us': Ordinary Intimacies in Emerson, Du Bois, and Baldwin," imagines Baldwin in conversation with these two esteemed interlocutors; however, the intimacies do not extend into the sensitive area of race or racism.[44] But she does quote Emerson and his conclusion that "the civility of no race can be perfect whilst another race is degraded."[45]

Several reviewers take umbrage at Glaude's concentration on *No Name in the Street* and his neglect of Baldwin's fiction, which might have brought considerable gravitas to the limited discussion of homosexuality. Elaboration on Baldwin's attempted suicides, a fuller explanation of the call for reparations, Trump's incipient fascism, and a deeper dive into Black Nationalism with the same exigency he gave white nationalism, as well as more on the nation's statutes rather than its statues would have provided additional resonance to a book packed with relevance.

Glaude is a perceptive traveling companion, a veritable Sancho Panza to Baldwin's laceration of America's windmills of lies. Baldwin once said that "to begin again demands a certain silence, a certain privacy that is not, at least for me, to be found elsewhere."[46] It is not so much a silence Glaude has found but a voice that he has summoned with a profound understanding of his purpose and direction, and a way of blending past and present, a Sankofa way of going forward by looking back. Baldwin's "after times" are never more current than the next beat of your heart.

Notes

1 Peter Slen, host of "In Depth" on C-SPAN, 6 December 2020, www.c-span.org/video/?477970-1/depth-eddie-glaude (accessed 28 January 2021).

2 *Ibid.*

3 James Baldwin, qtd. in "Symposium: The Negro's Role in American Culture," *Negro Digest*, XI:5 (1962), p. 81.

4 Eddie S. Glaude, Jr., *Begin Again: James Baldwin's America and Its Urgent Lessons for Our Own* (New York, Crown, 2020), p. xxiv.

5 *Ibid.*, p. xxvi.

6 *Ibid.*, p. xxv.

7 *Ibid.*, p. xviii.

8 *Ibid.*

9 Glaude borrows the phrase "furious passage" from Fern Eckman's 1966 biography, *The Furious Passage of James Baldwin.*

10 The original Baldwin source for this line is *No Name in the Street* (New York, Vintage, 1972), p. 149.

11 Glaude, *Begin Again*, p. 72.

12 *Ibid.*, p. 94.

13 Baldwin, *No Name in the Street*, p. 117.

14 Qtd. in Glaude, *Begin Again*, p. 121.

15 David Leeming and Magdalena Zaborowska, "Remembering Sedat Pakay," *James Baldwin Review*, 3 (2017), pp. 173–85.

16 Baldwin, *No Name in the Street*, p. 49.

17 *Ibid.*, p. 90.

18 Glaude, *Begin Again*, p. 99.

19 *Ibid.*

20 Bill Mullen, *James Baldwin: Living in Fire* (London, Pluto Press, 2019), p. 185.

21 Léopold Sédar Senghor, "Negritude and the Civilization of the Universal," in Carlos Moore, Tanya Sanders, and Shawna Moore (eds.), *African Presence in the Americas* (Trenton, NJ, Africa World Press, 1995), p. 21.

22 *Ibid.*

23 John E. Drabinski, "The Poetics of Beautiful Blackness: On Baldwin and Négritude," in D. Quentin Miller (ed.), *James Baldwin in Context* (Cambridge, Cambridge University Press, 2019), p. 240.

24 Mullen, *James Baldwin: Living in Fire*, p. 50.

25 Glaude, *Begin Again*, p. 129.

26 Robin Kelley, blurb for Bill Mullen's *James Baldwin: Living in Fire*, www.plutobooks.com/9780745338545/james-baldwin/ (accessed 29 January 2021).

27 Mullen, *James Baldwin: Living in Fire*, p. xiv.

28 Glaude, *Begin Again*, p. xxiii.

29 Baldwin, qtd. in Mullen, *James Baldwin: Living in Fire*, p. 91.

30 Nicholas Buccola, "How Do We Begin Again?," *The New Rambler: An Online Review of Books*, https://newramblerreview.com/book-reviews/literary-studies/how-do-we-begin-again (accessed 29 January 2021).

31 Glaude, *Begin Again*, p. 170.

32 Buccola, "How Do We Begin Again?"

33 Eddie S. Glaude, Jr., blurb for Nicholas Buccola's *The Fire Is Upon Us*, https://press.princeton.edu/books/hardcover/9780691181547/the-fire-is-upon-us (accessed 29 January 2021).

34 Glaude, *Begin Again*, p. 19.

35 Rustin qtd in *ibid.*, pp. 118–19.

36 James Baldwin, "The Dangerous Road Before Martin Luther King" (1961), in *Collected Essays*, ed. Toni Morrison (New York, Modern Library, 1998), p. 656.

37 Lester Fabian Brathwaite, "Hilton Als on the Many Faces of James Baldwin," *Newnownext.com*, 11 February 2019, www.newnownext.com/hilton-als-on-the-many-faces-of-james-baldwin/02/2019/ (accessed 28 January 2021).

38 *Ibid.*

39 "What Books Should Biden Read? We Asked 22 Writers," *New York Times*, 20 December 2020, www.nytimes.com/2020/12/20/books/joe-biden-book-recommendations.html (accessed 29 January 2021).

40 Glaude, *Begin Again*, p. 31.

41 *Ibid.*, p. 215.

42 *Ibid.*, p. 8.

43 Nell Irving Painter, *The History of White People* (New York, W. W. Norton, 2011), p. 139.

44 Prentiss Clark, "What 'No Chart Can Tell Us': Ordinary Intimacies in Emerson, Du Bois, and Emerson," *James Baldwin Review*, 5 (2019), p. 23.

45 *Ibid.*, p. 25.

46 Baldwin, qtd. in Glaude, *Begin Again*, p. 129.

Works Cited

Baldwin, James, "The Dangerous Road Before Martin Luther King" (1961), in *Collected Essays*, ed. Toni Morrison (New York, Modern Library, 1998), pp. 638–58.

_____ *No Name in the Street* (New York, Vintage, 1972).

Brathwaite, Lester Fabian, "Hilton Als on the Many Faces of James Baldwin," *Newnownext.com* 11 February 2019, www.newnownext.com/hilton-als-on-the-many-faces-of-james-baldwin/02/2019/ (accessed 28 January 2021).

Brim, Matt, *James Baldwin and the Queer Imagination* (Ann Arbor, MI, University of Michigan Press, 2014).

Buccola, Nicholas, *The Fire Is Upon Us: James Baldwin, William F. Buckley Jr., and the Debate Over Race in America* (Princeton, NJ, Princeton University Press, 2019).

_____ "How Do We Begin Again?," *The New Rambler: An Online Review of Books*, https://newramblerreview.com/book-reviews/literary-studies/how-do-we-begin-again (accessed 29 January 2021).

Clark, Prentiss, "What 'No Chart Can Tell Us': Ordinary Intimacies in Emerson, Du Bois, and Emerson," *James Baldwin Review*, 5 (2019), pp. 23–47.

Drabinski, John, "The Poetics of Beautiful Blackness: On Baldwin and Négritude," in D. Quentin Miller (ed.), *James Baldwin in Context* (Cambridge, Cambridge University Press, 2019), pp. 233–43.

Glaude, Jr., Eddie S., *Begin Again: James Baldwin's America and Its Urgent Lessons for Our Own* (New York, Crown, 2020).

Leeming, David, and Magdalena Zaborowska, "Remembering Sedat Pakay," *James Baldwin Review*, 3 (2017), pp. 173–85.

Maxwell, William J., *F.B. Eyes: How J. Edgar Hoover's Ghostreaders Framed African American Literature* (Princeton, NJ, Princeton University Press, 2015).

Mullen, Bill, *James Baldwin: Living in Fire* (London, Pluto Press, 2019).

Painter, Nell Irving, *The History of White People* (New York, W.W. Norton, 2011).

Senghor, Léopold Sédar, "Negritude and the Civilization of the Universal," in Carlos Moore, Tanya Sanders, and Shawna Moore (eds.), *African Presence in the Americas* (Trenton, NJ, Africa World Press, 1995).

Slen, Peter, "In Depth," C-SPAN, 6 December 2020, www.c-span.org/video/?477970-1/depth-eddie-glaude (accessed 28 January 2021).

"Symposium: The Negro's Role in American Culture," *Negro Digest*, XI:5 (1962), pp. 80–98.

"What Books Should Biden Read? We Asked 22 Writers," *New York Times*, 20 December 2020, www.nytimes.com/2020/12/20/books/joe-biden-book-recommendations.html (accessed 29 January 2021).

Contributor's Biography

Herb Boyd is an awarding-winning author and journalist. He has written or edited over 28 books and published countless articles for national magazines and newspapers, including New York's *Amsterdam News*. His 2008 book *Baldwin's Harlem: A Biography of James Baldwin*, was a finalist for a 2009 NAACP Image Award. *Brotherman: The Odyssey of Black Men in America: An Anthology* (One World/Ballantine, 1995), co-edited with Robert Allen of the Black Scholar journal, won the American Book Award for nonfiction. In 1999, Boyd won three first place awards from the New York Association of Black Journalists for his articles published in the *Amsterdam News*. Among his most popular books are *Black Panthers for Beginners* (Writers & Readers, 1995), *Autobiography of a People: Three Centuries of African American History Told By Those Who Lived It* (Doubleday, 2000), *Race and Resistance: African Americans in the 21st Century* (South End Press, 2002), *The Harlem Reader* (Crown Publishers, 2003), *We Shall Overcome: A History of the Civil Rights Movement* (Sourcebooks, 2004), and *Pound for Pound: The Life and Times of Sugar Ray Robinson* (Amistad Press, 2005). Two of Boyd's most recent publications—*Harlem Renaissance Redux* (Third World Press, 2019) and *Black Detroit: A People's History of Self-Determination* (Amistad, 2017)—have been widely praised. Boyd has been inducted into the Literary Hall of Fame for Writers of African Descent, the Madison Square Garden Hall of Fame as a journalist, and National Association of Black Journalists Hall of Fame. Along with his writing, Boyd is national and international correspondent for *Free Speech TV*. A graduate of Wayne State University in Detroit, Boyd is an adjunct instructor at City College of New York in the Black Studies Department.

CREATIVE NONFICTION

The Fire Inside

Aleksander Motturi
Translated by Kira Josefsson

Abstract

In this semi-biographical short story, the relationship between James Baldwin and Attorney General Robert F. Kennedy, and its culmination in their epic confrontation in New York City on 24 May 1963, is portrayed through the lens of an unidentified fictive narrator. In the midst of heightened racial tensions, Baldwin has been tasked with bringing together a delegation of prominent Black US personalities to meet with the Attorney General and share their views on the measures necessary to combat segregation and racism. The meeting has barely begun before the naivety of the administration's view of the national situation becomes clear, and the atmosphere in the room grows increasingly strained. "The Fire Inside" has never before appeared in print. An earlier version of the story was broadcast by Swedish Radio on 29 November 2019.

Keywords: James Baldwin, Robert F. Kennedy, Jerome Smith, Lorraine Hansberry

James Baldwin Review, Volume 7, 2021, © The Authors. Published by Manchester University Press and The University of Manchester Library
http://dx.doi.org/10.7227/JBR.7.12

We tried to cleave the fire. There is, we said, a fire that burns because we need it, a fire humans learned to control, by necessity, back in the early days, when they still dressed in animal pelts. There is, too, another fire, which has always lived its own life, which has transformed buildings, cities, civilizations; anything that stands in its way is turned into gray and white fields of ash. We tried to cleave the fire in order to understand it. There is, lastly, a fire that lives inside us, which glows in the spark of life, and erupts when dreams are cut short.

This is the fire that horrifies them now, the fire they describe as looting and destruction, as barbaric violence unfolding in our streets. When people talk about the fire it's always this fire they associate with us, with the Black Americans, the Negroes, who exist nowhere else in the world. Everyone is asking when and where it will erupt next time.

"It doesn't matter what you say about the violence," Jimmy had noted, commenting on the most recent uprisings, which he had prophetically foretold would break out in Birmingham. The violence exists, regardless of our thoughts on it. As long as there is a will to live in this world haunted by the nightmare of race, it will always erupt.

Jimmy was not alone in putting words to our experiences, but when he spoke nobody was left unmoved. This was true for both sides of the color line, not just for us. He was the first person to succeed in getting under the skin of the white liberal, forcing him into his own; nobody else had made them see what it means to be a citizen of the United States.

Jimmy always had white friends. Without them, he wouldn't be the person he's become: the author James Baldwin. We know this, those of us who go way back with him, all the way back to his childhood when his teacher was a woman named Bill, those of us who watched him mingle with artists and other bohemians at The Calypso in the Village, before he went to Paris and finished his first novel. It was good to have him back. He knew that we were at the cusp of an era that would come to define the future of the United States.

"Who are the Negroes other Negroes listen to?" Bobby Kennedy had asked.

Jimmy had the answer to Bobby's question. They would listen to no politician; they would listen only to people who could put words to our experiences for the simple reason of having, themselves, deep knowledge of them. The crucial thing was knowing how to speak honestly and straightforwardly about things that confused them. And it was those people who the Attorney General wanted to invite to a gathering. He wished to hear what was on our minds, what we wanted to achieve with the protests.

It all came together with lightning speed. When Jimmy asked for my opinion the decision to hold the meeting had already been made. If there is one thing I've learned from all these years of knowing Jimmy, it's to grasp the moment when it arrives.

"I guess it can't hurt," I said and thought about everything Kennedy had done to get James Meredith into the university, despite how badly they'd handled the situation with troops meant to quell the protests that broke out at Ole Miss. But I also thought about the President's call to Coretta, and their efforts to free Martin from jail. If there is anyone among the obtuse white liberals who can help make America what America must become, it is him.

Jimmy laughed at my words, which I had borrowed from his most recent book.

"So you've read *The Fire* now?"

"Of course," I nodded, bashful.

In truth I had only had time to page through it. I liked the ending, the idea that the price the whites must pay for their own liberation is our full liberation. I wasn't saying that Kennedy had been convincing in his fight for civil rights—only that there was nobody else.

"The total liberation of the Blacks is an exceedingly high price to pay for he who has built his whole identity on being white," Jimmy replied; he had no delusions that progress would come overnight.

This was what made him so unique; he had the ability to see things from their point of view, and not just from the point of view of what would, sooner or later, become inevitable. And for them, our rights were a crime against the natural order, as if the sun were to shine from a starry sky. Perhaps this was the reason he always hesitated when I grew too optimistic. I did not understand how frightening this upheaval of the universe would appear.

"But if not even the Attorney General can push new laws through Congress," I asked, "who can?"

For some reason there was nevertheless a hopeful tone to his voice when we met up. Once we'd sat down there was no doubt in him that we were in the midst of an event that would determine our country's future. The Attorney General wanted to hear our thoughts, and what he heard were things he was not prepared to hear.

The time for reforms had passed. This was the problem with the administration: they had no grasp of the urgency of the situation we were in. Even if they understood the scale of the problem of segregation, all they wanted to discuss was how much time it would take to change the structures.

I arrived a little before the others, but they let me in while they prepared the buffet. I knew that Jimmy had met Bobby a few times before; he'd told me about a perverted White House feast honoring Nobel laureates from the Western Hemisphere. That's what Jimmy was like, he was able to gain the trust of any scene that had even an ounce of openness. At the same time he was hard, philosophical, never engaged in ad hominem attacks. It was the ideas at the core of the inequality that interested him, not the person.

"It's up to you," he'd told a journalist who interviewed him. "As long as you think you're white there's no hope for you. Because as long as you think you're white I'm going to be forced to think I'm Black."

This was what made him so beloved and respected, but also feared and hated. James Baldwin's name was on everyone's lips at this point. His recent books were displayed in bookshops all across the world, and his face was everywhere, in magazines, on posters, and in the televised debates he took part in, where he often outdid philosophers and pundits with his fiery tongue. And yet, he was what he'd always been: late.

Jimmy was known for it. He was always late to meetings, it didn't matter who he was joining. During this period he had appearances and talks almost every day. He was even late to the breakfast meeting at the Attorney General's house before the gathering. After just two hours of sleep that night he'd missed his flight to Virginia, or maybe it was the plane that had been delayed.

In any case, it was a truncated breakfast with Kennedy at Hickory Hill in McLean. Half an hour. They served poached eggs and coffee and all seven children were seated at the table along with their parents, chewing on pieces of bacon. Bobby took a fork and scraped what Jimmy didn't touch on his plate onto the plate of one of his daughters. After breakfast Ethel, who was pregnant, went upstairs to rest. The Attorney General had to run to another meeting.

"My driver is already waiting in the car," he said and took one last sip of coffee.

Before leaving he asked Jimmy if he'd give his autograph to the maid who was clearing the table. She was overcome at such a thoughtful suggestion. The most recent issue of *Time*, with Jimmy on the cover, was upstairs. Bobby proposed that he sign the cover. Evidently he had read Jimmy's essay, which was on the night-stand along with *Time*. Though he'd studied up for their breakfast get-together there was no time to get to the details. Just a short conversation about the meeting Jimmy had had with the Nation of Islam. Nevertheless, what they did get into was very interesting from Bobby's perspective, and he looked forward to the gathering with the delegates.

I don't know that we were looking forward to it in the same way. In truth it was a bit unclear what the purpose of it all was. Formally, we'd been invited to a luncheon, but of course the Attorney General would want something concrete from it. He'd always been a pragmatic person. He wanted to know how to stop the violence. The situation was getting to be untenable. Especially after the events in Birmingham. Chaotic.

I'd walked past 24 Central Park South many times, never knowing who the owners of the building were. The grand apartment had a view of the park. Some days you could see through the foliage of the trees, and behind the noise from the traffic on the street down below you could hear the sounds of children playing in the distance. Despite the lack of advance planning for the gathering a good number of the invitees had made it, several of them celebrities: Lena Horne, Lorraine Hansberry, Harry Belafonte. Jimmy turned up with his brother. But there were people like me there too, and others who didn't say much. At one point there had been murmurs about Dr. King coming, but he was busy with his work in Chicago; in fact, he was quite skeptical of Kennedy's intentions. He had dispatched his counsel and attorney.

Among the attendees was Jerome Smith, who was known for his zealous nonviolent resistance. Even though he'd been beaten up by the cops—and he stuttered when he talked about the attack he'd suffered in McComb, where a white mob almost took his life with brass knuckles—he continued to defend the principle of nonviolence. Some people called him Gandhi II. He'd spent his whole life arguing against those who believed violence would ultimately be inevitable in the struggle to end white oppression.

In other words, we were there because the frustrated Black masses listened to us rather than the politicians of the country. What could we say? How could we encourage a new attitude from the politicians?

First, we said nothing.

Maybe that's why Bobby and his adviser started talking about all the things they'd done for us. It didn't impress anyone. In fact, there was raucous laughter when he started listing the measures he'd passed. We'd heard this talk many times before, and if there was a point to the meeting it was not for us to give our blessing to their planned reforms.

Maybe the fire had stopped burning. In Birmingham the smoke had dissipated. But it was just a matter of time before the protests would erupt again, either there or elsewhere in the United States. It wasn't just cars that were on fire—there were reports of whole busses ablaze with flames like dragon tongues as they approached the station where Klansmen were waiting with clubs and weapons. Not in a hundred years had the military been called in to quell the uprisings that spread from the outskirts to the cities' incensed interiors. Not even sites of worship were safe from reactionaries, from persecution and acts of revenge. It would only get worse, but Kennedy did not understand this.

A buffet table was set in the salon with wild salmon, green salad, and mushroom-stuffed potato croquettes. Already at this point, the chasm was evident. On the walls hung framed black-and-white photographs of some distant Swedish relative of the family, who had been a missionary at the Zambezi River in South Rhodesia.

We knew from the outset that the Attorney General didn't intend to arrange a group sing or anything like that. Bobby was, after all, known for his critique of the segregationists' stubborn resistance to Black students at the universities. And there were many other things he'd done that indicated good will and good intentions. Few politicians were his equals on this topic. In other words, if there was anyone who could do something for us, it would be him.

That's why Jimmy had agreed to arrange this delegation. But the problem was that Bobby had not understood the depths of the experiences that were at the center of the conflict; had not understood the frustration, why so many had found their way to the radical separatists, the Black Muslims. He had no sense whatsoever that forceful action from the country's leaders was necessary, that vague promises of political change did not cut it.

"You," Jerome suddenly said, "have no idea what the trouble is."

That much was clear from the newspaper reports that followed the event. At this point, the Attorney General proclaimed that as the grandson of Irishmen and Catholics, he understood very well the feeling of being oppressed. He said that his father and his grandparents had endured discrimination themselves, and not only in the United States; the British had once viewed them as "white monkeys," so he could very well understand, he said, the despair that was spreading among the

Blacks. Bobby even tried to instill a sense of hope by saying that we might have a Black president in this country—forty years from now.

"There you go, the problem distilled," Jimmy flashed. "We've been here for far longer than three generations, and we did not arrive out of our own free will. But while your family is at the top, we are still crawling in the gutter."

Bobby attempted to preserve the friendly atmosphere with a speech about the efforts the Justice Department had made in Black voting rights cases. It was soon after that things derailed. There we were, once again having to explain "the problem." Before anybody could start talking, Jerome said that he felt physically nauseated just having to be in the same room as Kennedy. The minister listened while his press secretary crunched a croquette between his teeth. Then he repeated, almost like a mantra, that "these things take time." In that moment it was clear that they still lived in another world, and that nothing would change.

"We don't have that time anymore," Jerome interrupted and set the tone for the rest of the meeting. "Can't you see that? Because I'm close to the moment where I'm ready to take up a gun."

Jerome's proclamation shocked everyone, not just the Attorney General and his advisers, who started shifting anxiously.

"When I pull the trigger you can kiss it goodbye."

It was evident that Bobby was upset. He took it personally. So he turned his back to Jerome in the hopes that the other members of the delegation would provide him with a more courteous response to the question they had gathered to discuss. This, he did not get. Instead, someone, I can't remember who, though it might have been Lorraine, said:

"I can't see why I should tell my children to fight for democracy when it's in the name of democracy they are being chased by police dogs, when it's in the name of democracy firefighters set off their water cannons to quell the uprisings, though all they did was walk peacefully in the streets to make use of their democratic rights. And here you are, beating your chest for having called in the military to deal with the warzone that exists down there."

The others started fidgeting but they kept quiet because they saw the Attorney General's face flushing. Jimmy held off on saying anything, he just listened very carefully. But at one point he asked Jerome if he would fight for the United States in Cuba.

"Never," he responded. "*Never, never.*"

Bobby, who had lost a brother in World War II, was shocked into silence. He could not understand this lack of patriotism, but none of us had any sympathy for his reaction.

"If there is anybody you should listen to in here, it is this man," Lorraine said and pointed at Jerome.

Essentially, we were all in agreement: what Jerome had said could not be dismissed as barbarism. The revolts were not just about the bomb attacks on Dr. King and his brother. Nor can they be explained by pointing to the brutal police torture of a twelve-year-old boy, which had caused his five-year-old sister to suffer a psychosis.

The worst part of it was the calculated indifference. The silence of the large, innocent masses, as though they were numb to these kinds of events, as though everything was the way it should be, inevitable. It wasn't just in the South that people had begun to seek out the radical groups, not just there the separatists rattled guns in their hideouts. It was not just the South that had groups of people who had ceased putting their faith in this talk of reforms long ago, generations ago, groups that did not see how the authorities, even if they had the support of J. Edgar Hoover, could guarantee their safety—all over the country, Blacks had grown tired of symbolic action.

"What is needed is a change in attitude, a moral commitment the president must pioneer, a miracle."

It didn't matter how the others tried to translate Jerome's fury into language the Attorney General could process—he'd already stopped listening. This was clear in the days that followed the meeting, when he made a statement to the *New York Times*.

"None of them had the slightest understanding of the meaning of political process. They don't even know what laws we have in this country. They don't know what the facts are. You can't talk to people like that. All you get is emotion, hysteria—they stood up and orated—they cursed—some of them wept and left the room."

I've never seen Jimmy as upset as he was when he read the newspaper reports.

"Instead of taking responsibility, instead of initiating true change, he reduced us to a group of ungrateful hysterics."

I didn't quite know what to say, so I placed my hand on his arm and watched my own fingertips dance nervously like a butterfly over his white shirt, before he took hold of my wrist, moved my hand to his cheekbone, over his eyes, his feverish forehead.

"The government asked us what Black people want. I mean, I have the answer. I know what we want and anyone who's learned to walk and talk knows what we want. Maybe I should have told Bobby. If you know what *you* want, then you know what *I* want."

But that's not how the meeting had ended, Bobby wasn't lying about that sequence; we had left the room. Lorraine had stood up and said:

"Mr. Attorney General. I am deeply concerned about the state of a civilization that produced that photograph of the white cop—this specimen of white masculinity—standing on that Negro woman's neck in Birmingham."

Then she thanked him for his time, and walked out. The rest of us followed.

Contributor's Biography

Aleksander Motturi (b. 1970) is a Swedish writer and the artistic director of the independent organization Clandestino Institute, where James Baldwin's legacy has been explored in various programs. After finishing his doctoral thesis in philosophy (on Ludwig Wittgenstein's remarks on James G. Frazer), Motturi has published both literary nonfiction and fiction in the form of novels, short stories, and plays. His auto-fictional novel *Broder* (Brother) won Swedish Radio's prestigious literary prize in 2018.

Translator's Biography

Kira Josefsson is a literary translator, writer, and editor working between English and Swedish. The recipient of a 2017 PEN/Heim translation award and multiple grants from the Swedish Arts Council and others, her work has appeared in *Granta, Vulture/New York Magazine, Words without Borders, Svenska Dagbladet, The Nation*, and elsewhere.

Manchester University Press

CREATIVE NONFICTION

Baldwin's Perfect Storm

Maureen Kelleher

Abstract

James Baldwin's arrest in Paris in December 1949 gave birth to his perfect storm. His ten days in Fresnes jail weakened him physically and emotionally. He made it out, but upon release he was mired in self-doubt and enveloped in a bout of depression. He returned to his hotel, ready to try to get back to his life, however daunting that effort would be. The hotelier's demand that he settle his bill, and do it quickly, awakened his obsession with suicide. He simply could not handle one more obstacle in his path; he chose to kill himself in his room. Ironically, he saved his life when he jumped off a chair with a sheet around his neck. In a matter of seconds his death wish was replaced by his equally obsessive need to write, witness, think, party, drink, challenge, and love.

Keywords: jail, suicide attempt, Paris, hotel, bedsheet

James Baldwin Review, Volume 7, 2021, © The Authors. Published by Manchester University Press and The University of Manchester Library
http://dx.doi.org/10.7227/JBR.7.13

D ecember 27, 1949, Paris: James Baldwin had one hour to pay his hotel bill or go. He had survived Harlem, New York City, and the United States, and he was beginning his second year in France. The hurdles he had faced as a young Black man—and one who wanted to earn a living as a writer—had been difficult, but he had been strong and resourceful enough to get over each one as it cropped up. But the hotel bill that day and his frame of mind were unusually grave. On the one hand he didn't have the money, and, on the other, he had no place to go to. Baldwin's outlook suggested three options: pay, leave, or die.

Ten days earlier: Baldwin found himself in the eye of a perfect storm. His friend had taken a sheet from one hotel and brought it with him to the Grand Hôtel du Bac where Baldwin was staying. Somebody took umbrage that a sheet from Hôtel des Deux Arbres was in Hôtel du Bac and the police were called. They found the sheet on Baldwin's bed. Baldwin was charged with receiving stolen goods and taken to jail. The perfect storm was born.

That Baldwin, an African American, was arrested because of a bedsheet—the same thing commonly worn in the USA by the Ku Klux Klan—put a fine point of irony on the genesis of the storm. For Baldwin, a sheet could be as lethal as a gun when the Klan wore it; it caused him to be arrested when his friend stole it; and it provided the means to hang himself when all he had was nothing worth living for. If given a second thought—which he did—a cotton sheet screamed subjugation of his people. In bygone days—but not that far gone—"King Cotton" strolled his fields filled with hundreds of his slaves; his grandmother, Barbara, was one them. But in the fall of 1949 Baldwin was thousands of miles from the Klan meetings back in Alabama. He was on a different continent, across the Atlantic Ocean, and a sheet, of all things, kicked up the storm.

The irony of the basis of his arrest gave way to the fact that he was, bottom line, just another arrested man when he got to the jail. He was weaker than most and he couldn't speak French. From the existential perspective who he was in the world was thrown off-kilter. His arrest and jail time brought him face to face with the question of his right to be alive.

Baldwin's body—often his Achilles' heel—made the arrest especially difficult. In late fall he had been hospitalized twice. He was not fully recovered when he was walked out of Hôtel du Bac, under police escort. It's hard to imagine that ten days in a jail cell in December didn't chip away at his already diminished health. He knew some French, but he wasn't fluent. He couldn't speak for himself in court. An interpreter had to be secured for him, thus delaying his court appearance and extending his time in jail. Like every other man in the cell he was, in everyday parlance, a nobody. Fame had not yet attached itself; he enjoyed no favors, from any quarter, for anything. And he was penniless. The idea of release, based on his own recognizance or by posting bail, was laughable. He couldn't get out of jail under his own power. He was terribly stuck.

Baldwin's arrest in France undermined his own sense of himself; for in the eyes of the French criminal justice system he was, like his white friend who stole the sheet in the first place, just an American. The color of his skin didn't matter; it was meaningless here. In one fell swoop, his quick, pugilistic Harlem intellect no longer provided a solid stance for throwing a punch. He was, vis-à-vis all the ways he had previously prepared for a fight, unarmed.

Lastly there was the ever-present voice in Baldwin's head that began in childhood. Under the right circumstances, it counselled him to take his own life. Baldwin's obsession with suicide was like a tiny bullet lodged precariously in his frontal lobe that could not be surgically removed. Something could jostle it just enough and he'd decide that killing himself was the right thing to do. What usually jiggled the mortal lead was a fight with a lover.

As a youngster he and all the kids heard about the neighbor boy who shot himself in the head, at the doorstep of unrequited love. The boy was black as coal. The girl he loved was just too fine—too fair—for the affection of a boy so dark. The young Baldwin could not get the image out of his mind: blood running out of the boy's head and onto the welcome mat at the girl's front door. A few years later his friend, Eugene Worth, jumped off the George Washington Bridge. In Baldwin's world, death was always an option to stop unbearable pain. That day in Hôtel du Bac he needed to stop his pain.

Mugshots. He turned left, right, then looked straight into the camera. He remembered when he threw a mug at a waitress in a Trenton, NJ diner. She had refused to serve him. *Yes, I threw it, it cracked that mirror, and I ruined, if only for a few very satisfying minutes, the Island of White where an American citizen who works hard—yes, sir, massa, laying track is hard—and looks like me can't even order a hamburger.* Baldwin had lost his patience with the racist system that had, twice that night, denied him a no-frills, affordable meal. The cracked mirror had to be replaced. That expense was not as big of a shock to the diner's receipts as the terror that interrupted the white patrons' dining pleasure. The sound of breaking glass brought them all to attention. The enraged Black man had a target on his back when he ran out, but he had survived. A successful denunciation of the system from a little righteous impatience. Both had felt good to him.

He lived to tell his mug-throwing tale, but he had to admit he almost died because of it. He stepped back and assessed himself from every angle imaginable after that episode. He was, after all, a thinker.

What he knew: he didn't want to end up in prison, he didn't want to die of an overdose, he must not be goaded into striking out in violence by the scared white society. He must not work against himself out of frustration and impatience. And he knew he wasn't like most of the people he ran into. Baldwin put it best: "I knew I was black, of course, but I also knew I was smart." What he wanted: to live his real life, not the spirit-crushing existence White America forced on him. *No safety net.* Unfettered by caution, Baldwin decided he would write, love, and witness full bore.

He walked down the hall handcuffed and in leg irons. When he felt the baton tap, he stopped. The guard pointed with it and indicated which way to turn at every stop. He made another right turn and saw the cell's entrance, a waffle-like, wall-to-wall grid of bars from floor to ceiling.

The guard outside the door, stick thin with red hair, had a wad of keys attached to his hip. He unlocked Baldwin's cuffs, leg irons, and then the cell door. He pulled it open and suggested the path with a sweep of his free hand, like the doormen did at the ritzy buildings back in New York. *Thank you, Red. I'm Black.*

The cell was cold. There were twenty men on benches along the three walls. A few of them leaned on each other as they slept. Some rocked back and forth, arms folded across their chests, and stared at the floor. Nobody talked. One guy with food in his beard paced from the back wall to the cell door, and to the wall again, non-stop. *Twelve, thirteen, fourteen. Stop. Turn. One, two, three, four.* Baldwin thought about the jaguar he saw on a school trip to the zoo. The black cat did the same thing along the front fence of his cage. *He's gone mad.*

He was thirsty and hungry. It had been a long day of questions and trying to make himself understood. But mostly it was waiting. He was tired. He folded his arms across his chest, just like the others, lowered his head, and closed his eyes. *Not a word of this in my letter home.*

A paper cup hit him on the forehead, followed by a young guy who crashed across his lap, sucker punched by the brute sitting by the cell door. Baldwin took out his handkerchief. He wet it with the bit of water left in the cup and dabbed the blood off the fighter's lower lip. *I am my mother's son.* "You're just a kid," Baldwin said, *who doesn't have enough sense to stay away from the biggest man in here.* A smear of the kid's blood ran across Baldwin's shirt.

Red unlocked the cell door; five more men walked in. He noticed Red's godawful acne. The new five took up the extra bit of room; now everyone had to sit up. The bench made Baldwin's bones hurt. It was difficult to find a comfortable position, one his spine could tolerate.

White piss, Black piss, French piss, Arabic piss. He felt an odd solidarity with the men as he stood on the edge of the hole in the center of the cell that served as a toilet. *Spanish piss, German piss, bloody piss, and piss that refuses to flow.* He relieved himself into the abyss. *We're all just animals in here.* Back on the benches they snored, belched, wheezed, and farted. Sleep was the best way to cope with the anxiety and boredom.

His father slapped him across his head. His ring left a small cut on Baldwin's ear. His brothers Wilmer and George were next, then his father came back to him. "You say you lost that mother fucking dime?" He covered his face with his hands in anticipation of the next slap. Red saw Baldwin's hands go to his face. "Américain!" Red yelled and put the prisoners' sandwiches down on the table by the door. Baldwin woke up. Red put a hand to his face and made buffoonish cries, mocking Baldwin. He got a good look at Red's acne. *Cigarette burns, they're cigarette burns. Some monster tortured him. At least daddy didn't leave scars on my face.*

He walked to the bars and to the back wall a few times. The movement relieved the aching in his back. *Why don't they call my name? Something is wrong.*

Day four: the sergeant and Red chained five prisoners together; he was the last man on the coffle. The sergeant led them down a passageway to a door that fed them right into the prisoner benches in the courtroom. They filed in and filled the second row. A large French flag hung majestically behind the judge. *Liberté, égalité, fraternité. My own tale of two cities.* At eleven years old he fell in love with Charles Dickens and his classic work. He had wanted to be Mr. Darnay so he could marry the fair-skinned beauty, Lucie.

Each man stood, with chains clanking, when the clerk called his name. He counted fifteen cases over the next few hours. The judge pounded his gavel, stood up, and opened an invisible door to the right of the dais. Baldwin panicked and jumped up. "Your Honor! My name wasn't called. Wait!" Two court officers rushed him and pushed him back down. "You didn't call my name!" He yelled his plea at the attorney in charge. "Why didn't you call my name? "Je m'appelle James Baldwin! Je m'appelle James Baldwin!" The clerk stood and hurried right up to the front row of prisoner benches. He tore his spectacles from his face; veins were throbbing at his temples. "Monsieur Américain! You must wait for an interpreter!"

Back in the cell he took refuge in Dickens again, but remembered the classic tale in more detail. *Nobody came for Darnay.* He lost his appetite for the sandwiches Red brought in.

Day five, middle of the night: a kid woke them all up with his screams in Spanish. Red was furious when he woke up. He ran his baton across the bars. The kid, a haggard teen, yelled louder, went to the bars, and spit through them. Red entered the cell; all but the kid retreated to the back wall. The Spanish kid spit again and hit Red in the chest. Red's baton glanced the kid's ear and with another crack the kid was on the floor, his whole body shaking. *He's catching a fit.* He had seen a girl at school have a seizure. Red took a step toward the kid; the guy who spoke German kneeled over the kid and pinned his arms to the floor. "Look!" Baldwin yelled and Red turned from the kid. Baldwin held the Spanish teen's pack of cigarettes inches from Red's face. Red took the pack and pulled the cell door shut behind him. Urine streamed from between the kid's legs.

Baldwin returned to his spot. *Thank you, Reverend Baldwin, good friend of the Great God Almighty.* Tears streamed down his cheeks. *You didn't give me much, but I'm not afraid of Red's baton.*

The next day the sergeant called the kid's name. "Bonne chance," Baldwin whispered to him. The Spaniard gestured like he was making a phone call. Finally Baldwin understood; he gave the kid the address of his friend, Tom. An old man scooted down the bench and offered him cheese and bread. "Merci," Baldwin said. "Eat," the old man commanded. Baldwin was surprised; "You speak English?" It was the first time he heard the old man talk. Baldwin scratched his neck and shoulders. The lack of a shower had accumulated on his body.

"Père Noel!" Red yelled out as he put the sandwiches on the table and then pretended to hobble like the old man. *It's Christmas.* Tears welled up. He lowered his head and put a hand over his eyes. *I'm failing miserably here, momma. I'm dying.*

The teen's blood on his shirt had turned brown on the edges. *I need a goddamn clean shirt.* His back ached all the time now; the bench felt like concrete. He could feel the mass of phlegm in his chest when he coughed; he breathed through his mouth. The men spit into the toilet hole as much as they urinated into it.

"Américain!" He was shackled and walked back to the courtroom. It was a public spectacle. The clerk read the day's docket; people in the gallery laughed when the chief attorney held up the stolen sheet. Baldwin looked at the people: *You're only there because I'm here.*

Hours passed, six men were released, and his name wasn't called. *What am I, the invisible American now? Does nobody see me here?* Finally he caught the interpreter's eye and motioned for her to come to him. "They have to sentence a man, then we will proceed with your case," the woman whispered. A prisoner was brought in from the back. The chief attorney handed the judge a piece of paper and he read from it. The prisoner's head fell to his chest; a woman in the gallery let out a screaming wail.

He had heard the same cry from women back home at funeral masses. The mother of the dark-skinned boy who killed himself—Johnny on the Spot they all had called him—screamed and moaned and then fell on the floor as her son was eulogized. The saints circled around her, sang, patted, and praised. The remnants of slavery had commingled with racism and insidiously trickled their way through the generations in Harlem. Johnny was simply too dark; he got the message. The little girls, oblivious to the psychological damage, spread the same fatal message on the sidewalks of Harlem. "Johnny on the Spot, she loves you not, shot-your-self-in-the-head," they sing-songed rhythmically as they skipped rope. He had wanted to whip his little sister with that damn rope.

The judge declared something, the interpreter turned to him, and the old man gave him a nudge. "You home, Américain."

He signed the paper and headed toward the exit. "Monsieur!" the clerk in the property cage called out. She passed his belt and an envelope through the small opening in the wire mesh. *My belt, right.* He opened the envelope and saw paper francs inside. He pulled out a piece of paper with precise handwriting: "Jimmy, glad to help. Tom." The old man hobbled to the property cage; Baldwin put the lion's share of Tom's money in his hand. He walked out of the Palais de Justice and crossed the street. *Sturm und drang the Germans would say.*

The storm dumped a spent and rickety Baldwin into Hôtel du Bac. The landlady was right there, watching him. She came from behind the counter to see the disheveled Baldwin with monster red eyes and the kid's blood across his shirt. "Mon Dieu!" she exclaimed. Her daughter came from the back room to see what was wrong. The women stared at him. He took the rest of Tom's money out of his pocket and put it on the counter. *Just one night's sleep in a bed.* His voice was almost gone and with very little French all he could implore was "s'il vous plait." The daughter picked up the money and put it in her apron pocket.

He stood outside his room. A woman and a small child walked past silently. He found his room key, went inside, and locked the door. *Hello, my little friend.* He gave his typewriter a pat and pulled the curtains shut. He laid down; it felt so good to be on a bed. There was a hard knock on his door; he opened his eyes. "Monsieur

Baldwin!" the landlady's daughter said loudly through the door. "Monsieur Baldwin! Une heure!" He had one hour to settle his bill or leave. Baldwin's perfect storm continued to blow.

He put a sheet of paper into his typewriter and began pecking the keys. "The courtroom, the cell, the flag, a judge, the court officers, cell keys, the attorney in charge, the gawkers, Red, bars, bailiff, blood, benches, cold, the interpreter, the hunger, shivering, beatings, the Spanish teen, thirst, hallways, a German, the batons, the stench, cigarettes, the man with food in his beard, sandwiches on the table, Red's cigarette burns, the screaming, the pacing, the old man. And the toilet hole. The lives of men reduced to a filthy hole they're forced to stand around like brute animals." He held down the shift lock key; "WHY AM I HERE?"

He swatted his papers to the floor—*I don't have any more money! I don't have a goddamned anything*—and took the sheet off the bed. He threw it over the pipe above. He stood on the chair and put the sheet around his neck.

Relax. Say goodbye, Jimmy. He felt a tingle of relief; Mr. Hindsight took control. He pulled off the sheet and sat down. He saw Eugene on the bridge's railing. *Eugene, take my hand. Thank you, Jimmy.*

"You can go fuck yourself, lady! I don't owe you shit," a man yelled from the hallway, and brought him out of his memory. He remembered the woman with her child. *He didn't pay her. The son of a bitch didn't pay her.* His reflection in the mirror added his two cents: *The daughter is going to beat the hell out of you.*

The perfect storm had left him perfectly alone. There was nobody to care that he was Black, that his hair was wiry, that his lips were big, that his eyes bulged, that he was poor, that he loved men, that he wrote, was really smart, and a good conversationalist. No one seemed to care that he was from Harlem, was a ton of fun, and had a lot to say, that he had written insightful essays, that he came from slaves, that he'd buy you a drink if he had the money, or offer to share his if he didn't. Nobody knew his name, or that he loved his family and missed them all very much.

Nobody saw his deep pride. He was his mother's helper; he was proud of her trust in him. He raised his brothers and sisters; he was proud that he named his baby sister, Paula. He stood on the chair again, and put the sheet back around his neck. *Why did Red have to beat that Spanish kid?* He stepped off the chair.

The chair fell back and the sheet pulled taut for just a moment. The water pipe broke clean through from his weight. The black hole of his psyche cracked wide open. The Holy Spirit, in all the hubbub, zoomed right in as he fell to the floor.

He looked up at the pipe. *What the hell?* Water came running down, right onto his face. He spit and sputtered to get a breath. He leaned on an elbow to get more air and a better look at the pipe. Instantly he realized he was reacting and moving and thinking differently, like his real self. He leaned back into the flow and took in a few gulps.

The water felt divine in his mouth: on his tongue, under it, on the roof of his mouth, on his gums and the inside of his cheeks. It felt good going down his throat. It pooled in his stomach. He felt the cells in his lips and his gut coming alive. His eyeballs and arms and ears and nose were soothingly wet. The water made its emotional conversions. A perfect storm's deluge washed over him as he gurgled with joy. He felt giddy. He was coming back to his real life, inside and out. *Renaissance!*

He stood up and pulled the curtains open. "I'm alive again!" he shouted to the children playing in the courtyard below. He yelled out a second time from sheer delight. He was delighted to be so delighted. He had forgotten what that felt like.

He wagged a finger at his friend in the mirror. "Nature abhors a vacuum. Don't you know that, man!" *No more of this craziness.*

That afternoon, Baldwin wanted to die; he did everything right to make that happen. He should have died, but, unwittingly, he jumped straight into the arms of a renewed *joie de vivre*. Suicide interrupted, the perfect storm ceased its morbid gales. All praise and respect to it and its component parts.

Baldwin chose suicide by hanging, not by jumping out of a window. The fall would have killed him. He chose to hang from a pipe overhead, not the back of a door. A door—and especially one in a huge, old Parisian hotel—would not have given way, but the water pipe did. The pipe, a limbless object, in its unique way pulled him back from the edge. And it conveyed its contents to where it was needed most.

Water, potable water. It gives life, it takes life, and it saves. Baldwin's perfect storm blew him from the bottom of a black fog to the peak of that afternoon's brilliant sun.

He gathered his clothes and collected his papers. He flung his duffel bag over his shoulder and tucked his typewriter under his arm. "Momma raised a gifted child," he said as he descended the stairs. *Daddy tried his best.* He got to the first landing. *Run!*

Man on the street. *Jimmy Baldwin, victorious!* The sun was glorious; he felt loved by its warmth. Purged, renewed by the storm, the air about him was clear, clean, fresh as it filled his lungs. He couldn't wait to get to Café de Flor and bum a drink and a cigarette.

Contributor's Biography

Maureen Kelleher is a private investigator in New York City. Prior to moving to the New York area she lived in New Orleans, Louisiana, where she worked as a criminal defense investigator, and specialized in fact investigations. Her field of expertise is old, cold, death row cases where an "actual innocence" legal claim is regarded to be highly possible by death row attorneys. She has helped get three men off Louisiana death row, and worked with Innocence Project New York to help exonerate Andre Hatchett in 2016. She is also a visual artist.

Manchester University Press

IN MEMORIAM

Cheryl Wall, *In Memoriam*

Edited by Cora Kaplan   University of Southampton

Abstract

The distinguished critic Professor Cheryl A. Wall (1948–2020) was the Board of Governors Zora Neale Hurston Professor of English at Rutgers University, New Brunswick. Her path-breaking scholarship in two highly influential monographs, *Women of the Harlem Renaissance* (1995) and *Worrying the Line: Black Women Writers, Lineage, and Literary Tradition* (2005), helped to ensure that twentieth-century Black women writers were recognized and valued for their power, genius, and complexity. Her most recent book, *On Freedom and the Will to Adorn: The Art of the African American Essay* (2018), places the essay form at the center of African American literary achievement. Throughout her long career she supported and enabled Black students, and championed racial diversity and gender equality at every level of the university. An Associate Editor of *James Baldwin Review*, she was the most generous and astute of readers, as well as a wise editor. In this memorial section, fifteen colleagues, former students, and interlocutors share their remembrances and honor her legacy.

Keywords: Cheryl A. Wall, *Women of the Harlem Renaissance, Worrying the Line: Black Women Writers, Lineage, and Literary Tradition, On Freedom and the Will to Adorn: The Art of the African American Essay*, tribute, Rutgers University

James Baldwin Review, Volume 7, 2021, © The Authors. Published by Manchester University Press and The University of Manchester Library
http://dx.doi.org/10.7227/JBR.7.14

Figure 1   Cheryl Wall (Photograph courtesy of Camara Epps)

Introduction

Cora Kaplan   University of Southampton

We were shocked and saddened to learn of the death, in April 2020, of Profes-sor Cheryl A. Wall, the Board of Governors Zora Neale Hurston Professor of English at Rutgers, New Brunswick. Her path-breaking scholarship shifted the critical conversations about Black women's writing and representation and, lat-terly, the African American essay. Professor Wall was an Associate Editor of *James Baldwin Review*, and we will greatly miss her wise, enabling advice and enthusi-asm. A symposium in her honor, organized by her Rutgers colleague Professor Evie Shockley to mark the occasion of her retirement, was scheduled for the spring of 2020, but unfortunately deferred because of the pandemic. It is now expected to take place in the spring of 2022, alas without her guiding presence. In the meantime, the journal has invited Cheryl's colleagues, students, and interlocutors to remember and celebrate her life and her work. The fifteen moving, personal tributes which are gathered here comprise a collage of vivid portraits that speak of a remarkable thinker and writer, colleague, teacher, mentor, interlocutor, and friend. Praised by all for her generous and collaborative spirit, her intellectual brilliance was matched only by her bold creativity in her field and in her institution.

Born in Manhattan and brought up in Jamaica, Queens, Cheryl Ann Wall was the daughter of Reverend Monroe Wall, a pastor of the Mount Calvary Baptist church in Harlem, and Rennie Ray (née Strayhorn), an English teacher in the city's public schools. She earned her BA in English at Howard University and gained her PhD in the History of American Civilization at Harvard. She joined the Douglass College faculty at Rutgers in 1972. In the almost five decades of her distinguished career at Rutgers, she was dedicated to transforming and enriching the curriculum, the classroom, and the faculty, making each more racially diverse. She was passionately committed to making the university environment welcoming, supportive, and democratic for students and teachers alike. The generations of postgraduate students whom she mentored, many now professors or educators themselves, speak eloquently of her enormous intellectual generosity and her kindness. Rutgers, New Brunswick, was the destination for an unusually large cohort of first-generation college students, reflecting New Jersey's markedly heterogeneous population. Asked about her vision of the shape and priorities of the "Future University" in a 2016 interview, she responded that undergraduate education should always remain at its center. Encouraging Black students to major in English, and supporting their trajectory at Rutgers and beyond, was at the heart of that practice. Cheryl Wall chaired the English Department at Rutgers from 1997 to 2003.

One of her first major publications, the edited volume *Changing Our Own Words: Essays on Criticism, Theory, and Writing by Black Women* (1989), now an indispensable classic, grew out of a conference she organized with others at Rutgers in 1987, in which critics and scholars of Black women's writing came together for "an intense and extended conversation among Black women writers and their readers" to reflect on the "overarching question" of "how to bring the terms *criticism, theory and writing by black women* into conjunction." In her prescient introduction to the collection, Wall hoped that the productive debates, at the live event and in the book, would, as it surely did, move that conversation on.

In that introduction too, Wall suggested that "from the margins, various strategies may be deployed, and varied, indeed contradictory propositions set forth," and she argued that the differing positions among Black feminist critics was itself a "response to the false universalism" of literary critical traditions that "rendered black women and their writing mute." A major achievement of Wall's first monograph, *Women of the Harlem Renaissance* (1995), is to move these African American women writers, Jessie Fauset, Nella Larsen, and Zora Neale Hurston, as well as artists and singers, Gwendolyn Bennett and Bessie Smith, from the margins to the center of the Harlem Renaissance where they belonged, and now happily reside.

Their wider importance to the longer traditions of African American and American writing is revealed both by "locating them in multiple contexts"—the heroine of Nella Larsen's *Quicksand* in relation to the phenomenon of Josephine Baker for example—as well as reading their work "alongside each other." Zora Neale Hurston's career and work was an abiding interest for Wall, from her first fleeting encounter with Hurston's writing in graduate school. She edited two collections of Hurston's work for the Library of America, as well as two volumes of criticism on her fiction.

The deep connection between the blues and African American writing is caught in Wall's resonant title for her next book, *Worrying the Line: Black Women Writers, Lineage, and Literary Tradition* (2005), which fast-forwards from the interwar years to the 1970s, coincidentally the beginning of her own career and the moment when an astonishing cohort of Black women writers were transforming the literary landscape—among them Lucille Clifton, Gayl Jones, Audre Lorde, Paule Marshall, Toni Morrison, Gloria Naylor, and Alice Walker. "Worrying the line" is a blues term, here refigured to highlight the ways in which Black women's writing at this conjuncture uses similar strategies of interruption, embellishment, and reworking. It refers simultaneously to the unanswered question of genealogy that arises in the work of so many of these writers, and to the radical re-vision of literary traditions that their writing both consciously pursues and collectively represents.

On Freedom and the Will to Adorn: The Art of the African American Essay (2018) brings the African American essay center-stage as an open and speculative genre in which African Americans excelled, one in which the personal and political are intermingled, and in which form and content are inextricably joined. The study takes a long view of the African American essay and its evolution over two centuries—from the free black Bostonians David Walker and Maria Stewart in the 1820s through Alain Locke, Hurston, Ralph Ellison, James Baldwin, June Jordan, and Alice Walker, to the combined print and online activism of Ta-Nehisi Coates and Brittney Cooper.

In each and all of these densely researched, elegantly written studies, and in her allied essays, Wall reimagined the terrain and the terms through which gender and genre in African American writing were considered. Praising her as a "leading, pioneering scholar," Henry Louis Gates, Jr., cited in Sam Roberts's *New York Times* obituary, describes the diamond quality of Wall's research and writing as "characterized by the careful meticulous attention to detail of a great literary historian and the exquisite mastery of form that marks the work our best literary critics—a combination all too rare among scholars of American literature today."

Cheryl Wall interpreted "changing words" as both a challenge, "talking back," and as "exchange": the collective and collaborative conversations she enabled with students and fellow scholars alike were essential to the radical research and scholarship she championed and practiced. In her long career she seized her time, found her subject, and helped to shape it. As her colleague Professor Evie Shockley has said "when black women writers were publishing, being recovered and receiving national attention in greater numbers than ever before," Cheryl Wall made "a 45-year career of helping to ensure that these writers and their writings are valued in all of their power, genius and complexity." It is now our shared task, to which the eloquent tributes below contribute, to ensure that her extraordinary work, life, and career, embodying in all its aspects what anthropologist David Scott has termed the "receptive generosity" and "the ethics of responsibility" of our most admired intellectuals, is valued in the same way.

Contributor's Biography

Cora Kaplan is Professor Emerita of English at University of Southampton. She was a General Editor, with Professor Jennie Batchelor, of Palgrave's 10-volume *History of British Women's Writing*. With Professor Bill Schwarz she organized a major conference on James Baldwin at Queen Mary, University of London, in 2007, and with him co-edited *James Baldwin: America and Beyond* (University of Michigan Press, 2011). She counts herself privileged to have had Cheryl Wall as a colleague at Rutgers from 1989 to 1995, and as a long-distance friend in the succeeding years.

Remembering Cheryl Wall as Educator and Mentor

Amy Barenboim   Columbia University

It would be more than possible merely to count and recount the ways in which Dr. Cheryl Wall touched me personally and intellectually. Yet I have found the role Dr. Wall played, and continues to play, in the formation of my time as a young scholar to be a uniquely un-unique story; I am all the time meeting her former students—now graduate students, professors, and educators—who attribute their success to her. I could also detail her pioneering scholarship and countless publications, her work on Zora Neale Hurston and the Harlem Renaissance, and her most recent and last monograph, *On Freedom and the Will to Adorn: The Art of the African-American Essay*.

However, I want to linger on the interstitial moments of Dr. Wall's time as an educator, moments that will not be revealed in a curriculum vitae or biography. Indeed, in her typical humility, Dr. Wall always described herself as an educator first and a scholar second, working in a long tradition of Black feminist educator-scholar-activists. While waiting outside her office for our meeting one day, I could not help but overhear Dr. Wall with another student, a freshman who had been struggling with her paper for their Toni Morrison seminar. Dr. Wall went through the student's paper line by line, guiding her through grammatical corrections as well as giving suggestions on content. Few, if any, scholars of her stature would take the time to support undergraduates with their writing.

In the same vein, Dr. Wall was always uniquely attentive to the class dynamics at Rutgers University, where the majority of students are either first-generation college students, commuters, or have full-time jobs in addition to their studies. I observed her understanding toward students in our James Baldwin seminar who would have to miss class for work or to take care of children. As one of the founders of the Rutgers English Diversity Institute, a summer preparatory program focused on creating more diversity in the humanities that brings students from around the country who are interested in pursuing PhDs in English literature, Dr. Wall took special care with students from other states and smaller schools. She took particular care with one student who had come from a college in Mississippi that had a student body of only five hundred people, always checking in with her, sitting with her at meals, and generally making sure she was comfortable in the new environment.

Dr. Wall's scholarly openness also translated into a long line of students, both my peers and students who went before me, who dedicate their work to her and her memory. As a lost undergraduate who wanted to go to graduate school but had no specialty, Dr. Wall encouraged me to study African American literature, welcoming me into a field I felt it was not my place to be in, and setting me on a path I might never have found. My graduate career, and beyond, is due to Dr. Wall's generosity, warmth, and desire to cultivate students who think critically about American history and literature, and who care about democratizing education. As I heard her state many times: "Diversity and excellence are not mutually exclusive."

I recount these moments of Dr. Wall's generosity to show that they were optional; at no point was she required to spend time and energy editing students' writing, mentoring them through graduate school applications, or founding programs to create openings for students of color to become scholars. It was from her own drive, intellectual kindness, and selflessness that Dr. Cheryl Wall dedicated her life to her students.

Contributor's Biography

Amy Barenboim is a PhD student at Columbia University in the department of English and Comparative Literature. She studies African American and African Diaspora literature and Critical Theory.

To Worry the Line

Rich Blint   The New School

In June 2007, a serious cadre of writers and scholars gathered at Queen Mary, University of London, to mark the twentieth anniversary of James Baldwin's death. This was the first in a series of ad hoc international conferences on the author staged in cities from New York to Boston, Montpellier, and Paris. I arrived in the country excited, but a bit harried. I had organized a panel to be chaired by my mentor and colleague, Hortense Spillers, and both of our planes were late. I jumped into a waiting black cab organized by local friends, located the building with some effort, and made my way to the front of the lecture hall. I sat down and gazed at my paper and the conference program while my colleagues (sans Spillers) shared insights about the great man and his work. When my turn came, I began my presentation in the style peculiar to our profession, read a couple of paragraphs, and then stopped. Placing my paper on the table, I quickly took emotional and intellectual inventory, appraising my discovery that this was a concurrent panel in familiar academic fashion. I'm not at all sure what I expected, but I remember pulling up short. I was several years into graduate school and had only seriously studied Baldwin on my own. I suppose that explains it: The growing knowledge that such an intimate relationship as the one I imagined I enjoyed with the author could be shared outside the hearing of all assembled on so solemn an occasion; that considerations of his insurgent legacy could be delivered via such common and well-rehearsed protocols.

I recall saying something to this effect and launching into a kind of missive concerning the relevance of his work beyond the gates of the university. This went over well enough and one of the conference organizers was very kind in her comments afterwards. But it was Cheryl Wall's plenary presentation the following morning that made clear to me how one might properly "worry the line" in relation to Baldwin's corpus. In the context of the condition of contingency and precarity that remains a defining feature of global Black life, scholarly discussions of Baldwin's commitment to a liberatory aesthetics must themselves break pitch, shout, and interrupt conventional narrative procedures. Squarely within the blues tradition that provided the title for Wall's volume on the literary activity of a cohort of contemporary Black women writers, the act of worrying the line is subversive in its insistence on emphasis and clarity. With a voice of quiet authority, a smile that always reached the eyes, and a generous, patient intelligence, Wall brought Baldwin's decades-long quarrel with the deep contradictions of American identity to elemental life. She captured a sense of what bearing witness to the violence raging openly in our intensely racialized society cost Baldwin. One caught a glimpse of the interior damage wrought by always being in battle, of the great burden of assimilating premature Black death—from marquee assassinations to the slow but sure. This was my introduction to the embodied wisdom of Cheryl Wall.

Thanks to the careless misplacement of my luggage by the handlers at Heathrow, my planned jaunt to Paris had to be cancelled. Instead, I had the great pleasure of reveling in Cheryl's convivial spirit through the kind offices of Hortense Spillers. We ate Caribbean food in Brixton, over-priced Italian in central London, and spent hours talking life and politics at the South Bank Center. The next time I saw Cheryl would be at Vanderbilt University for the inaugural board meeting of Issues in Critical Investigation: The African Diaspora. Convened by Spillers and attracting the labor of first-class intellectuals, Cheryl's

characteristic wisdom and commitment to clearing a way for the next generation of thinkers was on full display. Over the years, I would witness her subtle
redirection of conversation in productive ways, share a stage as she imparted her
extensive knowledge on Zora Neale Hurston, and marvel at her remarkable
capacity for institution-building.

I saw Cheryl for the last time at the MLA in Seattle last year. She was dazzling
with that ready, knowing smile and we enthusiastically agreed to meet for dinner
back east. She had only just written to fix a date when I learned she had left us, that
her rare beauty, brilliance, and expansive spirit had departed for the celestial. I
have to believe that someone like Cheryl who did so much good remains with us
not only through her life-shaping impact on students and colleagues. I imagine
she must also regularly check on her work, passing through just to make sure no
one is messing with her legacy. So then this is how we honor and mourn: In gratitude that she stayed with us long enough to model how to gracefully navigate the
actively hostile terrain of the American academy with a transformational inten-
tionality. Like Ursa Corregidora and blues singers before her, Cheryl Wall was
possessed by the injunction to sing a song of lineage, to "leave evidence," to worry
the line just so and long enough that the life and death gaps in our shared history
might yet be sutured.

Contributor's Biography

Rich Blint is Assistant Professor of Literary Studies and Director of the Program
in Race and Ethnicity at The New School. Co-editor of a special issue of *African
American Review* on James Baldwin (2014), Blint is author of the upcoming *A
Radical Interiority: James Baldwin and the Personified Self in Modern American
Culture.*

Herb Boyd   City College of New York

My personal regard and respect for Dr. Cheryl Wall began years ago, and back
in the summer of 2017 when I was finishing my book on the Harlem Renaissance I turned to her for a blurb, given her scholarship on the subject. "I'm still
trying to finish the revisions on my own manuscript—as well as writing tenure
and promotion reports for colleagues at Rutgers and elsewhere," was her email
reply.

That response was indicative of Cheryl's activity and pursuits, all of which came
to an end on 4 April when she died in Highland Park, NJ. She was 71. According
to her daughter, Camara Epps, the cause was complications from an asthma attack,
an ailment which made her all the more vulnerable in this season of the coronavirus pandemic.

From her post at Rutgers University she was scheduled to retire in May of
2020. Cheryl was widely hailed for her devout commitment to Black studies,

particularly African American literature with a focus on women writers and the Harlem Renaissance. These attributes were going to be highlighted in a symposium celebrating her legacy that had to be postponed because of the pandemic. "In a period when black women writers were publishing, being recovered and receiving national attention in greater numbers than ever before," Professor Evie Shockley, who was organizing the symposium, said, "Cheryl found it possible to make a 45-year career of helping to ensure that these writers and their writings are valued in all of their power, genius and complexity." More on this can be found in Sam Roberts's obituary in the *New York Times* (21 April 2020).

Exemplary of her research was the charitable review of Zora Neale Hurston's memoir *Dust Tracks on a Road*, a book "she did not want to write," Cheryl noted, "and many of her admirers wish she had not written." The book falls far short of a conventional autobiography and is fraught with inaccuracies and contradictions; even so, Cheryl commented, "passages in *Dust Tracks* are as engaging as any Hurston wrote." In *The Oxford Companion to African American Literature* her profile of Hurston is nearly definitive.

On the Rutgers University website, Cheryl is listed as the Board of Governors Zora Neale Hurston Distinguished Professor of English and the author of numerous books, including *Worrying the Line: Black Women Writers, Lineage, and Literary Tradition* and *Women of the Harlem Renaissance*, and as the editor of *Changing Our Own Words: Criticism, Theory, and Writing by Black Women*. She was the editor of two volumes of writing by Zora Neale Hurston for the Library of America—*Novels and Short Stories* (1995) and *Folklore, Memoirs and Other Writings* (1995)—as well as two volumes of criticism on Hurston's fiction: *'Sweat': Texts and Contexts* (1997) and *Their Eyes Were Watching God: A Casebook* (2000). She was the section editor for "Literature since 1975" in the *Norton Anthology of African American Literature* (2003). She served on the editorial board of *American Literature* and on the advisory boards of *African American Review* and *Signs: Journal of Women in Culture and Society*.

A former chair of the department, Cheryl remained active in university affairs. In 2003, she was co-principal with Mary Hartman of the Institute for Women's Leadership on "Reaffirming Action: Designs for Diversity in Higher Education." This Ford Foundation-funded initiative examined the strategies higher education institutions successfully employ to enhance racial and gender equity. Most recently, she was selected by Rutgers University President Richard L. McCormick to serve as vice chair of the Steering Committee on Implementation, a body organized to enact sweeping changes in undergraduate education at Rutgers. She had just become co-chair, with President McCormick, of the President's Council on Institutional Diversity and Equity.

She received the Warren I. Susman Award for Excellence in Teaching, and was named a Board of Governors Professor of English in December 2006, and named the Board of Governors Zora Neale Hurston Professor of English in January 2007. Her marriage to C. Roy Epps in 1979 ended in divorce.

In a follow-up to my request for a blurb, Cheryl wrote: "I'm traveling now, but I'll be home a week from today." She resides now in her eternal home and may she rest in peace.

This piece first appeared as an obituary in *New York Amsterdam News* on 30 May 2020, http://amsterdamnews.com/news/2020/apr/30/dr-cheryl-wall-distinguished-literary-scholar-dies/ (accessed 16 June 2021).

Contributor's Biography

Herb Boyd is an adjunct instructor in the Black Studies Program at the City College of New York.

Wesley C. Brown

I've struggled with how to explain to myself Cheryl's presence in my life and now her absence. Among the words—who, what, why, when, and where—that might help me, the 'who' of Cheryl is the only one I feel I can begin with, though I will, inevitably, fail to adequately answer my question.

There was the first time I met her at my interview for a teaching position at Rutgers University in 1978. I was asked many questions by the English Department faculty. I have very little recollection of what I or anyone else said. But I do have an indelible memory of Cheryl looking at me; and having the feeling that underneath her listening, she was also reading my words closely as I spoke them. That put me at ease, making me aware that she was hearing what I had to say, which encouraged me to want to be heard. I grew to greatly appreciate this quality in Cheryl. It made me more mindful of the importance of becoming an attentive listener in order to expect to be heard.

This probably wouldn't surprise anyone who came to know Cheryl within the community of her nearly five decades at Rutgers. Even while navigating her way through the maze of university life, there was an always unhurried seriousness she brought to her teaching and writing. This was evident in her seminal contributions to the study of African American women writers. Cheryl's commitment spoke across every page of her scholarship, leading us to the thunder in the words of the writers with no need to raise the temperature of her prose. She understood the power of language, giving voice to a generous, open-handed offering to readers, seasoned with a healthy dose of understated attitude and calling up comparisons to song stylist Carmen McRae. To paraphrase Audre Lorde, Cheryl celebrated the kingdom of Black women writers without shouting. And it would not be an exaggeration to say that even her silences were articulate!

I will always treasure our mischievously, often laugh out loud, conspiratorial call-and-response sessions, where we loosened our wits over the literary sweepstakes and the changing/same of the body politic. But despite the loss of those indispensable shared confidences and the failure of words to come close to expressing the fullness of 'who' Cheryl was for so many, my grief is made bearable by 'what' memories I have of her that will remain and 'why' the gift of Cheryl's life within my own will be there 'when' and 'where' I feel the need to summon her.

Contributor's Biography

Wesley Brown is the author of three published novels, a short story collection and four produced plays. He has taught at several colleges and universities, among them Rutgers University and Bard College at Simon's Rock. He lives in Lawrenceville, Georgia.

For Cheryl Wall, My Friend: A Very Short Introduction

Abena P. A. Busia

The Forty Years

The railway station, New Brunswick, NJ; this is where we first saw each other. I was arriving for my interview almost exactly forty years ago, she was waiting to meet me; in those pre-digital, pre-computer, pre-cell or smartphone, non-social-media days, two Black women with only our eyes searched along the antique railway platform, and found each other.

There are too many memories.

The following Fall, negotiating the start of the new year at our different Rutgers campuses, our paths seldom crossed naturally. Then several weeks later I got a phone call, an invitation, and another short ride. This time it was to what would have been a "store front" theater in a redbrick factory building lodged in a corner of a parking lot, except there were three risky flights to climb up to reach the makeshift stage. Cheryl had just become the first Board Chair of Crossroads, a new Black theater company in town, and took me to see to one of the bravest performances I have ever experienced: Charles Gordone's *No Place to be Somebody* (1969). With one generous invitation she introduced me to the world I had entered; a lesson for the ages. I still remember how that experience felt; it made me a believer. Forty years later I am still a subscriber and today on its board of trustees working with the last remaining founder of an organization which, but for her bravery, would never have been established. But for her courage to deal with who we are and where we wish to go there is much that would not have been established. She mentored future scholars at every level, including me.

The field of Black women writers itself! Douglass Library boasts mimeographs of her course on Black women writers, said to be the first in the country back in the mid-1970s when no one even knew our work could constitute a field of study. The first time I myself heard her give a paper, it was the day of an unseasonably huge snowstorm at a small conference on Black women writers, one of the first, at a high school in Montclair, NJ. The riches we had in one day; Nikki Giovanni, Toni Cade reading from the draft of *Those Bones Are Not My Child*, and the great Gwendolyn Brooks, reading and being Miss Brooks. The two critics among the writers were Cheryl A. Wall, who was fully present and spoke elegantly and wisely, and Hortense Spillers, but Hortense had been caught in the storm. She walked in late, but right on her closing presentation cue, still impeccably dressed with her short natural hair, and delivered a most perfect concluding talk, like she had been listening in on all the conversations, including Q&A, though she had missed the entire day. Once again Cheryl was driving, in a raging blizzard; we had dinner with Hortense at the long since disappeared Wooden Nickel before she continued on in the storm back down the turnpikes to Haverford.

Cheryl was working on *The Women of the Harlem Renaissance* and our vision of that world has never been the same.

I wrote my poem "Liberation" that very night: "we are all women, and we have that fire within of powerful women who can laugh beauty into life, and still make you taste the salt tears of our knowledge."

I remember our two mothers in Cheryl's first married home on Seaman Street; Mother Rennie Strayhorne Wall lifting her granddaughter into my once midwife mother's lap the week after the birth of Camara Rose. We had come to honor the ceremonies of the eighth day, bringing mother and daughter something white to mark her arrival and stay on this earth.

About a decade and a half later, standing in the parking lot of Murray Hall, with Cheryl uncharacteristically exasperated with that one and only child, refusing to be placated by Sharon Lewis's attempt to console her that the current adolescent storm was just the hormonal season, the three of us bursting into laughter at Cheryl's characteristic riposte both fierce and funny: "I had hormones, you had hormones, we all had hormones, but not in my mother's house!" Mother Cheryl Lena Younger Wall: "*In my mother's house there is still God.*"

And another decade after that, Cheryl in my mother's house in Accra: she really did see us at home, mother with her two granddaughters playing at her feet, bridging that gap, what a joy! She broke bread in my house in Ghana as I had during so many conversations around pot luck at her kitchen table, or the cornucopia that was her family Thanksgiving table; Cheryl, sister, and daughter hosting an assemblage of folks such as me, my waif and stray daughter, their fatherless nieces, and her ex-husband's great aunt.

We shared so many moments; marriages, divorces, present and absent daughters, the labors of creation; unfinished projects, half-finished books, award-winning publications, including invitations to the White House, all of it discussed and lauded around that small kitchen table. Or across her office desk.

She had way of looking over her glasses when she sensed you (or I, at least) were on the verge of saying something questionable, then lifting them onto her head when the look hadn't been enough to stop you—before sighing slowly and saying gently, "Well you know, you might want to reconsider that." When Cheryl suggested I might well want to reconsider something, I sat myself down and reconsidered!

And I don't think she ever understood how the friendship and love never diminished the admiration and the awe.

To this day I like to read her words aloud, I always have, because to do so is to hear the arc of her voice in the fine scan of her prose; a piano player's phrasing, each paragraph a musical score.

I have missed her more than I would have anticipated these last three years away. I took for granted the ability to knock at her office next door, or just cross the river to sit on her front doorstep and wait for her to come home.

And she will never come to that home again.

The Forty Days

Saturday 4 April 2020, 9:00 p.m. Brasilia time; my bedroom, after dinner a phone call from Stefan and the unendurable counting started.

Wednesday 8 April 10:00 a.m. Brasilia time, five grieving days later; an English department meeting over an unstable zoom connection; in these days we cannot meet to touch, I am grateful just to join colleagues in what is the only ritual of remembrance I can share, of this friendship guarded so jealously for four decades; to hear someone say they too loved you, and be comforted.

Saturday 11 April, Brasilia: the cycle of seven days of absence completed. Were I at home in Ghana, or you a Ghanaian anywhere in the world, family and friends would gather, pour libations, sing hymns, celebrate your life. Instead, I rattle distracted around this house, empty-handed, broken-hearted, leaden-footed. "*What ceremony else?*"

Thursday 17 April, thirteen days: I should have been at Rutgers today for the symposium honoring "the enduring legacy of your work." Is it blasphemy to say the timing was churlish? To ask the good Lord what it is He had in mind? We wanted just two more weeks to throw you your lifetime achievement party! That the date had already been moved six months is an inconvenient COVID truth we will let pass. You called to say you hoped I could still come; as if there were ever a question.

Wednesday 14 May: today the forty days are over. Your soul must be unfettered to reach home. Stefan had written "In these already trying times, we will have to find new ways and forms of grieving," so it is he and Evie I contact to confess I haven't been able to sleep a single Saturday night in April. Grief is a strange devouring beast: we find new forms of appeasement, we exchange your own words, and read other words of mourning: I offer "I Am Standing Upon the Seashore" and wonder what it was like for you; who were the "other eyes watching ready to take up the glad shout Here she comes" at your dying?

Coda at Forty Weeks

As this new year turns,
Sad is not the word for what I am
as I struggle to fix these memories,
for you are free now:

Through your will to adorn
everything about this life,
you have worried all the lines to
savour the salt of your lasting renaissance.

Consider these patches of memory
the distressed funeral cloth I could not wear for you,
its erratic lines of mourning
the white threads of repair stark against
my indigo cloth of grief.

Let's re-write this casebook for the blues:
This first year your anniversary falls on Resurrection Sunday.
I will wear white and remember you
With Love.

Contributor's Biography

Abena P. A. Busia, Ghana's current ambassador to Brazil, was Cheryl Wall's colleague at Rutgers for forty years. She has published widely, lectured extensively, and taught workshops and master classes on curriculum transformation in the areas of gender, race, and African Diaspora studies. She is also a published poet and one of the three project co-directors and series editors of the award-winning four-volume *Women Writing Africa* project, published by the Feminist Press (2002–08).

"I'll Change as Many Words as I Darn Well Please": Tribute to Cheryl Wall

Cheryl Clarke   Rutgers University

> Who said we had to call ourselves "African-American" instead of "Black?"
> Nobody asked me.
>
> Cheryl A. Wall, c. 1989

The chronological approach would take almost fifty years of memory. And there's only so much memory and only so many words. (I am already *over* my word limit.) Cheryl Wall was of a generation of Black feminist thinkers who, in their writing and their teaching, heralded the brilliance of African American women writers. Cheryl and I ended up in the same institution, Rutgers, that was intent upon being in the running with US university literature departments championing the literature of African Americans (men), and if Black women must be among them, then so be it. (Though when I first entered Rutgers in 1969, only one faculty person, Walter Bezanson, had even heard of Bessie Smith.)

I first met Cheryl Wall in 1972, when she moved to New Brunswick, NJ, where I had lived since 1969. We were, in fact, both graduates of Howard University—Cheryl in 1970 and I in 1969. And we lived in the same shabby high-rise apartment building, Bishop Towers, overlooking the banks of the Raritan River. (And best of all, the bus line to Manhattan stopped right in front of our building every hour.) We shared the same spelling of our first names, after pre-baby boomer Cheryl Crane, Lana Turner's fated and fateful (lesbian) daughter.

Cheryl was among a number of Black and white faculty who caused progressive changes in the curriculum, culture, color, sex, and faculty of the Rutgers English Department. Cheryl was a scholar, teacher, preacher's daughter, and *gentlewoman*. She laughed easily. Her laugh was affecting and infectious—characteristically cupping her hand over her chuckling. We had many years of conversations on Black literature: from Wheatley to Wright, Harper to Harper, Walker to Walker, of Amiri Baraka and ntozake shange, of Toni Morrison and Toni Cade Bambara, of Gwen Brooks and Ann Petry, of Nikki Giovanni and Maya Angelou (neither of whom are my favorites, nor Cheryl's).

Cheryl introduced Toni Morrison the first time she came to Rutgers to speak in 1973—after her first novel, *The Bluest Eye,* and just before the publication of *Sula*. In her days as a summer intern at Random House, Cheryl had known Morrison, an editor. Cheryl was among the first people to whom Morrison showed the galleys of *The Bluest Eye*—such was the charisma of Cheryl and such was her brilliance. Morrison came to Rutgers many times after 1973, and Cheryl was always close at hand to make her more at ease. Shortly after Morrison's death, when we talked on the phone, Cheryl said, "Even though I had been told for the last year Toni was very ill, I found it hard to accept her death. We think some people will be here forever." *We do think that, Cheryl. Then, with such suddenness and finality, there you were—not here. No chance to go back. No time for a grudging last profession of affection. No occasion for a halting admission of some youthful nonsense. And the finish. And then that "Girl. Girl. Girl" Sula-Nell moment.*

I am remembering the four-day conference, "The Black Woman Writer and the Diaspora," convened in 1985 in East Lansing at Michigan State University. In her closing remarks, Akasha (Gloria) T. Hull says the conference pulled together "black women writers, critics, readers from our various places throughout the world—particularly Africa, the Caribbean, and North America—so that we could share our love of our selves [sic] and our writings with one another" (*The Black Scholar*, March/April, 1986, p. 2).

Toi Derricotte, Jewelle Gomez, and I drove there from New Jersey. Cheryl was there as well, and in fact had also driven from New Jersey with Abena P. A. Busia.

(They drove back to New Brunswick with critic Hortense Spillers, who drove on from there to Haverford, PA.). We were there with the likes of Maryse Condé, Audre Lorde, VèVè Clark, Alexis De Veaux, Ellen Kuzwayo, and many other luminaries whose names I cannot remember. Cheryl and I first encountered one another at the book display tables, where I was selling *Conditions Magazine*, which I co-edited at the time. This was one of the most transformative experiences of my life, because of the panoramic vision shone upon the diasporic oeuvre of Black women. Cheryl and I continued to bump into one another happily for the duration of the conference. Every time calling out to one another: "Cheryl Clarke." "Cheryl Wall." "Cheryl Wall." "Cheryl Clarke."

"Changing Our Own Words: A Symposium on Criticism, Theory, and Literature by Black Women" in 1988 was and is one of my most satisfying experiences as a Black feminist at Rutgers or anywhere else. As organizer, Cheryl assembled her planning committee, which included an energetic crew of faculty, deans, graduate students, administrators, and a wonderful visiting scholar. Cheryl's acknowledgments in *Changing Our Own Words: Essays on Criticism, Theory, and Writing by Black Women* will give readers an idea of how stupendous a symposium it was.

I was involved with "Changing Our Own Words" because I was Cheryl's friend and believed in the project. I also wanted to stand up for Black lesbian writers as actors in the African American tradition and as resisting its respectability strictures. I did my best. This one-day event was radical for the intelligence that it radiated, though the issue of sexuality was not addressed explicitly. Mae G. Henderson, Deborah E. McDowell, Valerie Smith, Hortense J. Spillers, Hazel Carby, Claudia Tate, Abena P. A. Busia, and Susan Willis made marvelous contributions, exploring and exploiting language, form, history, and genre— redefining Black women's writing and literary criticism in a Black feminist image. Two years ago, at a colleague's retirement party, Hazel Carby, whom I had first met at "Changing," expressed to me that it remains an unforgettable experience for her.

Cheryl Wall chaired my dissertation committee (1996–99). We had been having conversations about Black literature for almost thirty years by 1999. So they (the conversations) might as well have culminated in my dissertation defense. Cheryl disagreed with me unrelentingly over my opinion of ntozake shange's *for colored girls (who have considered suicide when the rainbow is enuff)* as a closeted exploration of lesbianism in the "black community." I still think it is. And Cheryl never changed her mind.

Cheryl delivered a remarkable talk on Black bibliophiles at the "Black Women Writing across Genres in the Late 20th Century" symposium at Penn in February 2020, to which we had both been invited. Organized by Professor Barbara Savage and Senior Curator Lynne Farrington, we were called upon to celebrate the gift from Ms. Joanna Banks of 5,000 books by Black women writers to Penn's Van Pelt Library. Cheryl's talk placed Ms. Banks, a Black lesbian collector and Baltimorean, in the school of Black bibliophiles who, unlike their (Black bibliophile) predecessors, including Arthur Schomburg, did not "apologize for" but rather extolled the African American literary tradition. After that lovely symposium, Cheryl and I taxied to the famed 30th Street Station in Philly to catch the Amtrak back North. Unable to sit together, we parted, and I watched her back as she proceeded to another car. She detrained at the Metro Park, NJ, station, and I rode on to Penn Station in Manhattan. Two weeks later, masks descended over New Jersey, New York, and the rest of the country. Then that April morning, Barbara Balliet, my partner of 27 years, who knew Cheryl from Rutgers and Women's Studies (1990–2013), haltingly, thickly announced, "Something terrible has happened." She held out the Facebook post on her iPad. I took it to my breast as to either squelch or to let its pronouncement seep into my weak heart. I had no words. And barely any breath.

A year ago now, in Philly, the night before our panel, I saw you from the street at the front desk of the Hilton Inn at Penn. I was foiled at surprising you. You knew I was approaching and called me out: "Cheryl Clarke," you greeted, bending over your signature left hand, un-turning. "Cheryl Wall. I shoulda known I couldn't sneak up on you," I confessed.

Xmas of the year we met, 20,000 tons of bombs exploded over Hanoi. One-stress last names. Clarke. Wall. One, common Irish; one, blurry conceit. A resonance of uplift. "New Negroes." Postwar. Howard co-eds. Black Arts. The "race's" literary sophistication declaimed unabashedly to each other all night in those early days: "Listen to this ... Hey. Listen."

Contributor's Biography

Cheryl Clarke is a Black lesbian feminist poet and the author of five books of poetry: *Narratives: Poems in the Tradition of Black Women* (1982), *Living as a Lesbian* (1986), *Humid Pitch* (1989), *Experimental Love* (1993), and *By My Precise Haircut*, winner of the 2016 Hilary Tham Award from Word Works Books; and of the chapbooks, *Your Own Lovely Bosom* (2014) and *Targets* (2018). With her life partner, Barbara Balliet, she is co-owner of Blenheim Hill Books, a used and rare bookstore in Hobart, NY, and she maintains a teaching affiliation with the Graduate Faculty of the Department of Women and Gender Studies at Rutgers, the State University of New Jersey.

Remembering Cheryl

Paula J. Giddings Smith College

There are people you like right away; you know, as soon as you meet, a steady friendship is in the offing. That's how it was when I first met Cheryl more than five decades ago.

We were of the same generation, experienced the same thrills when the likes of Toni Cade Bambara, Alice Walker, and Toni Morrison came on the scene to feed our hungry souls. Over the years we were impressed by each other's work too. But there was something else.

I think (we actually never talked about this) we shared an emotional makeup that was impassioned but disciplined—maybe even a little repressed—by the insistence of humility hammered into us as children. With me, Cheryl could brag a little and know that I wouldn't take it the wrong way, and vice versa. I can still see one of those can't-help-myself smiles in the telling of her triumphs over grad-school doubters at Harvard; of Toni Morrison choosing her to present a paper side by side with her at an important forum; and my favorite, the time when the then president of Rutgers, in an effort not to lose Cheryl to a competitor, sent a limousine and driver to her house with a counter-offer that couldn't be refused. I especially liked to tell these stories at gatherings with self-congratulatory talk and where Cheryl was demurely silent.

We both had a kind of wild-child-dying-to-get-out syndrome, tame by today's standards, but which we were able to realize, in part, when we rented an apartment one summer in Harlem. We threw parties featuring our specially made, multi-liquored Sangria, and got great satisfaction from the fact that its storied effect on our guests made us a little infamous in our group.

One day I was reading a newspaper over lunch and saw that Aretha Franklin was to feature at the Newport Jazz Festival and in fact was singing that very evening. No words were spoken, we just got up from the table, tumbled into my old Rambler (which sometimes required the passenger to use a stick to raise the accelerator that could get stuck) and made our way to Rhode Island. We decided not to tell anyone who might worry about us until we got there. There had been a lot of angry protests at the festivals in past years and we didn't want to chance an order to desist.

Cheryl and I didn't even think of reserving a place to stay the night, or even checking if there would be tickets available. We weren't even sure we would arrive in time to hear the Queen.

I remember how balmy Newport was and the beauty of the ocean. I remember that Cheryl and I somehow got tickets and got to the concert just in time to hear Aretha. I remember at that moment that was all that mattered.

Contributor's Biography

Paula J. Giddings is the Elizabeth A. Woodson Professor (Emerita), Africana Studies, at Smith College. She has published four books, including *Ida, A Sword Among Lions: Ida B. Wells and the Campaign Against Lynching* (Amistad, 2008)—winner of the *Los Angeles Times* Prize in Biography, the Letitia Woods Brown Prize from the Association of Black Women Historians, and a finalist for the National Book Critics Award. She is a member of the American Academy of Arts and Sciences.

Passing the Torch, Sharing the Light

Melanie R. Hill   Rutgers University

In Scripture, the latter set of verses in Proverbs assert, "She opens her mouth with wisdom and the teaching of kindness is on her tongue." As my gracious mentor, Dr. Wall, you were the definition of God's love and all of its attributes; you were patient, benevolent, attentive, altruistic, and compassionate. In 2020, the *New York Times* aptly named you "Champion of Black Literary Writers." As my mentor, though, you were more than a champion whose erudition, life, and legacy continue to envision the world not as it is, but as it *should* be. Comporting yourself with grace, humility, and dignity, you were the model and ingenious embodiment for so many Black women literary scholars. In your book, *Worrying the Line: Black Women Writers, Lineage, and Literary Tradition*, you mark the blueswoman as a figure who is not only represented in the works of contemporary Black women writers but who also uses her life's creativity to empower others. The blueswoman's art enables others' work and creativity. Just as the blueswoman in your work empowered others, your work and life, Dr. Wall, have also empowered me. By passing the torch and sharing the light, you were affable in your mentorship.

I officially met you in 2018 while I was a postdoctoral fellow at Rutgers University. You took me under your wing, and you always had a listening ear for me. As I approach the first year since your passing, I hold your material culture even closer to me, both literally and figuratively. *Your* material culture, encompassing the depth of Black women writers, defines the newfound imprint and legacy you have left in my life and the guiding light for my career.

There were several times when you and I would unexpectedly appear at the same events. In the spring of 2019, we met at the Toni Morrison reading at 92Y in New York where Phylicia Rashad and Andre Holland were reading from Morrison's *The Source of Self Regard*. Surprisingly, while I was waiting for the event to start, the elevator doors opened and you appeared! A few months later in October 2019, New Jersey convened a Crossroads Gala honoring Denzel Washington. After the event was over, I was preparing to leave and suddenly you were right in front of me! There were other events, but for these, each time I saw you, I exclaimed with glee and was so happy to see you.

Dr. Wall, because of your example, I know how to comport myself and be the best professor that I can be. I knew that any advice that I would need, I could call and talk to you without hesitation. In 2018 in Atlanta at the National Women's Studies Association conference, I remember you admiring a renowned author after the keynote address. As we both stood toward the front after the event, you said, "This author is the most centered woman I have ever seen or experienced." The same centeredness that you admired in that author, I also admired in you. I can still hear the tranquility in your voice and the cadence and intonation of joy in your laughter. Your father, Reverend Monroe Wall, was a Baptist preacher, so we were able to bond intellectually over my research interests of literature, music, and theology. You knew the art of the sermon, so you were able to speak with me about my passion and work on Black women preachers, musicians, and how the art of the sermon manifests through literary, musicological, and theological realms. You were able to discuss that in-depth with me, and I will be forever grateful to you. I miss you so much. You were also a huge fan of the Queen of Soul, Aretha Franklin. We both had a deep love for her sacred music:

> When our work here is done,
> And the life's crown is won
> And our troubles and trials are o'er
> All our sorrow will end
> And our voices will blend
> With the loved ones who've gone on before…
> in the land where we'll never grow old.

As Aretha Franklin sings these lyrics so mellifluously, I think of your work, legacy, and what you left with me. I know that you will be a constant guiding light in heaven for us all.

I always say that it inspirits me now more than ever to continue to do the good work my soul must have. Two weeks before you passed, I shared good news with you, and you said to me, "When this pandemic is over, we're going to go out and celebrate!" Although our dinner celebration never came, I celebrate you, Dr. Wall, through my work and my passions of literature and music. I celebrate the beautiful mentor that you were to me. I celebrate your gentle spirit. I celebrate you welcoming me with open arms. I celebrate our mutual love for Aretha Franklin. Through your life, you have taught me what it means to value the work that fuels me. I miss you tremendously, and when I'm confronted with a situation, I always ask myself, "What would Dr. Wall do?" or "How would Dr. Wall respond?" With your books in one hand and a violin in the other, I honor your legacy, Dr. Wall, today and forever!

Love,
Melanie

Contributor's Biography

Melanie R. Hill, PhD, professor, scholar, and gospel violinist, is an Assistant Professor of American Literature in the Department of English at Rutgers University, Newark. Her research examines the intersections of African American literature, music, and Black theology.

Ricardo Khan

Before this
all there was was one crazy notion.
An idea, a new view, of ourselves imagined
so differently.

It was a bridge too far for too many. But we hadn't the restraint of imagination some thought we should have, nor the appetite to sit at someone else's table when we knew we could manage the meal ourselves.

We didn't know any better!

And in the swirl and glow of our own young, Black impatience,
with dream in hand and uncaring of what might lie ahead in our way,
we were introduced to the precious soul who would become our first *Co-dreamer*,
Cheryl A. Wall, Crossroads Theatre Company's first Board President.

It would have been easier for a soul of sane mind to say, "Nice dream, fellows, keep it up and keep in touch." In fact, most did. But not Cheryl Wall. With Cheryl, it was "I hear you, I'm with you." Simple. Full stop.

It would have been easier to walk away. But people like Cheryl wouldn't … couldn't. For even back then, she seemed to know something of what she was meant to do and be to us on this earth, in this dream. After all, she was a brilliant mind.

The Crossroads Theatre Company is here today because in its first days, when some listened interested, Cheryl Wall listened and responded fiercely! No bravado, no leader's pride, no raised voice, no fear.

Just the souls of Black folk pounding in her heart.

Contributor's Biography

Ricardo Khan is a director, writer, and the co-founder and Artistic Director Emeritus of the Tony Award-winning Crossroads Theatre Company. Recently, Khan produced and directed the opening night ceremonies for the Smithsonian's new National Museum of African American History and Culture in Washington, DC, and wrote the NAACP award-winning *FLY*, about the Tuskegee airmen of World War II.

Today, My Gratitude Looks Like Grief

Brian Norman   Simmons University

What I remember is the music.
In her graduate seminar on the African American essay, Cheryl Wall began each session with an offering from the Black song book as we filed in. Billie Holiday, Nina Simone, Thelonius Monk. Before we opened a text to peer inside with any theoretical instruments at hand, we entered a cultural space as a community

234234234234234234234234234234234444444423444444444444444444444444444444444442344444444234234234234234234234234234234234234234234234342342342342342342342342342342342342342342344444234234234234234234234234234234234234423423423423423423423423423423423423423434234 understand my responsibilities and my limits. She didn't have to do this. My world is bigger for her generosity.

I learned of Cheryl's passing from a friend and fellow mentee. We were gutted by the loss and its abruptness. A diaspora of friends, colleagues, and mentees had been set to convene for a symposium on Black feminist literature on the occasion of her retirement and in honor of the field that she helped build. But those plans had just been scuttled by the early days of the COVID-19 pandemic. Now, it was a fundamental injustice that we would not get to give Cheryl her flowers, that day or ever. Instead, the diaspora had to gather in grief from afar—in phone calls, on social media, in elegies—to try to find words to mark the loss and what Cheryl meant to us, and the world. Here is my own offering from that day:

Let us hold up Cheryl Wall today. She was a towering intellect, gracious soul, and generous mentor to so many, including me. She shaped worlds. Today my gratitude looks like grief. Rest well, Professor.

Contributor's Biography

Brian Norman is Dean of the Gwen Ifill College of Media, Arts, and Humanities at Simmons University where he is also Professor of English. His most recent book is *Dead Women Talking: Figures of Injustice in American Literature* (Johns Hopkins University Press, 2013).

Claudine Raynaud   University Paul-Valéry Montpellier 3

Cheryl A. Wall was scheduled to take part in the Toni Morrison symposium that we were organizing at the University Paul-Valery in Montpellier in March 2020. Her talk would have been entitled "Toni Morrison's Sublime Word-work," a wording borrowed from Morrison's 1993 Stockholm lecture: "Word-work is sublime [...] because it is generative: it makes meaning that secures our difference, our human difference—the way in which we are like no other life." The global pandemic decided otherwise, but word-work is what Cheryl Wall and all of us, scholars, writers, critics, are indeed engaged in, and all the more so in these harrowing circumstances. Amid a mounting feeling of disarray, helplessness, and incredulity, we had to reschedule the conference when the news came in the mail in early April that Cheryl had passed away. The shock was immense to our community of Morrison and African American scholars and to me especially, since we had last talked at the CAAR Zora Neale Hurston conference in Orlando the year before. I last saw her in Eatonville, FL, Zora Neale Hurston's hometown. The Montpellier conference, which finally took place in September 2020, both via videoconference and on-site, paid homage to Cheryl, whose major book on the black female literary tradition, *Worrying the Line. Black Women Writers, Lineage, and Literary Tradition*, was mentioned on the call for papers. Her work was a prism through which we wanted to revise our readings of *Song of Solomon*.

Our first meeting was in 1991, at the University of Tours, when I invited her to one of the first conferences I organized upon my return from the United States, where I had studied at the University of Michigan. Michel Fabre and all the French African American university researchers around him that made up the CEAA gathered, as we would until his death in 2007 (*Voix éthniques, Ethnic Voices. GRAAT* #14, 1996). She came with Mae Henderson and we spent a lot of time at the local police station, since Cheryl had been robbed at the railway station. She was laughing to have been caught unawares in a small provincial French town, when she was so streetwise in the urban metropoles of the United States. This event started a lifelong relationship with both scholars, whom I would meet on sundry occasions in Europe or the United States. Cheryl was working at the time on what would become *Women of the Harlem Renaissance*, her path-breaking feminist contribution to the scholarship that was then thriving in a reassessment of that crucial period for Black pride and artistic achievements. Her meticulous scholarship placed Black women writers at the forefront, as she categorically asserted that "the Harlem Renaissance was not a male phenomenon." Marita Bonner, Jessie Fauset, Nella Larsen, Zora Neale Hurston, Georgia Douglass Johnson: all these women writers would gain prominence and visibility thanks to her intervention, and the appraisal of the Harlem Renaissance was changed forever, as was the scholarship that followed in her wake.

She had been a pioneer in Black feminist literary criticism (along with Barbara Christian, Deborah McDowell, and Mae Henderson) with her book-length study, *Changing Our Own Words: Criticism, Theory, and Writing by Black Women*. She was a key figure in that field, "troubling" established truths, "worrying" a tradition. Her last book, *On Freedom and the Will to Adorn: The Art of the African American Essay*, addresses the African American genre of the essay in which so many Black writers have illuminated themselves: Baldwin, Ellison, June Jordan, and Alice Walker, but also the new generation, Ta-Nehisi Coates, Brittney Cooper. Her decisive contribution definitely alters the appreciation of generic categories in the African American literary tradition.

Cheryl Wall, whose professional title was Board of Governors Zora Neale Hurston Professor of English at Rutgers University, went on to edit the two volumes for the Library of America (1995) that gather Zora Neale Hurston's works, in which she incorporated the unedited version of *Dust Tracks on a Road*, which I had analyzed as part of my PhD dissertation at Robert Hemenway's suggestion. She also co-edited two volumes of articles on Hurston's *Sweat* and her celebrated novel *Their Eyes Were Watching God*. Analyzing Hurston's contribution to Black literature and culture was a link that joined us across the Atlantic, for one needs other kindred spirits, benevolent mentors, thinking partners, in order to move forward. A community of scholars.

Our paths crossed multiple times over the years. I, for instance, vividly recall meeting her in London at another scholarly event, a Baldwin conference at Queen Mary University in 2007, where Caryl Philips was also guest speaker. When I applied for a Zora Neale Hurston visiting professorship at the University of

Central Florida, I turned to her to write a recommendation letter. I am so thankful for her support, her kind and generous words. As I carry on working on Hurston, I am wondering to whom I should now turn to read and critique my work. Thoughts of Cheryl come up and I see her face in my mind. And I feel the pain of loss, the pang of mourning. Cheryl was an accomplished scholar, a trailblazer in Black feminist literary criticism, a shaper of the tradition of Black letters. She was also a kind, beautiful person. I miss her.

Contributor's Biography

Claudine Raynaud is Professor Emerita of American Studies at University Paul-Valéry Montpellier 3 and W. E. B. Du Bois Fellow (2005). She recently published a translation of Sojourner Truth's *Narrative* (PURH, 2016), and "The Uses of Enchantment: Instances of Magic Realism in Morrison's Later Writing," in *The Palgrave Handbook of Magic Realism in the Twenty-First Century* (2020).

Tribute for my Mentor, Professor Cheryl A. Wall

Heather D. Russell   Florida International University

Cheryl Wall oozed Black literary tradition and she suffused us with it. By "tradition" I am not speaking of the kind imposed on and used against Black scholars during the culture wars, the "nagging" word we were warned of in 1972 by Mary Helen Washington—the word which "has so often been used to exclude or misrepresent…." Tradition for Dr. Cheryl Wall was about respect for the vexed, complicated, and vanquishing history of more than two hundred and fifty years of Black letters, the profundity of a body of work that didn't just come up all willy nilly. No solitary solipsistic masturbatory writing here. Black literature, criticism, and theory in and as community—*that* is how she trained us.

I was fortunate to enter the MA/PhD program at Rutgers in 1991 as one of a cadre of young Black graduate students (four ahead of me, two of us contemporaries, and perhaps another five admitted in the subsequent two years) who formed, I now realize, a safeguard against the then *en vogue* of all things African American studies. We were the stealth weapon against the potential dilution, diffusion, and dismissal of a field still young, tenuous, and precariously placed within the ivory halls of the academy. Two years before, Cheryl (and I did not dare call her "Cheryl" until the end of my first year, and only with her permission) had published the germinal *Changing Our Own Words: Essays on Criticism, Theory, and Writing by Black Women*. That collection was as important to many of us emerging Black feminist critics as the publication of Toni Cade Bambara's *The Black Woman* (1970) had been to Black women writers, activists, and newly minted Black and Women's Studies scholars nearly two decades before.

Changing Our Own Words gave us the critical taxonomy we needed and eventually learned to wield—Mae Gwendolyn Henderson's heteroglossia/glossolalia (or speaking in tongues), Spillers on Freudian theory and race, Wall on "changing words." Theirs was discursive armor in the incredibly alienating hypertheoretical world of Foucault, Derrida, and Lacan, where many of us sat wondering *when or where we entered.* Impostor syndrome had not yet been coined. At her home, Cheryl hosted monthly gatherings for the Black graduate students in English. There we could laugh, cry, drink, signify, specify, and give the lie to the idea that we did not belong. The year I began studying for my comprehensive exams, which originally were to comprise four approved bibliographies (major author, genre, theory, and a hundred-year historical period), we were told that the graduate faculty had instituted a significant change. *If* we wanted to focus on African American literature as our historical period, we would be expected to know more than 250 years of it. We would need conversance from Wheatley to Wideman. We complained to our Black professors, Cheryl Wall, Donald Gibson, Abena Busia, and Wesley Brown, only to learn that *they had led the initiative.* Of course, they had.

On the first day of my first graduate course in African American literature, a class jointly taught by Cheryl and Dr. Gibson, I vividly remember her entrance. Dr. Cheryl Wall was the epitome of easy brilliance, grace, humility, and fierceness. She was, to use today's terminology, an unequivocal *boss.* They introduced themselves; and as she affirmed the generative and foundational work of her co-leader, she gently, chidingly, humorously, and pointedly reminded him and us that his classic work, *Five Black Writers,* published in 1970, featured essays on "five writers, all of whom were men."

Cheryl and I last met in Eatonville, Florida, in February 2019. I had not seen her in a few years, although we had kept in touch from time to time. It was the thirtieth anniversary of the Zora Neale Hurston Festival of the Arts and Humanities. As one of the leading Hurston scholars, she was of course an invited speaker. For some years prior, I had been privileged to lead several NEH Landmarks in American History teacher-training workshops for the Florida Humanities Council, on Zora Neale Hurston and her Eatonville roots (working with more than five hundred teachers from all over the country). Cheryl's inspiriting influence was with me whether planning reading materials, interviewing Eatonville residents, standing beside Zora's grave in Fort Pierce, or watching my mentor wax brilliant in the documentary we showed every year, *Zora Neale Hurston: Jump at the Sun* (2008).

It is said by some who I have come to love and trust while doing that work that Zora picks her literary daughters (we might think of Alice Walker here) very intentionally. Surely, Cheryl was one of Zora's daughters, preserving and forwarding her complicated, powerful, and affirming legacy, and unapologetic love of Black people, Black speech, Black culture, Black women's right to full and free expressivity. I was gifted Zora Neale Hurston by Cheryl Wall in that same class. Little did my 20-year-old Rutgers graduate student self know that nearly two decades later, while myself a professor in Miami, I would be entrusted with furthering Cheryl's work, ensuring that in Social Studies and Language Arts classrooms throughout the country, teachers and students would be *changing words* on Zora.

Cheryl and I got to hug, catch up, take pictures, laugh, and reminisce a little that day in Eatonville. I got to sit in her presence once more as her student, bearing witness once again to her largesse, her scholarly generosity, and her sheer brilliance of mind. There will never be another Cheryl Wall. Her passing has left an indescribable lacuna in the field. The best we can do by way of ending is to affirm that we, the purveyors of Black literary tradition because of her, shall carry on.

Contributor's Biography

Heather D. Russell, formerly Heather Andrade, is Professor and a Senior Associate Dean in the College of Arts, Sciences & Education (CASE) at Florida International University. For several years she led the Florida Humanities Council's flagship seminar "Jump at the Sun: Zora Neale Hurston and her Eatonville Roots." She attended Rutgers University and attained a BA in English (1987–91) and PhD in English (1991–97) where she was taught, mentored, and trained by Dr. Cheryl A. Wall.

In Memory of Cheryl Wall: A Beginning

Evie Shockley   Rutgers University

I've never faced a more difficult challenge as a writer than this one of composing a brief tribute in memory of Cheryl Wall, a mentor and dear friend whose life and work meant so much to so many people. She deserves much more celebration, detail, and artful writing than I am able to muster in my current state of pandemic-arrested grieving, so I offer the following as an attempt at beginning, a draft, a work-in-progress.

Cheryl Wall very materially helped make the space, the field, I entered when I started graduate school: a space that would invite me and other Black women as students, scholars, readers, and writers, without denying entry to anyone else who knew how to behave themselves. Her edited collection *Changing Our Own Words: Essays on Criticism, Theory, and Writing by Black Women* was one of the two volumes recommended to me as pre-reading for my return to literary studies. In the volume's introduction, she wrote: "Making our positionality explicit is not to claim a 'privileged' status for our positions. Black and white male critics have written perceptively about black women's texts. Making our positionality explicit is, rather, a response to the false universalities that long defined critical practice and rendered black women and their writing mute." Within just its first few pages, her essay cited and celebrated a whole constellation of creative and critical Black women writers whose powerful truths, formal brilliance, incisive analysis, and theoretical daring, she argued, had already forged a path through the wilderness, a path that was now ours to enhance, expand, and extend. Cheryl's words thus welcomed me into a space defined by work, community, and joy—not simply a space, but, in multivalent ways, a methodology, a network, and a practice of making.

She was later to welcome me into the English Department at Rutgers University: the department which she had earlier chaired, and the university at which she spent her entire career. I can never convey how fortunate I was to be mentored and befriended by Cheryl Wall. Her office was right across the hall from mine for a decade. I knocked on her open door innumerable times: to ask for her advice, to congratulate her, to compare notes on something we'd both read or seen, to share some good news, to make plans for the program (REDI) we co-directed, to see if she was free for dinner, or—did I mention this?—to ask for her advice. Over the years, from across the hall and at many other connection points, I came to see how much generosity she showed her students, how gracious and engaged she was with colleagues, how carefully she considered problem-solving strategies, how devotedly she researched and revised her scholarship—which is to say, how tirelessly she worked. And by "tirelessly," I mean that she was unceasingly in demand and very often quite tired, but dedicated to principles of equity, resistance, change-making, and future-building that she prioritized over rest more often than not (and arguably more often than she should have, though that is for no one but her to judge).

But she also—in the process of working and on her own time—placed great emphasis on nurturing her relationships: with colleagues at Rutgers and internationally, with a wide-ranging and eclectic group of friends, with members of her church, and with cherished family. She also made time for the cultural experiences she enjoyed most: theater, music, travel, food, and, of course, the books of her favorite authors. As a result, it seemed to me, even if she was not always well rested, she was at least regularly rejuvenated in spirit. The smile of a Cheryl Wall who had been teaching Black literature in Paris or talking with sister scholars at a Black feminist symposium in Atlanta, who was describing an Aretha Franklin concert or a production of an August Wilson play, who had spent the evening with a new Toni Morrison novel or the weekend with her daughter—this was radiance.

While Cheryl taught me (and many) by her living example, she has thankfully also left a beautiful legacy—a model we can continue to aspire to—in her writing and in the memories of generations of scholars. She brought her pleasures and her values with her into the academy and worked to make it accommodate them, rather than contorting herself to fit within its pre-existing structures. She understood the significance of Black literature and culture—Black women's cultural production, in particular—and she made it her business to give and help obtain for that work the critical attention, historical contextualization, theoretical scaffolding, and institutional space it deserves. Her *Women of the Harlem Renaissance*, for instance, remains foundational for considerations of gender in literary studies of the period. Cheryl demonstrated repeatedly that the scholarship she produced in and for the academy could, in its register and concerns, simultaneously served non-academic people, whose lives often inspired Black women's cultural production and who were quite crucially among the (intended, desired) audiences for that work. I remember her noting with delight, after she published *Worrying the Line: Black Women Writers, Lineage, and Literary Tradition*, that church groups invited her to talk with them about the book and accounted for a number of its sales. She saw her scholarship positioned not over and apart from the creative work she studied, but alongside and in collaboration with that work. She loved the writers and thinkers she studied, and, joy of joys, she loved the hours she spent reading, teaching, and writing about their work—which is to say that, at its core, Cheryl Wall loved her work. In this way—in all these ways—her legacy is love.

Contributor's Biography

Evie Shockley is Professor of English at Rutgers University, New Brunswick. Among her publications are *Renegade Poetics: Black Aesthetics and Formal Innovation in African American Poetry* (Iowa University Press, 2011), and the award-winning poetry collection *semiautomatic* (Wesleyan University Press, 2017).

Deborah Gray White   Rutgers University

I miss Cheryl as much today as I did almost a year ago. Not a day goes by that I don't think of how we, two colored girls from New York City, connected over stories about Clio and Latta, South Carolina—the two towns our people were from. We sat through Chairs meetings, and sitting together we communicated without ever opening our mouths. A throaty groan or grunt, under our breaths, was all we needed to know what we each thought about whatever was being discussed. Our body language was decipherable only to us, I think. Cheryl was gracious and elegant. She was the most generous person I will ever know, generous almost to a fault. We gave each other "just say no" cards because we were so often called upon for service work. Cheryl answered the call a whole lot more than I did and I thanked her for it because if she had not been so generous I would have had to answer more calls than I did. I only wish that she could have used her "just say no" card last April. I miss her so.

Contributor's Biography

Deborah Gray White is Board of Governors Distinguished Professor of History at Rutgers University. She is a specialist in the history of African American women; author of *Ar'n't I A Woman? Female Slaves in the Plantation South* (W. W. Norton, 1999) and *Too Heavy a Load: Black Women in Defense of Themselves, 1894–1994* (W. W. Norton, 1999); she also is editor of *Telling Histories: Black Women in the Ivory Tower* (University of North Carolina Press, 2016).

Tribute to Professor Cheryl A. Wall

Magdalena J. Zaborowska   University of Michigan

I first met Professor Cheryl A. Wall after she had given a beautiful keynote about James Baldwin's *No Name in the Street* (1972) at the first International James Baldwin Conference at Queen Mary's College in London in 2007. I was finishing my first book on Baldwin in Turkey then, and introduced myself afterwards, curious that she had picked as her subject the book I also found fascinating and, like her, thought rather curiously underappreciated in the field. As we chatted about Baldwin's fourth essay volume and its innovations, I felt an immediate connection to her not only as a junior colleague in African American literary studies, but also as a certain kind of reader, one who prized deep dives into the text, its cadence, imagery, and syntactic power. We were lit-crit kindred spirits. Meetings like that don't happen very often.

After that, Professor Wall became my steadfast supporter who always provided revealing and nourishing conversation whenever we encountered each other in professional settings. Dignified, charismatic, kind, and soft spoken in a way that invited listening and leaning in, she was an academic elder who invited emulation and admiration. I knew from a former graduate student, who spent her postdoc with Professor Wall at Rutgers, that she was a supportive and patient, exacting and rigorous mentor. Her books, *Women of the Harlem Renaissance* and *Worrying the Line: Black Women Writers, Lineage, and Literary Tradition*, are models of painstaking literary scholarship that few can pull off these days. They confirm the need for deep, thoughtful, close readings as the foundation of any meaningful academic work in the humanities. In that sense, she is still mentoring us and will be there for our students, which is a truly comforting thought in these days of scourge and sorrow.

On a lighter side of things: When we ran into each other on a great walking tour of Baldwin's Paris that seemed to have no end despite its advertised limit of four hours, we both hit on the same idea: We ran into a cab that had miraculously appeared in the narrow street we were walking with the group, abandoning the tour suddenly, somewhat joyously. Having apologized in unison, "So sorry, we have to get ready for the conference!" we commiserated on our way back to the hotel that we were tired and wanted to catch a breath before the evening session. It was the scary year of 2015, following the terrorist attacks in Nice and Paris, with police armed to the teeth scattered all over the city. We were attending another Baldwin conference, at the American University in Paris, and had to get through heightened security and show our passports every time we wanted to get into the conference venues. Being in the presence of likeminded folks who loved Baldwin, though, compensated for all that. The year my *Me and My House* book came out, we ran into each other again during the very cool, jazzy evening organized by *JBR* at the ASA conference in Atlanta. Professor Wall came up to me, smiling, gave me a big hug and told me how much she enjoyed my book: "Thank you for writing it!" No review gave me as much joy and pleasure.

She was to speak about her most recent, terrific book, *On Freedom and the Will to Adorn: The Art of the African American Essay*, at a lecture series in Afroamerican and African Studies in April 2020 that I was running. When the University of Michigan was about to shut down due to the pandemic, we exchanged hurried emails on 14 March, confirming her lecture's unfortunate cancellation.

She wrote in response to my message:

Dear Magadelena [sic!],

I had looked forward to the lecture on April 1st but had assumed it would be canceled. All public events at Rutgers are canceled as well. I very much hope that it can be, as you say, a pleasure deferred. I would very much look forward to visiting Ann Arbor again.

These are indeed chaotic times—unlike anything I have experienced before. But there are moments of grace as well. One such moment for me was reading your review of <u>On Freedom and the Will to Adorn</u> *in* <u>Literature and History</u>*. I could not have hoped for a more thoughtful or generous analysis of my work. I came across it at a time when I was beginning to despair that anyone would review the book. Yours was the first review—and so far the only—review I've read. What a gift. Thanks so much for the care you took in writing it.*

I will miss the opportunity to continue a discussion of the African American essay with you in person next month. But I look forward to having that opportunity in the not-too-distant future.

Warm regards,
Cheryl

Then, merely two weeks later or so, I heard via friends that she had died.

Let me close this brief tribute with a few words from my review of her book that we didn't get to discuss in Ann Arbor last April, *On Freedom and the Will to Adorn: The Art of the African American Essay*:

Awaited eagerly by this reader, and many of those in the fields of American Literature and African American and Black Studies, this exciting book is the first (to my knowledge) comprehensive study of the cultural and stylistic foundations of the African American essay. Taking as her inspiration Zora Neale Hurston's claim that the "will to adorn" characteristic of black English changed how southern whites spoke by transforming not only their language but also their attitude toward it, Prof. Wall builds a deep and complex cultural history of the genre while offering groundbreaking theoretical analyses and interpretations of its great practitioners and shapers. A sweeping panorama that portrays the essay as a vehicle for the "subject that has preoccupied black writers for three centuries"—freedom—this book delights with rigorously researched analyses and painstaking close readings that span literary productions from the eighteenth to the twenty-first century.

I hope you will read it.

It is still hard for me to believe that she is gone. I miss her, though I am also profoundly grateful that her work and spirit have not left us, and never will. Thank you, Professor Wall!

Contributor's Biography

Magdalena J. Zaborowska is Professor of African American and American Studies in the Departments of Afroamerican and African Studies and American Culture at University of Michigan. Her most recent books are *Me and My House: James Baldwin's Last Decade in France* (Duke University Press, 2018), and the MLA award-winning *James Baldwin's Turkish Decade: Erotics of Exile* (Duke University Press, 2009).

MANCHESTER
1824
Manchester University Press

BIBLIOGRAPHIC ESSAY

Trends in Baldwin Criticism, 2017–19

Terrance Dean   Denison University

Abstract

Reading works on Baldwin from 2017 to 2019, the author tracks the significance of Baldwin within the Black Lives Matter movement and our growing need for police reform in conjunction with a revaluation of the lives of racial and ethnic minorities within the oppressive systemic biases of American social and political life.

Keywords: James Baldwin, Black Lives Matter, Joseph Vogel, Eddie S. Glaude, Jr., Magdalena Zaborowska, Nicholas Buccola, police reform

James Baldwin Review, Volume 7, 2021, © The Authors. Published by Manchester University Press and The University of Manchester Library
http://dx.doi.org/10.7227/JBR.7.15

This essay looks at trends in James Baldwin scholarship from 2017 to 2019, the crucial years of Black life under President Donald Trump, a reality television star who became leader of the free world. This project builds on previous writing in *James Baldwin Review* that has explored Baldwin's works and impact on the Black Lives Matter movement, particularly the outbursts of protest in major cities from New York and Los Angeles to Chicago, Atlanta, and Detroit. Black, brown, and other ethnic minority groups—as well as many who identify as white—have been distressed over the Black lives taken by police officers, and the judicial system that has failed to produce any justice for the victims. Along with the protests in the streets, people have protested virtually on social media platforms including Twitter, Instagram, and Facebook. Posts on these platforms have gone viral as they use Baldwin's words and texts, which serve as historical reminders of Black life in the face of continued racial opposition from the civil rights movement through today. The lives of Black persons continue to be marred by violence, racism, and systemic structures of oppression well into the twenty-first century. Many scholars and thinkers, such as James Cone, Michael Eric Dyson, Toni Morrison, James Vogel, Nicholas Buccola, Vincent Lloyd, Eddie Glaude, Jr., Bill V. Mullen, and Magdalena J. Zaborowska, have added further nuance to the prophetic message of Baldwin, shedding light on his life, writings, and voice in an effort to make sense and meaning of Black life in the twenty-first century.

The texts reviewed here locate Baldwin in the American landscape against the backdrop of racism, political upheavals, social dissonance of Black life, and police brutality. From 2017 to 2019 Baldwin's words resonated even more strongly, illustrating the racially patriarchal systems that became more evident under the leadership of President Trump. In 2019, Atatiana Jefferson was shot and killed by police as she played video games with her nephew in the living room of her home in Fort Worth, Texas. A neighbor called the police after noticing Jefferson's front door open. When police arrived, they peered through a window and saw Jefferson and shot her through the window, killing her in front of her nephew. In 2018, Stephon Clark was standing in his grandmother's backyard when he was confronted by a swarm of police officers in Sacramento, California. They believed Clark was holding a gun and shot him more than twenty times. He was holding his cell phone. Also in 2018, Botham Jean was shot and killed by an off-duty police officer who entered his home in Dallas, Texas, and shot him. The officer claimed she entered Botham's apartment believing it to be her home, and thought he was a dangerous intruder.[1]

These killings highlighted an already hostile climate of racial divide under the Trump presidency. His antics and rhetoric on racial division fueled notions of white nationalism and American nationalism. In 2016, former San Francisco Giants football player Colin Kaepernick, along with his teammate Eric Reid, refused to stand for the national anthem. Instead, Kaepernick and Reid both kneeled in protest due to the unjust killings of Black persons by police officers. News outlets and social media were abuzz with people chiming in on Black Lives Matter and the objective of kneeling during the national anthem at sports events.

The continued attacks by President Trump, targeting Kaepernick's actions as anti-American, fueled the formation of white nationalist groups such as the Proud Boys. Trump's vitriol against NFL players shaped the next four years of his presidency, which included continued attacks on Black life. Social unrest and racial angst would erupt over two deaths during the COVID-19 pandemic year of 2020, a year of health disparities and law enforcement failures. The deaths of George Floyd and Breonna Taylor, both killed by police officers, sparked a new fire within the Black Lives Matter movement. Taylor was asleep in her home with her boyfriend when police rushed into their apartment, shooting and killing Taylor. Police claimed they had a search warrant when they entered the apartment looking for drugs, yet no drugs were recovered. Floyd's death prompted calls for empathy and marches across the world. Floyd attempted to pass a twenty-dollar counterfeit bill at a local store. The store clerk called the police, which ended with him in police custody and an officer kneeling on Floyd's neck for more than eight minutes while he pled for his life. Floyd's final moments were captured on video which circulated around the world, sparking anew pleas from many to stop the killings of Black, brown, and other ethnic people.

The threat against Black life rang loudly, signaling a national call and response from protestors, particularly racial and ethnic minorities, to proclaim that Black Lives Matter and that threats against humanity under the guise of political and social unity were un-American, unethical, immoral, and anti-Black. James Baldwin became an essential voice of revolution within the movement for Black lives and against white patriarchy. In 2019, the Pulitzer Prize-winning Black gay writer Hilton Als produced a gallery installation titled, "God Made My Face: A Collective Portrait of James Baldwin" at the David Zwirner Gallery in New York City. The exhibit included works by James Welling, Kara Walker, Diane Arbus, and Beauford Delaney.[2] For the past several years, openly gay, Grammy-nominated recording artist Me'Shell Ndegeocello has created yearly musical theater tributes, *Can I Get A Witness?* and *No More Water/The Fire Next Time: The Gospel According to James Baldwin*, based on Baldwin's seminal text, *The Fire Next Time* (1963). Ndegeocello stated that Baldwin's writings spoke to her as a lesbian, and she wanted to find a way to bring him to life for others. In her descriptions of the musicals, Ndegeocello has said: "There's a sermon and music, and I fit my ideas into that framework. We read his text as if it were his gospel, full of proverbs."[3] Ndegeocello captures the essence of Baldwin and how he wrote for the marginalized and oppressed. She homes in on Baldwin's prophetic voice, and how the preacher in him shows up in his writings and lectures. Baldwin's legacy and prophetic words continue to renew interest in the prolific writer. Black gay men and lesbians are recovering his work to help them affirm their sexual identities. In this way, he has become a hero, a prophet, guiding many to self-love and self-worth. But, why Baldwin? What is it about Baldwin's words in the twentieth century that continues to resonate with us in the twenty-first?

Baldwin's gifted writings and fiery speeches represent many things to many people. On 20 December 1987, a few weeks after his death, Toni Morrison wrote a public eulogy in the *New York Times*, "Jimmy: You Crowned Us." The essay was reprinted in 2019 as "Eulogy for James Baldwin," in *The Source of Self-Regard: Selected Essays, Speeches, and Meditations*. Morrison's eulogy illumines Baldwin's prophetic immanence. Morrison paints him as an unparalleled phenomenon who resonates in the spheres of love, truth, and humanity. Morrison analogizes Baldwin's friendship to that of the Three Wise Men, who came bearing gifts to the newborn king, Jesus. As Morrison writes, "Well, the season was always Christmas with you there, and like one aspect of that scenario, you did not neglect to bring at least three gifts."[4] Morrison highlights Baldwin's gifts as language, courage, and tenderness.[5]

With each of these gifts, Morrison frames Baldwin as a man who loomed larger than life. He enveloped those he encountered, and their worlds were forever changed. These gifts transformed people, because Baldwin gave them unselfishly, unyieldingly. She writes,

> The difficulty is your life refuses summation—it always did—and invites contemplation instead. Like many of us left here, I thought I knew you. Now I discover that, in your company, it is myself I know. That is the astonishing gift of your art and your friendship: you gave us ourselves to think about, to cherish.[6]

Morrison also highlights a Baldwin virtue that Cornel West revered: truth. "In place of intellectual disingenuousness and what you called 'exasperating egocentricity,' you gave us undecorated truth," she writes.[7]

> You replaced lumbering platitudes with an upright elegance. You went into that forbidden territory and decolonized it, "robbed it of the jewel of its naiveté," and ungated it for black people, so that in your wake we could enter it, occupy it, restructure it in order to accommodate our complicated passion.[8]

Baldwin restructured the hierarchy of white dissonance, and held white America accountable for its role in a distorted history that many refused to admit had ever happened. And, as Morrison ends her eulogy, alluding to Baldwin's insistence that Black America's crown had already been bought and paid for, and all we had to do was wear it, she writes, "And we do, Jimmy, you crowned us."[9]

As Morrison's final words make clear, Baldwin shaped a discourse that helped the world see itself as it should be, to envision what was possible in love, justice, and righteousness. If the world were able to remove the blindfold, shake the distorted lies of its fictive history, Baldwin's message of Black liberation—steeped in Christian rhetoric, biblical language, stories, and texts—would be heard clearly. Baldwin the preacher used his gifts to deliver a prophecy to all the people of America. Indeed, the spirit of Baldwin's words has become a fixture in the discourse of the day because many people are searching for meaning in a world filled with racism that has persisted since the civil rights era. Black and white relations remain strained in the midst of increasing police brutality, poverty, and unemployment among people of color—and especially among Black people.

The father of Black liberation theology, James Cone, writes that James Baldwin was the catalyst for his own desire to quell a burning flame within him. In his text, *Said I Wasn't Gonna Tell Nobody: The Making of a Black Theologian* (2018), Cone writes, "Reading Baldwin helped me sing my theological blues in *Black Theology and Black Power*, as I struggled to make sense out of the urban disasters in the 1960s."[10] Cone writes that while reflecting on the urban riots that were taking shape in 1967—during which twenty-seven people were killed in Newark and forty-three in Detroit—"I picked up Baldwin's 'Fire' again, as I wrestled with the fire burning hot inside me."[11] It was Baldwin's fiery attack against America, condemning the country for its failure to make amends for continued atrocities against Black people, that would compel Cone to conceive of a Black liberation theology freeing Black folks from a white Christian theology. Cone would take note of Baldwin's religious foundation undergirding *The Fire Next Time* and extend the dialogue to white Christianity. "I was the angriest black theologian in America!" Cone writes.[12] He continues,

> Like me, James Baldwin was brought up to be a preacher who understood something about the black religious experience. No one can read *Go Tell It on the Mountain* and not know that for James Baldwin God was real. He had been on the "threshing floor" all night, "passed through the fire," as the saints prayed him through, got up and left God's house to preach the gospel of love to the world, which he couldn't do in the church.[13]

Cone reveals that it was Baldwin who was the catalyst for his academic training and scholarly engagement when tackling religious thinkers and philosophers who maintained the hold on, mainly white, religious theology. Cone says, "I started to read Baldwin and couldn't stop. I was captivated by his eloquence and religious insights about the 'sun-baked' 'criminal Jew' from Galilee and his relentless and devastating criticism of the Christian church. He spoke to me like no other writer."[14]

Cone made use of Baldwin's words, prophecy, and anger to fuel his Black liberation theology against theological giants such as Karl Barth and Reinhold Niebuhr. The significance of Baldwin for the next generation, and those to follow, is what Baldwin often refers to as "witnessing" Black resistance and Black rebellion. Black people utilize Baldwin to resist the patriarchal and systemic structures that have for far too long kept them imprisoned in race and racism. Cone says that he "saw in Baldwin what I liked in Martin and Malcolm—blackness and love, defined by justice for all and a vision of hope in the face of the enduring power and absurdity of white supremacy."[15] In *Said I Wasn't Gonna Tell*, Cone continues to illustrate the political, social, and religious differences between Martin Luther King, Jr., Malcolm X, and James Baldwin. Yet it is Baldwin who most resonates and speaks to Cone's religious ethos: "Nobody could preach love like Martin;

nobody could talk black like Malcolm; and nobody could write with eloquence about love and blackness like Baldwin."[16] What Baldwin's words and example as a witness meant for Cone and the Black liberation theology movement persists within the Black Lives Matter movement of today, harnessing the eloquence of Baldwin's message on love and Blackness, proclaiming Black spaces, and reclaiming Black life.

Two essential texts in the timeframe examined here explore James Baldwin and his relationship with two US presidential eras. Michael Eric Dyson's *What Truth Sounds Like: RFK, James Baldwin, and Our Unfinished Conversation About Race in America* (2018) and Joseph Vogel's *James Baldwin and the 1980s: Witnessing the Reagan Era* (2018) examine critical moments in Baldwin's career, writings, and outlook on race during John F. Kennedy's presidency in the 1960s and Ronald Reagan's presidency in the 1980s.

In *James Baldwin and the 1980s*, Joseph Vogel reminds us that many critics had written off Baldwin during the 1980s because they felt he had not been able to keep up with the times. Various critics and scholars complained that Baldwin's novels, like *Just Above My Head* (1979), and his nonfiction work *The Evidence of Things Not Seen* (1985) suffered because Baldwin's personal bitterness and ideological rigidity significantly reduced the rich complexity of his previous writing. Others felt that Baldwin had lost touch with the main currents of late twentieth-century American life and that he was simply repeating themes from previous books. Despite what many felt was Baldwin's decline, Vogel argues that Baldwin actually made crucial strides during the ever-changing climate of the 1980s and post-civil rights era. Vogel situates Baldwin's putative "decline" through a look at his late works, helping to unveil his powerful and provocative writing. For Vogel, Baldwin "holds up as one of the most prescient observers of the post-civil rights landscape."[17] Vogel reimagines Baldwin's messaging on race during the 1980s to be a complexly mixed address to, and assessment of, the assumptions undergirding the contemporaneous white literary establishment and Baldwin's own position within—or, rather, outside—the Black Power movement. Baldwin failed to make traction within the Black Power establishment because he refused to lay claim to their conservative identity politics.

Vogel also addresses the rise of actor-turned-president Ronald Reagan, who marched into office seeking to reclaim America not only as an economic and political power, but also a nation of masculinist patriarchy. Not only were West-ernized systems of power manifested through the ideal of masculinity that was on explicit display during the 1980s, mimicking Reagan's on-screen persona as the typical macho cowboy, but popular culture also shifted to become a crucial forum for sexual identity. Vogel writes:

> Reagan held himself up as the living embodiment of the American Dream: an ordi-nary boy from Illinois who made it to Hollywood, an ordinary actor who now aspired to the highest office in the land. If he could do it, anyone could. If he could succeed, so could America … This context is significant to understanding *Just Above My Head*,

a novel profoundly interested in the efficacy of the American Dream. Baldwin's narrative complicates Reagan's myth—most obviously by recognizing its entanglement with race, gender, and sexuality.[18]

With this backdrop in mind, the 1980s saw the rise of gender-bending artists such as Michael Jackson and Prince. The ideal of hyper-masculinity was now blurred with effeminate notions of male expression. In his 1985 essay, "Freaks and the American Ideal of Manhood," Baldwin described and critiqued a nation desperately struggling to retain—or rescue—its manhood. Those who crossed borders, those who occupied that liminal space "in between," incited panic precisely because they exposed the lie that propped up Reagan's black-and-white fantasy of American purity.

Vogel also examines the effect of AIDS in America and its drastic impact on the queer community. Many sought Baldwin's insights on the gay community as an openly gay man, as well as his perspectives on the gay revolutionary movement. For example, Vogel weaves a critical thread connecting Baldwin's unpublished text, "The Welcome Table," not only to the AIDS epidemic that raged in the 1980s, but also to the contemporary LGBTQ movement:

> As a prominent gay author, Baldwin has been criticized for his reluctance to be more outspoken about AIDS (and gay rights more generally), as he was for black civil rights in the 1960s. He was, however, abundantly clear about the legitimacy, dignity, and humanity of LGBTQ individuals. There was nothing wrong with us, he asserted; nothing immoral about our orientation or desires; nothing abnormal about loving another human being.[19]

Located on the periphery of social and political life, three black women, two of whom are queer, Alicia Garza, Patrisse Cullors, and Opal Tometi, founded the Black Lives Matter movement, which highlights their position in the fight for justice, dignity, and humanity.

Vogel also explores Baldwin's last published essay, "To Crush the Serpent," to reveal the ways religion and religious ideologies played a destructive role in American politics. Vogel critically examines *The Evidence of Things Not Seen*, which he cites as Baldwin's "most overlooked book," and illustrates how that text can be seen as a prophetic book as we bear witness to the police killings of young Black and brown men and women across the country. The wave of racial violence during the 1980s child killings in Atlanta foretells "the 'post-racial' violence that continued in the Obama era."[20] During both of these periods, Black lives were considered expendable. Baldwin repeatedly emphasized that "history is not the past. It is the present. We carry our history with us. We are our history."[21] President Barack Obama shared the same sentiment following the George Zimmerman verdict in 2013. On the public stage in front of America, President Obama acknowledged that if he had a son he would look like Trayvon Martin, "but recognized that the incident was part of a history that doesn't go away."[22]

Vogel provides a poignant examination of Baldwin in a new time, space, and place. He works intentionally to extend Baldwin's importance as thinker and critic in the 1980s against a backdrop of naysayers who insisted that Baldwin had lost his voice. With great sophistication, Vogel strategically places Baldwin in the future of pop culture, highlighting works such as *Just Above My Head* and "The Welcome Table," placing them in revealing historical contexts and unpacking their relevance through salient critique and studied analysis. Vogel mounts an exemplary study of Baldwin and his relevance during the late twentieth century in popular media and the ways he helped to transform our cultural life.

In *What Truth Sounds Like: RFK, James Baldwin, and Our Unfinished Conversation About Race in America*, Michael Eric Dyson further explores the impact of history on the complex issues of race in America. In May of 1963 Baldwin assembled a delegation to meet with then US Attorney General Robert Kennedy— brother of then president John F. Kennedy—to hear the views of intellectuals, artists, activists, and Black leaders on the topic of segregation and discrimination, particularly in the South. The movement in Birmingham, Alabama, brought national attention to the discriminatory practices in the South and the protests taking shape that resulted in widespread boycotts. Martin Luther King, Jr., had been meeting and organizing with other leaders in Alabama, but tensions mounted and President Kennedy was attempting to quell the South's segregation problem. The invitation to the Black celebrity elite to meet with Robert Kennedy was an attempt to hear what Black leaders had to say on the problem. Baldwin assembled playwright Lorraine Hansberry, celebrities Lena Horne and Harry Belafonte, psychologist Kenneth Clark, and Freedom Rider Jerome Smith. The optimism of Kennedy in gathering Black intellects, thinkers, and leaders to discuss racial issues would, however, backfire. Dyson illustrates the unfortunate dynamic:

> When he invited James Baldwin to assemble an intimate gathering of friends to discuss race in May 1963, [Robert Kennedy] had no idea that he was setting himself up for a colossal failure. He didn't anticipate the sober lesson ahead; even elite Negroes, no matter their situation, feel the pain of their less fortunate brothers and sisters; they remain in touch with their people, and indeed, with their very humanity.[23]

Dyson illustrates a key point about Black celebrities and white audiences—that Black elitism is read as the mediating voice for Black pain and suffering. He draws a parallel among key moments in racial unrest, and how white leadership often seeks to mediate race relations through Black celebrity. As Dyson reveals of the three-hour meeting between Baldwin and Kennedy, "the unvarnished, unfiltered truth got loose; the reality of black perception without blinders or shades became clear; the beautiful ugliness of our existence got vented without being dressed up and made presentable, or amenable or acceptable, to white ears."[24] Kennedy was disappointed with what he felt were irrational Black leaders who would not condone an agenda of asking Black people in the South to wait. "They don't know what the facts are," Kennedy raged, "they don't know what we're doing or what we're trying to do. You can't talk to them the way you can talk to Martin Luther King or Roy Wilkins. They didn't want to talk that way."[25] One can only imagine that in a room filled with activists who held strong convictions that Baldwin would resist not sharing his true sentiments.

Dyson asserts that Black artists have always expressed racial contention through their art. "Black artists have rarely, if ever, enjoyed the luxury of making work that is divorced from black culture."[26] The rage against racial injustices, which Dyson highlights throughout his text, still persists. He rails, with great importance, against the seeming necessity for celebrity activists to make use of their platforms to address race, despite criticism or the damage it may cause their careers. Dyson argues that modern-day celebrities, like Baldwin then, continue to carry this burden, listing intellectuals, artists, athletes, and politicians such as Vice-President Kamala Harris, writers Ta-Nehisi Coates and Farah Jasmine Griffin, artists Jay-Z and Beyonce, and sports figures Muhammad Ali and Colin Kaepernick. Dyson concludes with a reference to the mythical city of Wakanda, as featured in the blockbuster film *Black Panther* (2018). It is not a utopian dream deferred for Dyson, but a real location and destination for Black people:

> Wakanda is the place of our unapologetic blackness, a blackness that is beautiful and ugly, that is uplifting and destructive, that is peaceful and violent, that is, in a word, human in all of its glory and grief, with no special pleading for its virtue, no excuse made for its wickedness, except that wickedness exists, and in its existence, we find it necessary to address it, to fight it, to remove it, but not to defend ourselves against the belief that it represents all black people.[27]

The hostile racial climate of the 1950s and 1960s is a continual theme in Nicholas Buccola's *The Fire Is Upon: James Baldwin, William F. Buckley Jr., and the Debate over Race in America* (2019). This historical debate helped to solidify Baldwin's place in the civil rights movement; moreover, it situated Baldwin as an oratorical genius. Buccola provides a stunning account of the televised 1965 debate on the theme "The American Dream is at the expense of the American Negro," between James Baldwin and William F. Buckley, Jr., at Cambridge University. But it is the comparative examination of Baldwin's and Buckley's lives, from childhood to the debate, that cements *The Fire Is Upon Us* as an important contribution. The book intricately examines two vastly different worlds, one rich, white, and privileged, and the other poor, Black, and oppressed. Buccola illustrates the career of these two writers up to the debate. "Both guests of honor were about forty years old, both were American, and both had risen to prominence as writers, but that was about all they had in common."[28] He maintains that Baldwin and Buckley reached the heights of their careers at the same time. "Right in the middle of that timeline, the movements that each man would do so much to shape—the civil rights movement and conservative movement, respectively—were born."[29] Buccola spends the book examining their lives and the ideas that shaped them into the men they would become, and would ultimately inform their debate.

Buccola locates a central theme of Baldwin's speech from the Cambridge debate, which has become a popular outtake for social media during the Black Lives Matter movement: "It comes as a great shock to discover the country which is your birthplace, and to which you owe your life and your identity, has not in its whole system of reality evolved any place for you."[30] Baldwin's trenchant observation is as relevant to the situation of Black lives today as it was when he uttered these words in 1965. Segregation and discrimination in the South foreshadowed the entanglement of the haunting storied past in the present-day racial tensions plaguing American cities. What many had hoped for then, access to the American Dream, would only uncover the deeply racist ideologies that lie at the center of our country's culture. By juxtaposing the two vastly different worlds of Baldwin and Buckley, Buccola's rich and insightful interrogation demonstrates how they shaped each man's view. Buckley would have the spoils of rich America, while Baldwin's world involved intense poverty and police surveillance. According to Buccola's recounting, Buckley's is a story of triumph, illustrating the conservative perspective of those who inherited the privilege of America's deserving elite. Baldwin's perspective, on the other hand, is the story of attempting to escape the grip of white supremacy strangling the Black community.

Buccola guides the reader through the historical moment of the Cambridge debate. With meticulous precision we are given an account of Buckley and Baldwin, toe-to-toe, addressing race, segregation, and the fate of Black Americans in white America. As Buccola notes, "The students voted for Baldwin, Buckley surmised, not because he was right or offered superior arguments but because they wanted to affirm his identity and join him in deploring the United States."[31] Baldwin won the debate by a vote of 544 to 164 among the audience's mostly white, male students. However, in Buccola's account, Buckley won a strategic victory that would have momentous implications for the future of American race relations. "He was actually proud of what happened that night."[32] Buckley figured that his appearance at the debate, expressing his conservative views, had actually proved his rightful place in America. Despite the loss, Buckley would make use of his conservative ideals and position on race and democracy. He continued to attack Baldwin in interviews and the media, calling him a militant, a Marxist, and a socialist. Baldwin, in later years, said in an interview that "Buckley needed and deserved to be beaten over the head with a coffee mug on the set of *Open End* because he believed black folks living in the slums deserved their fate and refused to listen to anyone who challenged him on this point."[33] Years later, Buckley would announce his candidacy for mayor, depicting New York City as a city ripe for potential racial uprising if harsh measures were not put in place. Though he would lose his mayoral bid, Buckley's conservative ideology and white supremacist philosophy would endure, as Buccola points out:

> In the forty years that passed between Buckley's meetings with Baldwin and his death, Republicans became the conservative party, achieved almost total control of the South, won the White House in seven out of ten elections (losing only three to

moderate southern Democrats), and movement conservatives were to be found wherever there was power to be had: in the judiciary, bureaucracy, think tanks, legis-latures and statehouses, and corporate hierarchy as well as on the school boards.[34]

Buccola, ever-attentive to the implications that our past has for our present, con-tinues:

> Through their words and deeds, Baldwin and other civil rights revolutionaries laid bare the utter depravity of white supremacy, and yet decades later we find ourselves still caught in its merciless grip. The story of Baldwin and Buckley reminds us that moral righteousness is often not sufficient to gain political power. This is a sad truth, but it is a truth we ignore at our peril.[35]

In Bill V. Mullen's biography, *James Baldwin: Living in Fire* (2019), readers are offered a unique look into the much-explored life of Baldwin. Mullen's approach seeks to explore the political life and development of Baldwin, examining the fire burning within him as he "relentlessly rage[d] against those who made him burn."[36] Mullen argues that much of the work on Baldwin has under-explored his political life, particularly "his willingness to organize, march, contribute money, write letters, sign petitions, and, where necessary, lead campaigns for social jus-tice."[37] Mullen seeks to draw upon Baldwin's politics to provide a more nuanced view of how this shaped his writing and activism in the civil rights movement. Baldwin's gender and sexual politics, along with his racial politics, were the driv-ing force of his writing. Mullen establishes Baldwin as a Black queer public figure, as well as his radical internationalism on matters in France, Turkey, and Algiers. Through detailed coverage of each iteration of Baldwin's life and his engagement with various political and social historical moments—the Vietnam War and pro-tests, the Young People's Socialist League, the Communist Party in America, the Palestinian liberation movement, the Nation of Islam, Black Power, Malcolm X, and the FBI's relentless and crushing surveillance of Baldwin and Black radicals—Mullen highlights Baldwin's substantial role in the political and literary worlds from the 1940s to the 1980s. What is most critical to note is Mullen's astuteness in detailing the impact of Baldwin on the Black Lives Matter movement, which insists that Baldwin's legacy live on prophetically, and instrumentally, for the next generation of Black leaders, thinkers, and activists.

Several critical essays from 2017–19 provided new analyses of Baldwin's insights into the social, political, and religious racial discourses pervading our world. These scholars identify unique theoretical perspectives, extending the scholarship on Baldwin in fascinating analytical ways. In "'Something Unspeakable': James Baldwin and the Closeted-ness of American Power," David C. Jones takes an important critical departure from Eve Kosofsky Sedgwick's theoretical concept of the epistemological closet, redressing Sedgwick's homosexual closet, with which she traces "the construct of heterosexual identity through a defiled homosexual other."[38] As Jones notes,

The closet simultaneously forecloses that which threatens to violate heterosexual privilege and reaffirms this privilege through the same process of exclusion. In doing so, the closet sets the parameters of normative discourse. The existence of a defiled homosexuality at its threshold orients heterosexuality, mapping the representational terrain on which sexual identity may legitimately be constructed.[39]

Smartly, Jones reimagines the concept of the closet through Baldwin's race writings and positions the closet within a discourse of racial oppression. Analogously, race, or rather African Americans, become America's unspeakable—its closeted discourse. Jones notes that, because of Sedgwick's failure to address race within her framework of homosexuality, in many regards her argument recenters whiteness and upholds the notion of power, privilege, and class in the closeted discourse. Making use of Baldwin's racial, gender, and sexual politics, Jones is able to open the closet on race:

It is precisely because the historical experiences of African Americans are "hidden" that the mythology of "freedom loving heroes" can be naturalized. Any role blackness does have in the symbolic order of the United States, Baldwin suggests, is merely as a function of whiteness, with a repudiated black otherness serving as what he describes as "the fixed star" and "immovable pillar" that orients the white world's sense of "reality."[40]

Drawing upon Baldwin's *The Fire Next Time*, Jones is able to keenly illustrate the ways in which Baldwin tackles America's feigned innocence on race. Baldwin opens the closeted door to address the stain on America:

To acknowledge the historical claims of African Americans is to erode the very foundations on which the United States' existing social order is premised. Therefore, the ignorance and silence for which innocence is a synonym serve a vital epistemological function that corresponds to the power relations mobilized by the homosexual closet. In the same way that the closet helps ward off the potential of what Sedgwick terms a "definitional crisis" in the realm of gender and sexuality, white Americans' innocence in relation to the historical experiences of African Americans becomes a way of containing a discourse that threatens the United States' national self-image.[41]

For Jones, it is Baldwin's gendered sexual politics that forces open a discreetly hidden door into the vortex of America's open secret on race. The closet becomes a new familial secret of which we all are aware, yet white America refuses to acknowledge the dark cousin, brother, and sister. Jones points us to Baldwin to address this familial tie of this unspeakable communal bond, kept closeted in America.

The discourse of race and trauma have become part of the twenty-first-century Black power chant, particularly within the Black Lives Matter movement, recentering the healing of Black life as we navigate years of pain, present and historical, of brutal racial trauma. In "Losing Real Life: James Baldwin and the Ethics of Trauma," Mikko Tuhkanen examines the ways in which the culture of trauma pervades academia as "pride," noting that it is "deemed politically and ethically imperative to persist in one's trauma, for it designates a singularity that must not be dissipated by such ideologies as the liberal ethos of commonness."[42] According to Tuhkanen, trauma is a "set of firmly established onto-ethical assumptions concerning the subject's orientation in a world of radical differences."[43] Mainly in white spaces and institutions, privilege asserts itself when students make use of their oppressed positionality, notably within the categories of gender, sex, sexuality, class, and other defining lines, in an effort to mark their individuality. In this vein, they create and formalize groups based on their common trauma, through the voice of outrage, attempting to overthrow or disarm that which is a threat against the individual or group. Tuhkanen posits, "The demands for trigger warnings and safe spaces are ways to flexibly encounter the irreducibly different ways people experience the world … As the unprocessed—importantly, unprocessable—cut that births the subject, trauma has become a site where people insist on their unnamable individuality."[44] Unfortunately, Black people in the real world are not afforded the opportunity of safe spaces and trigger warnings, as threats against their lives persist, and they can name the institutions that put their lives at risk. For Black people it is historical. Tuhkanen critically argues that white elites and institutions hide behind the academic veil, and instead of pointing the damning finger at the real enemy—white supremacy—trauma pride fails to name the real culprit of the individual's outrage.

Tuhkanen makes use of Baldwin's *Notes of a Native Son* and *The Fire Next Time* to illustrate how the impact of real world racism, a historical thread, induces trauma in the writer who stands in as representative concerning the pain and oppression of Black people. In *Notes of a Native Son*, Tuhkanen notes that when Baldwin encounters the white waitress in the restaurant who tells him that they do not serve Negroes, his rage surfaces and he grabs a glass of water and throws it at her. The waitress ducks and the glass shatters the mirror behind her. The source of Baldwin's rage is not simply the white waitress who refuses to serve him, for Tuhkanen, but diasporic modernity's tragic script of race and racism. Reflectively, Baldwin inscribes in the text that rage pushes him to consider committing a murder: "I saw nothing very clearly but I did see this: that my life, my *real* life, was in danger, and not from anything other people might do but from the hatred I carried in my own heart."[45] It is the real world and the real encounter that pushes Baldwin to react. It is the historical trauma of racism, for which the waitress stands in as a messenger, reinforcing modernity's persistent opposition to Black people, against which Baldwin finds himself reacting. Black people face a real threat of death in their lives. "Unlike the celebrants of trauma pride in contemporary academia, Baldwin insists that allowing trauma to become the mode of negotiating the frictional world constitutes a devastating error."[46] Black people do not have the luxury of relishing their lived experience as fictional trauma, for they live in a world that positions their identity as a threat. Tuhkanen usefully examines trauma to shift the racial discourse within institutions of higher learning.

Jesse A. Goldberg notably situates Baldwin as a theorist of law who becomes a prison abolitionist. In "James Baldwin and the Anti-Black Force of Law: On Excessive Violence and Exceeding Violence," Goldberg focuses on *The Fire Next Time* and *No Name in the Street*, as he grounds his critical argument in conversation with theorists such as Saidiya Hartman, Jacques Derrida, Alexander Weheliye, and Christina Sharpe. He argues that "policing in the United States is inherently organized by a(n) (il)logic of anti-Blackness that necessitates racist violence as a structural component of its practice."[47] In this regard, Black subjectivity is formed through excessive violence, and according to Goldberg, Blackness exceeds this violence. The law holds Blackness as hostage. Goldberg situates Baldwin's interrogations of law, police, and prisons at the center of our nation's determination to rid society of Black bodies. Law and rights over Blackness historically framed enslaved persons as constitutionally bound, notably "three-fifths" human. However, Goldberg notes that in *The Fire Next Time*, Baldwin shows the shift in positionality of Black Americans to American Negroes. The shift from American to Negro denotes their status under law, from free Americans to forever-bound Negro property. In *The Fire Next Time*, Baldwin notes how he was under police surveillance in his Harlem community, always subject to the law, but it is his interaction with the police that produces his Blackness as violence. Thus, Goldberg maintains that "The law of slavery is what gives the Negro his existence as a recognizable piece of the US political structure, and so in the case of Blackness, race is produced by law."[48] If race is produced by law, then the police who uphold the laws see Blackness as a violation to be violently held in check. Baldwin is harassed and his body experiences violence from the police officers who grab and snatch him because they are upholders of the law. Baldwin knows his positionality not as Negro but as a continued enslaved person, property of the state. Goldberg states,

> He does not believe that America as it was at the time was capable of making Black freedom truly possible, since America's condition of possibility was and is Black unfreedom. At the same time, Baldwin absolutely believes in his and any Black person's right to shape the laws that govern the United States.[49]

Goldberg places Black life into the discourse of freedom and liberty, and particularly the law, through Baldwin's writings and public presence as a possible figure of humanness and Americanness who frees other Black persons to see themselves in a world that despises them and militates against them within the law. In other words, Baldwin disrupts the law and centers blackness within America and the American ideology of freedom, liberty, and justice.

As stated earlier, the words of Baldwin resonate hauntingly, from past to present and into the world wide web of social media, living forever in an ethereal space. In the essay, "Tweets of a Native Son: The Quotation and Recirculation of James

Baldwin from Black Power to #BlackLivesMatter," Melanie Walsh reminds us that the recirculation of Baldwin from the real world to out there, in infinite time and space, sustains the power of his words. In 2014, Kim Moore was the first to quote Baldwin's words on social media in relation to another police killing of a Black person. Using the social media platform Twitter, she situated Baldwin in the Black Lives Matter movement by making use of a quote from Baldwin along with the hashtag #BlackLivesMatter. Her tweet went viral, as Walsh explains:

> These Twitter users collectively recirculated Baldwin's words throughout the social media network but in the process they also used Baldwin's rage to forge a network of social, political, and historical connections: between individuals rallying around a common political cause; between the similar fates of different black people under a system of institutionalized racism and state-sanctioned violence; and between multiple moments in American history from the civil rights era of Baldwin's prime to Ferguson on August 9, 2014.[50]

What Walsh keenly illustrates is that not only were Baldwin's words meaningful during the civil rights era, but they would hauntingly serve as crucial truths more than fifty years later with the Black Lives Matter movement. Walsh brilliantly reminds us that within the historical recovery of Black voices who can speak to present-day issues of race and racism, Baldwin is the most significant figure. "By drawing on an archive of over thirty-two million tweets sent between June 2014 and May 2015 that mentioned #BlackLivesMatter or forty-four related hashtags and keywords (such as #Ferguson, Mike Brown, or #TamirRice), I find that 'James Baldwin' was referenced in at least 7,326 tweets and retweets."[51] Walsh notes that Baldwin was the most invoked African American writer on Twitter relative to all other writers. During the civil rights era, Baldwin appeared twice on the cover of *Time* magazine; he continues to show up through digital formats and social media, marking his role and prophetic works as critical and necessary. Baldwin was not only a man of his time, but of all time.

A turn toward theology and religion is in the wheelhouse for much of Baldwin scholarship. Due to Baldwin's religious upbringing, and his teen years as a preacher, his writings have always foregrounded his religious faith, making use of scripture, spirituals, and Black religious cultural symbols. In this regard, Religion scholar Eddie Glaude, Jr., further explores America's failure to address racial disparities within the framing of white supremacy. In "The Magician's Serpent: Race and the Tragedy of American Democracy," Glaude directly links Walt Whitman's 1871 text *Democratic Vistas* with Baldwin's *No Name in the Street*, in an effort to illustrate Whitman's disavowal of race in his later writings. Whitman seemingly negates Black life and Black persons in an effort to address American democracy, particularly those who have access to it. Glaude makes use of Whitman's metaphor of the magician's serpent, which Whitman claims eats up all other serpents, or rather eats up America's storied and dark past, and that money making is the magician's serpent which eats up all the others. After the Civil War, America's new vision of itself was no longer to create democracy and moral values for its citizens, but capitalism. And with American's new focus on economy, for Glaude, "The manic pursuit of money emptied out the spirit of the country and distorted what sort of people we could reasonably aspire to be."[52]

Glaude perfectly inserts Baldwin as a response, a well-read interlocutor to Whitman, noting that "Like Whitman who writes in the shadows of the carnage of the Civil War, Baldwin writes *No Name* in the 'after times' of the civil rights movement."[53] Baldwin writes about the soulless nation of America, especially after losing his three friends in the movement, Medgar Evers, Malcolm X, and Martin Luther King, Jr. "For Baldwin, the assassinations revealed the depth of the sickness that infects the American soul."[54] After the Civil War, Whitman desperately wants to move beyond race and America's dark closet of the enslaved Black bodies lingering in its history. Glaude notes that "By the time we get to *Democratic Vistas*, race is, effectively, erased. It has been swallowed whole. Not by greed; however, instead, by his commitment to the belief that white people matter more than others."[55] For Glaude, Baldwin highlights America's moral obligation to its citizens, its democratic processes, reminding it of race and Black people's place in its democracy. Glaude posits that the history of democracy is yet to be born because the "appeals and petitions of black folk fell on barren soil, because a different way of being in the world, one not disfigured by the nastiness of white folk, had yet to be born."[56] Whitman fails to address race relations because he does not figure Black persons in the progress and democratic process of the nation. Yet, as Glaude notes, "Baldwin, with Whitman in hand like a child's head forced to confront what he does not want to see, faces the serpent head on—and imagines us anew."[57] Baldwin contends with the demons that America refuses to acknowledge. The failure to adequately address race and racism, even to engage with them, earmarks the future with which America finds itself contending in the twenty-first century. The fight for Black people's visibility, presence, and viability is the proverbial thorn in America's side.

As religion has been a sustainable form of hope and deliverance for black people, race within religion also serves as a permeating discourse, as stated earlier with regard to James Cone, father of Black liberation theology. Thus, religion scholar Vincent Lloyd takes up the racial discourse in his essay, "The Negative Political Theology of James Baldwin." Lloyd argues that Baldwin's negative concept of theology saves Black theology and Black Christianity. Lloyd suggests that the white Christianity that Baldwin's father held onto caused his religious demise, as well as that of other Black people who clung to a white religious ideology. Yet for Baldwin, a political theology is grounded in love. "James Baldwin transformed, rather than rejected, his father's Christianity. The components of that Christianity— ideas about innocence, salvation, sin, truth, and much else—are reworked by Baldwin, and in their new form they are inextricably linked with Baldwin's political vision."[58] Lloyd masterfully traces the racially charged religious incidents in Baldwin's life. He notes,

But then, Baldwin grew up. Unlike his father, he was able to acknowledge his own hatred and to see how it could detrimentally affect his life. He saw how his father's Christianity was motivated by his hatred, how its apocalypticism and denial of the world were a product of American race relations—and how they would not remedy racial justice.[59]

Baldwin locates himself within the hatred and changes course, moving from destruction to love and truth. For he believes that these will save both Black and white Christians from their own idolatries. For love and truth "are both, for Baldwin, spiritual practices."[60] Salvation is within the grasp of Black hands and Black life. It lives within the concept of love, and as Lloyd argues, "When we love an object, we see it in truth, its imperfections as well as its virtues. We are compelled to be honest about both."[61] Baldwin reminds us that as Black Americans we have a right to critique those we love, even our home, America. It is not above reproach. Its ills and its successes are to be discussed, including the ills of its racial divide. As Lloyd notes, "Baldwin asserts that blacks are privileged lovers of America because the stakes are so high in their ability to see America rightly: their life depends on it."[62]

I conclude with Magdalena J. Zaborowska and her stunningly sophisticated approach to Baldwin as place, time, and matter. She examines the writer and activist within the context of his own material matters. In *Me and My House: James Baldwin's Last Decade in France* (2018), Zaborowska explores Baldwin's time in France, particularly his home in Saint-Paul de Vence, known as *Chez Baldwin*, and brings together what she says are three entities that undergird Baldwin's 1977 essay, "Every Good-bye Ain't Gone," and are evident throughout his career—home, blackness, and me. Zaborowska writes that she wants to

> explore the domestic and intimate parts of James Baldwin's story, and places where he lived and wrote in his late life, and to link his national house-rebuilding efforts—his critique in virtually all of his works of U.S. national identity as exclusionary and divisive—to the complex politics and poetics of racialized, gendered, and sexualized social space.[63]

The writer makes a critical play of situating Baldwin's body as home, place, and location within his home in France—a material location and space. The mapping of Baldwin's body becomes a symmetrical mapping of his travels, writings, and ideologies.

Zaborowska asserts that Baldwin's final home in France inspired an attention to Black domesticity in his late works of fiction, life writing, and drama, including *Tell Me How Long the Train's Been Gone* (1968), *No Name in the Street* (1972), *If Beale Street Could Talk* (1974), *The Devil Finds Work* (1976), *Just Above My Head* (1979), *The Evidence of Things Not Seen* (1985), and the unfinished play, "The Welcome Table." She notes that "the myriad roles that domesticity and its representations play in Baldwin's works have not yet been interrogated with any consistency."[64] Zaborowska uses a keen reading, in an effort to nuance Baldwin's words and characters, charting their territorial political and social residency of gender, sex, and race. The book is an exemplary contribution to the American and international reclamation of Black lives, particularly the gender-sexual politics of Baldwin. Zaborowska notes that she wants scholars to begin "rethinking how we preserve the material legacy of literary black lives against their systematic and systemic erasure—a queerly raced matter, indeed."[65] Zaborowska interjects herself into the narrative study of Baldwin's house as place and material matter. She provides the reader with snapshots and memorializations of her visits to *Chez Baldwin* throughout the years. She guides the reader through Baldwin's writings and the sociopolitical scene taking shape in the United States. The book recounts the many visitors and guests at *Chez Baldwin*, such as Maya Angelou, Toni Morrison, and Bernard Hassell. Zaborowska also provides readers with glimpses into Baldwin's final years, woven together from interviews with neighbors and family friends. It is through her eyes, and the *Architectural Digest* interview (1987), that *Me and My House* constructs Baldwin's residence as another "home." Her moves through the empty house, a shell of itself, create a nostalgic desire for place and gathering.

With this insightful and notable sojourn, Zaborowska reminds readers why we longingly revisit Baldwin. Despite his home, the material is nothing but the ether of imaginative hope and desire: "Baldwin's writings explored and exploded the meanings of 'blackness' and 'home' as historical, economic, social, and cultural creations and representations, products, and constructs located in social space."[66] Today's activists seek to explain and proclaim Black life, and the mattering of Blackness over and against oppressive systems. As these systems and ideologies continue to undermine Black mobility, Black access, Black success, and simply put, Black lives, Baldwin's prophetic witnessing may help to ground and heal us still.

Notes

1 Alia Chughtai, "Know Their Names: Black People Killed by the Police in the US," Al Jazeera, 22 January 2020, https://interactive.aljazeera.com/aje/2020/know-their-names/index.html (accessed 17 June 2021).

2 Coralie Kraft, "Hilton Als on Giving James Baldwin Back His Body," *New Yorker*, 16 January 2019, www.newyorker.com/culture/photo-booth/hilton-als-on-giving-james-baldwin-back-his-body (accessed 2 March 2021).

3 Geoffrey Himes, "Me'Shell Ndegeocello Gives a Reading from the Scripture of James Baldwin," *Washington Post*, 13 December 2018, www.washingtonpost.com/goingout-guide/music/meshell-ndegeocello-gives-a-reading-from-the-scripture-of-james-baldwin/2018/12/13/8c60e91c-f7e4-11e8-8d64-4e79db33382f_story.html?utm_term=.a9406b944a1d (accessed 2 March 2021).

4 Toni Morrison, *The Source of Self-Regard: Selected Essays, Speeches, and Meditations* (New York, Knopf, 2019), p. 229.

5 *Ibid.*

6 *Ibid.*

7 *Ibid.*

8 *Ibid.*, p. 230.

9 *Ibid.*, p. 232.

10 James Cone, *Said I Wasn't Gonna Tell Nobody: The Making of a Black Theologian* (Mary-knoll, NY, Orbis Books, 2018), p. 149; see also Cone's *Black Theology & Black Power* (1969) (Maryknoll, NY, Orbis Books, 2019).

11 Cone, *Said I Wasn't Gonna Tell Nobody*, p. 149.

12 *Ibid.*

13 *Ibid.*, p. 145.

14 *Ibid.*, p. 146.

15 *Ibid.*, p. 149.

16 *Ibid.*, p. 159.

17 James Vogel, *James Baldwin and the 1980s: Witnessing the Reagan Era* (Chicago, University of Illinois Press, 2018), p. 2.

18 *Ibid.*, pp. 26–7.

19 *Ibid.*, p. 70.

20 *Ibid.*, p. 117.

21 *Ibid.*, p. 18.

22 *Ibid.*

23 Michael Eric Dyson, *What Truth Sounds Like: RFK, James Baldwin, and Our Unfinished Conversation About Race in America* (New York, St. Martin's Press, 2018), p. 9.

24 *Ibid.*, pp. 16–17.

25 *Ibid.*, p. 40.

26 *Ibid.*, p. 87.

27 *Ibid.*, p. 217.

28 Nicholas Buccola, *The Fire Is Upon Us: James Baldwin, William F. Buckley, Jr., and the Debate over Race in America* (Princeton, NJ, Princeton University Press, 2019), p. 2.

29 *Ibid.*, p. 7.

30 *Ibid.*, p. 381.

31 *Ibid.*, p. 357.

32 *Ibid.*

33 *Ibid.*, p. 358.

34 *Ibid.*, p. 364.

35 *Ibid.*, pp. 365–6.

36 Bill V. Mullen, *James Baldwin: Living in Fire* (London, Pluto Press, 2019), p. xi.

37 *Ibid.*, p. xx.

38 David Jones, "'Something Unspeakable': James Baldwin and the 'Closeted-ness' of American Power," *James Baldwin Review*, 3 (2017), p. 49.

39 *Ibid.*

40 *Ibid.*, p. 50.

41 *Ibid.*, p. 53.

42 Mikko Tuhkanen, "Losing Real Life," *James Baldwin Review*, 4 (2018), p. 116.

43 *Ibid.*

44 *Ibid.*, p. 117.

45 *Ibid.*, p. 119.

46 *Ibid.*, p. 120.

47 Jesse A. Goldberg, "James Baldwin and the Anti-Black Force of Law: On Excessive Violence and Exceeding Violence," *Public Culture*, 31:3 (2019), p. 522.

48 *Ibid.*, p. 525.
49 *Ibid.*, p. 527.
50 Melanie Walsh, "Tweets of a Native Son: The Quotation and Recirculation of James Baldwin from Black Power to #BlackLivesMatter," *American Quarterly*, 70:3 (2018), p. 531.
51 *Ibid.*, p. 533.
52 Eddie S. Glaude, Jr., "'The Magician's Serpent': Race and the Tragedy of American Democracy," *James Baldwin Review*, 5 (2019), p. 11.
53 *Ibid.*, p. 17.
54 *Ibid.*
55 *Ibid.*, p. 13.
56 *Ibid.*, p. 18.
57 *Ibid.*
58 Vincent Lloyd, "The Negative Political Theology of James Baldwin," in Susan J. McWilliams (ed.), *A Political Companion to James Baldwin* (Lexington, KY, University Press of Kentucky, 2017), p. 172.
59 *Ibid.*, p. 174.
60 *Ibid.*, p. 191.
61 *Ibid.*, p. 185.
62 *Ibid.*
63 Magdalena J. Zaborowska, *Me and My House: James Baldwin's Last Decade in France* (Durham, NC, Duke University Press, 2018), p. 17.
64 *Ibid.*, p. 23.
65 *Ibid.*, p. 198.
66 *Ibid.*, p. 15.

Works Cited

Buccola, Nicholas, *The Fire Is Upon Us: James Baldwin, William F. Buckley, Jr., and the Debate over Race in America* (Princeton, NJ, Princeton University Press, 2019).

Chughtai, Alia, "Know Their Names: Black People Killed by the Police in the US," Al Jazeera, 22 January 2020, https://interactive.aljazeera.com/aje/2020/know-their-names/index.html (accessed 17 June 2021).

Cone, James, *Black Theology & Black Power* (1969) (Maryknoll, NY, Orbis Books, 2019).

_____ *Said I Wasn't Gonna Tell Nobody: The Making of a Black Theologian* (Maryknoll, NY, Orbis Books, 2018).

Dyson, Michael Eric, *What Truth Sounds Like: RFK, James Baldwin, and Our Unfinished Conversation About Race in America* (New York, St. Martin's Press, 2018).

Glaude, Jr., Eddie S., "'The Magician's Serpent': Race and the Tragedy of American Democracy," *James Baldwin Review*, 5 (2019), pp. 9–22.

Goldberg, Jesse A., "James Baldwin and the Anti-Black Force of Law: On Excessive Violence and Exceeding Violence," *Public Culture*, 31:3 (2019), pp. 521–38.

Himes, Geoffrey, "Me'Shell Ndegeocelo Gives a Reading From the Scripture of James Baldwin," *Washington Post*, 13 December 2018, www.washingtonpost.com/goingoutguide/music/meshell-ndegeocello-gives-a-reading-from-the-scripture-of-james-baldwin/2018/12/13/8c60e91c-f7e4-11e8-8d64-4e79db33382f_story.html?utm_term=.a9406b944a1d (accessed 2 March 2021).

Jones, David, "'Something Unspeakable': James Baldwin and the 'Closeted-ness' of American Power," *James Baldwin Review*, 3 (2017), pp. 46–64.

Kraft, Coralie, "Hilton Als on Giving James Baldwin Back His Body," *New Yorker*, 16 January 2019, www.newyorker.com/culture/photo-booth/hilton-als-on-giving-james-baldwin-back-his-body (accessed 2 March 2021).

Lloyd, Vincent, "The Negative Political Theology of James Baldwin," in Susan J. McWilliams (ed.), *A Political Companion to James Baldwin* (Lexington, KY: University Press of Kentucky, 2017), pp. 171–94.

Morrison, Toni, *The Source of Self-Regard: Selected Essays, Speeches, and Meditations* (New York, Knopf, 2019).

Mullen, Bill V., *James Baldwin: Living in Fire* (London, Pluto Press, 2019).

Tuhkanen, Mikko, "Losing Real Life," *James Baldwin Review*, 4 (2018), pp. 114–27.

Vogel, James, *James Baldwin and the 1980s: Witnessing the Reagan Era* (Chicago, University of Illinois Press, 2018).

Walsh, Melanie, "Tweets of a Native Son: The Quotation and Recirculation of James Baldwin from Black Power to #BlackLivesMatter," *American Quarterly*, 70:3 (2018), pp. 531–9.

Zaborowska, Magdalena J., *Me and My House: James Baldwin's Last Decade in France* (Durham, NC, Duke University Press, 2018).

Contributor's Biography

Terrance Dean is an Assistant Professor in Black Studies at Denison University. He received his BA from Fisk University and his MTS from Vanderbilt Divinity School. He also earned his MA and PhD in Religion from Vanderbilt University. His research interests include gender, sex, sexuality, Black religion and homiletics, African diaspora, Black Cultural Studies, James Baldwin, and Afrofuturism. Dean has served as special guest editor for *Palimpsest: A Journal on Women, Gender, and the Black International*. The special issue, entitled "Thirty-Year Retrospective of Black Queer Studies," also includes Dean's essay, "Don't Forget About Us: James Baldwin, the Black Church, and Black Queer Identity." He has also served as special guest editor for *Black Theology: An International Journal*. The special issue, entitled "Afrofuturism in Black Theology–Race, Gender, Sexuality, and the State of Black Religion in the Black Metropolis," also includes Dean's essay, "Fire This Time: James Baldwin, Futurity, and a Call and Response." His book, *Black Grace: First Ladies of the Black Church*, is forthcoming with Beacon Press.